Absolute Music

This book is born out of two contradictions: first, it explores the making of meaning in a musical form that was made to empty its meaning at the turn of the nineteenth century; secondly, it is a history of a music that claims to have no history – absolute music. The book therefore writes against the notion of absolute music which tends to be the paradigm for most musicological and analytical studies. It is concerned not so much with *what* music is, but why and how meaning is constructed in instrumental music and what structures of knowledge need to be in place for such meaning to exist. Instead of existing in a pure and autonomous form, music is woven back into the epistemological fabric, and tangled with the discourses of theology, visual perspective, biology, philosophy, gender, chemistry, politics, physics. Such contextualisation, far from diminishing the significance of music, actually demonstrates the centrality of music in the construction of modernity. From the thought of Vincenzo Galilei to that of Theodor Adorno, Daniel Chua suggests that instrumental music has always been a critical and negative force in modernity, even with its nineteenth-century apotheosis as 'absolute music'.

The book discusses the ideas of thinkers such as Vincenzo Galilei, Descartes, Diderot, Rameau, Rousseau, Kant, Hegel, Schopenhauer, Hanslick, Wagner, Max Weber and Adorno and considers the works of composers such as Monteverdi, C. P. E. Bach, Haydn, Mozart and, most importantly, Beethoven, whose music defines the notion of absolute music for the nineteenth and twentieth century.

New perspectives in music history and criticism

GENERAL EDITORS

JEFFREY KALLBERG, ANTHONY NEWCOMB AND RUTH SOLIE

This series explores the conceptual frameworks that shape or have shaped the ways in which we understand music and its history, and aims to elaborate structures of explanation, interpretation, commentary and criticism which make music intelligible and which provide a basis for argument about judgements of value. The intellectual scope of the series will be broad. Some investigations will treat, for example, historiographical topics – ideas of music history, the nature of historical change, or problems of periodisation. Others will apply cross-disciplinary methods to the criticism of music, such as those involving literature, history, anthropology, linguistics, philosophy, psychoanalysis, or gender studies. There will also be studies that consider music in its relation to society, culture and politics. Overall, the series hopes to create a greater presence of music in the ongoing discourse among the human sciences.

ALREADY PUBLISHED

Leslie C. Dunn and Nancy A. Jones (eds.), *Embodied voices: representing female vocality in Western culture* 0 521 58583 X

Downing A. Thomas, *Music and the origins of language: theories from the French Enlightenment* 0 521 47307 1

Thomas S. Grey, *Wagner's musical prose: texts and contexts* 0 521 41738 4

Absolute Music

And the Construction of Meaning

DANIEL K. L. CHUA

CAMBRIDGE
UNIVERSITY PRESS

PUBLISHED BY THE PRESS SYNDICATE OF THE UNIVERSITY OF CAMBRIDGE
The Pitt Building, Trumpington Street, Cambridge CB2 1RP, United Kingdom

CAMBRIDGE UNIVERSITY PRESS
The Edinburgh Building, Cambridge, CB2 1RU, UK http://www.cup.cam.ac.uk
40 West 20th Street, New York, NY 10011-4211, USA   http://www.cup.org
10 Stamford Road, Oakleigh, Melbourne 3166, Australia

First published 1999

Typset in 10/12pt. Adobe Palatino in QuarkXPress™   [SE]

A catalogue record for this book is available from the British Library

Library of Congress cataloguing in publication data

Chua, Daniel K. L., 1966–
Absolute music and the construction of meaning / Daniel K. L. Chua.
    p.   cm. – (New perspectives in music history and criticism)
Includes bibliographical references and index.
ISBN 0 521 63181 5 hardback
1. Absolute music.   2. Music – Philosophy and aesthetics.
I. title.   II. Series.
ML3854.c5   1999
781.1'7 – dc21   98-42733   CIP   MN

ISBN 0 521 63181 5 hardback

Transferred to digital printing 2004

CONTENTS

Contents

ILLUSTRATIONS

ACKNOWLEDGEMENTS

This book has only been made possible by the support and encouragement of many friends and colleagues. I offer my heartfelt thanks to them both for their input and for what they had to put up with.

Irene Auerbach, Sam Barrett, Olav Beckmann, Andrew Bowie, Scott Burnham, Tim Carter, David Chung, John Deathridge, Laurence Dreyfus, Cliff Eisen, Annegret Fauser, Michael Fend, Berthold Hoeckner, Brian Hyer, Paul Jordan, Jeffrey Kallberg, Scott Kim, Gudrun Pebody, Beate Perrey, Alex Rehding, Ulinka Rublack, Penny Souster, Joan Steigerwald, Henry Stobart, W. Dean Sutcliffe, Christopher Wintle, Alison Winter.

ON THE PREFACE

A preface often speaks of anxiety. When Giulio Caccini published his *Le nuove musiche* of 1602 he attached a preface to annotate his notation; the notes, he says, 'are written in one way, but to be more graceful [they] are affected in quite another'.[1] His words carry the anxiety of Baroque performance practice, a fear that always lurks behind the notes whenever a text demands the creative interaction between the performer and the notation; in such cases, the preface greets the reader as a defence mechanism to safeguard the author's intentions, lest the text be misinterpreted. So it is not simply out of politeness that I greet you. This preface is written out of an anxiety about your performance practice. How will you read this book? Will you get it? Let me invoke three words both to guide your reading and to allay my anxiety:

1. CONSTELLATION: this word murmurs with the aura of Walter Benjamin. For Benjamin things simply refuse definitions, for a concept cannot live up to the thing it names, but limits the meaning by making it identical to the concept. Similarly, absolute music cannot be defined; its identity is nebulous and its history too volatile to pin down with precision. To write about it as if it were a single, stable concept would miss the point, for its meaning is situated in an ever-changing constellation of elements. This book is therefore arranged as a constellation of tiny, fragmentary chapters that gather around the object, often in an extreme manner to exaggerate the tensions between the concepts, without collapsing everything into the black-hole of absolute music or by allowing one star to outshine the others. There is no attempt to exhaust the history of absolute music or to focus on a single period. What I present are selected splices of time, which are momentary flashes of thought made to illumine the object without overcoming it. The story I tell is an invisible thread that connects these momentary glimmers together, like a sign of the Zodiac picked out from among the stars.

---

[1] Giulio Caccini, *Le nuove musiche* (Florence, 1602), ed. H. W. Hitchcock (Madison: A-R Editions, 1970), 50.

2. ARCHAEOLOGY: this word relates to the historical method of Michel Foucault. His attempt to dig out deep epistemological layers is designed to remove the subject as the agent of history, replacing it with a clinical structure. The question, for Foucault, is not 'who makes history?' but how things are ordered. So in this book it is not so much who makes absolute music but what structures of knowledge need to be in place before absolute music can exist at all. This means that absolute music cannot be confined to the history of music as if it were purely musical, circling in its own autonomous sphere. What it claims to be is embedded in structures outside music(ology), and it is only by excavating these sites that the meaning of absolute music can be reconstructed.

3. DIALECTIC: this word is meant to conjure up the apparition of Theodor W. Adorno, who, unlike Hegel, offers no synthesis in his dialectical process. And neither is there one in this book; the constellation remains in tension and the epistemological sediments do not mingle. Moreover, this immiscible concoction of the stars and the earth also demands a dialectic between the twinkling particulars, which function as forensic details that might clinch the case, and the general epistemological shift that bulldozes all differences in the name of totality. Benjamin and Foucault do not mix, and Adorno's dialectic does not arbitrate between them but maintains as necessary the unresolved dissonance at the core of Western knowledge. This dissonance also disturbs the centre of absolute music which claims to be both general (the absolute) and particular (the work) at the same time. The dialectical strain between a flash of thought and the epistemological strata or between the analysis of a work and a general theory of music is a condition of absolute music itself. Either/or is not an option.

These three words – constellation, archaeology, dialectic – have no absolute power over you; they are not magic spells designed to instil the fear of the author or to constrict the imagination of the reader. Quite the opposite; these words are meant to put the onus on the reader to perform in the gaps between the stars or along the geological lines. To paraphrase Caccini, the text is 'written in one way, but to be more graceful [it should be] affected in quite another'.

PART 1

The Garden of Eden

1

On history

Glass objects have no 'aura' . . . glass is the enemy of the secret.
(Benjamin)[1]

Absolute music has 'no history'.[2] It denies that it was ever born. The fact that it emerged at the turn of the nineteenth century was not a birth, it claims, but an emancipation, a discovery unveiled by the German Romantics, as if absolute music had always been there, eternal and absolute. After all, an absolute by definition cannot have a history; God – the absolute absolute – cannot be historically grounded, and neither can the surrogate absolutes of the secular world such as Reason or the Transcendental Ego; they all claim to start from nothing, as a self-sufficient method or metaphysical entity, without genealogy or narrative. Absolutes only have histories when they self-destruct to reveal their false identity. This means that absolute music can only have a history when it is no longer absolute music.

The emergence of absolute music was muttered rather than announced by the early Romantics.[3] In fact, the Romantics were so reticent about the subject that they did not even call absolute music 'absolute music'; that task was left to Wagner, who, ironically, was trying to expose its mendacious claims by negating it in his dialectics of music history.[4] Absolute music is therefore a murky concept, born without a

---

[1] Walter Benjamin, *Gesammelte Schriften* (Frankfurt: Suhrkamp, 1972–9), 2:217.

[2] Wilhelm Heinrich Wackenroder and Ludwig Tieck, 'Symphonien', *Phantasien über die Kunst für Freunde der Kunst* (Hamburg, 1799), in *Werke und Briefe von Wilhelm Heinrich Wackenroder* (Berlin: Verlag Lambert Schneider, 1938), 255. Tieck added several essays to Wackenroder's *Phantasien über die Kunst*, including the essay entitled 'Symphonien'; this has raised problematic questions concerning authorship. It is for this reason that I have included Tieck's name in the authorship of the publication.

[3] I shall use the term 'Romantic' to refer to the *early* Romantics only, which include writers such as the Schlegel brothers, Novalis, Tieck, Wackenroder, early Schelling and, to some extent, E. T. A. Hoffmann.

[4] See Richard Wagner, *Das Kunstwerk der Zukunft* (1850) and *Oper und Drama* (1851) in *Sämtliche Schriften und Dichtungen* (Leipzig, 1911–16), 3:42–177 and 222–320; also see Klaus Kropfinger, *Wagner and Beethoven: Richard Wagner's Reception of Beethoven* (1974), trans. P. Palmer (Cambridge: Cambridge University Press, 1991), 115, Carl Dahlhaus, *The Idea of Absolute Music*, trans. R. Lustig (London and Chicago: University of Chicago Press, 1989), 18–19, and Thomas S. Grey, *Wagner's Musical Prose: Texts and Contexts* (Cambridge: Cambridge University Press, 1995), 1–2.

proper name. Indeed, its retrospective baptism calls the legitimacy of its birth into question.[5] However, the Romantics did call instrumental music 'pure music',[6] and this can be taken to be almost 'absolute', for its purity was deemed to be the essence of music itself, as if its spirit could be filtered through a symphonic sieve. So for the Romantics music became equated with Spirit,[7] something too ethereal to have a history and too transcendent to be soiled by the muck of contextualisation. To avoid the possibility of contamination, the Romantics removed music from historical reality altogether and enclosed it in its own 'separate world',[8] where its signs could reflect each other within an autonomy so pure that its being discovered itself as tautology: music is music. In this equation, music's purity is self-evident truth; it just is; it needs no historical or external validation; there is nothing extraneous. By circling in its own orbit, music finally discovers its identity as 'Music', and so begins to preen itself of all that is not 'Music', discarding such elements as extra-musical appendages.

Absolute music therefore discriminates. Indeed, it defines itself by exclusion. The category of the 'extra-musical' was invented in the nineteenth century as the negative other of the 'purely musical'.[9] But this binary opposition is only a tactic designed to be mistaken as truth – as if such categories actually existed. What, after all, is an 'extra-musical' object? It is obviously not Music, but neither is it non-music. Would the concept even be possible without the existence of absolute music? Or, to put the question the other way round, would absolute music exist without positing the extra-musical? Perhaps the extra-musical is merely a deflection that diverts one's attention from the dubious nature of the 'purely musical'. Just try interrogating absolute music's purity. What is it? What does it mean? What is this essence that so powerfully discriminates between what is and is not Music? There is no answer; or, at least, when asked to disclose the criteria for musical purity, absolute music deliberately draws a blank. Its signs signify nothing. Indeed it cleverly champions this nothingness as its purity. The sign and referent cancel each other out in such a frictionless economy of exchange that no concept or object is left over. Thus the meaning of absolute music resides

---

[5] See Mark Evan Bonds, 'Idealism and the Aesthetic of Instrumental Music at the Turn of the Nineteenth Century', *Journal of the American Musicological Society*, vol. 50 nos. 2–3 (1997).

[6] See, for example, Friedrich Schlegel, *Athenaeum Fragments*, no. 444, in *Philosophical Fragments*, trans. P. Firchow (Minneapolis: University of Minneapolis Press, 1991), 92.

[7] See, for example, Wackenroder, *Werke und Briefe*, 207 and 255. Also see Johann Gottfried Herder, *Kalligone* (1800) in *Sämmtliche Werke*, ed. B. Suphan (Berlin: Weidmann, 1877–1913), 22:187.   [8] Wackenroder, *Werke und Briefe*, 189, 245 and 255.

[9] The issues here are developed from a lecture by Lydia Goehr entitled 'Wagner and the Quest for the Autonomous Musical Voice', given at the Institute of Advanced Musical Studies at King's College, London (14 January 1998).

in the fact that it has no meaning; the inchoate and the ineffable become synonymous. Consequently, there is no way of teasing out an explanation from absolute music for its utterances are ineffable. This is why its purity is not a fact that is open to investigation, but a secret whose power resides in the inaccessibility of its sign. No wonder the early Romantics venerated instrumental music as a mystery that wraps 'mysterious things in a mysterious language'.[10] As 'the ultimate mystery of faith', absolute music was not something to be examined but believed in.[11] Its purity is entirely opaque.

In this ideology of the pure, history is something that is outside music. It is an added 'extra', if not an optional 'extra'. And as proof, absolute music bedazzles the historian with its opaque and mysterious purity where no history is possible. But, of course, this purity is not a condition of truth; it is simply a method whereby absolute music renders its own history unreadable. It is a strategy designed to silence the historian. After all, the only response that befits an ineffable music is speechlessness. This is why the social phenomenon that accompanied the ideology of absolute music was the eradication of audience chatter. The hushed expectancy that descended upon the concert halls of Europe by the 1840s was an acknowledgement of music's ineffability.[12] Absolute music therefore stifles critique – there is no way of talking about it. Or, to borrow Theodor Adorno's metaphor, there is no direct way into these 'windowless monads'.[13] Writing a critical history of absolute music becomes a moral dilemma, for to break in to steal the meaning of these monadic objects would constitute a breach of music's aesthetic autonomy. Any attempt to pry open these self-adhering signs to unlock what Lawrence Kramer calls 'hermeneutic windows',[14] will involve a defenestration of absolute music's purity. You forfeit absolute music by gaining access to it. By unlatching such windows, one reduces the ineffable sign to concrete objects that can never live up to the purity and totality of absolute music. The sign must remain a secret if music is to remain absolute. To give it away is seemingly to fail. So absolute music does not only make its history unreadable but the decipherment of its history undesirable.

This is not to say that histories of absolute music do not exist, but that

---

[10] Wackenroder, *Werke und Briefe*, 255.   [11] Ibid., 251.

[12] See James H. Johnson, *Listening in Paris: A Cultural History* (Berkeley: University of California Press, 1995), 257–80.

[13] Theodor W. Adorno, *Aesthetische Theorie*, ed. G. Adorno and R. Tiedemann (Frankfurt am Main: Suhrkamp, 1970), 15. There are two English translations of *Aesthetic Theory*, one by C. Lenhardt (London: Routledge, 1984), the other by Robert Hullot-Kentor (Minneapolis: University of Minnesota Press, 1997). Hullot-Kentor's is the more accurate translation, but I have used Lenhardt's where it seems more appropriate.

[14] Lawrence Kramer, *Music as Cultural Practice: 1800–1900* (Berkeley: University of California Press, 1990), 1–20.

they are often written under its spell. But why should absolute music set the conditions for its critique? Must musicology always perpetuate its ideological claims? This book attempts to answer these questions by writing a history of absolute music without absolute music. It asks: what would happen if the concept of absolute music were removed as the epistemological ground of Western music? What would it be like?

First, absolute music would not be 'Music'. After all, the Romantics did not compose; they merely talked. They fabricated from the symphony the *discourse* of absolute music.[15] So far from standing speechless before its ineffable utterances, the Romantics spoke absolute music into existence. It is a music emancipated from language *by language*; 'were it not for the poetic conceit of unspeakability', writes Carl Dahlhaus, 'there would have been no words available for reinterpreting the musically confusing or empty into the sublime or wonderful'.[16] This is not to say that the symphony does not exist, but that the process of naming changes the meaning of the symphony. This is why a history of absolute music cannot be a history of *music*. Rather, it is a history of a discourse. Or, to turn absolute music against itself, absolute music is an extra-musical idea. As such, absolute music does not have a fixed meaning, but is subject to the mutations of those who speak about it. And since its dialogue was played out as a heated argument in the nineteenth century, the history of absolute music is not the elaboration of a *single* idea, but a clamour of contradictory discourses, each vying for power in the construction of its meaning. Thus absolute music has a decentred and fragmented identity that can only be elucidated as a constellation of discursive ideas. Its history does not add up to the totality that it claims for itself.

Secondly, absolute music would not be absolute. Without its purity, absolute music would no longer be able to transcend history as an immutable sign and orbit in that ethereal, autoletic world of essences where it can discriminate against everything that does not aspire to its uncontaminated condition. If music is no longer absolute, then it can no longer constitute the unconditional ground of knowledge. Instead, it would find its being embedded within various epistemological structures that shape its existence. In other words, the unconditioned (the absolute) becomes conditioned. Its history would therefore resemble the archaeology of knowledge pioneered by Michel Foucault,[17] which will be a grubby operation that will not leave absolute music pure. Its pristine features will be sedimented within the formations of theology,

---

[15] On discourse see Diane MacDonell, *Theories of Discourse: An Introduction* (Oxford: Blackwell, 1986).

[16] Dahlhaus, *The Idea of Absolute Music*, 63.

[17] See Michel Foucault, *The Order of Things: An Archaeology of the Human Sciences* (London: Tavistock/Routledge, 1974).

cosmology, cartography, philosophy, zoology, anthropology, physiology, biology, chemistry, physics, mechanics, mathematics, politics, linguistics, aesthetics, economics, magic, agriculture and sex. Admittedly, such excavations may not resemble a history of music at all, since they dig up the extra-musical debris against which absolute music purifies itself. To the 'purist' it may not even look like musicology. But this may be the only way of writing a meaningful history of a music that claims to have no history.

To write a history of absolute music is to write against it.

2

On modernity

Why should absolute music claim to have no history? Surely such a radical denial already betrays a historical consciousness. Its ahistorical stance is therefore a symptom of history, an allergic reaction for which the only cure is denial. This is not simply the truism that absolute music, like any other object, is governed by the fluctuations of time. Rather, absolute music embodies history itself. It is *modern*. Indeed, it was called 'modern music'[1] at the very time when the French Revolution brought history into crisis and initiated a historical consciousness within German philosophy. Absolute music was therefore born at the time when time itself was under critical scrutiny. If this music is shaped by its context, then its history is about history. But why should it conceal this fact, claiming to transcend history when it lives off the very progress of modernity?

Because human history failed. Or rather, humanity failed to make the future it hoped for. Seventeen eighty-nine turned out to be the catastrophe of history as the ideals of the Revolution collapsed into the barbarity of the Terror. By the end of the eighteenth century, modernity had lost faith in itself; the promises of the Revolution, the progress of technology, the Utopian visions of the Enlightenment were no longer inevitable truths that time would unfold. Rather, history became more contingent and the future less attainable. Under such uncertain circumstances, the teleology of history risked degenerating into the ephemeral fluctuations of time, where modernity would merely be a matter of passing fashions. Without direction, modernity is only modish. Something from within modernity needed to legitimise history, to become its absolute and stand as an eternal emblem that could mark the progress of humanity and stabilise the vision of the future; the elevation of 'Art' as some kind of divine utterance, purged of all function and fashion, seemed to provide modernity with the meaning it needed; 'Art' became a religion of modernity, and absolute music, as the condition to which all art should aspire, was its god. And so, like God, this music exists outside history to make history; it transcends fashion to endorse

---

[1] See James Webster, *Haydn's 'Farewell' Symphony and the Idea of Classical Style* (Cambridge: Cambridge University Press, 1991), 347–57.

8

progress. This is why many German critics of the nineteenth century, such as A. B. Marx, Wilhelm von Lenz and Richard Wagner, considered Beethoven's *Eroica Symphony* a monument of modernity – a contradictory object that is simultaneously eternal (monumental) and progressive (modern).[2] The celebrated C♯ in the seventh bar, for example, was regarded by Wagner as an epoch-making event: it is the very first note of modernity, he was reported to have said.[3] But the modernity he speaks of here is not the superficial and fashionable modernity that he denounced as 'Jewish',[4] for this C♯ is no mere passing-note of fashion; it is the fundamental structure of modernity – the paradox of the 'modern classic'. The *Eroica* will always be in vogue, a heroic deed that transcends history in the very act of making it.[5] So although absolute music claims to have no history, what it validates is modernity itself, creating a timeless norm out of the fashions of time.[6]

So absolute music is modern – indeed, it is the monument of modernity itself. But is this such a radical concept? After all, musical instruments are necessarily products of technology; although instrumental sound has not always been absolute by nature, it has always been modern in the sense that it is inextricably bound to technological progress. Compared to the eternal *voice* of nature, its mechanised utterances seem to articulate the advance of modern culture. Instrumental music was already modern before the early Romantics discovered 'absolute' music; the idea was not something new to the nineteenth century. Many commentators would like to think that absolute music burst into history on Teutonic soil, as though its birth was some revolutionary rupture, late in coming but strong in securing the hegemony of German culture, but absolute music was not born under a Beethovenian star. Rather, like the C♯ of the *Eroica*, it is only a dissonance within the harmonic progression of modernity, marking a critical juncture of modern self-consciousness.[7] To grasp the meaning of this moment one has to understand the modernity of instrumental music *prior* to Romanticism, for the Romantics merely gave a twist to an existing discourse to turn instrumental music into absolute music.

Exactly when the world became modern is difficult to gauge. This is

---

[2] See Adolf Bernhard Marx, *Ludwig van Beethoven: Leben und Schaffen* (Berlin, 1859), 2: 275, Wilhelm von Lenz, *Beethoven: Eine Kunststudie* (Hamburg, 1855–60), 3:291, and Richard Wagner, 'Ein glücklicher Abend' and 'Beethovens "heroische Symphonie"', in *Sämtliche Schriften und Dichtungen*, 1:147 and 5:169–70. Also see the chapter in this volume 'On Monuments'.

[3] *Cosima Wagner's Diary*, trans. G. Skelton (London: Collins, 1978), 1:378 (17 June, 1871).

[4] See Richard Wagner, 'Das Judenthum in der Musik', *Sämtliche Schriften*, 5:66–85.

[5] Richard Wagner, 'Ein glücklicher Abend', ibid., 1:147.

[6] See Jürgen Habermas, *The Philosophical Discourse of Modernity*, trans. F. Lawrence (Cambridge: Polity Press, 1987), 9.

[7] See the chapter in this volume, 'On the Apocalypse'.

partly because the modern condition is one that perpetually sees itself as the culmination of history, leaving a trail of epochs that posit themselves as new. The Reformation, the Renaissance, the Enlightenment, the Romantic era, are all 'modern ages'. Modernity is therefore driven by a need to overcome the past in the name of progress, so that the 'new' is constantly consigned to be 'old' by history. Its only point of reference is an idealised 'ancient world' against which it defines itself by an endless process of self-mutation. Unlike the ancient cosmos, the modern world is no longer grounded in a static, hierarchical structure in which one is simply born with pre-assigned duties, but is fashioned by a historical pressure that turns the world into a mass of potential waiting to be transformed by the assertion of the human will.[8] The endeavours of man and the exercise of reason seemed to promise a Utopian future in an open and infinite universe. The globe seemingly expanded with the 'discovery' of 'new worlds' in the fifteenth century;[9] the Reformation brought orthodox Christianity into theological flux;[10] modern science interrogated a formerly immutable nature through the powers of reason and technology.[11] And, similarly, the music of modernity, from *Ars Nova* to the avant-garde, is driven by the same process of human control and assertion over space, time and matter.

Within this history of human progress, the concept of instrumental music plays a negative, antagonistic role. The newness of its sounds only came into prominence when modernity came into crisis. Its empty signs were made to articulate moments of negation when the transformative potential of the new fizzled out into a kind of historical inertia. Thus instrumental music only figures in the modern discourse when modernity needs to overcome its own failure. In such instances, the immutable nature of the ancient world is seen in a different light; no longer is the past a superstitious dead-end for the thrust of scientific progress, but an Arcadian world of static perfection which modernity yearns for, believing that its future perfection lies in the revival of some ancient practice; ancient becomes modern. It is this narrative that my book will try to trace as it sifts out the meanings of instrumental music. There are two stages to the story.

First, at the turn of the seventeenth century instrumental music was

---

[8] See Anthony J. Cascardi, *The Subject of Modernity* (Cambridge: Cambridge University Press, 1992), 6–7.

[9] See David Woodward, 'Maps and the Rationalization of Geographic Space', in *Circa 1492: Art in the Age of Exploration*, ed. J. A. Levenson (New Haven: Yale University Press, 1991), 85–7.

[10] See Peter Berger, *The Heretical Imperative: Contemporary Possibilities of Religious Affirmation* (New York: Anchor Press, 1979), 1–31.

[11] See Alexandre Koyré, 'Galileo and Plato', *Metaphysics and Measurement: Essays in Scientific Revolution* (London: Chapman and Hall, 1968).

denounced as modern; it was perceived as detrimental to the future, for its mechanised sounds seemed to echo the emptiness of the present. As early as the 1580s, Vincenzo Galilei blamed instrumental music for the impotence of modern composition, claiming that its polyphonic sounds had depleted the ancient power of monodic song.[12] By denouncing instrumental music, modernity actually affirmed its belief that the present could be surpassed and that a new society would emerge from the historical momentum of music; if instrumental sounds were removed then Utopia would follow as Arcadia.

However, by the turn of the nineteenth century, with the aftermath of the French Revolution, the same emptiness was embraced as the reality of the modern condition. This is the second stage, where the future could no longer be secured by a simple faith in human progress. The early Romantics idealised the ancient world to such a point of unattainability that future perfection was rendered impossible. So instead of denouncing instrumental music, the Romantics yearned for Utopia negatively in the figure of the vacant sign, as if a double negative could somehow make a positive. At the point when the future seemed to meander aimlessly, instrumental music was made absolute in the hope that the present, like the C♯ of the *Eroica*, would resolve within a teleological structure yet to be articulated. Although in both these stages of its history instrumental music signals a loss, its emptiness took on different meanings as modernity came to terms with its own emptiness. In other words, the optimism of modern progress is inversely proportional to the prestige of instrumental music. Or to put it another way: the rise of instrumental music is dependent on the fall of modernity.

[12] See Vincenzo Galilei, *Dialogo della musica antica e della moderna* (1581) in Oliver Strunk, *Source Readings in Music History* (New York: Norton, 1950), and the chapter 'On Opera' in this volume.

3

On disenchantment

For the German sociologist Max Weber, modernity is marked by the 'disenchantment of the world [*Entzauberung der Welt*]'. What segregates the modern from the ancient world is a process of 'de-magification', whereby Western society exorcises itself of its fear of demons, ghosts and goblins.[1] Modern humanity no longer submits itself to the spell of superstition and the sacred rituals of power, but has demystified its existence through the calculations of science and the bureaucratic apparatus of state. What was supernatural has been rationalised as merely the natural; the 'fear of things invisible', as Thomas Hobbes puts it,[2] has been dispelled by the clarity of reason; the authority of religion has been replaced by the politics of state. The modernisation of society is therefore its secularisation; humanity, by disenchanting the world, needs believe in no other god than itself.

But for Weber secularisation is a fateful process. He sees the seed of this catastrophe in the fruit of knowledge that enticed humanity with the promise of enlightenment. Weber's sociology replays the narrative of Eden in secular terms: 'The fate of an epoch which has eaten of the tree of knowledge', he writes, 'is that it must know that [it] cannot learn the meaning of the world from the result of its analysis.'[3] Modern knowledge is staged by Weber as a Fall that expels man from paradise, for the self-exorcism of humanity gains knowledge only by losing its meaning; it organises itself through the endless analysis of *facts*, but these facts have no binding *values*. Hence modern science cannot produce an ethics out of its own system of truth (facts).[4] Disenchantment, then, is a form of knowledge, and Weber defines this

[1] Max Weber, 'Science as Vocation' (1917), translated in *From Max Weber*, ed. H. H. Mills and C. Wright Mills (New York: Oxford University Press, 1946), 155.

[2] Thomas Hobbes, *Leviathan* (1651), ed. C. B. Macpherson (London: Penguin, 1968), 1:168. Also see Cascardi, *The Subject of Modernity*, 44–9.

[3] Max Weber, *Methodology of the Social Sciences*, ed. E. A. Shils and H. A. Finch (New York: The Free Press, 1949), 57.

[4] See Weber, 'Science as Vocation', 141–56, Michael Polanyi, *Personal Knowledge: Towards a Post-Critical Philosophy* (Chicago: University of Chicago Press, 1958), 3–17, Alasdair MacIntyre, *After Virtue* (London: Duckworth, 1981), 35–59, and Lesslie Newbegin, *Foolishness to the Greeks: The Gospel and Western Culture* (London: SPCK, 1986), 21–41 and 65–94.

knowledge as *instrumental reason*. It is instrumental precisely because reason is used as a *tool* that dissects the world as an object of investigation, distancing the human subject in the process as an outside observer. Instrumental reason is therefore knowledge as a *means* of control, a *technique* that is both ruthlessly direct and relationally remote. On the one hand, through these tools of knowledge, humanity can grasp the divine power of the ancient cosmos as its own, transforming a formerly immutable world of essences into a malleable one that can be endlessly modernised in the name of material progress. Everything is open to technological manipulation; nature can be colonised, society engineered and the self transformed. But on the other hand, this new sovereignty, with all its instrumental prowess, turns out to be the Midas touch of reason. Everything the sovereign touches turns into facts; and these facts can only be used as a means without meaning; they are truths drained of their sacred and moral substance. Instrumental knowledge only knows *about* the world; it can never *know* the world. Enlightenment therefore alienates humanity from Eden and ultimately leaves it empty handed. This is what Weber means when he states that modern society can never 'learn the meaning of the world from the result of its analysis'.

Music, too, according to Weber, is subject to disenchantment.[5] It has lost its magic. The cultic melodies that had once enchanted the world have now been modernised to become an efficient means of harmonic production, he claims. By explaining the rationalisation of music as a shift from melodic incantation to harmonic calculation, Weber rehearses a trope that has haunted modernity since the end of the sixteenth century, namely, the disenchantment of song through instrumental harmony.[6] Weber explains the disenchantment by isolating equal temperament as the most modern mode of musical rationalisation. Music, by bowing to the regulations of $^{12}\sqrt{2:1}$ demanded by the technology of fretted and keyboard instruments, forfeits its power to enchant.[7] The modern semitonal system is therefore instrumental reason as instrumental music, for it is the mechanisation of sound that rationalises the scale with the kind of efficiency and pragmatic economy that Weber

---

[5] See Max Weber, *The Rational and Social Foundations of Music*, trans. D. Martindale, J. Riedel and G. Neuwirth (Carbondale and Edwardsville: Southern Illinois University Press, 1958).

[6] See the chapters in this volume 'On Opera', 'On the Body' and 'On Absolute Music' which deal with the Florentine Camerata, Rousseau, Rameau and Wagner.

[7] Weber is mistaken in assigning the development of equal temperament to keyboard instruments, although by the time the piano was established equal temperament was invariably used. However, equal temperament is required by fretted instruments such as the lute and viol. See, for example, Vincenzo Galilei, 'A Special Discourse Concerning the Unison', in Claude V. Palisca, *The Florentine Camerata: Documentary Studies and Translations* (New Haven: Yale University Press, 1989).

associates with modern societies. This is why he claims that modern tuning, as a rationalisation of harmonic production, has desensitised modern ears with a 'dulling effect' and has shackled music in 'dragging chains'.[8]

Weber therefore implies that the history of Western music is a process of incarceration – a narrative that Theodor Adorno would complete in his account of modern music. The twelve-note chain of the 'tempered half-tone system', he notes, is the underlying logic of the 'twelve-tone technique';[9] serialism, as the product of equal temperament, completes the disenchantment of music and so signals the end of modernity – indeed, of history itself, he claims.[10] For the philosopher, dodecaphonic music is instrumentalised to the point of 'total rationality'.[11] If the ordering of sound reduces 'the magic essence of music to human logic', he writes, then the 'total organisation of serialism' is the ultimate alienation of music under the domination of human control.[12] It is the final revelation of modernity's progress towards self-destruction. The 'twelve-tone technique is truly the fate of music', says Adorno, echoing the catastrophic tones of Weber, and 'fate', he writes, 'is disaster'.[13]

If Weber and Adorno are correct, then tuning turns out to be the apocalypse of modernity. The slightest adjustment between intervals, it seems, can cause catastrophe. But why should we believe this disaster of semitonal proportions announced by Adorno? Why should Weber's 'fatal comma' be so fateful?[14] After all what is a mere diesis between an ancient and modern world? Surely Weber has blown the ratio of 256:243 out of all proportion; he is mistaken to hear so much in so small an interval. Or is he?

The very fact that tuning seems such a marginal if not an irrelevant explanation of music's meaning today testifies to a disenchanted world. Tuning, for the ancients, was a magical formula; its numbers tempered the cosmos.[15] If music was ever absolute then this was the only time in history that music was genuinely absolute music. It harmonised every-

---

[8] Weber, *The Rational and Social Foundations of Music*, 102–3.

[9] Theodor W. Adorno, *Philosophie der neuen Musik* (1949), 126, translated by A. G. Mitchell and W. V. Blomster as *Philosophy of Modern Music* (London: Sheed and Ward, 1987), 61.

[10] See Thomas Mann, *Doctor Faustus*, trans. H. T. Lowe-Porter (London: Secker and Warburg, 1949), and the chapter in this volume 'On Suicide'.

[11] Adorno, *Philosophy of Modern Music*, 69.   [12] Ibid., 65 and 69.

[13] Ibid., 67.   [14] See Weber, *The Rational and Social Foundations of Music*, 99.

[15] For a brief history of tuning and the theoretical problems it created for early modern music, see Michael Fend, 'The Changing Function of *Senso* and *Ragione* in Italian Music Theory of the Late Sixteenth Century', and Klaus-Jürgen Sachs, 'Boethius and the Judgement of the Ears: A Hidden Challenge in Medieval and Renaissance Music'; both articles are in *The Second Sense: Studies in Hearing and Musical Judgement from Antiquity to the Seventeenth Century*, ed. C. Burnett, M. Fend and P. Gouk (London: Warburg Institute, University of London, 1991).

thing. What the Romantics discovered as absolute music was a mere shadow of what Pythagoras formulated two thousand years earlier, for the absolute music he bequeathed to humanity was not so much a music to be composed as a music that composed the world.[16]

Thus any comparison between the ancient and modern world must involve measuring the difference between a universe composed by music with one manufactured by instrumental reason. But it would be a mistake to see this as an opposition between modern rationality and ancient illogicality. The ancient world was not an irrational sphere of magic. In fact, irrationality is a modern condition, an emotional reaction that arises from the underbelly of instrumental reason.[17] If anything, the ancient world was far more rational in its organisation of the cosmos than the modern world, for its music was *ratio*-nality itself; this is why music was not classified as an art but belonged with geometry, astrology and arithmetic in the sciences of the quadrivium. In Plato's account of creation,[18] music tunes the cosmos according to the Pythagorean ratios of 2:1, 3:2, 4:3 and 9:8, and scales the human soul to the same proportions. This enabled the inaudible sounds of the heavens to vibrate within the earthly soul, and, conversely, for the audible tones of human music to reflect the celestial spheres, so that heaven and earth could be harmonised within the unity of a well-tuned scale. This scale came to be pictured as a monochord that connected the stars to the earth like a long piece of string that vibrated the structure of the universe (plate 1). Its geometric and astral mathematics represented the binding order of an immutable and crystalline world. So music, as the invisible and inaudible harmony of the spheres, imposed a unity over creation, linking everything along the entire chain of being. It functioned, says Giambattista della Porta, 'as a rope stretched from the first cause' to the ultimate end by a reciprocal and continuous connection that 'if we touched one extremity of that cord it will make tremble and move all the rest'.[19] When music moves, the earth moves with it. Thus music was not simply an object in a magical world, but the *rational agent of enchantment*

---

[16] See, for example, Joscelyn Godwin, *Music, Mysticism and Magic* (London: Routledge, 1986), Ruth Katz, *The Powers of Music: Aesthetic Theory and the Invention of Opera* (New Brunswick: Transaction Publishers, 1994), Jamie James, *The Music of the Spheres* (London: Little, Brown and Company, 1994), 140–58, Gary Tomlinson, *Music in Renaissance Magic* (London and Chicago: University of Chicago Press, 1993), 67–100, Claude Palisca, *Humanism in Italian Renaissance Musical Thought* (New Haven: Yale University Press, 1985), 161–88, and John Hollander, *The Untuning of the Sky* (Princeton: Princeton University Press, 1961), 3–51.

[17] See Max Weber, 'The Esthetic Sphere' and 'The Erotic Sphere', in *From Max Weber*, and Michel Foucault, *Madness and Civilization*, trans. R. Howard (London: Routledge, 1989).

[18] See Plato, *Timaeus* 34b–47e.

[19] Giambattista della Porta, *Magiae naturalis libri viginti* (1589), quoted in Foucault, *The Order of Things*, 19.

itself. As the monochord, it animated the cosmos and tuned its very being. To disenchant music is therefore to untune the entire world. This is why tuning has apocalyptic overtones. The slightest change in global temperament can cause a collapse of the cosmic order.

Exactly when the world went out of tune is difficult to gauge. Its intonation probably slipped unevenly if not imperceptibly, but perhaps the dying echoes of its magical strains can be heard at the end of the fifteenth century. According to Gary Tomlinson, the Neo-Platonic structure of the Renaissance world still functioned within a 'magical episteme' or ground of knowledge.[20] For writers such as Marsilio Ficino, Ramos de Pareia and Henry Cornelius Agrippa music remained absolute in the Pythagorean sense, commingling with astrology, geometry and arithmetic within the quadrivium that interpreted the cosmos. As Egidius Carlerius puts it in his treatise on church music: 'Music is dependent on numbers, for number encompasses and perfects everything . . . all things bounded by the heavenly orbit – their being, their life – are based on a numbered arrangement. Music in its general sense, therefore, is found everywhere because of number'.[21] This made the nature of music somewhat diffuse, or at least seemingly so, for this music embraced the most eclectic elements within its numerical vibrations. The entire cosmos was the notation of absolute music. As the 'score' of the world, absolute music was an all-inclusive, syncretistic form of knowledge that notated the most bizarre configurations through a system of resemblances. These resemblances, as Foucault notes, 'organised the play of symbols [and] made possible the knowledge of things visible and invisible' within the Renaissance world.[22] That human phlegm, the moon and the hypodorian mode could inhabit the same site of logic in the writings of Ramos de Pareia was therefore not due to an aberration of reason but to a harmonic logic that spun a web of similitude around the world. Enclosed within this system, Ramos could tap into the absolute music of the cosmos to influence the sublunar and celestial realms, binding the modes (*musica instrumentalis*) to the planetary spheres (*musica mundana*) to affect the bodily humours (*musica humana*) along the length of the monochord.[23]

To disenchant the world, modernity had to sever the umbilical link of

---

[20] Tomlinson, *Music in Renaissance Magic.*

[21] Egidius Carlerius, *Tractatus de duplici ritu cantus ecclesiastici in divinis officiis* (c.1470), in *On the Dignity and the Effects of Music*, trans. J. D. Cullington, ed. R. Strohm (London: Institute of Advanced Musical Studies, King's College London, 1996), 26–7.

[22] Foucault, *The Order of Things*, 17.

[23] See Bartolomeo Ramos de Pareia, *Musica Practica* (1482), ed. J. Wolf (Leipzig, 1901), and Tomlinson, *Music in Renaissance Magic*, 77–84. On *musica instrumentalis, musica mundana* and *musica humana*, see Anicius Manlius Severinus Boethius, *De institutione musica*, translated by C. M. Bower as *Fundamentals of Music* (New Haven: Yale University Press, 1989), 9–10.

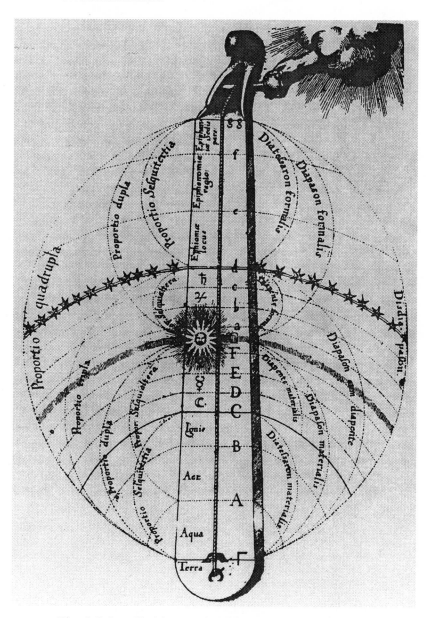

Plate 1 Robert Fludd, monochord from *Utriusque cosmi*. Instrumental sound as divine order: the hand of God tunes the string of the cosmic monochord that stretches from heaven to earth to embrace all the elements within the unity of its harmonic ratios.

the monochord, disconnecting itself from the celestial realms in order to remove music as an explanation of the world. With its supernatural aura demystified as natural and its inaudible, invisible essences dismissed as non-existent, modern music became an autonomous object open to the manipulations of instrumental reason. Significantly it was Vincenzo Galilei, father of Galileo, the astronomer who disenchanted the universe,[24] who was among the first to cut the ancient monochord in a series of experiments conducted in the 1580s,[25] by subjecting instrumental sound to the instrumental reason of empirical science. Indeed, Stillman Drake suggests that Galilei's experiments with sound may have 'led to the origin of experimental physics', inspiring his son to interrogate the world to verify the laws of nature as empirical fact.[26] Galilei wanted to 'demonstrate real things', he said, in the spirit of Aristotle and not the numerological abstractions of Pythagorean mysticism.[27] He collapsed music into 'reality' as an audible *fact* divorced from celestial *values*.[28]

Galilei in these experiments exercised an instrumental rationality in two ways. First, he objectified music as a neutralised matter for experimentation. Numbers were not sonorous in themselves, he claimed, but had to be 'applied to some sonorous body'.[29] Music does not exist as some perfect numerological system out there in the celestial realms as Pythagoras and indeed Galilei's teacher, Zarlino, believed;[30] rather sounds are emitted from bodies whose differing components colour the aural perception of their harmonic ratios. Why believe in the ancient ratio of 2:1, for example, if, as Galilei demonstrates, the diapason can be variously obtained between strings whose length is in duple proportion, or weights in quadruple proportion, or pipes in octuple proportion?[31] Empirical reality simply did not match up with the ancient integers that were supposed to organise the universe. Music is therefore *particular* for Galilei, rather than cosmic. And what makes it particular

[24] See Koyré, 'Galileo and Plato', *Metaphysics and Measurement*.

[25] Indeed, Galileo may have taken part in his father's experiments. See Stillman Drake, *Galileo at Work, His Scientific Biography* (Chicago: University of Chicago Press, 1970), 15–17, 'Renaissance Music and Experimental Science', *Journal of the History of Ideas*, vol. 31 (1970), 497–8, and Palisca, *The Florentine Camerata*, 163.

[26] Drake, 'Renaissance Music and Experimental Science', 488.

[27] Vincenzo Galilei, 'A Special Discourse Concerning the Diversity of the Ratios of the Diapason', in Palisca, *The Florentine Camerata*, 183–5.

[28] See Drake, 'Renaissance Music and Experimental Science'.

[29] Vincenzo Galilei, 'A Special Discourse Concerning the Diversity of the Ratios of the Diapason', in Palisca, *The Florentine Camerata*, 183–5.

[30] On the difficult relationship between Zarlino and Galilei and how it coloured Galilei's writings, see D. P. Walker, *Studies in Musical Science in the Late Renaissance* (London: The Warburg Institute, 1978; Leiden: E. J. Brill, 1978), 14–26.

[31] See Galilei, 'A Special Discourse Concerning the Diversity of the Ratios of the Diapason', in Palisca, *The Florentine Camerata*, 183–5.

are its imperfections. Galilei counters Pythagoras by showing how musical ratios are contingent upon the particular dimensions and material structure of the instruments which are variable in their construction and so yield *inexact* ratios. In such cases, there are no perfect, immutable sounding numbers that stabilise music, only the variability of lines, surfaces, solids, gut, steel, copper. Even the unison, from which the unity of the ancient world emanates, fails to persuade Galilei's ear of its perfect equation: sounds, he writes, 'are unisonant only insofar as the diversity of material of which they are made allows'. There are disparities among unisons 'depending', he says, 'on the quantity of sound . . . the diversity of agents that strike [the instruments], the thickness, height and length of the body on which they are stretched, and the force with which they are struck'.[32] For Galilei, empirical reality was simply out of tune with the ancient world.

Secondly, having demythologised music with an empirical rationality, he subjects it with an instrumental efficiency that re-tunes music for modern ears. If, as his experiments proved, sounds were necessarily imperfect and unrelated to simple numbers, then there was no reason why the irrational tuning of Aristoxenus, that is equal temperament, should not be imposed upon music played on or accompanied by instruments.[33] Indeed, the chromatic and enharmonic nature of modern music demanded it, and just to underline the point, Galilei composes 'a song' which if sung with perfect intonation would be out of tune with reality (see example 1): the chromatic and enharmonic clashes of modern harmony can only be eradicated if played on instruments tuned to equal temperament. 'Voices, being naturally perfect', writes Galilei, 'cannot sing well a song that is not composed according to their perfect usage, but an instrument tempered according to the imperfect usage [of Aristoxenus] in which this song is imperfectly composed, on the other hand, can play it.'[34] In other words, imperfect music requires the imperfect tuning of an imperfect reality.

An imperfect piece can no longer be absolute music. Indeed, instrumental music and absolute music are diametrically opposed at this juncture of modernity, for equally tempered music cannot connect with the cosmos as sounding numbers. Galilei has therefore modernised music by writing a piece that is instrumental in both mode and method. In fact, the song is not even a composition, but an experiment, a demonstration of instrumental rationality itself. Hence the system of equal temperament that the piece advocates means nothing other than its rationalisation. It is a method, whereas Pythagorean tuning is an ethos;

[32] Galilei, 'A Special Discourse Concerning the Unison', in ibid., 201.
[33] Vincenzo Galilei, 'Discourse Concerning the Various Opinions that the Three Most Famous Sects of Ancient Musicians had Concerning the Matter of Sound and Tunings', in ibid., 175.   [34] Ibid., 207.

19

Ex. 1 Demonstration of the need for equal temperament from Vincenzo Galilei's *Discorso particolare intorno all'unisono*.

the first is the product of an instrumental knowledge, the second an emanation of substantive reason; equal temperament reduces music to a quantitative sameness, Pythagorean tuning structures the world with a qualitative difference. One is grounded in supernature, the other is the pragmatic result of empirical nature. Equal temperament and Pythagorean tuning therefore stand against each other as opposing structures of rationality.

The difference between modern and ancient rationality can be stated as a difference of tuning: Pythagorean tuning harmonises the octave, while equal temperament partitions it equally. Ancient rationality unifies; modernity divides. This division already lurks within the writings of Galilei, who, on the one hand, champions a modern pragmatism, yet (as a later chapter will explain), laments the loss of ancient meaning in the very music he disenchants.[35] But it is with the early Romantics that this sense of division becomes a conscious dilemma. The Romantics knew that modernity, in dividing to rule, risks possessing nothing but its own divisions, creating a world without God, without magic and without meaning. Friedrich Schiller, in the final years of the eighteenth

---

[35] Galilei's scientific work actually contradicts his desire to re-enchant the world through monodic singing; see the chapter 'On Opera' in this volume, and also Daniel K. L. Chua, 'Vincenzo Galilei, Modernity and the Division of Nature', *Music Theory and Natural Order: From the Renaissance to the Early Twentieth Century*, ed. S. Clark and A. Rehding (Cambridge: Cambridge University Press, forthcoming).

century, already speaks of the 'disenchantment of the world'; in fact, Max Weber's narrative is a retelling of Schiller's aesthetics as sociology. For the poet the 'all-unifying nature' of the ancient world has been replaced by the 'all-dividing intellect [*Verstand*]' of the modern age.[36] The machinery of state, the rationalisation of labour and the specialisation of knowledge have brought modernity into a crisis of division. 'Everlastingly enchained to a single little fragment of the whole', says Schiller, 'man himself develops into nothing but a fragment.' Humanity has forfeited the magic of music in the dragging chains of the mechanised world; with 'the monotonous sound of the wheel that he turns', man, he states, 'never develops the harmony of his being'.[37] Schiller's chain of reasoning runs as follows: the ancient world is an enchanted totality; to disenchant is to divide; to divide is to be modern; to be modern is to be in crisis. And Hegel agrees: 'Modern culture', he writes, has 'driven [humanity] to the peak of harshest contradiction.' Man has become 'amphibious', split between himself and his environment, and unable in his self-styled sovereignty to mediate between object and subject, freedom and necessity, sense and reason, fact and value.[38] Having dismantled the coherence of a harmonic cosmos, modernity's desire to construct a new unity out of itself merely produces a divided totality. What was needed was a new harmony, and Schiller's achievement, according to Hegel, was to construct the aesthetic as the way of reconciliation.[39]

It is out of these divisions that the Romantic idea of 'absolute music' arose as an *aesthetic* totality; the early Romantics revitalised the music of the spheres in the hope of reconciling the world to itself:[40] 'Music', writes Schelling, 'is nothing other than the aurally perceived rhythm and harmony of the universe.'[41] But this reharmonisation of the cosmos was merely a speculative abstraction in a world without the monochord; stars no longer sang, and scales no longer laddered the sky. To re-enchant a rationalised world, the Romantics could not reconstruct a system of resemblances that would validate celestial truths that are eternal and external to their subjectivity; they only had an aesthetic system which searches for truths from the *particularity* of their own ego,

[36] Friedrich von Schiller, *On the Aesthetic Education of Man: In a Series of Letters*, trans. E. Wilkinson and L. A. Willoughby (Oxford: Clarendon Press, 1967; reprinted 1985), 33.

[37] Ibid., 35.

[38] Georg Wilhelm Friedrich Hegel, *Aesthetics: Lectures on Fine Art*, trans. T. M. Knox (Oxford: Clarendon Press, 1975), 54. [39] See ibid., 61–2.

[40] On the revival of Pythagoreanism in early Romanticism, see John Neubauer, *The Emancipation of Music from Language: Departure from Mimesis in Eighteenth-Century Aesthetic* (New Haven: Yale University Press, 1986), 193–210.

[41] Friedrich Wilhelm Joseph von Schelling, *Philosophie der Kunst* (1802–3), in Peter le Huray and James Day, *Music Aesthetics in the Eighteenth and Early-Nineteenth Centuries*, (Cambridge: Cambridge University Press, 1981), 280.

hoping to find some meaning among the rubble of facts. The Romantic concept of absolute music is therefore Neo-Platonicism in *subjective* form, the cosmology of a transcendental ego in search of an unattainable wholeness. They turned the ancient world on its head. This is why absolute music for the Romantics is posited as a *work* and not a system of tuning; it starts from the particular because the modern subject, in its delusion of genius, tries to create a universe out of itself, hoping to find a global system that might restore its fragmented existence. Thus between the absolute music of Ramos de Pareia and that of the Romantics the absolute had changed irrevocably. The aesthetic system designed to retune the world was only a necessary figment of the Romantic imagination. For Ramos the metaphors of cosmic harmony were literal,[42] but for the Romantics they were literary; both believed in an absolute music, but for the Romantics the absolute was an 'infinite yearning' for the 'spirit realm'[43] that Ramos knew as enchanted reality. Absolute music is therefore doomed by the Romantics as a fictional 'as if'. The ancient idea of absolute music is not so much revitalised by the Romantics but brought into a modern condition.

Thus the rebirth of absolute music in the nineteenth century turns out to be a symptom of a disenchanted world rather than a solution. By hibernating in the aesthetic sphere instead of marshalling the universe, absolute music syncopates against reality as an autonomous work that seems to divorce art from truth. 'The symphony of the universe', as Novalis calls it, is only a nostalgia for enchantment in a world where there is nothing to enchant. As J. M. Bernstein writes, 'every conception of the alienation of art from truth is simultaneously a work of remembrance, a work of mourning and grief, even for those philosophers who doubt that such an "original" state of union ever existed. In modernity beauty is not only alienated from truth, but grieves its loss; modernity is the site of beauty bereaved – bereaved of truth.'[44] Absolute music is therefore only absolute in that it recalls the past when music was once absolute reality. Today absolute music simply curls up in its own orbit as a microcosm of some unknown universe, discovering an aesthetic freedom in an autonomy that is out of tune with the cosmos. It dreams of Pythagoras in equal temperament.

---

[42] See Tomlinson, *Music in Renaissance Magic*, 211 and 246.

[43] E. T. A. Hoffmann, 'Review of Beethoven's Fifth Symphony', *Allgemeine musikalische Zeitung*, vol. 12 (1810), ed. D. Charlton, trans. M. Clarke, *E. T. A. Hoffmann's Musical Writings: Kreisleriana, The Poet and the Composer, Music Criticism* (Cambridge: Cambridge University Press, 1989), 238–9.

[44] J. M. Bernstein, *The Fate of Art: Aesthetic Alienation from Kant to Derrida and Adorno* (Cambridge: Polity Press, 1992), 4.

4

On division

So modernity, by disenchanting the world, divides it. Modern music is therefore divided. One of the first signs of this division is the expulsion of music from language, as if tones and words were separate entities vying for power. This is why the history of modern music is staged dialectically as a struggle between instrumental and vocal forces grappling for totality.[1] Music's progress and its desire for meaning are both generated by a split that is the mark of its modernity.

Hegel claimed that the Reformation witnessed some of the earliest stirrings of modern consciousness.[2] Once again, modernity is born out of division; it broke out of a cataclysmic fracture that not only split Christianity but divided Europe into warring factions. Thus it is hardly surprising that modern progress should move schismatically for Hegel, pushing itself forward through a continual conflict of reformation and counter-reformation which the philosopher would conceptualise as the dialectic of history. What is modern about the Reformation for Hegel is that humanity finally discovers its individual freedom as a kind of 'heretical principle';[3] humanity liberates itself from the past through an exercise of individual reason, embodied in the figure of Martin Luther nailing his theses on the door of the Wittenburg church. However, the freedom of modern subjectivity which Hegel speaks of is the very freedom that Max Weber describes as an incarceration; the rationality of the Protestant work ethic closes in on humanity like an 'iron cage'.[4] It is not so much Luther that Weber has in mind as the Puritans who pushed the logic of the Reformation to an extreme practice. 'Ascetic Protestantism', claims Weber, is the origin of modernity's 'ascetic rationalism'.[5] The disenchantment of the world is therefore Puritanism secularised; instrumental reason is instrumentalised religion. If this is the case, then perhaps it is with the ascetic reformers, whom Luther himself

---

[1] See the chapters in this volume 'On God', 'On Conscious Life-forms' and 'On the Apocalypse'.

[2] Georg Wilhelm Friedrich Hegel, *The Philosophy of History*, trans. J. Sibree (New York: Dover, 1956), 412–547.   [3] See Berger, *The Heretical Imperative*, 1–31, 56–8 and 128.

[4] Max Weber, *The Protestant Work Ethic and the Spirit of Capitalism*, trans. T. Parsons (London: George Allen and Unwin, 1976), 181.   [5] Ibid., 183.

denounced as 'zealots',[6] that music is first disenchanted and divided from language as mere tone. Indeed, in certain churches the Word of God became so rationalised as intelligible speech, that the unintelligible sounds of music were eradicated from the service altogether. In 1525, the city council of Zurich, under Huldrych Zwingli, silenced music from its worship, isolating musical tones as the absent 'other' of congregational speech.[7] Nothing could be a clearer sign of music's disenchantment than the removal of music from ritual. For Zwingli, music was not necessary because it no longer connected the earth to the heavens; there was no more magic in its substance to influence the celestial realms. The nature and meaning of music therefore changed with the division of Christianity.

What is different about the word-tone debate is not primarily the question of intelligibility or morality, which, after all, are arguments that the ascetic reformers could easily glean from their reading of St Augustine; it is rather the question of disenchantment that effects the relationship between word and tone, forcing music into a kind of instrumental functionalism where tones are no longer things with a magical ontology but tools of efficient utility. In Foucauldian terms, the analogical unity created by the system of resemblances is replaced by a representational system where tones are made to represent words to achieve a unity of thought.[8] This unity, however, divides.

Prior to the Reformation, music was not 'pure' music as if it were a separate entity of pitches and rhythms. The ancient concept of 'vox' (voice) incorporated both vocal and instrumental sound; indeed, the voice was regarded like an instrument with the tongue functioning as a plectrum that played the air of the wind pipe.[9] Moreover, music was mixed media – sonic, visual, calligraphic and textual; the experience was cultic, coloured and encrusted with symbols. Far from being a pure sign, music was a hidden signature, embedded in the world through a system of resemblances where it could articulate the diversity of the cosmos within the unity of the octave; it was the *discordia concors* of the world.[10] Within this system, the differentiation of instrumental and vocal music was not structured hierarchically as a binary opposition as it is in modernity; rather sound and text found their being in the rationality of the celestial spheres. One could imitate the transcendental ratios,

---

[6] Martin Luther, '*Preface*' from Johann Walther, *Geystliche gesangk Buchkleyn* (1524).

[7] Friedrich Blume, *Protestant Church Music: A History* (London: Victor Gollancz, 1975), 509. [8] Foucault, *The Order of Things*.

[9] See Aristotle, *De anima*, 420b27–8. On 'vox', see Charles Burnett, 'Sound and Its Perception in the Middle Ages', in *The Second Sense: Studies in Hearing and Musical Judgement from Antiquity to the Seventeenth Century*, ed. C. Burnett, M. Fend and P. Gouk (London: Warburg Institute, University of London, 1991), 46–9.

[10] See Tomlinson, *Music in Renaissance Magic*, 50 and 85.

says Cicero, both 'on stringed instruments and in singing' to reflect the 'divine truths' of the heavens,[11] no doubt because such noetic harmonies were both instrumental and vocal, emanating from the hum of the crystal spheres[12] and from the sirens which, according to Plato, perched on each ring.[13] Speech and sound were therefore equated in the heavens. Or as Agrippa puts it, 'harmony and words are composed of numbers';[14] they shared the same rationality. They also shared the same substance. In Ficino's magical formulations, sounds and words were both conceived 'as an airy, spiritual, animate material similar or even identical to a disembodied spirit or demon'.[15] Thus the magic depended on a music that was composite in structure and heterogeneous in its unity.

With the religious schism, the magic of music found its mixture sifted out by the rationality of the new liturgy; the composite elements were segregated into separate spheres. Of course, the alignment of word and tone had always been a significant aspect of text expression,[16] but with the Reformation the relationship between text and music came into friction on both sides of the religious divide, and this changed the method and meaning of the concept of word-tone integration. At the extremes of both the Reformation and counter-reformation, music was forced to submit to words to make worship intelligible. But how could it submit to words unless a division had already taken place between word and tone? Under the new regime, sound withdrew from the world as the husk of language. Music suddenly lost its rational substance and became a sonic void. It only regained its meaning by following the contours of the text. This is why text underlay became such a critical issue from *c.* 1530; the question of word-tone unity had become a question of word-tone identity.[17] The melismatic setting of text in earlier music suddenly *appeared* arbitrary, for the epistemic shift in the sixteenth century had narrowed *logos* down as the intelligible utterances of the mind of God or man which music must imitate in a declamatory fashion. Music represents words.

It was the Protestant ascetics who most vehemently split music to

---

[11] Cicero, *Republic*, quoted in Edward Lippman, *A History Of Western Aesthetics* (Lincoln: University of Nebraska Press, 1992), 7.

[12] See Macrobius, *Commentarii in Somnium Scipionis*, vol. 2, ed. J. Willis (Leipzig: B. G. Teubner, 1970), comm. 1.4, 2–3.   [13] See Plato, *Republic*, 616d–17c.

[14] Tomlinson, *Music in Renaissance Magic*, 62.

[15] Ibid., 136. Also see D. P. Walker, 'Ficino's *spiritus* and Music', in *Music, Spirit and Language in the Renaissance*, ed. P. Gouk (London: Variorum Reprints, 1985), VIII, 131–50.

[16] See Don Harrán, *Word-tone Relations in Musical Thought from Antiquity to the Seventeenth Century* (Neuhausen-Stuttgart: American Institute of Musicology and Hänssler-Verlag, 1986).

[17] See Honey Meconi, 'Is Underlay Necessary?' in *Companion to Medieval and Renaissance Music*, ed. T. Knighton and D. Fallows (New York: Schirmer, 1992).

rearrange reality as an opposition between the word that clarifies the world and the tone which mystifies it. Within this system, music had to be brought under the rational control of the word in case it should lure the Puritan soul back to the superstitions of the past – if not of the Pope. Music was therefore dangerous. An irrational fear of church organs seized Puritan communities, as if the sounds blown from its pipes reminded them of the airy spaces that were once inhabited by disembodied spirits. To disenchant the music, physical and verbal violence was applied; they melted the organ pipes into tin and exorcised the air by conceptualising it with the Word. So instead of floating nebulously as some disembodied spirit, music became a physical phenomenon for the Puritans. From now on, it was only the word that was spiritual, belonging to the disembodied mind; conversely, for John Calvin, music was material, a mere ornament that titillated the senses. Its magical allure had become a form of sensual enticement 'solely for the pleasure of the ear'.[18] Calvin literally despiritualised music by giving it a body which enabled him to denounce music as sensual and to validate the word as the product of the rational soul. The division of body and soul therefore relegated music as mere matter for the mind to dominate through the word lest 'the ear be more attentive to the harmony of song than is the mind to the spiritual meaning of words'.[19] As with the organ pipes that were melted into tin to make pewter utensils,[20] sound was desensualised and reduced to a tool. It became a function of intelligibility, quite literally an instrument, which Calvin described as a 'funnel [entonnoir]' to channel the words to the heart.[21] Thus music, as a sonic funnel, had to have its ornamental protuberances removed to facilitate the flow of the text. In a Protestant anthem such as Tallis' 'O Lord in Thee is all my trust', the music is pared down with a homophonic asceticism and sealed syllabically in case its magic should seep out and overcome the senses (see example 2). The music is instrumentalised as a means for words; it conveys rather than connects; it rationalises ritual instead of ritualising religion. The injunction of the English Reformation to set 'a playn and distincte note, for every sillable',[22] aims to control music; it does not attest to the unity of words and music but the division of words and music which is then forced into a uniform identity by instrumental reason. Modern rationality divides and rules.

So what took place in the Puritan communities of the sixteenth

---

[18] John Calvin, *Institution Chrétienne*, quoted in *The New Oxford History of Music: The Age of Humanism*, ed. Gerald Abraham (Oxford: Oxford University Press, 1968), 4:442.

[19] Ibid.

[20] See Robert M. Stevenson, *Patterns of Protestant Church Music* (Durham, NC: Duke University Press, 1953), 16.   [21] Blume, *Protestant Church Music*, 517.

[22] Royal Injunction of 14 April 1548, to the Dean and Chapter of Lincoln Minster; quoted in Gustave Reese, *Music in the Renaissance* (New York: Norton, 1954), 796.

Ex. 2 Thomas Tallis, 'O Lord in Thee is all my trust'.

O Lord, in Thee is all my trust, Give ear un-to my woe - ful cries;

Re-fuse me not that am un-just, But bow - ing down thy hea - ven-ly eyes

century was a form of rationalised devotion, where music no longer mirrored the ineffable songs of the angelic hosts, but 'funnelled' concepts from the mind to the heart. The Puritan soul turns in towards itself, withdrawing from the magical world of resemblances to experience the indwelling Word of God. Indeed, the Papists live in sin for Calvin precisely because their music remains within the superstitious system of resemblances, which mistakes for reality the 'figurative' language of the Old Testament. Their attempt to employ 'instrumental music . . . to imitate the practice of God's ancient people', says Calvin, merely apes the Old Testament in a 'senseless and absurd manner, exhibiting a silly delight' in an ancient worship which merely prefigures the Gospel. The light of Christ has dissipated the 'shadows of a departed dispensation' he says.[23] For the Puritan, the enlightened Word of God has superseded the penumbra of resemblances; the ancient world is as distant from the modern age as the old covenant is from the New Testament. Thus instrumental music no longer means anything in the modern era of Christ, the Word made flesh, because the system of resemblances no longer stands as truth. In the new dispensation, sound and text, instrument and voice, polyphony and melody, become binary oppositions where *logos* dominates over *harmonia*. A music that had enchanted the world by weaving its mixture as an invisible bond between heaven and earth is now cordoned off to harmonise with itself beneath the articulation of words as a sign without signification. To adapt the words of Foucault: the 'tautological world of resemblances finds itself dissociated, and . . . split down the middle', with the tools of

---

[23] John Calvin, *Commentary on the Book of Psalms* (Edinburgh, 1847), 3:494–5, quoted in Stevenson, *Patterns of Protestant Church Music*, 14.

analysis on one side and the 'murmuring resemblance of things' on the other.[24]

The division of music was a Puritanical act. The repercussions were not confined to the Puritan communities, but were felt across Europe from the Scottish Psalter to Palestrina's polyphony in Rome. In such cases, intelligibility was sanctioned as a verbal formula that would reform music. But the putative rationality of the Protestant ethic should not be mistaken as the modern condition itself; it is modernity's *pre*-condition. As Weber points out, the asceticism of the Puritans was a calling; it was a choice of obedience and not a burden.[25] However rational their worship, it was still spiritual and ethical. What forges the 'iron cage' of rationality for Weber is the *secularisation* of Puritan asceticism that turns divine calling into human fate. 'This new order', writes Weber, 'is now bound to the technical and economic conditions of machine production which today determines the lives of all the individuals born into the mechanism . . . with irresistible force'.[26] The rationalised worship of Protestantism is still religious worship. Music, to borrow the language of the reformers, was still grace and not yet work. But what does this worship sound like when it is secularised as a commodity under the conditions of machine production that Weber speaks of? What is the music of ascetic Protestantism in secular form?

---

[24] Foucault, *The Order of Things*, 58.   [25] Weber, *The Protestant Work Ethic*, 181.
[26] Ibid.

5

On opera

To dis-*enchant* the world is to leave it un-*sung*. Modernity registers its songlessness by trying to re-enchant the world with its own voice. The revelation of this unsung condition occurred in the final decades of the sixteenth century, which witnessed an obsession with song as an Edenic mode of expression. The vocal turn in music, from which opera is born, is a symptom of disenchantment. Opera sings in an unsung world as nostalgia for an ancient age enchanted by music. Perhaps this is why the earliest operas were all pastorals,[1] set in Arcadian landscapes emptied of dung and toil, and filled with singing nymphs and demigods mingling among the shepherds and lovers. The pastoral is the world as a garden, a secular Eden conjured by the desires of the urban imagination,[2] where work is play because the only implement that works nature is the very lyre that enchants it. This Orphic lyre, (mis)represented by the Renaissance as a *lira da braccio*, colonises the landscape with its harmonies, modulating the brutality of nature into the grace of culture.[3] And the figure who dramatises the Arcadian landscape is Orpheus, the son of Apollo, the god of music. He is the one who undulates the landscape with the drones of the *lira da braccio*; his song is the eco-system of the enchanted world. Music is the magic that makes the pastoral.

As a genre, the pastoral drama is a product of modernity; it is the modern dream of a Golden Age. Giambattista Guarini, the author of the most celebrated pastoral of the sixteenth century, *Il pastor fido*, says that its form is 'something modern'.[4] And his critics agreed; this tragi-comic genre, far from reviving antiquity, is an impure mix of Greek drama. Modern in form, ancient in content, the pastoral embodies the split which modernity makes to measure itself against the past. Indeed,

---

[1] See Nino Pirrotta, 'Early Opera and Aria', in *New Looks at Italian Opera: Essays in Honor of Donald J. Grout*, ed. W. W. Austin (Ithaca: Cornell University Press, 1968), 72–89, Ellen Harris, *Handel and the Pastoral Tradition* (London: Oxford University Press, 1980), 25, and Katz, *The Powers of Music*, 142–8.

[2] See Frank Kermode, *English Pastoral Poetry from the Beginning to Marvell* (London: Harraps, 1972), 14.

[3] On Arcadian landscapes see Simon Schama, *Landscape and Memory* (London: HarperCollins, 1995), 517–78.

[4] Giambattista Guarini, *Compendio della poesia tragicomica* (1599), quoted in Harris, *Handel and the Pastoral Tradition*, 16.

modernity cannot define its orientation without this division. Opera too, as a type of pastoral, shares the same fissure, but it attempts to dress the wounds by using music both to recount the ancient magic and to demonstrate it as a modern practice. Music brings the reality of the pastoral's past into present experience. So although opera was conceived more than a hundred years after the earliest pastoral, it was already latent in the pastoral as the magical component.[5] In this sense Romain Rolland was correct when he called the very first pastoral, Angelo Poliziano's *Favola d'Orfeo* (*c*.1480) 'l'opéra avant l'opéra'.[6] All the constituents of opera are already there: Poliziano brings together Platonic theory, Orphic mythology and the Arcadian eclogues of Ovid to dramatise the magical powers of music, a magic vocalised by actual songs on stage and realised by the machinery off stage.[7] Moreover, Poliziano's pastoral inaugurates opera's most celebrated plot, that of Orpheus in the underworld, and connects directly with Monteverdi's *Orfeo*, which in its original ending imitates the same final scenes of Dionysian dismemberment. What distinguishes Monteverdi's *Orfeo* from Poliziano's is that the music is no longer a realistic element called for by the narrative but saturates the entire spectacle. For Poliziano music was only required at strategic moments in the plot, whereas for Monteverdi music becomes the plot itself. By 1607, the subject had become the medium; the content is the form. Hence Poliziano's *Favola d'Orfeo* is retitled *L'Orfeo, Favola in musica*; Monteverdi's opera is music about music; it is both *in musica* and *de musica*. And just to make it clear, the music tells you. In Monteverdi's prologue, the Florentine practice of a narrator singing with a lyre is reinterpreted with *Musica* herself personified on stage as the one who controls the narrative.[8] She defines herself: 'I am music', she sings, after which she proceeds to elaborate the theory of her own powers; she moves, she allures, she enchants, for the lyre in her hand is the Orphic lyre of the opera. The magic on stage is the magic you experience, presented and demonstrated before your very ears; she is both the content and intent of opera. By the time of Monteverdi's *Orfeo*, the question of enchantment had become the question of music itself.

Obviously something had happened to music in the 130 years that

---

[5] See Gary Tomlinson, 'Pastoral and Musical Magic in the Birth of Opera', in *Opera and the Enlightenment*, ed. T. Bauman and M. P. McClymonds (Cambridge: Cambridge University Press, 1995).

[6] Romain Rolland, *Musicien d'autrefois* (Paris: Librairie Hachette, 1908), 19.

[7] See Nino Pirrotta and Elena Povoledo, *Music and Theatre from Poliziano to Monteverdi*, trans. K. Eales (Cambridge: Cambridge University Press, 1982), 3–36, Tim Carter, *Music in Late Renaissance and Early Baroque Italy* (London: B. T. Batsford, 1992), 152, and Roy Strong, *Art and Power: Renaissance Festivals 1450–1650* (Woodbridge: Boydell Press, 1973), 37.   [8] See Pirrotta, *Music and Theatre*, 120.

separate Poliziano's *Orfeo* from Monteverdi's. Why does music reflect upon itself in the guise of opera in the early years of the seventeenth century? Why does it need to define its identity – 'I am music' – and explain its own practice? Why does it have to demonstrate in reality the magic it recounts as ancient history? Perhaps it was because modernity finally realised that its disenchantment of the world was the unsinging of music. After all, the group who allegedly created opera, the so called 'Florentine Camerata' of Giovanni Bardi, which included Vincenzo Galilei and Giulio Caccini, were driven by a sense of loss and the need to regain an ancient magic. Although it would be simplistic to claim that the Camerata invented opera,[9] the theories they espoused in the 1580s register the disenchantment of music that is the anxiety behind opera. They wanted to revive the bardic magic of monodic song, for modern music, they claimed, had come into a crisis of identity: music had lost its power. If it were still magical, argues Galilei, then where are the 'miracles' today that are described in the ancient texts?[10] 'Pythagoras cured alcoholics, and Empedocles the mad, and Xenocrates someone possessed of a devil', says Bardi, but modern music is merely a polyphonic confusion of affections that cannot work its magic on the soul.[11]

A hundred years earlier, magic was a musical practice for a musician like Ficino;[12] by the time of the Camerata, it could only be proposed as a theory for the re-enchantment of reality. Their discussions testify to a disenchanted world disenchanted with itself, and so mark a critical moment of self-realisation in modernity's progress. From now on, music's future becomes a matter of recovery; its drive towards the new is haunted by an idealised past. Like Arcadia itself, 'ancient music', says Galilei, is 'lost . . . and its light has so dimmed that many consider its wonderful excellence a dream and a fable'.[13] Thus the Camerata instigated a new strategy for modernity: it denounced the present as a pale imitation of music's 'first and happy state'[14] to propel the ancient strains back to the future as a paradise regained. Consequently, modernity,

---

[9] See, for example, Claude V. Palisca, 'The Alterati of Florence, Pioneers in the Theory of Dramatic Music', in Austin, *New Looks at Italian Opera*, 9–11. The theories of the Camerata were not unique; however, I shall use the Florentine Camerata as a focus for the new theories of music discussed within the humanist circles of sixteenth-century Italy.

[10] Vincenzo Galilei, *Dialogo della musica antica e della moderna* (1581) in Strunk, *Source Readings in Music History*, 305. Much of Galilei's argument here is taken from a letter he received in 1572 from Girolamo Mei; see Palisca, *The Florentine Camerata*, 45–77.

[11] Giovanni Bardi, *Discourse Addressed to Giulio Caccini, Called the Roman, on Ancient Music and Good Singing*, in Palisca, *The Florentine Camerata*, 111. Again, the material is adapted from Mei's letter to Galilei; see above.

[12] See Walker, 'Ficino's *spiritus* and Music', in *Music, Spirit and Language in the Renaissance*, VIII, 131–2, and Tomlinson, *Music in Renaissance Magic*, 144.

[13] Galilei, *Dialogo*, 310.   [14] Ibid.

from the Camerata to Adorno, mourns for an unsung world by projecting a melodious past as its Utopian hope; with the disenchantment of
the world, music becomes a site of both nostalgia and anticipation,
where Arcadia and Utopia, fixed at either end of history, yearn for harmonisation.

To put it another way, the Camerata inaugurated the pastoralisation
of music theory. Their ideas, as the impulse behind opera, created an
Arcadian dream evident in the flurry of pastorals by Peri, Caccini and
Cavalieri that purport to be the 'birth of opera' around the dawn of the
seventeenth century.[15] It is a controversial matter whether these
Florentine pastorals really constitute the 'birth of opera',[16] but they certainly produced, as their afterbirth, the modernity of instrumental
music. The problem with the Camerata's strategy is that it is necessarily divisive: it has to denounce the present to idealise the past as its
future. If opera heralds the promise of Utopia, then the songless present
has to be overcome. Instrumental music must be surpassed. Opera is
therefore the pre-condition of absolute music's modernity, not only
because its overture anticipates the sinfonia, but because it forced
instrumental music into an emptiness of being which speaks of a
modern despair.

The logic is simple: what happens to music when the world is
unsung? It becomes instrumental. A disenchanted world vocalises its
hope by projecting its loss as instrumental music; its unsung tones only
make sense as a negation of the past, drained of Arcadian presence. In
opposition to the pastoral, instrumental music is an empty sign, lacking
the magical presence that only the voice can represent. 'After the loss of
[ancient music] men', according to Galilei, 'began to derive from . . .
instruments . . . rules . . . for composing and singing several airs
together.' A music without speech is therefore made to explain the disenchantment of music. This is why Galilei, following his teacher
Zarlino,[17] calls instrumental music 'artificial'; its music is a simulation
of nature. But whereas Zarlino idealised nature as a metaphysics of
numbers, for Galilei it was an Edenic state of pure expressivity which
had been lost. Thus Galilei does not only undermine instrumental
music but *all* modern music. The vocal polyphony manufactured by the
abstract contrapuntal laws of Zarlino is equally artificial for him. This is
because the origin of polyphony, claims Galilei, is instrumental. It was
invented by ignorant musicians who started to play 'several airs in con-

---

[15] See, for example, Claude V. Palisca, *Baroque Music* (Englewood Cliffs, NJ: Prentice Hall,
1981), 29–38.

[16] See Lorenzo Bianconi, *Music in the Seventeenth Century*, trans. D. Bryant (Cambridge:
Cambridge University Press, 1987), 161–89.

[17] See Fend, 'The Changing Function of *Senso* and *Ragione* in Italian Music Theory of the
Late Sixteenth Century', 211.

sonance' on the cithara, solely 'to tickle the ear' with their clever inter-vallic calculations. Instrumental music is therefore the original sin of modern music. The 'modern contrapuntists' may write for voices, but their music is already unsung, because humanity has eaten from the tree of instrumental knowledge, which excludes modernity from the garden of Arcadia.[18] Instrumental music is therefore the stigma of modernity, the very sound of disenchantment.

In this way, the humanism of the Camerata has a curious affinity with the Protestant ascetics; it rehearses the Puritan ethic in secular form, transforming a rationalised liturgy into a secular spectacle, which, by the 1640s, would become arguably the first musical commodity within the economics of operatic production.[19] Like the Puritans, the Camerata divided music into body and soul, where instrumental music functions as a sensual 'tickling' that hovers in the ear 'without sense, movement, intellect, speech, discourse, reason or soul' in contrast to the disembodied word which 'expresses the conceptions of the mind'.[20] It is 'self-evident', writes Bardi, 'that just as the soul is nobler than the body so the text is nobler than counterpoint'.[21] Once again, tone is forced to submit to words; like Calvin's funnel, the function of music is to channel human verbiage from the mind to the heart to align concept with passion. The result was a monodic style of singing, derived from bardic improvisation, but controlled by an ascetic minimalism, where, at least in theory, music is pared down in range and cleared of all contrapuntal clutter to concentrate its ethical affect as sung speech. Monody is the rationalisation of song, what D. P. Walker aptly calls a form of 'musical Puritanism'.[22]

Thus it is hardly surprising that the Camerata's theory, far from inaugurating the return of an ancient magic, actually eradicated it. Their revival of monodic song turned an ancient practice into a modern condition, for what monody cannot tolerate is precisely the mixture that characterises the ancient world of resemblances. Galilei lamented the 'composite and different natures' of modern contrapuntal music, echoing the complaints of his mentor, Mei;[23] today's music, says Mei, 'does not work any of the miracles [known to the ancients], since it conveys to the soul of the listener at one time diverse and contrary signs of affections as it mixes indistinctly together airs and tonoi that are completely dissimilar and of natures contrary to each other'; modern polyphony, he adds, 'differs haphazardly from one part to another . . .

[18] Galilei, *Dialogo*, 308, 310, 312 and 315; translation slightly modified.
[19] See Bianconi, *Music in the Seventeenth Century*, 180–9, and the chapter in this volume 'On Machines'.   [20] Galilei, *Dialogo*, 312.
[21] Bardi, *Discourse Addressed to Giulio Caccini*, 115.
[22] See Walker, *Studies in Musical Science in the Late Renaissance*, 63–5.
[23] Galilei, *Dialogo*, 118.

the soprano hardly moves, while the tenor flies and the bass goes strolling in slipper-socks'. Worst of all, this results in 'the disordered perturbation, mix-up and mangling of words' that befuddles the mind.[24] Clearly, music for the Camerata was no longer that composite mixture of the ancient world, where speech and tone could co-exist without being identical. The seemingly haphazard underlay of words beneath the melismas of ancient music is discarded by the Camerata for a music that follows the inflections of speech, hugging the contours of language as if *identity* constituted the unity of the word-tone divide. In monody there is no waste; the melody is meant to determine the verbal meaning by fixing the emotions, to denote, define and communicate a message without the blurred edges of polyphonic connotations.

But what kind of unity is this? The unity only works if the division of tones and words is forced together by the will of the monodic self. The unity is not a condition of the universe but the coercion of the ego; it is not cosmic but particular, located in the individual who controls the world by the force of rhetoric.[25] Monody is therefore an instrumental totality, for the voice is used as a *tool* that no longer requires the vertical validation of the celestial spheres but moves horizontally 'to induce in another the passion that one feels'.[26] It controls the 'other'. The magic that the Camerata wants is, ironically, the very magic of instrumental reason that disenchants the world. Thus monody signifies an ontological shift: the harmony of the spheres has collapsed into the song of the self. As a consequence, the metaphysics of being is no longer grounded in a cosmology but an anthropology, in which song becomes the origin of humanity, lost in some Arcadian past which modernity must recover to regain the plenitude of being which instrumental music lacks. This eventually gave rise to the speculative histories of language in the eighteenth century, most famously articulated by Rousseau, which claimed that the first intelligible utterances of humanity were sung.[27] The effect of opera was to divide nature into subjective and objective states, with an interior realm of sung speech alienated from the cold corridors of the external world.

Giulio del Bene said as much in 1586 when he gave a speech to another Camerata in Florence, the *Accademia degli Alterati*, proposing

---

[24] Girolamo Mei, 'Letter [to Vincenzo Galilei] of 8 May 1572', in Palisca, *The Florentine Camerata*, 61, 62 and 63; translation slightly modified.

[25] See Katz, *The Powers of Music*, 62–75 and 130–4.   [26] Galilei, *Dialogo*, 317.

[27] See the chapter in this volume 'On the Body'. Also see Downing A. Thomas, *Music and the Origins of Language* (Cambridge: Cambridge University Press, 1995), and Jean-Jacques Rousseau, *Essai sur l'origine des langues* (1764) in *The First and Second Discourses together with the replies to Critics and Essay on the Origin of Languages*, ed. and trans. V. Gourevitch (New York: Harper & Row, 1986).

that music should be transferred from the quadrivium to the trivium, that is, from the immutable structure of the medieval cosmos to the linguistic relativity of rhetoric, grammar and dialectics.[28] In the trivium, music becomes *human* and can be made infinitely malleable by the power of rhetorical persuasion. This shift allows man to bend music according to his linguistic will, twisting and distorting its intervals to vocalise his passional self. Monody deliberately breaks the harmonic laws of the cosmos to legitimise humanity as the new sovereign who creates his own laws out of his own being. This new style of singing, by 'transgressing through several forbidden intervals', as Caccini puts it,[29] articulates the heretical ego of the new humanity. Singing is its being; or to borrow Derrida's term, singing brings out from the recesses of the ego the 'metaphysics of presence' in an unsung world, bereft of divine presence.[30] The shift from the quadrivium to the trivium signals a modern ontology.

In this sense, the monodic statement 'I am music' in Monteverdi's *Orfeo* is really the 'I am' of the new humanity. The prologue is a manifesto that renegotiates the meaning of the self as a monodic presence with power to influence the world. Nothing could be more modern than this supposedly ancient method of singing through which *Musica* simultaneously explains and demonstrates her instrumentality. Whereas in the past, humanity was fixed like alphabets upon the cosmic page, with opera, man has become a flexible, linguistic being; he is now the prologue that *author*ises the text. Opera transforms what Foucault calls the 'prose of the world', by using music to interiorise the script as the inflections of self-presence.[31] This contrast can be seen, suggests W. J. T. Mitchell, by comparing medieval and modern cartoons. In the medieval cartoon speech is pictured as a scroll, which emanates from the hand, as if this were the scholastic space of canonic texts and endless commentaries. In the modern cartoon, however, language balloons out of the mouth as a bubble of the soul. And it is monody that first makes audible this disembodied bubble of the 'invisible interior' that is the modern subject; it negates the 'scriptive space' of resemblances for the sung speech of self-*represent*ation.[32] So it is not the text itself that is fundamental to opera but its intonation. In other words, the unscriptable inflections of language, notated as music, carry the sound of Arcadian

---

[28] See Palisca, 'The Alterati of Florence', 14–15.

[29] Caccini, *Le nuove musiche*, 44; translation modified.

[30] See Jacques Derrida's discussion of Rousseau's *Essai sur l'origine des langues* in *Of Grammatology*, trans. G. C. Spivak (Baltimore: Johns Hopkins University Press, 1976).

[31] See Foucault, *The Order of Things*, 34–42, and Gary Tomlinson, *Monteverdi and the End of the Renaissance* (Berkeley: University of California Press, 1987), 3–11.

[32] W. J. T. Mitchell, *Picture Theory* (Chicago: University of Chicago Press, 1994), 91–2.

Ex. 3 Claudio Monteverdi, *L'Orfeo*: Prologue – bs 22–4.

[And now, with noble anger, now with love,   I can inflame the coldest minds.]

presence. This is why modernity has to sing itself into Utopia in the seemingly bizarre if not silly unreality of opera. The self must perform; it cannot be read; it must find itself as melody whose rhetoric distorts the written grammar. The false relations and 'forbidden' dissonances of the second practice through which *Musica* claims to incite anger and inflame passion do not picture the affective states with the kind of madrigalism that Galilei, in fact, disparages;[33] rather the so called *stile rappresentativo*, re-presents the soul as music, animating the words with an immediacy of meaning (see example 3). One 'speaks in tones', writes Caccini, 'to move the affects of the soul' in another.[34]

Such a notion is not without precedent. The tonal inflections of monody that form the invisible script of the text are a secular version of the sacred vowels of the Hebrew language, which, because they were never written down, gave rise to all kinds of magical speculations during the period. The language was only made alive when read aloud, like the word of God which has to be *breathed out* to accomplish its purposes.[35] 'In Hebrew the vowels are not letters', writes Spinoza:

That is why the Hebrews say that 'vowels are the soul of letters' and that bodies without vowels are 'bodies without soul'. In truth, the difference between letters and vowels can be explained more clearly by taking the flute, which is played with the fingers. The vowels are the sound of music; the letters are the holes touched by the fingers.[36]

In opera, the ancient belief that Hebrew is the language of Eden is secularised by modernity to make spoken music the language of

---

[33] Galilei, *Dialogo*, 127.

[34] Caccini, *Le nuove musiche*, 44–5. On the idea of the voice as a presentation of the beautiful soul in seventeenth-century Italy, see Iain Fenlon and Peter N. Miller, *The Song of the Soul: Understanding Poppea* (London: Royal Musical Association, 1992), 36–9.

[35] See Maurice Olender, *The Language of Paradise: Race, Religion, and Philosophy in the Nineteenth Century*, trans. A. Goldhammer (Cambridge, MA: Harvard University Press, 1992), 1–36.

[36] Baruch Spinoza, *Abrégé de grammaire hébraique*, ed. J. Askénazi and J. Askénazi-Gerson (Paris: Librairie Philosophique J. Vrin, 1968), 35–6, quoted in ibid., 24.

Ex. 4 Claudio Monteverdi, *L'Orfeo*: structure of the Prologue.

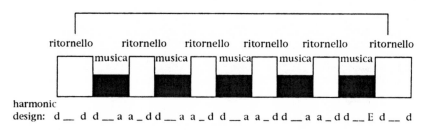

harmonic
design: d __ d d __ a a _ d d __ a a _ d d __ a a _ d d __ a a _ d d __ E d __ d

Arcadia, where, as Giambattista Doni writes, 'music was natural and speech almost poetic'.[37] The music of the voice carries the secret vowels of the soul; it intones an unwritten presence, whereas the instrumental mechanism forms the clatter of consonants that are like 'holes' on the flute – that is, a sign of absence.

So it is the function of instrumental music to form the empty consonants for the voice to animate in performance. When *Musica* sings in the prologue of Monteverdi's *Orfeo* her presence on stage is signified by the absence of the instrumental ritornello *off-stage* – the unseen consonants for her vowels. The ritornello functions as aural scenery; it encloses the prologue like a perspective set, framing the voice as the outer sections and punctuating the monologue as the space in which *Musica* moves and poses (see example 4).

In contrast to *Musica*'s improvisations, the ritornello is fixed. It is static in structure, not only encasing *Musica* with a symmetrical design, but reflecting the same spiral within itself as a closed system, where the bassline rotates down the 'arpeggio' of the mode from D to D, alternating flat and natural hexachords; and with each step, the bass oscillates up then down a fifth, as if to define, on the most atomistic level, the structural fixity of perpetual return in the form (see example 5): the ritornello is truly a ritornello. Moreover, the upper instrumental voices reinforce this self-reflexive stance by exchanging their lines and register in a counterpoint that confuses the location of melodic presence. It is only by homing in on the unison at the final cadence that the true identity of *Musica* emerges out of the instrumental texture as voice. *Musica*'s entry is a moment of individuation.

This is the revelation of the monodic self, the individual whose rhetorical presence can transform and mutate the static world of the ritornello. As *Musica* says: 'I am music. With my sweet accents I can make every restless heart peaceful and inflame the coldest minds, now with

---

[37] Giambattista Doni, *Trattato della musica scenica* (1633–5), quoted in Harris, *Handel and the Pastoral Tradition*, 26.

Ex. 5 Claudio Monteverdi, *L'Orfeo*: Prologue – bs 1–5.

anger, now with love'. Thus in *Orfeo* it is vocal music that is instrumental in method, and it is Orpheus himself who demonstrates *Musica* in style and action; through him, writes Susan McClary, 'we learn how manipulated we truly are: we hang on his every pitch as though he constructs reality for us – which indeed he does'.[38] He possesses the magic of *Musica* who at the very start is able to change her lines over an unchanging bass to exhibit her rhetorical prowess. She is the one who can conjure up passion with wayward intervals that do not need to return to the final; she opens out the harmonies, to the fifth (bars 14, 24, 35, 46) then to the dominant of the fifth (bar 57), that the ritornello has to close; she flouts the laws of dissonance which the ritornello keeps, and she distorts the melodic contours that it delineates. What *Musica* does in the prologue Orpheus pursues to extremes in the opera.

But what of the ritornello, the shadow of *Musica*? As scenic architecture, can it have a role? After all, it cannot speak. *Musica* is capable of self-exegesis, but the ritornello, says Philip Pickett, is 'capable . . . of projecting almost any emotion',[39] which is to say that it projects nothing at all. It has no rhetorical power; it is just an empty structure that outlines its form for *Musica* to move in. That the ritornello means nothing, however, does not mean that Monteverdi is incapable of making its nothingness meaningful. Indeed, its presence, or rather its absent pres-

[38] Susan McClary, *Feminine Endings: Music, Gender and Sexuality* (Minnesota: University of Minnesota Press, 1991), 42.

[39] Philip Pickett, 'Behind the Mask', liner notes for his recording with the New London Consort of *Claudio Monteverdi: L'Orfeo*, CD 433 546–2 (L'Oiseau-Lyre, 1991), 18–19.

ence, is critical in the opera as a signification of nothing. It returns as an architectural pillar at the end of Act II and at the beginning of Act V as if to frame the scenes of hell itself – the abyss of the 'King of Shadows' as Orpheus puts it.[40] These structural returns mark the moments of loss in the opera: first the loss of Euridice on earth (Act II), then secondly, the loss of Euridice in hell (Act IV). Thus what surrounds *Musica* in the prologue is the very absence that will swallow Euridice, and, indeed, *Musica* herself, for, despite the symmetrical structure that the ritornello imposes on the opera, *Musica* never returns. Like Euridice, she disappears. What recurs in the final act is only the ritornello; it returns to trace the same location that began the opera, but this time in terms of a loss: 'These are the gardens of Thrace', sings Orpheus, 'and this is the place where sorrow pierced my heart with the bitterest news'.[41] But although the ritornello returns, the landscape has changed, for the music that sets the scene is a ritornello from hell; instead of leaving the instrumentation unspecified, as on the previous occasions, Monteverdi now calls for the same instruments that had orchestrated the descent into Hades in Act III – the cornet, trombone and regal. These are traditionally the sounds of the underworld. In the final act, the ritornello brings the abyss into Arcadia, and the plenitude that started the opera is now unsung. Orpheus may sing, but his music no longer enchants nature; the dancing nymphs and melodious shepherds have deserted the landscape, and Orpheus is left alone within the void constructed by the ritornello, alienated from nature with only the voice of his echo returning 'each last word' of his lament. Indeed, with his echo, Orpheus becomes an allegory of the ritornello's solipsistic structure where presence is only a reverberation that orbits autonomously in the hollow of the empty self. He has become instrumental music in the echo-system of his own ego. And to underline the point, Monteverdi changes mode, from the soft (*cantus mollis*) to the hard (*cantus durus*) hexachord to symbolise the indifference of an obdurate nature that can only reply with the disenchanted echoes of the mountains.[42] Orpheus represents the modern ego whose rhetorical sovereignty alienates humanity from nature; and the echo, a symbol of unrequited love, becomes the sound of an unrequited music that returns to itself to leave the world unsung.[43]

Thus latent in *Orfeo* is the story of opera's own disenchantment: Orpheus the man who controls the passion of others with the power of

---

[40] Monteverdi, *L'Orfeo* (1607), ed. C. Bartlett (Huntington: King's Music, 1993), 51.

[41] Ibid., 108.

[42] See Eric T. Chafe, *Monteverdi's Tonal Language* (New York: Schirmer, 1992), 154–5.

[43] In Guarini's *Il Pastor Fido* the echo creates a secret prophetic statement by stringing the final syllables of each line together. In *Orfeo* the echo simply dies away and reveals nothing of the future. See Silke Leopold, *Monteverdi: Music in Transition*, trans. A. Smith (Oxford: Clarendon Press, 1991), 96–8.

Musica cannot control his own passions and so exchanges for Utopia an alienation from nature and his desires. In the end, he is divided from Euridice, and is isolated in an Arcadia which has hardened into an indifferent landscape as cold as the symmetry and structural calculations of the ritornello. The dualism that started with the oscillations of vocal and instrumental textures in the prologue spawns a series of extreme fissures in the opera between joy and sadness, light and dark, Arcadia and Hades, gods and men, and it culminates in an unintentional dualism that is the impasse of the final act: there are two endings. And both of them are an undoing of the monodic self; either Orpheus flees from the Bacchantes or else he requires some *deus ex machina* (Apollo) to winch him out of the impotent interior of his monodic subjectivity. If opera attempts to re-enchant an unsung world through the modern ego, then *Orfeo* is not the birth of opera, as is sometimes thought: it is already its end.

6

On machines

> As Euridice was seen. *Everything* must be understood from that
> viewpoint. (Adorno)[1]

Opera is the symptom of which it claims to be the cure. It is a performative contradiction, presenting the quadrivium while demonstrating the trivium, so that the ancient magic it wants is negated by the method it uses. Antiquity and modernity simply cancel each other out as a contradiction of content and form.

It is tempting to hear opera within the magical episteme that it tries to conjure up on stage. Nature is painted as an enchanted idyll where Orpheus sings of the celestial spheres in ways not dissimilar to Ficino's incantation of magical songs. Indeed, if Poliziano's *Orfeo* is an opera in embryo, then opera's lineage is surely related to the improvised style of incantatory speech which Poliziano knew from Ficino himself.[2] Is not Monteverdi's *Orfeo* drawing from the same source of Orphic mysticism? When Orpheus intones his prayer to Apollo, accompanying himself on the *lira da braccio*, is he not performing the magical rituals prescribed by Ficino? No, because for Ficino magic was a practice that worked in reality, whereas in opera it is a performance staged in the reality of the work.

Moreover, there is no direct line that connects Poliziano's *Orfeo* to Monteverdi's. Opera is knitted together from many strands. As a magical spectacle that eventually became a spectacular commodity, opera's mechanism of authority combines Orphic wizardry with the visual propaganda of the Italian courts that hosted elaborate tournaments, fêtes, jousts, fireworks, water displays and royal entries – events designed to project a show of power. The media image of the monarch depended on these spectacles, which were advertised, prolonged and propagated through commemorative books that documented the magnificence of the occasion.[3] The significance of music in such an *optic* form of propaganda was not primarily through its sonic medium, although

---

[1] Theodor W. Adorno, *Beethoven: The Philosophy of Music*, ed. R. Tiedemann, trans. E. Jephcott (Cambridge: Polity Press, 1998), 6.   [2] See Katz, *The Powers of Music*.
[3] See Strong, *Art and Power*, 21

music was performed, but in its meaning. Music was employed as an emblem of power. The recurring theme of these Renaissance fêtes, as Roy Strong suggests, is the harmony of the spheres, visualised on stage, to mirror the harmony of the princely state. There is a commingling of Orphic mysticism and human power in these 'pre-operatic' spectacles. On the one hand, this attests to the composite nature of the ancient episteme where magic, music and politics could co-exist within an ontic cosmology. Yet inherent in this Neo-Platonic universe is the instrumentality that would ultimately disenchant the cosmos, for the epistemic line between cosmic magic and instrumental domination is blurred at the point where the monarch assumes a divine right which he prosecutes through the machinery of state. The microcosm of the celestial spheres on stage is also a microcosm of the monarch's rule. These Renaissance festivals, writes Strong, 'enabled the ruler and his court to assimilate themselves momentarily to the heroic exemplars' in the celestial realms,[4] as if their regime were somehow validated by a higher power. In this way, the microcosm of the spectacle could easily reflect a macrocosm of harmonic coercion.

How does this optic regime work? There are two stages to the process: a backstage and a frontstage.[5] The backstage was cluttered with machines. The rituals of magic that imitate the invisible forces of the supernatural world through the descent of deities from clouds and the flying of furies from the pit of hell were controlled with an Oz-like wizardry from behind the scenes.[6] Such stage machinery was something of a 'crowd puller' that winched in the audiences, particularly with the commodification of opera in the seventeenth century, but it also had a disenchanting effect by turning the world into clockwork. In these engineered spectacles, the invisible realm of essences, which had kept the ancient world spellbound by superstition, is demystified by an unseen realm backstage,[7] filled with the ropes and levers of stage machinery.[8] What is mystical on stage is merely the puppet of a mechanised magic, whose cogs are concealed by the set and whose creaks are masked by the music. However much the event enacts a superstitious ritual, the fear of the invisible has already been overcome because the invisible is

---

[4] Strong, *Art and Power*, 40.

[5] The idea of a backstage–frontstage division of knowledge and power is indebted to the work of Simon Schaffer in a paper given in Clare College, Cambridge, entitled 'Enlightenment Machines and Darkened Spaces: Managing Access to Practical Knowledge' (1997).

[6] See, for example, the description of Caccini's opera, *Il Rapimento di Cefalo* (1600), in A. M. Nagler, *Theatre Festivals of the Medici: 1539–1637* (New Haven: Yale University Press, 1964), 96–100.

[7] On machines and the control of nature, see Leonard Goldstein, *The Social and Cultural Roots of Linear Perspective* (Minnesota: MEP Publications, 1988), 28–59.

[8] See Pirrotta and Povoledo, *Music and Theatre from Poliziano to Monteverdi*, 47.

ultimately knowable as an interaction of levers, pulleys and pumps. The backstage is therefore the site of modern science; the ancient magic that the Camerata sought is only possible through modern technology. For all its magic, opera is a machine world of cause (backstage) and effect (frontstage). So upstage there might be an ancient cosmos with rotating spheres and ethereal beings in full flight, but the magic is thoroughly modern, purely instrumental and entirely human. As Roy Strong puts it:

The world of the court fête is an ideal one in which nature, ordered and con-trolled, has all its dangerous potentialities removed. In the court festival, the Renaissance belief in man's ability to control his destiny and harness the natural resources of the universe find their most extreme assertion. In their astounding transformations, which defeat magic, defy time and gravity, evoke and dispel the seasons, banish darkness and summon light, draw down even the very influences of the stars from the heavens, they celebrate man's total comprehen-sion of the laws of nature. The Renaissance court fête in its fullness of artistic creation was a ritual in which society affirmed its wisdom and asserted its control over the world and its destiny.[9]

One of the earliest contraptions that reified the magic of the cosmic order was designed by Leonardo da Vinci for the *Festa del Paradiso* to cel-ebrate the marriage of Gian Galeazzo Maria Visconti to Isabella of Aragon in 1490.[10] Such ducal marriages were designed to create lines of power across the map of Europe, and Leonardo's presentation of the Ptolemaic universe, with its starlit heavens that opened to reveal musi-cians and singers, was not merely a talismanic ritual to draw down astrological influences upon the happy couple, but a machine that vali-dated a new political harmony. Hence the planets, personified as singers, backed the new order by paying their tribute to the duchess.

Exactly how much this cosmic automaton consciously reflected an instrumental mentality is difficult to gauge given the epistemic blur of ritual, art and power in the final decade of the fifteenth century. But latent in the construction of the spectacle is the rationality of the modern world. Almost a hundred years later, the same scenario would be reenacted, but this time the staging would actually gesture to the instru-mental domination of nature, conjuring up the elements of fire, earth, water and air to conflate the Neo-Platonic magic of Ficino with the sci-entific exploitation of modernity.[11] In a way, the theme is a reflection of the mechanics of the spectacle itself, which was engineered by Bernardo Buontalenti and organised by Giovanni Bardi who orchestrated the event as a re-creation of ancient music in the manner of his own Camerata. The collaboration of music and mechanics in these famous *intermezzi* of 1589 was designed to celebrate the marriage of Christine of

---

[9] Strong, *Art and Power*, 40–1. [10] See ibid., 36. [11] See ibid., 136

43

Plate 2 The musical cosmos in perspective: Bernardo Buontalenti's design for the first *intermezzo* for *La Pellegrina* (1589), 'The Harmony of the Spheres'.

Lorraine to the Grand Duke Ferdinando I de Medici, but they inadvertently staged the divorce of the ancient and modern world; Buontalenti wanted to emulate the ancient science of Hero of Alexandria and Bardi the ancient music of Orpheus, but Buontalenti's magic that blew clouds across the stage and pulled up mountains before the eyes was as instrumental as Bardi's monodic manipulation of the world. There is a fundamental dissonance at the heart of the spectacle, despite the descent of Rhythm and Harmony in the final *intermezzo* to soothe the burdens of humanity and to bring society into an Arcadian dance.[12]

The modern dissonance backstage is echoed frontstage. Simply compare Buontalenti's scenic designs for the opening *intermezzo* with earlier representations of cosmic harmony (plate 2). Buontalenti's scenery is in *perspective*. Whereas in the past the monochord unified an aggregate space through the system of resemblances, the linear perspective in Buontalenti's design unifies the musical cosmos by depositing it as an object in a rationalised, geometrical space. The eternal essence of music is slotted into what Martin Jay calls an 'eternal container of objective processes'.[13] By putting the harmony of the spheres in perspective the ancient cosmos collapses, because the infinity of the universe, which for the ancients could never be grasped by human vision, has been made finite; cosmic infinity has been replaced by the infinity of the vanishing point which puts the human eye at the centre of perception. With this monocular vision, music no longer looks down upon humanity but is looked upon as an object; in Erwin Panofsky's words, the new perspective on music creates 'an objectification of the subjective'.[14] It disenchants the very enchantment it projects. Perspective, writes Panofsky,

seals off religious art from the realm of the magical . . . where the miraculous becomes a direct experience of the beholder . . . Perspective, in transforming the *ousia* (reality) into the *phainomenon* (appearance), seems to reduce the divine to a mere subject matter for human consciousness.[15]

The vertical connection in Neo-Platonic thought between the stage and the stars has been severed by the monocular vision that re-positions the subject as the sovereign eye (I), particularising the cosmos in the retinal bowl of the ego. And where should the sovereign be placed in the *Teatro Mediceo* that staged the *intermezzo* than at the viewpoint where the linear co-ordinates of perspectival space converge as the centric rays of princely vision, as if his eye were at the centre of the visible world.

---

[12] For a detailed description of the spectacle see Nagler, *Theatre Festivals of the Medici*, 70–92.

[13] See Martin Jay, *Downcast Eyes: The Degeneration of Vision in Twentieth-Century French Thought* (Berkeley: University of California Press, 1993), 53.

[14] Erwin Panofsky, *Perspective as Symbolic Form* (1927), trans. C. S. Wood (New York: Urzone, 1991), 66. [15] Ibid., 72.

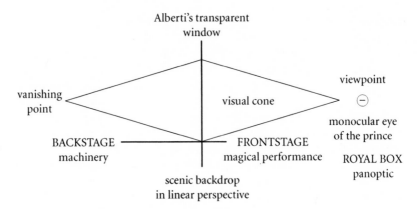

Fig. 1 Opera in perspective

The entire cosmos spirals into his focus as the vanishing point is to infinity.[16] From viewpoint to vanishing point, from infinity to infinity, the sovereign sees the world as it was once seen by God. But in the sovereignty of his vision, he is also alienated from the world he objectifies; the 'transparent glass', as Leon Battista Alberti famously calls it,[17] that intersects the visual cone from viewpoint to vanishing point is in fact the entirely opaque plane of the picture (see figure 1). It is the axial backdrop in the theatre, a window that Buontalenti frames with a proscenium stage that divides the subject which sees from the object that is seen; 'the spectator', writes Jay, withdraws 'entirely from the seen (scene), separated from it by Alberti's shatterproof window'.[18] The cost of assuming divine control afforded by perspectivism is a vision so remote from the object that the subject can only manipulate it with an instrumental distance. Thus what is extended through the eye of the prince beyond the backdrop is the stage machinery, which is screened from view by the opacity of Alberti's transparent window as if it has vanished with the vanishing point to manipulate the scene from the outside. The remote vision of the monocular subject is extended by remote control; it is an instrumental vision operated by an instrumental reason. In this way the frontstage and backstage meet to neutralise the space of enchantment as observable fact, creating a panoptic regime, where visual power is an invisible instrumentality that controls the site (sight) of Arcadia.[19] In its very representation of the ancient world, what

---

[16] See Leon Battista Alberti, *Della Pittura* (1435), translated by J. R. Spencer as *On Painting* (New Haven: Yale University Press, 1966), 48, where he names the central ray the 'prince of rays'.   [17] *Ibid.*, 51.   [18] Jay, *Downcast Eyes*, 55.

[19] On the panopticism see Michel Foucault, *Discipline and Punish: The Birth of the Prison*, trans. A. Sheridan (New York: Vintage Books, 1977), 195–228.

E. J. Dijksterhuis calls 'the mechanisation of the world picture' is already in operation to set the scene for modern science.[20]

Some commentators regard the *intermezzi* of 1589 as seminal to opera, not least because the composers involved included Peri, Caccini and Cavalieri who vied to be the progenitors of the form.[21] Moreover, the scenes of heaven, hell and Arcadia are those of the earliest operas, and Buontalenti's internal arrangements of the *Teatro Mediceo*, because of the mass dissemination of his designs, standardised the Baroque theatre which staged the perspectival scenery of opera. But perhaps the connection is not so much the style of music or its staging as the mechanism of power behind the spectacle. If the music of the spheres in the *intermezzo* is staged as the machinery of state emanating from the vision of the sovereign by whose invisible control society cadences in Arcadia, then it is hardly surprising that the same regime would appear in the operas performed for the 'machine King' himself, Louis XIV, who would sometimes appear as the *deus ex machina*, the Sun King, Apollo, as a kind of theophany of power. In the staging of Cavalli's *Ercole amante* (1662), for example, given in honour of the royal wedding, the King himself not only turned up on stage as the Sun, but also as Pluto and Mars to establish his cosmic presence.[22] But even without such divine appearances, the royal machinery is felt; when Apollo descends in the final part of Lully's *Alceste*, this engineered deity 'is not so much a historical figure', remarks Jean-Marie Apostolidès, 'as the king himself'. In the opera, the machine king becomes the 'King machine' to fuse his body with the apparatus of state: he is both spectator and machinery.[23] As Charles Cotin wrote in 1665, the King,

clearly sees that his mind is . . . the soul of the world. If this soul did not reconcile all the differences in one perfect temperament that establishes the harmony of the universe, the universe could disintegrate; and if the monarch's intelligence does not control the whole machinery of government, the machine falls to pieces.[24]

Such megalomania, however, is not confined to kings. As Foucault points out in his famous analysis of *Las Meninas*, it is 'man' who pictures himself in 'the place of the king' in modern society, assuming a sovereign gaze that objectifies and mechanises the world as his own possession.[25] Opera, once divested of its humanistic theories and courtly

[20] Edward Jan Dijksterhuis, *The Mechanisation of the World Picture: Pythagoras to Newton*, trans. C. Dikshoorn (Princeton: Princeton University Press, 1986).

[21] See, for example, Pirrotta, 'Early Opera and Aria', 39–46.

[22] See Bianconi, *Music in the Seventeenth Century*, 239.

[23] Jean-Marie Apostolidès, *Le roi-machine: Spectacle et politique au temps de Louis XIV* (Paris: Les Éditions de Minuit, 1981), 128–31.

[24] Charles Cotin, *Réflexions sur la conduite du roi* (Paris: P. le Petit, 1665), 9.

[25] Foucault, *The Order of Things*, 307–8.

function, reflects the machinery of the king as capitalist power. In 1637, opera became the first musically fungible spectacle with a ticket price.[26] It went into mass production; it was purchased, consumed and disposed of with the kind of capitalist mentality that turns the world into commodified forms. If the invention of perspective coincided with the commodification of oil painting,[27] then it is quite plausible that the perspectival space of opera also packaged music as a detached commodity; opera even resembles the space of capitalist venture that divides the system into a backstage of production and a frontstage of consumption, concealing labour for the buyer to view the 'pleasing prospect' of some Arcadian property. Lorenzo Bianconi suggests that the commercialisation of opera in Venice is the beginning of the genre, or, at least, that there is a difference in kind between the early operas and their commercial counterpart.[28] But the commodification of opera is really a completion of the instrumentality inherent in the earlier forms. As a disenchanted object which pictures an enchanted world, opera finally succeeded in turning the music of the spheres into what Weber calls the 'cosmos of the modern economic order'.[29]

Thus opera, as ideology and commodity, is a symptom of the modern condition which it tries to cure with an ancient music. Monocular and monodic, opera is the singular affair of the sovereign eye/I and passionate voice. It is not the Arcadian community or the festival that it depicts on stage, but the modern subject that Descartes would later define as the cogitating ego for whom the world is arranged as objects in a perspectival world for rational manipulation.[30] He tried, he said, 'to be a spectator rather than an actor',[31] observing the world as fact rather than living with the uncertainty of myth. This strangely makes the Cartesian ego into the image of Orpheus. After all, what demythologises Orpheus and alienates him from nature is his gaze, namely, his need to objectify Euridice as observable fact. 'How can I know that she is following?' he asks, aware that if he were to glance back, he would lose her forever (Act IV). Nevertheless, he turns. This is the moment – the *Augenblick* – in the opera where magic, monody and vision collide with such force that they repel each other as a kind of epistemic fissure between the ancient and modern world. Orpheus, the monodic self, sings; he sings of his monocular powers – 'I see you now, I see . . .' – as if the certainty of vision and the monodic manipulation of his voice could reconcile him to the object of his desires in a moment of Arcadian magic (see example 6). But there is no magic, because there is no music. There is a gap. For all its

[26] Bianconi, *Music in the Seventeenth Century*, 163.   [27] See Jay, *Downcast Eyes*, 58–9.

[28] Bianconi, *Music in the Seventeenth Century*, 161–70.

[29] Weber, *The Protestant Work Ethic and the Spirit of Capitalism*, 181.

[30] See Jay, *Downcast Eyes*, 69–79.

[31] René Descartes, *Discourse on Method, Optics, Geometry, and Meteorology*, trans. P. J. Olscamp (Indianapolis: Bobbs-Merrill, 1965), 24.

Ex. 6 Claudio Monteverdi, *L'Orfeo*: Act IV – bs 131–4.

[O sweetest eyes, I see you now, I see ...
but what eclipse obscures your light?]

rhetorical power, monody fails in this instance of vision; for Monteverdi, no music can articulate this juncture of irredeemable loss. What should have been the ultimate moment of presence – the sight of Euridice – is a moment of absence. The magical component of the pastoral withdraws, and Orpheus is literally left speechless in the revelation of loss and disenchantment. His monody breaks off into stunned silence: 'I see . . .' He sees Euridice as fact, but that fact is so devoid of value that no music can define its truth. The Euridice he sees is unsung. And to underline the irreversible nature of this vision, there is a harmonic disjunction either side of this gap that cannot be resolved, with a flatward slippage on one side of the hexachordal divide that belongs to a world of substantive reason, and a sharpward shift from a C minor to an E major sonority on the other side to symbolise a world of instrumental distance. This gap, articulated by this extreme harmonic upheaval and a change of orchestration,[32] is an epistemic fissure not only of this opera, but of opera itself. Its unsung reality articulates the point of disenchantment where Orpheus and Euridice, as subject and object, are torn apart by a monodic and monocular rationality to leave the enchanted world irretrievably lost as a memory.

Opera, writes Jean-Laurent Lecerf, 'is a painting that really speaks';[33]

---

[32] See Chafe, *Monteverdi's Tonal Language*, 151–4.

[33] Jean-Laurent Lecerf de la Viéville, *Comparaison de la musique italienne et de la musique française* (Brussels, 1704–06), 1:196, quoted in Georgia Cowart, *The Origins of Modern Musical Criticism: French and Italian Music, 1600–1750* (Ann Arbor: UMI Research Press, 1981), 74.

like Orpheus it sings, 'I see'. The painting that the voice animates is the ancient world, sealed by a perspectival window with proscenium frames. What speaks is the modern magic of self presence. This is a contradiction: the presence of the voice is cancelled out by the absence of the observer. But the contradiction is not a mark of transition from one epoch to another, but a sign of opera's modernity. To picture the world is modern, claims Martin Heidegger. 'To be new', he says, 'is peculiar to the world that has become a picture.'[34] Modernity styles itself through an objective representation of the past which is always distanced by the definition of the frame. But the modern subject not only pictures the past, but yearns for it as its future. Hence it is the voice, with its passional immediacy that retrieves the past as present experience to goad modernity back to the future. Thus picturing the world is the vision that *defines* modernity; singing that vision is the machine that *drives* it forward. The modernity of opera is the mechanisation of sight through the immediacy of music.

[34] Martin Heidegger, 'The Age of the World Picture', in *The Question Concerning Technology and Other Essays*, trans. W. Lovitt (New York: Harper and Row, 1977), 132.

7

On space

Linear perspective is a *visual* logic. If it has any influence on music then this must be *seen* as a shift in the visualisation of sound. However, Filippo Brunelleschi's invention of artificial perspective in 1425 does not map on to the polyphony of the early sixteenth century, as is sometimes suggested.[1] Do the contrapuntal constructions that conceive of sound horizontally and vertically really correspond to the illusion of visual depth in painting? It is true that the rationalisation of both space and sound in the Neo-Platonic world encapsulated a divine order as a microcosm for a humanistic society to perceive and harness,[2] but that does not mean that music and image can exchange their historical forms without friction. The contrapuntal lines of music are not the perspectival lines that systematise space as a grid in order to locate objects behind a window of reality; its harmonies are not empty spaces in which meaning is deposited, and neither is the counterpoint the vanishing point for the ear to grasp the totality of the cosmos.[3] In fact, far from being parallel structures, music and vision came into conflict, creating an epistemic rift by the end of the sixteenth century between the ancient and modern world.

'The sixteenth century', writes Lucien Febvre, 'did not see first; it heard and smelled, it sniffed the air and caught sounds. It was only later, as the seventeenth century was approaching, . . . that vision was unleashed.'[4] Similarly, Robert Mandrou suggests that the ancient world

---

[1] See Edward E. Lowinsky, 'The Concept of Physical and Musical Space in the Renaissance (A Preliminary Sketch)', in *Papers of the American Musicological Society*, ed. G. Reese (1946), and Goldstein, *The Social and Cultural Roots of Linear Perspective*, 76–7.

[2] See Martin Kemp, 'The Mean and Measure of All Things', in *Circa 1492: Art in the Age of Exploration*, ed. J. A. Levenson (New Haven: Yale University Press, 1991), 95, and Samuel Y. Edgerton Jr., *The Renaissance Rediscovery of Linear Perspective* (New York: Basic Books, 1975), 24.

[3] Jessie Ann Owens, in *Composers at Work: The Craft of Musical Composition 1450–1600* (Oxford: Oxford University Press, 1997), argues from the available manuscript sources that composers of sixteenth-century imitative polyphony continued to think in layers and in separate parts as their predecessors had. Despite the claims of Edward Lowinsky, there is no shift in 'perspective' that allows for a simple mapping of the new vision on to compositional technique. Also see note 15.

[4] Lucien Febvre, *The Problem of Unbelief in the Sixteenth Century: The Religion of Rabelais*, trans. B. Gottlieb (Cambridge, MA: Harvard University Press, 1982), 432, quoted in Jay, *Downcast Eyes*, 34.

was an aural habitat that relegated sight below sound and sense. 'The order of their importance was not the same', he writes, 'for sight, which is dominant today, stood in third position, a long way behind hearing and touch.'[5] However, both Febvre and Mandrou are mistaken because their categorisations of the senses are already a symptom of the modern 'eye that organises' – to borrow Mandrou's own words. The ancient world did not partition the world neatly into such categories; it did not hear first, at least, not on the way that Febvre describes it; in a sense, it heard nothing. Instead of hearing, the ancients *saw* with their *ears*. For them, music organised space.

In the enchanted world of the ancients, music was an airy substance; it did not occupy space, it was its very essence. Artificial perspective, on the other hand, drains out the substantive meaning of harmonic space to situate reality within an empty geometry. Prior to perspectivism, the musical sign, even when devoid of text, could not constitute what Kevin Barry calls an 'empty sign',[6] because there is no empty space in a musical universe. Zero ratios did not exist. Indeed, the Hindu concept of zero, imported from Indian mathematics in the thirteenth century,[7] was something of a theological problem in a cosmos infused with the divine presence of the one true God. 'An empty space (the space of geometry)', writes Alexandre Koyré, 'is utterly destructive to [the ancient] cosmic order', for there is no 'natural place' for the order of things to belong.[8] The ancient *uni*-verse numbered itself from one; zero did not figure in its calculations. Hence the invisible, inaudible sound of music starts from the unison (1:1). The celestial harmony, although mute like the numbers that inscribed its being, sounded its silence as the infinite calculations that ordered the differences and affinities of the entire cosmos. It structured the world, it did not create it *ex nihilo* as if reality were projected from some vanishing point.[9]

So what does this ancient musical space look like? As opposed to the unified grid of perspectivism, the spatial totality of music was simultaneously continuous and fractured: continuous because it connected the spaces of stars and angels with the earth, allowing the invisible and celestial intelligences to flow without friction;[10] and fractured precisely because these varied spaces had to be connected by the monochord.

---

[5] Robert Mandrou, *Introduction to Modern France 1500–1640: An Essay in Historical Psychology*, trans. R. E. Hallmark (London: Edward Arnold, 1975), 50.

[6] Kevin Barry, *Language, Music and the Sign* (Cambridge: Cambridge University Press, 1987).

[7] See Brian Rotman, *Signifying Nothing: The Semiotics of Zero* (London: Macmillan, 1987), 7–14. [8] Koyré, *Metaphysics and Measurement*, 28.

[9] On the relationship between zero and linear perspective, see Rotman, *Signifying Nothing*, 14–22; also see the chapter in this volume, 'On Nothing'.

[10] See Walker, 'Ficino's *spiritus* and Music', in *Music, Spirit and Language in the Renaissance*, VIII, 139–42.

Instead of coalescing space into a unified vision from which vantage point infinity can be perceived on earth, the transcendental vision of the ancient world was predicated on the shattering of space that defers the totality as an inconceivable vision that only God can grasp. In order for humanity to catch a glimpse of eternity, multiple glances had to be mapped over one another as decentred and fissured planes. Thus in medieval pictures, the surface is not seen through as if there were some empty space beyond, but filled in with a luminosity that colours the fissures with a kind of 'musical' substance, or what Panofsky calls a 'homogenizing fluid, immeasurable, and indeed, dimensionless'.[11] Medieval spaces were in some sense acoustic, particularly when they were liturgical in function. As Norman Bryson notes, such spaces did not pinpoint the individual as viewer, but accompanied a community in ritual, choreographing society cyclically, like the stained-glass windows that narrated the rotation of the church's calendar.[12] Indeed, the polyphony sung in the cathedrals was arranged in a cyclic pattern of fractured spaces, composed in layers and laid out in parts, for the sound of worship to fill in, colouring the visual gaps with an aural cohesion that only God can see as a 'score'.

By unifying the co-existence of different spaces without collapsing them into a monotonous vision, music sounded a divine, enchanted world. It formed the co-substantive space of the Holy Trinity, the transubstantial space of the Eucharist and the hypostatic space of divine incarnation, where flesh and spirit are one. If today 'faith has withdrawn from a disenchanted world',[13] as Anthony Cascardi notes, then it is because the perspectival vision of modernity can no longer tolerate the co-existence of different objects in the same space. The unison of form and content, subject and object, flesh and spirit become binary oppositions in perspectival thought: God and man become mutually exclusive, divine indwelling becomes an invasion, miracles become a transgression of nature.[14] Whereas the iconic fractures of harmonic space gesture to a depth beyond its surface as divine reality, perspectival depth is an illusion projected as reality for the instrumental practices of a disenchanted subject for whom the world is like an operatic stage. The sovereign ego subjugates the totality of what it sees with the mechanics of power backstage, but can never co-exist with the objects it manipulates on stage.

This puts music in a very difficult position, for the disenchantment of space disables the power of music which opera extols. When *Musica*

---

[11] Panofsky, *Perspective as Symbolic Form*, 49.

[12] Norman Bryson, *Vision and Painting: The Logic of the Gaze* (New Haven: Yale University Press, 1983), 96–8.   [13] Cascardi, *The Subject of Modernity*, 21.

[14] See Jeremy Begbie, *The Sound of God: Resonances Between Music and Theology* (Cambridge University Press: forthcoming).

appears in the prologue of *Orfeo* she is robbed of the ancient magic she boasts of the very moment she steps on stage. Her text suggests that she gestures to the plants and birds on the Arcadian backdrop behind her as if her voice could control them by the sheer force of her linguistic assertions, but she is unconscious of the fact that her voice has already been silenced by the backdrop. Her cosmic space has shrivelled to become an object under the perspectival gaze that locates her in a rationalised space. She lives in the delusion of rhetorical control when what is controlling her is a visual regime. Unfortunately, the scenic backdrop for *Orfeo* has not survived, but there is no need to assume that it was drawn in perspective, for the perspective has already been internalised in print. Simply look at the notation. The ritornello which shadows *Musica*'s movements as her sonic scenery is in *score*. Even when she emerges from the ritornello with her monodic presence, her voice is still contained within an instrumental grid that positions her every move with the figures that run along the bass axis. Her figured bass notation may appear to escape the cage-like lattice of the ritornello that graphs the music with its staves and barlines, but she is merely trapped in the same rationalised space; the difference with the grid of the basso continuo is that its score is invisible. It forms a transparent window through which she is made to perform. Music in perspective is notated in score.

By the end of the sixteenth century, music was no longer an organisation of space; it was visualised sound.[15] Although scores were not unknown in earlier centuries,[16] they were sporadic rarities that hardly resemble the rigid, grid-like structures printed in the sixteenth century; indeed, the typography even looks like a system of co-ordinates that locates and cages the pitches for the surveillance of the modern eye (plate 3). The old, congealed markings of neumes and ligatures found their blotches separated out into precise points that are aligned for the eye and boxed by barlines that no longer partition large sections, but order the page with a metronomic regularity. The score rationalises the fissured and layered patterns of medieval notation by containing music within a geometrical space that pictures the totality as a map. Indeed,

---

[15] On the early history of scores, see Owens, *Composers at Work*, Edward E. Lowinsky, 'On the Use of Scores by Sixteenth-Century Musicians', *Journal of the American Musicological Society*, vol. 1 (1948), 'Early Scores in Manuscript', *Journal of the American Musicological Society*, vol. 13 (1960), and David Charlton's article on 'Score' in *New Grove Dictionary of Music and Musicians*, ed. S. Sadie (London: Macmillan, 1980). Owens counters Lowinsky's notion that scores represented a change in compositional thought with the advent of complex imitative polyphony early in the sixteenth century; thinking or seeing in score was a much later practice that only became prominent towards the end of the sixteenth century. This later dating supports the connection between score-format and figured bass notation.

[16] For example, twelfth-century florid organum and some early thirteenth-century motets were written in score.

like the Ptolemaic co-ordinate system which was adopted by the early sixteenth century to chart an empty globe for the inscription of newly 'discovered' territories,[17] the handful of sixteenth-century scores presupposes an empty grid of parallels and meridians in the form of staves and barlines on which notes are inserted and newly discovered harmonies colonised. At times the number of notes does not even determine the spatial intervals between barlines; they are simply squeezed into a pre-existent lattice (plate 3).[18]

Thus scores objectify music for the gaze of an ego that no longer requires the multiple vantage points of communal participation that the notated ritual of, say, Ockeghem's *Missa prolationum* invites (see example 7a).

Any attempt to rationalise the Mass as score (see example 7b) will lose the spatial meaning of its original notation, where different temporalities are mapped over the same space and different staffs are dis-located to delineate the magic of the ratios. There is no perspective from which this notation can be grasped as a visual whole. Its totality can only be known in performance.[19] In contrast, the sixteenth-century score does not sound the cosmos as a play of proportions but measures music with a mechanical appetency; its calculations have no other meaning than their functionality; it is an efficient means to an end. The score grasps the totality for the individual ego, enabling it to possess the music as a commodity which it owns *but cannot play*.[20] It replaces the communal ritual with a distant control that so alienates the ego that it cannot perform the sounds it sees. It can only manipulate the music. This is why the earliest scores were not performed, but were didactic objects in text books; they opened music as a visual anatomy for the eye (I) to scrutinise.[21]

So what do you do with a score if you cannot perform it? What is the point of gaining the totality of music if you lose out on participating in it? Having pictured music with an analytical vision, the sixteenth century had to find a way of reducing the score into an instrumental format, so that the sound it sees can sit under the control of the ego's

---

[17] See Woodward, 'Maps and the Rationalization of Geographic Space', and Edgerton, *The Renaissance Rediscovery of Linear Perspective*, 91–123; also see Frank Lestringant, *Mapping the Renaissance World: Geographical Imagination in the Age of Discovery*, trans. D. Fausett (Cambridge: Polity Press, 1994).

[18] See plates 7–24 in Lowinsky, 'Early Scores in Manuscript'.

[19] See, for example, Owens, *Composers at Work*, 45, Margaret Bent, '*Resfacta* and *Cantare Super Librum*', *Journal of the American Musicological Society*, vol. 36 (1983), 376–9, and 'Some Factors in the Control of Consonance and Sonority: Successive Composition and the Solus Tenor', *International Musicological Society: Report of the Twelfth Congress, Berkeley 1977*, ed. D. Heartz and B. Wade (Kassel: Bärenreiter, 1981).

[20] The early printed scores were so expensive that they were probably more a luxury commodity for the glory of the patron or owner than a practical source for performance.

[21] See, for example, 'Score' in *New Grove*, 60–1 and Owens, *Composers at Work*, 42–5.

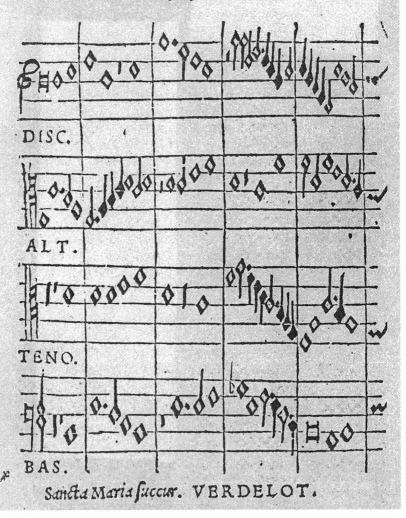

Plate 3 Lampadius of Lüneburg, *Compendium musices* (Berne, 1537).
The earliest modern printed score with barlines – music visualised as
spatial co-ordinates.

Ex. 7 (a) Johannes Ockeghem, *Missa prolationum*, Kyrie II, in original notation.

Ex. 7 (b) Johannes Ockeghem, *Missa prolationum*, Kyrie II, in score.

newly acquired sovereignty. Hence the sixteenth-century ego did not perform the score: it *realised* it. The continuo became an extension of the ego's visual control as the backstage mechanism that brings the score into sonic reality, as a fingering of the self. The realisation of figured bass is the self-realisation of the ego.

Why else would anyone want to instigate such a peculiar practice? What would be the logic of sounding the score within the music as a miniaturised totality inserted in the compositional texture if it is not to make audible a sovereign gaze? The development of the basso continuo is therefore bound up with the history of modern subjectivity. It did not simply evolve as a functional necessity demanded by the music of the later sixteenth century to abbreviate scores for rehearsals, for it participated in the performance. It was not simply a practical device invented to follow the flexible lines of bardic improvisation and monodic song, because these figures run along the *entire* basslines of the earliest operas; they are not just confined to recitatives. The scores of Peri's *Euridice,* Caccini's *Euridice,* and Cavalieri's *Rappresentatione di Anima, et di Corpo,* published within the first two years of the seventeenth century, are all marked with this strange ghosting and doubling of the music, which visualises the score as spectator and realises the event as machine, as if the perspectival and automated structure of opera is inscribed within the notation itself. Constructed by the horizontal axis of the bassline and the vertical axis of the figures, the rationalised space of the continuo contains and locates the rhetorical inflections of the voice. So, ironically, the ideas of the Camerata which seem to notate the triumph of bardic practice over the abstractions of theory, are nothing more than a frontstage performance manipulated by a backstage theory, where the strings of the continuo control the vocal puppetry. All the talk of vocal superiority, not least by *Musica* herself, is just rhetoric; what actually determines opera is an instrumental theory. But, of course, everyone believes *Musica* because no one sees the controls; perspectivism naturalises the instrumentality of the eye as surely as Galilei could only hear nature in monody and Alberti could only see reality through the 'transparent window' of linear perspective; the theoretical grid of figured bass is seemingly a neutral empty stage, where the perversely dissonant inflections of the monodic self can create the reality of its own nature.

For all of *Musica*'s posturing, it is ultimately the continuo that projects the ego's presence, albeit in an instrumental rather than an Arcadian form, because everything the ego surveys through the continuo is an extension of its presence. With the score under its control, the ego becomes panoptic, seeing all without being seen; it is continuous, like the continuo; its presence is always there even when it is inaudible. As C. P. E. Bach says, 'even in heavily scored works, such as operas performed outdoors, where no one would think that the harpsichord could be heard, one misses [the continuo] if it is not there'. It has to be played and heard from the vantage point of perspectival listening: 'if one listens to it from an *elevated position*', he says, 'one can hear every note clearly'.[22] Its presence is necessary because figured bass is the theoretical foundation of Baroque composition; thus its realisation forms a running commentary of the creative ego, especially when the composer himself directs from the keyboard. From 'what source other than the composer itself does [the basso continuo] spring forth?' asks Johann David Heinichen; 'the thorough bass', he adds, 'like composition itself, leads to the complete investigation of the *entire musical edifice*'.[23] Figuring the bass is therefore a kind of tactile analysis that places the

---

[22] Carl Philipp Emanuel Bach, *Versuch über die wahre Art das Clavier zu spielen* (Berlin, 1753–62), translated and edited by W. J. Mitchell as *Essay on the True Art of Playing Keyboard Instruments* (London: Cassell, 1949), 173; my italics; translation modified.

[23] Johann David Heinichen, *Introduction or A Musical Discourse on the Thorough-Bass and Music in General* (1728) translated in George J. Buelow, *Thorough-Bass Accompaniment according to Johann David Heinichen* (Michigan: UMI Research Press, 1986), 309; my italics. On the use of figured bass in composition, see Joel Lester, *Compositional Theory in the Eighteenth Century* (Cambridge, MA: Harvard University Press, 1992), 65–8.

performer inside the composer and so *author*ises the panoptic gaze of
that which is outside the performance. To put it another way, the continuo is both inside and outside the music but never quite coincidental
with it, just like the absolute sovereign for whom the lines of perspective meet to validate his remote vision off stage and his remote control
on stage. The basso continuo, as the site of composition and realisation,
is the viewpoint and vanishing point of the musical spectacle as sounding score.

Consequently, from the seventeenth-century opera to the eighteenth-
century symphony, the continuo was the centre and circumference of
music. It wielded absolute power. From its 'elevated position', it could
peruse and 'investigate the . . . musical edifice' and control the performance. In this sense, it was already absolute music in embryo, a sound
that could embrace and order the totality. The practice only became
redundant in the nineteenth century because its panoptic vision was
more powerfully evoked by the absolute ego as conductor. The conductor could dispense with the keyboard machinery, for his baton had
become the point of control in a society where the psychology of influence was founded on mesmerism;[24] the machinery no longer needed to
be concealed because the power was already invisible. Thus historically
and ideologically, the nineteenth-century conductor situates himself in
the place of the continuo player; he did not evolve from the time-beaters
of the Baroque who tapped tables and waved scrolls of paper in the air,
for his gestures are not about tactus but tactics.[25] He is more an incarnation of the machine King, who, in viewing the work through the transparent window of the score, extends his baton to mesmerise an
orchestra that is laid out before him like a perspectival cone that meets
at his podium. He is outside and inside the music, since he himself plays
nothing, yet manipulates everything; his presence is necessary whether
he twitches his finger or not, for he has the totality in his view, and realises it by operating an orchestra whose labour is hidden by the absolute
harmonies of pure music (see figure 2).[26]

In the genealogy of absolute music opera is therefore seminal: first,

[24] See Alison Winter, *Mesmerized: Powers of Mind in Victorian Britain* (Chicago: University
of Chicago Press, 1998). Also see the cartoon of Berlioz and Wagner conducting each
other to sleep (*Revue trimestrielle*, 9 January, 1864) in Elliot W. Galkin *The History of
Orchestral Conducting: Theory and Practice* (New York: Pendragon Press, 1988), 314.

[25] See George Houle, *Meter in Music, 1600–1800: Performance, Perception, and Notation*
(Bloomington and Indianapolis: Indiana University Press, 1987), 34, and Galkin, *The
History of Orchestral Conducting*, 241–85. Also compare in Galkin's book the diagrams of
the orchestral lay-out, particularly between the 'linear' arrangement in the eighteenth
century (151) and the 'perspectival' pattern in the nineteenth century, such as the plan
of the Leipzig *Gewandhaus* Orchestra under Mendelssohn in 1835 (153).

[26] See Jacques Attali, *Noise: The Political Economy of Music*, trans. B. Massumi (Manchester:
Manchester University Press, 1985), 66–7.

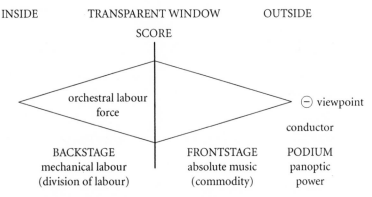

INSIDE   TRANSPARENT WINDOW   OUTSIDE

SCORE

orchestral labour force

⊖ viewpoint

conductor

BACKSTAGE
mechanical labour
(division of labour)

FRONTSTAGE
absolute music
(commodity)

PODIUM
panoptic
power

Fig. 2 The perspectival power of the absolute conductor

because it created the epistemological structures in which music could be objectified on stage for the perspectival gaze of the subject; and, secondly, because it inscribed this gaze as a score that is realised by the continuo. The symphonic site of absolute music and the spectacular site of opera are one and the same; they share the same mechanism of power, the same structure of modern subjectivity and the same vision of absolute control. Opera may style itself as the dialectical protagonist in the history of instrumental music, banishing instrumental sounds as the backstage mechanism for its vocal presence, yet against its own rhetoric, opera's visual structure actually brought instrumental music into perspective as sounding score. Absolute music secretly inheres within opera.[27]

Thus the structure of absolute music was already in place by the Baroque. Yet given these conditions, instrumental music did not become absolute. Why should this be the case in an era when instrumental music was flourishing, and the symphony already formed? What prevented an age of political absolutism from finding an absolute music?

---

[27] As Wagner was to discover with *Tristan*; see the chapter in this volume 'On the Beautiful and the Sublime'.

8

On style

The linguistic turn at the end of the sixteenth century transformed the mathematics of music into the rhetoric of music. Giulio del Bene, by transferring music from the quadrivium to the trivium, shifted music from the cosmos to man, giving humanity some vocal control over the magic of sound.[1] But the redistribution was somewhat lopsided. In the attempt to re-enchant the world with the voice, instrumental music was left discarded in the quadrivium as abstract theory. The transfer severed the identity of music: vocal practice, legitimised by the rhetorical flourishes of the will, was set against the mathematics of instrumental theory, and so split the nature of music between man (humanistic values) and the cosmos (scientific facts), a conflict most acutely articulated by Rousseau and Rameau later in the eighteenth century.

Monody signalled a new ontology for modernity: to sing was to be. But the new identity, however euphonious, created a problem. The eloquence of living in the trivium could not make sense of the world; the shift was meant to validate the monodic ego, but because the trivium has no cosmology, there is no objective world for the ego to ground itself in; it can only assert its influence rhetorically, with no theory to validate its practice. Of course, there was an agenda behind the shift; the monodists wanted to activate the human will as a pragmatic and passional force to break through the constipated intellectualism of scholastic thought.[2] As the Petrarchan saying goes, 'It is better to will the good than to know the truth.'[3] The Camerata therefore willed music as a virtuous act within the trivium and disenchanted the eternal truths of the quadrivium as aberrant theoretical speculations. If the quadrivium was of any scientific use at all, then it was only as a database for the trivium to manipulate. The 'science of music' (quadrivium), says Mei, provides 'truths' for the 'arts' (trivium) to 'exploit . . . for its own end'.[4] Music only

---

[1] See Palisca, 'The Alterati of Florence, Pioneers in the Theory of Dramatic Music', 14.

[2] See Tomlinson, *Monteverdi and the End of the Renaissance*, 3–11.   [3] Quoted in ibid., 6.

[4] Girolamo Mei, 'Letter [to Vincenzo Galilei] of 8 May 1575', in Palisca, *The Florentine Camerata*, 65. Palisca cites this passage as a source of inspiration behind Galilei's empirical experiments with sound; see Claude V. Palisca, 'Vincenzo Galilei's Counterpoint Treatise: A Code for the *Seconda Pratica*', *Journal of the American Musicological Society*, vol. 9 (1956), 85 footnote, and the chapter 'On Disenchantment' in this volume.

finds its moral value in the linguistic power of the will; the quadrivium furnishes the *facts* for the will to activate. Without the trivium, these facts are no longer a means to an end and therefore become meaningless calculations, seemingly inviolable to the theorist, but absolutely useless in reality. 'Observe this', says Galilei, 'if [ancient music] arose primarily to express the passions . . . and to communicate . . . then the rules observed by the modern contrapuntist as inviolable [are] directly opposed to the perfection [of music].'[5] And contrapuntal rules for Galilei are predicated on the artifice of instrumental composition.[6]

Thus instrumental music was rather awkwardly positioned in this epistemological shift. It found itself straddled between the quadrivium and trivium. It was strangely schizophrenic, functioning as a backstage theory that formed the mechanics of composition (thorough-bass), yet, as a practice frontstage, it had to be legitimised by the rhetorical ego which reduced it to a parasite of vocal presence. Although instrumental music as a theory was left in the quadrivium, as a *practice* it was hauled into the trivium where it was taught to speak properly. Instrumental music had to find a voice to find its meaning. Hence, Girolamo Frescobaldi says that his keyboard music is to be played in 'the modern style of the madrigals' as if they were following the expressive nuances and tempo fluctuations 'suggested by the mood and meaning of the words'.[7] The highly sectionalised nature of the pieces formed a kind of repository of rhetorical effects which the ego could activate at will; the performer, says Frescobaldi, 'may finish where he wishes, without being obliged to play them complete'.[8] So for all its theoretical rationality, instrumental music in the trivium developed a volatile, almost erratic texture to follow the expressive violations of the voice. But without words to ground the rhetorical excesses, Italian instrumental music, and in particular the sonata, came to epitomise the indiscriminate mixture of vocal effects that confused rather than articulated the identity of the ego. To the ears of the Northern Europeans, the diction of the Italian sonata was verging on sheer nonsense: 'Sonata, que me veux-tu?' was Fontenelle's famous interrogation of instrumental music.[9]

So what was wrong with the sonata? The Baroque had no problem lip-reading this kind of instrumental music as a dumb copy of the voice; there were standardised figures that could decode the grammar and

---

[5] Vincenzo Galilei, *Dialogo della musica antica e della moderna* (1581), in Strunk, *Source Readings in Music History*, 307. Also see Chua, 'Vincenzo Galilei, Modernity and the Division of Nature'.   [6] See the chapter in this volume 'On Opera'.

[7] Girolamo Frescobaldi, *Toccate e partite d'intavolatura di cimbalo* (1615), translated in Christopher Hogwood, 'Frescobaldi on Performance', in *Italian Music at the Fitzwilliam* (Cambridge: Fitzwilliam Museum, 1976), 18.   [8] Ibid., 19.

[9] See Jean-Jacques Rousseau, 'Sonate', *Dictionnaire de musique* (Geneva, 1781), 639.

meaning of the music;[10] instrumental music could just about 'speak'. The real problem with it was epistemological; instrumental music 'deconstructed' the very basis of musical knowledge. What the sonata reveals is the *linguistic relativity* inherent in the trivium. With music no longer tied to the harmony of the spheres, its melodies simply drifted on the currents of the rhetorical will. This may have enabled humanity to colonise and define new meanings for itself, but there was no way of stabilising these meanings as eternally valid truths. Rhetorical relativity risks meaninglessness, and it was the sonata that made audible this uncontrollable semiosis. Fontenelle confronted the sonata not because it signified nothing, but because it signified too much.[11] The excess of signification spilled over into an indeterminate relativism that decentred the vocal ontology of the ego and destabilised the trivium as the ground of meaning.

What do you do when the heterogeneity of the world no longer harmonises under the music of the spheres but disperses into random fragments? If there is no totality to organise the diversity then the only way to control the mess is to atomise each element in order to sort and file the world as a catalogue of definitions. In the trivium, the global and absolute is replaced by the local and particular; the meaning of the world is no longer an immutable structure, but has to be caught as momentary definitions within the linguistic flux. Absolute music is impossible in the trivium.

One of the earliest symptoms of linguistic relativity in music is the redefinition of musical meaning in terms of styles. The *stile rappresentativo* that arose out of the Camerata is really a style of styles, for this style represents reality as stylised figures.[12] But as the semiotics of the trivium, the *stile rappresentativo* only works as a communicative exchange from ego to ego; it is not a system of free-floating signs detached from the reality of the subject; it can only function as the signature of the self, for it is by fixing the sign to the self that the linguistic flux is momentarily anchored. Style locates and defines the ego to identify the individual in time and space. In this sense, monody is a

---

[10] See Mark Evan Bonds, *Wordless Rhetoric: Musical Form and the Metaphor of the Oration* (Cambridge, MA: Harvard University Press, 1991).

[11] See Maria Rika Maniates, '*Sonata, que me veux-tu?*: The Enigma of French Musical Aesthetics in the 18th Century', *Current Musicology*, vol. 9 (1969) for the background to Fontenelle's purported comment.

[12] See, for example, Claudio Monteverdi 's foreword to his *Madrigali guerrieri ed amorosi* (Venice, 1638), translated in Strunk, *Source Readings*, 413–14, and Johann David Heinichen, *Introduction or A Musical Discourse on the Thorough-bass and Music in General* (1728), translated in Buelow, *Thorough-Bass Accompaniment according to Johann David Heinichen*, 330–80. Also see Leonard G. Ratner, *Classic Music: Expression, Form, and Style* (New York: Schirmer, 1980), and Pirrotta, 'Early Opera and Aria', 52–3.

stylisation of the ego; it customises words with the idiosyncratic inflections of music. Indeed, Caccini conflates style with the self by using the same word – *affetti* – to stand for both the affects of the ego and the effects of the ornamental devices.[13] Style and the will are one and the same. The authenticity of monody depends on this double meaning that fuses the external figure with the internal passion, to stabilise meaning as the interior dialect of the soul. This is why style for the Camerata cannot be displaced from the integrity of the ego; if melodies carry 'the mutation of moral character [*costumi*]', as Bardi puts it, then the costume that one acquires in monody to communicate the affect of the soul cannot simply be an affectation.[14]

Style therefore betrays the identity of the self, for the ego cannot help but leave its mark on the object it produces. This enabled the Baroque to orientate the meaning of music without an absolute measure. Through style recognition, the listening ego can locate and define objects and pinpoint their co-ordinates within the linguistic relativity of the trivium. 'One must have a secure, clear and pure concept of each main style', writes Johann Mattheson later in the eighteenth century, and 'not improperly mix impression [inside] and expression [outside] with one another'.[15] So instead of ordering the being of music as a series of immutable ratios, the Baroque tabulated and classified music according to the variables of function, location, figure, affect, genre and grammar. With this identikit-aesthetic, music could be defined, documented and filed as a known identity. This is why the Baroque did not have a *Formenlehre* but an *Affektenlehre*. Forms are external abstractions that do not define the particular but subsume them as static, absolute shapes that cut across the stylistic boundaries. Style, on the other hand, is made up of tiny figures that provide the forensic details for detecting the origins of a work in an individual. Thus the Baroque defined music by a process of constant division and subdivision to create an inventory of discrete and distinct identities: first the genre, then the subgenre, followed by the style and its figures, with its 'main sentiment . . . subsidiary sentiments . . . dissected sentiments',[16] which are further honed by the idiosyncratic mannerisms of the performer whose ornamental additions actually whittle down the identity of the piece to the moment of performance; it is so punctual in its location that it cannot transcend the time and space of the individual. Indeed, at its most extreme, the music's

---

[13] See Caccini, *Le nuove musiche*, 45.

[14] Giovanni Bardi, *Discorso mandato a Giulio Caccini detto romano sopra la musica antica, e 'l cantar bene*, translated in Palisca, *The Florentine Camerata*, 109.

[15] Johann Mattheson, *Der vollkommene Capellmeister* (Hamburg, 1739), trans. E. C. Harriss (Ann Arbor: UMI Research Press, 1981), 225.

[16] Johann Nikolaus Forkel in his *Musikalischer Almanach für Deutschland auf das Jahr 1784* (Leipzig, 1784), 31–2.

ephemeral identity eludes the attempt to notate the style – notation is already too general. Caccini may have entitled his monodies of 1614 as a 'New Music and a New Way of Writing Them Out' (*Nuove musiche e nuove maniere di scriverle*), but, in practice, he would not pinpoint the style on the page. He tried to write the new practice down, but as Mattheson notes, the spontaneous affects of the Italian style 'do not occur on paper' – at least not on the printed stave.[17] They only appear in the 'preface' as instructions.[18] Style is an annotation of notation; the notes, says Caccini in the preface of his 1602 songs, 'are written in one way, but to be more graceful are affected in quite another'.[19] So style as a personal preference is a personal preface that already speaks of the anxiety of authenticity at the birth of Baroque performance practice.

Thus the Baroque score is not 'the work'; it was not an absolute notation to which one must be true;[20] it is more an attempt to fix the music as a commodity which must be unpacked and realised as one's personal style in the act of reproduction. Baroque notation is a fusion of humanism and materialism, an interface between the self and the commodity which does not allow music to exist as an eternal essence outside the location of interaction. It is inimical to absolute music, merely providing a rational space for the realisation of the ego's identity. As Buffon says, 'Style makes the man';[21] the score, on the other hand, does not make the composer. Hence Johann Jakob Froberger's Toccata I from his *Livre de 1649*, for example, does not look as it should sound (see example 8a). The notation is a mechanism for the fingerprint of the keyboardist to mark. The score does not contain the presence of the work, but the absence of the performer's identity. Thus Louis Couperin's realisation of the opening of this toccata imprints his style (or rather his imitation of Froberger's style) over the notation in a way so divergent from the 'original' that it almost robs the score of its contents (see example 8b). This is because there is no original. Even Couperin's realisation is a kind of *tabula rasa* for the individualisation of the performer. Each realisation is relative to an infinite number of possible realisations, and this holds true

---

[17] Mattheson, *Der vollkommene Capellmeister*, 217.

[18] Similarly, in the preface of Jacopo Peri's opera, *Euridice* (1600), the composer praises Vittoria Archilei, who sang the part of Euridice, for adorning the music 'with those graceful and charming turns which no amount of notation can express and which, if written down, cannot be learned from writing'; cited in Nagler, *Theatre Festivals of the Medici: 1539–1637*, 95. For similar examples and a discussion of these issues, see Tim Carter, 'Printing the New Music', in *Music and the Cultures of Print*, ed. Kate van Orden (New York: Garland Press, forthcoming). [19] Caccini, *Le nuove musiche*, 50.

[20] See Lydia Goehr, *The Imaginary Museum of Musical Works* (Oxford: Clarendon Press, 1992), 89–286, and 'Being True to the Work', *Journal of Aesthetics and Art Criticism*, vol. 47 (1989). See also the chapter in this volume, 'On Divinity'.

[21] Quoted in Laurence Dreyfus, *Bach and the Patterns of Invention* (Cambridge, MA: Harvard University Press, 1996), 217.

Ex. 8 (a) Johann Jakob Froberger's Toccata I from *Livre de 1649*.

Ex. 8 (b) Louis Couperin, 'Prélude à l'imitation de M. Froberger' from *Pièces de clavecin*.

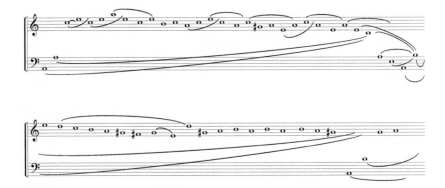

even for less improvisatory pieces, because the Baroque score is always open to the personal markings of ornaments, touch and articulation. So although Froberger notated his music, it was said at the time that no one could reproduce his style.[22] The same was said of Chambonnières whose touch was so unique that it was impossible even to copy the way he played a single chord.[23] An authentic performance of Baroque music is too particular to theorise and too ephemeral to authenticate, for there is no authentic essence, merely an authentic effect which is not available to the distant academicism of historical reconstruction. Style is so punctual that a second take is already too late.

This means that style, like its modish counterpart fashion, only has an ephemeral life-span. It lives for the moment. If one is in doubt about what style to play in, writes François Couperin, one should execute the

[22] See, for example, Rudolph Rasch, 'Johann Jakob Froberger and the Netherlands', in *The Harpsichord and its Repertoire: Proceedings of the International Harpsichord Symposium*, ed. P. Dirksen (Utrecht: STIMU, 1992), 127.

[23] See Pierre Le Gallois, *Lettre de M. Le Gallois à Mlle Regnault de Solier touchant la musique* (Paris: Michallet, 1680), reprinted at the end of Davitt Moroney's introduction to Louis Couperin, *Pièces de Clavecin* (Monaco: L'Oiseau-Lyre, 1985), 38–41.

piece 'in the style of today'.[24] Style updates the score.[25] So, although style locates the identity for that affective moment of monodic self-presence, it cannot sustain the effect, let alone surpass time and space as an eternal monument. The Baroque could not formulate a timeless norm out of its ephemeral, ever-progressing identity; it could only gauge music relatively through a comparative analysis of styles – whether, for example, a piece is sacred or secular, old or new, high or low, French or Italian. Taste was judged by the fittingness of style, genre and function.[26] But such measurements cannot guarantee the canonisation of music. The Baroque, to be sure, formulated a *repertory* of pieces that were re-printed and restylised but it never constituted a canon of works that could bypass time as 'modern classics'.[27] Modern music was either old or new – never eternal. Hence the cultural conflict that plagued the Baroque was known as the *querelle des anciens et des modernes*. The quarrel only stopped when the nineteenth century canonised Baroque music, particularly through the deification of Bach, in the eternal pantheon of absolute music.[28] The Baroque 'canon', in contrast, was a perpetual shuffle of binary relations between composers whose modernity was constantly relegated by the progress of history. Yves-Marie André, in an essay of 1741, noted that Lully, the emblem of French modernity, had recently 'become an ancient . . . relegated almost to the status of the Greeks'.[29] But Lully was only one composer in a chain reaction where Lully would be superseded by Rameau, and Rameau by Gluck and so on. And this process of stylistic relegation had no fixed meaning or canonic stability. One's judgement depended on which side of the *querelle* one was on: to become ancient was either to be 'classic' or out of date; conversely, to be modern was either to be a passing fashion or to be a sign of future perfection. André encapsulated the dilemma of the modern canon when he explained that the quarrel between the ancients and the moderns was an issue over whether beauty 'is fixed and

---

[24] François Couperin, *L'Art de toucher le clavecin* (Paris: Author, 1717), 61. On issues of performance style, see David Y. S . Chung, *Keyboard Arrangements of Lully's Music and Their Significance for French Harpsichord Music* (Ph.D. University of Cambridge, 1996).

[25] It is also clear from Peri's preface to *Euridice* that the addition of embellishments in performance is meant to update the score; he writes that the performers' inventions are there 'more to comply with the taste of our time than in the belief that only herein lay the beauty and power of our singing'.

[26] See, for example, Dreyfus, *Bach and the Patterns of Invention*, 103–68.

[27] On the difference between repertory and canon and the formation of a secular canon of music in the nineteenth century, see Joseph Kerman, 'A Few Canonic Variations', *Critical Inquiry*, vol. 10 no. 1 (1983), 110–14.

[28] See Carl Dahlhaus, *Foundations of Music History*, trans. J. B. Robinson (Cambridge: Cambridge University Press, 1983), 10, 111 and 157, and the chapter in this volume 'On Monuments'.

[29] Yves-Marie (père) André, *Essai sur le beau* (Paris, 1741), quoted in Cowart, *The Origins of Modern Musical Criticism*, 101.

immutable' or whether it is like the 'modes and fashions' that fluctuate with 'opinion and taste'.[30]

But the *querelle* itself was already a symptom of modernity; it attests to music's epistemological shift from the quadrivium to the trivium, for quarrelling is a method of positioning style within the relativity of the trivium. What other system is there within a sphere where truth is asserted as a matter of rhetoric? With cultural products freed from the confines of princely courts, a bartering of style was necessary within the market to affirm one's purchases as a mark of good taste. Quarrelling was therefore a strategy of the newly developed sphere of public opinion.[31] Quarrelling affirms modernity by forcing the monodic subject to interact with others within the trivium to form a critical consensus in a relativistic world. What the trivium demands, then, is not a cosmos but a forum in which music can be validated as a social sense rather than a global essence. The integrity of one's individual style finds external recognition as a shared style. This may not transcend humanity, but it can create a *sensus communis*, that is a style that forms a sense of community, cultivated through the rhetorical eloquence of the trivium.[32] Thus one's conviction is no longer based on facts, but on a trafficking of opinion; and truth becomes a matter of persuasion.

By quarrelling, the trivium turns into a public arena – what Jürgen Habermas calls an *Öffentlichkeit* – and this gave rise to the music critic who acts as the referee, bringing the stylistic factions into arbitration.[33] The proliferation of newspapers, critical journals and moral weeklies in the eighteenth century enabled the critic to form a mirror in which the public could debate about itself through the chit-chat of salon life and café society.[34] The task was to define public taste, and the idea of 'good taste' (*bon goût*) became the new criterion for assessing a culture in a relativistic society.[35] Although taste shares the same tongue as rhetoric, its task is not to formulate opinion but to validate it. Taste is a sense that is both distinctly individual, in that it is subjective, and curiously communal, in that it is invariably right: not everyone will agree with a judgement of taste, but, as Immanuel Kant says, everyone *should* agree

---

[30] Quoted in ibid., 99.

[31] See Jürgen Habermas, *The Structural Transformation of the Public Sphere*, trans. T. Burger (Cambridge, MA: MIT Press, 1991), 15–19, 37 and 39.

[32] See Hans Georg Gadamer, *Truth and Method*, trans. J. Weinsheimer and D. G. Marshall (London: Sheed and Ward, 1975), 19–30.

[33] See Cowart, *The Origins of Modern Musical Criticism*.

[34] See Habermas, *The Structural Transformation of the Public Sphere*, 42–3. On the role of music reviews in establishing a public forum for instrumental music in Germany, see Mary Sue Morrow, *German Music Criticism in the Late Eighteenth Century: Aesthetic Issues in Instrumental Music* (Cambridge: Cambridge University Press, 1998).

[35] See Cowart, *The Origins of Modern Musical Criticism*, 65.

with it.[36] The public tongue consists of individual taste buds that savour music with a kind of salival reaction that is shared by an *ideal* society.[37] It is only by a free trafficking of individual style that the social ideal of the public sphere could be reached.

This is one reason why style became distinctly mixed in the eighteenth century; the styles that divided Europe were deliberately brought into a consensus of taste. For example, François Couperin, in order to canonise Lully and Corelli, felt the need to arbitrate between their French and Italian styles by incorporating the elements of both into a single *goût-réuni*. In his *Apotheosis of Lully* (1725), published a year after his *Apotheosis of Corelli*, Couperin immortalises Lully on Mount Parnassus through a stylistic exchange with Corelli that culminates in an intersubjective duet for violins in which first Lully 'plays the subject with Corelli accompanying him', followed by a reversal, where the two composers swap roles (see example 9). The precision and mixture of the styles allows for the distinctive and communal nature of taste to sidestep the stylistic relativity to bring 'Peace . . . on Mount Parnassus'. Couperin, however, does not surpass or subsume the stylistic divide; he may weave the voices together, but the parts do not join organically into a whole, but remain within the atomistic aesthetic of the Baroque as discrete styles that can be identified and catalogued. It is not that the styles are so defined that they jangle dissonantly against each other; there is no breach of decorum. Indeed, Lully and Corelli begin with imitation at the unison as if to bury their differences; if anything, they accompany each other rather blandly. But Couperin cannot help but let style betray the voice of the composers by leaving tell-tale details in the score. It is essential to attribute the right lines to the right composer to authenticate the peace. There is no fusion of styles in the exchange; they simply coexist as precisely encoded and distinctively notated lines with 'an Italian treble clef for Corelli and a French violin clef for Lully', and appropriate ornaments to match.[38] In the mixture, the styles lose nothing of their punctuality or locality. In the end, the *goût-réuni* is not an anonymous blending of styles but a heterogeneity which leaves a mixed rather than a universal taste upon the tongue.[39]

Advocates of the mixed style, particularly in Northern Germany,[40] wanted to form a consensus of taste that would escape the boundaries of Europe, but their bilingual names for the mixed style – *glückliche*

---

[36] Immanuel Kant, *Critique of Judgement* (1790), trans. J. C. Meredith (Oxford: Oxford University Press, 1973), 50–60 and 82.   [37] See Gadamer, *Truth and Method*, 34.

[38] Dreyfus, *Bach and the Patterns of Invention*, 119.

[39] On a similarly rough mix of national styles in Fux's *Concentus musico-instrumentalis* (1701), see the discussion in ibid., 120, and in Cowart, *The Origins of Modern Musical Criticism*, 130–1.   [40] For an overview of the mixed style in Germany, see ibid., 128–39.

Ex. 9 François Couperin, 'Air Léger' from *L'Apothéose. de Lully.*

Mélange (Heinechen) and *gemischter Goût* (Telemann) – testify to the immiscibility of their project.[41] Ultimately, the mixed style is not so much the reunion of taste as the undoing of style. It is a canonic contradiction: first, because it cannot amalgamate the stylistic components into a single canonic style except as a kind of party trick of whistling and humming two languages at the same time; and secondly, because any stylistic amalgamation would confuse the distinct categories of the Baroque and turn the mixture into Babelic nonsense. Hence the mixed style, in the end, mixed up the arguments of its advocates. As Laurence Dreyfus observes, on the one hand, Johann Adolph Scheibe could write: 'one must take care, whether working in French, Italian or German styles, not to mix one with another, for the clarity of styles must be observed'. Yet a few pages later, he asks, 'would [it] not be possible to combine the most beautiful [qualities of the three nations] and apply them to one single piece?'[42] Perfection, he suggests, would ensue. But such perfection is impossible within the linguistic world of the trivium. The relativity of the mixed style brings confusion. 'I am a little worried', writes Mattheson, 'that as time goes by only a few or even perhaps not

[41] See Jeanne Swack, *The Solo Sonatas of Georg Philipp Telemann: A Study of the Sources and Musical Style* (Ph.D. Yale, 1988).

[42] Johann Adolph Scheibe, *Compendium musices theoretico-practicum* (1736), quoted in Dreyfus, *Bach and the Patterns of Invention*, 131–2.

a single one of these styles and genres might remain unadulterated and with distinguishing characteristics. For there is already such mishmash to be found in the style of many self-instructed composers, as if everything were deteriorating into a formless mass.'[43] The mixed style ended up articulating the very relativity that it set out to overcome.

It was instrumental music in particular that fermented this dangerous mixture of styles. Not only did the critics find the chopping and changing of national accents disorientating, but the incorporation of the Italian style necessarily involved the switching and mixing of affects which merely added to the confusion of the 'wordless rhetoric'.[44] There was simply no way of identifying the subject or authenticating its style without the text. With such music, style, far from being connected to the ego, reveals itself as peripatetic and transferable. After all, without this interchangeability, instrumental music could not be transferred into the trivium as something vocal in the first place; Frescobaldi does not import the madrigal into his keyboard pieces, but the 'modern *style* of the madrigal'. The cross-over simultaneously legitimises the music and accentuates the malleability and detachability of style that renders it relative, arbitrary and ultimately incomprehensible. The critics who accuse the sonata of spouting sheer nonsense were in fact looking in their own epistemological mirror – the tarnished face of the trivium.

The musicological myth that the mixed style somehow transmuted into the 'Classical style', transcending national boundaries of taste to form the language of absolute music, is an inversion of the facts. The Viennese Classical style has neither the purity nor clarity associated with Classicism. It was a confused style. Haydn's mischievous mixture was precisely the sort of immiscibility that disrupted the rhetorical clarity of the Baroque aesthetic, reducing the 'oratory of the pulpit', says the Revd William Jones, to 'the talk . . . of the tea-table'; it was just chattering nonsense, as if the public sphere had gone banal. The pieces of Haydn and Boccherini, Jones adds, 'are sometimes so desultory and unaccountable in the way of treating the subject that they must be reckoned among the wild warblers of the woods'.[45] And in terms of taste, the 'Classical style' was heard as such a hotchpotch of ingredients that it was more a recipe for disaster than for pleasure. Mozart's music, said one critic, was 'too highly seasoned'; his 'almost unadulteratedly spicy diet', said another critic, could easily spoil one's palate with its lack of

---

[43] Mattheson, *Der vollkommene Capellmeister*, 225.
[44] As Mary Sue Morrow points out, in the 1760s, the music critics in Northern Germany regarded Italian instrumental music as the renegade 'Other' against which to define their own cultural superiority, describing the Italian symphony as 'impotent . . . Vulgar . . . Farcical . . . Chopped-up'; see *German Music Criticism in the Late Eighteenth Century*, 45–65. [45] William Jones, *Treatise on the Art of Music* (Colchester, 1784), 49.

unity.[46] With its wayward mixture, the 'Classical style' signals the end of style, the ruin of taste and the undoing of rhetoric, because it reveals the stylistic relativity inherent in the trivium. Indeed, its wilful nature, by pushing the Baroque aesthetic to an extreme logic, marks the end of the Baroque itself. In a sense, what the early Romantics heard in the works of Stamitz, Haydn and Mozart was not an absolute music but a totally relativistic one. It was so modern that it seemingly fell off the cutting edge of progress into a heterogeneous form of discourse, which Friedrich Schlegel compared to the novel. 'The method of the novel', writes Schlegel, 'is that of instrumental music. In the novel, even the characters can be treated as wilfully as the music treats its theme.'[47] And the novel, for Schlegel, is uncategorisable; it can only be defined by its arbitrary mixture (*Mischung*) as a multiplicity of genres. In the same way, the Romantics heard in instrumental music a sound that was untheorisable, whose stylistic relativity left it without genre, without style and without definition. The trivium had reached aporia. If Guilio del Bene, by transferring music to the trivium, turned music into language, then the Romantics had to reverse the process by turning language into music in the hope of regaining the quadrivium for modernity.

---

[46] *Magazin der Musik* (1787) and *Teutschlands Annalen des Jahres* (1794) quoted in Otto Erich Deutsch, *Mozart: A Documentary Biography* (Stanford: Stanford University Press, 1965), 290 and 472–3.

[47] Friedrich Schlegel, *Literary Notebooks, 1797–1801*, ed. H. Eichner (London: The Athlone Press, 1957), no. 1359. Also see Philippe Lacoue-Labarthe and Jean-Luc Nancy, *The Literary Absolute: The Theory of Literature in German Romanticism*, trans. P. Barnard and C. Lester (Albany: State University of New York Press, 1988), 90–100, and Cascardi, *The Subject of Modernity*, 110–12.

PART 2

The Fruit of Knowledge

9

On being

By the turn of the nineteenth century instrumental music had been given a new ontology. It simply existed – a matter of being rather than meaning. It could miraculously generate itself from nothing. And not only was it given the sovereignty of auto-genesis, but it acquired the godlike ability to exist even if the entire world ceased to be, for music was its own cosmos, 'a self-enclosed world',[1] spinning itself out as its own origin, cause and totality. In its instrumental purity, music was hailed as absolute, which is to be assigned the original 'I AM' that had once belonged to a now marginalised deity. Indeed, it was worshipped with religious devotion;[2] the veneration of instrumental music, according to Carl Dahlhaus, was itself a religion.[3] To its followers music revealed itself as a *work* that had to be internalised as an aesthetic experience. It offered a kind of salvation of works through a Eucharist of criticism and analysis. This new ontology is the foundation of musicology.[4] But what is now a demystified object of investigation was then a mystical figure of initiation – a way to self-knowledge. The German Romantics were not simply making up metaphors to philosophise about music; musical ontology was an inner reality; it was a way for the romantic ego to come to terms with its own being.

The absolute autonomy of music is a romantic discourse. And it is only a discourse. In reality, music cannot simply exist. The aesthetic might assign it a divinity, it may even signify its autotelic delusions and conceal the umbilical links, but for music to be pure being it would have to be purely autistic. But far from effacing itself from the world, music, with its seemingly empty and meaningless signs, resonated with a fullness of meaning that touched the very identity of the romantic ego. Despite the ontological claims, music was not in fact pure being; it was

---

[1] Wilhelm Heinrich Wackenroder and Ludwig Tieck, *Phantasien über die Kunst für Freunde der Kunst* (Hamburg, 1799), in *Werke und Briefe von Wilhelm Heinrich Wackenroder*, 189.

[2] See, for example, Wilhelm Heinrich Wackenroder and Ludwig Tieck, *Confessions and Fantasies* (Berlin, 1797), trans. M. H. Schubert (University Park and London: The Pennsylvania State University Press, 1971), 146–60 and 174–97.

[3] Dahlhaus, *The Idea of Absolute Music*, 78–102.

[4] On the concept of work and its musicological implications, see Goehr, *The Imaginary Museum of Musical Works*, 89–286.

only a substitute, a *sign* of being that was an ideological tool for the Romantics. Music did not exist for itself but for the newly styled subject of German romanticism; it was the *subject* and not music that had to create itself out of nothing, constantly positing its own activity to cover up the impossible act of self-generation. And music, as an empty sign, was used to mask the emptiness that haunts all postures of pure autonomy. Indeed what better way to turn the tables on this nihilistic fear than to proclaim the vacant sign as the plenitude of romantic existence. Music as blind, mute and abstract became the mirror of the self, positing its own sovereignty on the very brink of its own emptiness. A secret symbiosis between man and music was used to conjure up the illusion of the subject as the first principle of being; the symphony, the sonata, the quartet were all repositories for the romantic ego. This was not an irrational move, as if romantic philosophy was a kind of speculative lunacy. In fact it was the opposite. The turn to aesthetics was a serious, intellectual solution to a crisis of philosophy in which music was forced to make sense of subjectivity and ultimately of the entire cosmos. The truth of absolute music is not in what it means but *why* it was made to mean.

But this is the end of a story. A hundred years earlier the indistinct and empty quality of instrumental music was recognised as precisely that – indistinct and empty. In fact, its very existence was an epistemological problem for the Enlightenment, given the increasing popularity of Italian instrumental music; the discourses that the eighteenth century wove around the music was an attempt to assign it a meaning that would make some sense within a newly emerging structure of knowledge.

There was, of course, nothing actually new about instrumental music; the eighteenth century did not stumble upon some novel invention, but accentuated the divisions and disenchantment of instrumental music in the seventeenth century.[5] What the Enlightenment discovered was not a new music but a new twist in the structures of meaning that set instrumental music out of joint. Its existence was a problem, for prior to that time, music, in a certain sense, did not exist at all; or at least its being was lost in the fabric of a cosmos so dense and interwoven into a pattern of things so fabulous that it was impossible to isolate music's existence as a question of meaning. But at certain imperceptible points in the seventeenth century, music was tugged out of its cosmological structure like a loose thread and was made to reformulate itself in a new epistemological space that focused on its existence while undermining the very ability of music to justify itself. Instrumental music could not quite slip into the new folds of thought and found itself awkwardly posi-

---

[5] See the chapters in this volume 'On Disenchantment' and 'On Division'.

tioned, conspicuously jutting out as an anomaly. The problem was that its being had nowhere to be.

As long as the old cosmological structure existed, music could reside in the heavens and emanate from the inaudible songs of angels and sirens or issue from the geometrical motions of the celestial spheres.[6] Like a 'taut string'[7] stretched between heaven and earth, music was able to conceptualise the unitary structure of the entire cosmos, blending the 'intellectual, celestial and corruptible' as Agrippa points out in the harmony of the monochord.[8] Under the sounds of the celestial canopy, one could temper the soul as one tempered a lyre; and in the system of resemblances, one could play upon the heart (*cordis*) as one would pluck the strings (*chorda*) of a harp.[9] But by the eighteenth century these were all mythical metaphors. The Copernican gaze had shattered the crystal spheres and music tumbled from the stars and could no longer take its place within a chain of being that connected music to a network of resemblances.[10] There were to be no more secrets hidden in the signatures of music that could decipher the structure of the universe.[11] No longer were the properties of rocks and plants and beasts ingrained with a harmony that differentiated their character. Music lost its ability to duplicate the world, to reside in things, to mime the forms of the celestial realms and to participate in a magic that mingled man with the cosmos.[12] There were to be no more musical myths retold as truths, no more 'occultic arithmetic'[13] in the calculations of sound, no more conjuring up of demons and spirits in the magic of incantation.[14] Chromatics lost their blackness of meaning, modes their planetary influence, and triads their resemblance to the Trinity.[15]

When in 1722 Rameau pronounced music a 'science'[16] he spoke for a new order that obliterated a music that had been documented for so long by such theorists as Boethius, Ficino, Kircher and Zarlino; their books placed music alongside the domains of fable, medicine, astrology,

---

[6] See, for example, Joscelyn Godwin, *Music, Mysticism and Magic*, James, *The Music of the Spheres*, 140–58, Tomlinson, *Music in Renaissance Magic*, 67–100, and Hollander, *The Untuning of the Sky*, 3–51.

[7] Plotinus, *De rebus philosophicis*, quoted in Tomlinson, *Music in Renaissance Magic*, 86.

[8] Henry Cornelius Agrippa, *De occulta philosophia* (1533), quoted in ibid., 61.

[9] Hollander, *The Untuning of the Sky*, 42.

[10] On resemblances, see Foucault, *The Order of Things*, 17–44. Much of the discussion that follows is indebted to Foucault's analysis of the sixteenth-century episteme.

[11] See James, *The Music of the Spheres*, 140–58.

[12] Tomlinson, *Music in Renaissance Magic*, 62 and 50.

[13] Gottfried Wilhelm Leibniz, 'Remarks on an Extract from Bayle's Dictionary', quoted in Hollander, *The Untuning of the Sky*, 12.

[14] Tomlinson, *Music in Renaissance Magic*, 64.

[15] Ibid., 67–100, and Thomas Christensen, *Rameau and Musical Thought in the Enlightenment* (Cambridge: Cambridge University Press, 1993), 87.

[16] Jean-Philippe Rameau, *Traité de l'harmonie réduite à ses principes naturels* (Paris, 1722), 1.

geometry, magic, body, soul, spirit, demons, angels and seemingly the entire content of the universe; there was a *musica mundana* that ordered the cosmos and changed the seasons, a *musica humana* that united the 'activity of the reason with the body' tempering their opposition 'into a single consonance', and a *musica instrumentalis* that was the practical manifestation of music.[17] Rameau, on the other hand, placed music merely in the realm of sound. The entire semantic network that connected music to the world was relegated as some kind of antiquarian quirk. Music by the middle of the eighteenth century became only that which was *heard*. From now on music was to be audible. 'Now since nothing at all can be heard', writes Mattheson in a dismissal of the music of the spheres and of the soul, 'we will not deal with them in this book'.[18] So it was that music in the Enlightenment had its existence simplified as acoustic. And if Descartes is a catalyst of Enlightenment thought, then his early treatise on music marks an epistemological shift. For the first time, the investigation of the monochord was to be based on an audible phenomenon as opposed to some metaphysical calculation: the treatise begins, 'the basis of music is sound'.[19] Or in Rameau's words, music is 'the science of sound'. 'Consequently', he continues, 'sound is the principal object of music' and the 'task of defining sound' was left to the purity of physics.[20] Instead of being interlaced in the meaning of things, music became a thing itself, defined by a space so natural and audible that the scaffolds of Enlightenment discourse that framed it were hardly visible.

In the Age of Reason, to tease out the resemblance between things was no longer an act of erudition but error. As Michel Foucault explains, signs were no longer 'part of things themselves' but became 'modes of representation'[21] that had withdrawn from the cosmos to function as a tool for the analysis of the world. Knowledge, in other words, was no longer the discovery of signs, but the use of signs. Indeed, the sign became so transparent in its re-presentation of objects that its system of thought was invisible to itself; it merely functioned.[22] Its task was to measure the object of its nomination, to order its being, tabling its identities and differences and displaying its progression from simple to complex structures.[23] First the 'relationship between harmonic ratios and proportions' to establish a fundamental base (bass) from which music can be measured; then – book two – the ordering of the 'nature and proportion of chords' by arranging their identities and differences along the lines of consonance and dissonance as states of equilibrium

[17] Boethius, *De institutione musica*, in Strunk, *Source Readings in Music History*, 85.

[18] Mattheson, *Der vollkommene Capellmeister*, 89.

[19] René Descartes, *Compendium of Music*, trans. W. Roberts (American Institute of Musicology, 1961).   [20] Rameau, *Traité de l'harmonie*, 1.

[21] Foucault, *The Order of Things*, 129.   [22] See ibid., 58–67.   [23] See ibid., 54–5.

and motion. This is the theoretical structure of Rameau's treatise on harmony. Its aim is to represent the *practical* reality of music in the principles of nature – book three, 'on composition', book four, 'on accompaniment'. Thus at the very heart of the analytical process of representation is what Max Weber terms the 'disenchantment of the world', in which music is demystified, mechanised and made transparent to knowledge. The Enlightenment's fear of the supernatural results in the neutralisation of music as natural – a state that Rameau's discourse forces music into.[24] But by stripping the magic to reveal its acoustical nudity, music lost all its cosmological legitimisation and was pushed out into its own autonomous sphere to find other ways of validating itself. Without the divine order that had organised music in the rituals of human life, a seemingly functionless music was possible: music could have a new existence as a disenchanted object.

In a sense, this new object was conjured up by the whole system of representation. After all, representation measured and ordered the very nature of sound. Indeed, it made music so audible, so transparent and even visible through the scientific observation of its physical properties that music was asked to share in the same autonomy as a system of signs, as a language whose mission was to represent. Representation named music as representation so that music might participate in the same structure of knowledge. Vocal music, operating within the trivium, had no problem with this, but music in its instrumental guise soon found itself in a terrible contradiction. On the one hand, its very being as sound was formulated by the system of representation, yet on the other hand, its inability to represent was denounced by the very system itself. In an age of representation, instrumental music could not represent; it could not answer back and join in the game of naming. So music found itself objectified by Enlightenment reason as a thing that could not mean because it could not name. If, as Foucault suggests, 'to know is to speak correctly', then instrumental music could not properly reside in the system of knowledge because it could not articulate itself with any precision.[25]

There is no sure way of mapping the *exact* co-ordinates of this epistemological shift across the landscape of seventeenth- and eighteenth-century history, but such a mutation of thought, despite all its local modifications, undoubtedly occurred on a level deeper than the proverbial categories of culture – the Baroque, Rococo, Classical, Romantic. Certainly, the 'untuning of the sky'[26] had been irreversibly accomplished

---

[24] On the Enlightenment's fear of the supernatural, see Max Horkheimer and Theodor W. Adorno, *Dialectic of Enlightenment*, trans. John Cumming (London: Verso, 1979), 3–42.

[25] Foucault, *The Order of Things*, 87.

[26] Hollander, *The Untuning of the Sky*, the title is adapted from the final line of Dryden's 'Song for St Cecilia's Day' (1687) – 'and Musick shall untune the sky'.

Variation	Canon at the	Planets
3	unison	Earth
6	second	Moon
9	third	Mercury
12	fourth	Venus
15	fifth	Sun
18	sixth	Mars
21	seventh	Jupiter
24	octave	Saturn
27	ninth	Fixed stars

Fig. 3 Bach's Goldberg Variations – canons at the unison to ninth: a cosmic order?

by the beginning of the eighteenth century. Music was left on the earth to the mechanics of a new philosophy, and instrumental music, assuming the capricious forms of symphonies and overtures, came from Italy to trouble the minds of the Northern Europeans. Of course, there were still vestiges of the old cosmology lingering in the earlier part of the century, but these were merely anachronistic murmurs to be silenced as superstition gave way to empiricism. The expanding intervals in the canons of Bach's Goldberg Variations may have echoed the structure of the Ptolemaic universe, but Bach was grasping at a cosmic order that had long collapsed by the 1740s (see figure 3).[27]

Meanwhile his son, Carl Philipp Emanuel, was writing a music whose meaning resided in the erratic depths of the human psyche. What had happened within a generation was that the ancient universe had disintegrated and its structure of meaning internalised within the self; ideas were no longer embodied in the cosmos but in the mind.[28] And music was relocated from the heavens into the human being. But in this new order, where could instrumental music find its meaning? It could neither find refuge in a cosmos that had collapsed nor reside in the rational soul for it was outside knowledge (representation). The only space left for it was the body – in the old space of the humours that *musica humana* had left behind. But that was it; it would merely move in the body, in the raw data of the senses, without migrating to the analytical processes of the mind and without any external validation.

This was why sound in the eighteenth century was explained by Newtonian physics and its meaning by physiology; music was *seen* as motion and its effect was in the body. The fusion of physics and physiol-

---

[27] See David Humphreys, *The Esoteric Structure of Bach's Clavierübung* III (Cardiff: University of Cardiff Press, 1983), 90–2.

[28] See Charles Taylor, *Sources of the Self* (Cambridge: Cambridge University Press, 1989), 144.

ogy resulted in a peculiar form of sonic passion: sound *moved the body*. And to be moved was literally to move – emotion was motion; 'wherever passion is concerned', writes Daniel Webb, 'a coincidence of sound and motion become . . . the native and proper language of the passions'.[29] The visibility of musical movement that the new discourse had brought into focus through the vibrations of strings and tubes was internalised as a physiological experience. Cosmic harmony was now a matter of pulsating nerve fibres and dilating blood vessels. Almost every music theorist of the eighteenth century believed in a kind of parallel tracking between the musical movement of sound and the emotional movement of the body. Mattheson writes:

The experts on nature know how to describe the manner in which our affections actually and so to speak physically function, and it is of great advantage to a composer if he also is not inexperienced in this . . . Since for example joy is an expression of our soul, thus it follows reasonably and naturally that I could best express this affection by *large* and *expanded* intervals. Whereas if one knows that sadness is a contraction of the subtle parts of our body, then it is easy to see that the *small* and *smallest* intervals are the most suitable for this passion.[30]

Thus music was not only heard, it was felt. It took on a materiality that could be grasped and analysed by the tools of Enlightenment reason. If its physical properties were dissected in the experiments on sound, its meaning was found in the physiology of the body.

---

[29] Daniel Webb, *Observations on the Correspondence Between Poetry and Music* (London, 1769), 150–1.   [30] Mattheson, *Der vollkommene Capellmeister*, 104–5.

10

On the mind

At first such a somatic experience of sound was a problem because the body at the beginning of the eighteenth century was not a living organism but a mechanical structure of levers, pumps and sieves (see plate 4). In fact it was no different from an inorganic object. 'To think', for Descartes, may have grounded the self in the 'I am' of being, but it also severed the body from the soul in the act of reflection, creating an ontological fissure at the very core of self-realisation.[1] The Cartesian, writes Charles Taylor, 'discovers and affirms his immaterial nature by objectifying the bodily'.[2] Somehow, by a peculiar twist of being, the mind (the rational soul) had to disengage its nature from ordinary experience and divide itself from the flesh as a disembodied entity in order to find its new epistemological footing as an external observer. The body became purely material, something to be reconstructed by the rational soul as mere mechanism and mere extension, emptied of all spiritual essences. Self-realisation became the instrumental control of reason over the body. It was in this way that the Cartesian mind banished the animistic principles that had inhabited the Renaissance body with a functionalism that left its own flesh as good as dead. This is why some historians of science claim that biology was impossible before c.1750; life simply could not be explained by laws different to those of the inanimate world.[3]

So, although sound resided in the body, the body itself could not validate musical meaning, since the thinking ego had basically mechanised it to death. If any life existed in instrumental music it was merely that of 'a marionette or a mechanical doll'.[4] For sound to have any real meaning at all it would have to ground itself in the *cogito ergo sum* of Cartesian ontology; it had to inhabit the mind. But how? Given its

---

[1] See René Descartes, *Les Méditations sur la philosophie première* (Paris, 1641), translated by J. Cottingham as *Meditations on First Philosophy* (Cambridge: Cambridge University Press, 1986), 16–23 and 50–62.   [2] Taylor, *Sources of the Self*, 146.

[3] See Thomas L. Hankin, *Science and the Enlightenment* (Cambridge: Cambridge University Press, 1985), 113–19.

[4] Nöel-Antoine Pluche, *Le Spectacle de la nature, ou Entretiens sur les particularités de l'histoire naturelle, qui ont paru les plus propres à rendre les jeunes-gens curieux, et à leur former l'esprit* (Paris, 1732–50), vol. 7 (1746), 115.

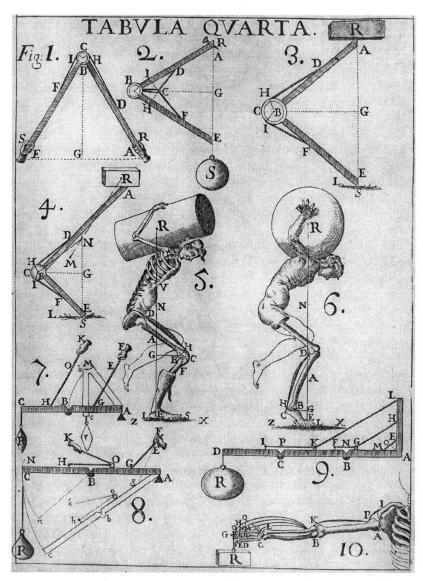

Plate 4 Giovanni Alfonso Borelli, illustration from *De motu animalium* (Rome, 1680). The body as machine – but is it alive?

inability to represent, how was music supposed to think? This was why music needed a voice, for the voice signified a rational presence, the thinking 'I am' that was the very identity of the self. Vocal music was the only kind of music that could authenticate its own being; the soul, as it were, inhered within it. As for instrumental music, it was derided as 'body without soul', which, in Cartesian thought, is to declare it 'a dead thing'.[5]

Thus Cartesian dualism set in motion the system of opposition between instrumental and vocal music that was to bedevil the eighteenth century; it delineated in music the contrast of body and soul, passion and reason, object and subject, and fuelled the debate in Northern Europe over the relative merits of French and Italian music. In the jostle of polemical ideas, what was sharpened by Cartesian thought was the question of rational mastery over two critical areas of mediation which reinforced the pre-eminence of vocal music – the domain of rational ideas that mediated between inward reason and outward reality, and the site of the passions which was the point of contact between body and soul and the focus of Descartes' moral philosophy. In fact, even with the eclipse of Cartesianism, these two realms of rational and passional control were the bridle that steered the discourses on music throughout the century.

First, in Descartes' system of reason, the question of truth was resolved by mingling both rational knowledge and empirical reality in the same metaphysical origin; both the innate ideas of the mind and the objects of the world carry the fingerprint of God. 'Innate ideas are the trademark which the divine workman has imprinted on his products', writes Ernst Cassirer. 'Reason, as the system of clear and distinct ideas and the world as the totality of created being, can nowhere fail to harmonize.'[6] Nowhere except, that is, for the realm of instrumental music, which seemed to clash dissonantly against the system. Certainty for Descartes needed 'clear and distinct' ideas, but instrumental music had no concept, it had no divine identity for the power of Cartesian thought to dissect and construct. 'Without intention or object', writes Jean d'Alembert, 'it would neither speak to the mind nor the soul.'[7] It was simply a body that was out of control. Instrumental sound, in the

---

5 Johann Christoph Gottsched, *Auszug aus des Herrn Batteux schönen Künsten aus dem einzigen Grundsatze der Nachahmung hergeleitet* (Leipzig, 1754), 202. Nöel-Antoine Pluche shares the same opinion; see *Le Spectacle de la nature*, 114–15.

6 Ernst Cassirer, *The Philosophy of the Enlightenment*, trans. F. C. A. Koelln and J. Pettgrove (Princeton: Princeton University Press, 1951), 95.

7 Jean d'Alembert, 'De la liberté de la Musique', in *Mélanges de littérature, d'Histoire et de Philosophie* (Amsterdam, 1770), 4:445, quoted in Bellamy Hosler, *Changing Aesthetic Views of Instrumental Music in 18th-Century Germany* (Ann Arbor: UMI Research Press, 1981), 48.

phonocentric order of music, became a kind of Derridian nightmare: it behaved like a decentred text of multiple voices that did not issue from the unity of the rational soul, but disseminated its identity in the web of its own material and across the motions of the body; its signifiers were 'labyrinths of tones' meaning nothing, leaving the body jangling with a noise that made the mind conceptually impotent.[8] The problem was not so much the lack of signification, but the uncontrollable polysemy of the new Italian music that seemingly flitted from one mood to another without rhyme or reason; it made sense to the body as a kind of ear-tickling sensation but left the rational soul morally vacant. The attempt to 'amuse the ear without presenting any thought to the mind', writes Noël Antoine Pluche, 'is directly contrary to the very nature of music, which is to imitate, as do all the fine arts, images and feelings which occupy the mind'.[9]

Having objectified music as sound in the system of representation, with all its meticulous measurements and calculations, the system of knowledge did not know what to do with it; it was forced to leave instrumental music at the margins of knowledge since it could not enter the realm of innate ideas, and called upon the voice to rescue music as representation. For the Cartesian, words objectify sounds; they convert music into clear and distinct concepts. 'As speech is a sign of our thoughts', writes Pluche, 'so is writing the sign of our speech . . . Music is speech', he adds, meaning, of course, a music fixed by words;[10] for only in this way could music participate in the divinely ordained realm of innate ideas that forms the bridge between concept and object, knowledge and reality. 'Instrumental music receives from vocal music a more determinate and certain meaning.'[11] The marriage of words and music was a divine institution, morally sanctioned to bring the body in line with the soul. It was vital that reason controlled music by an act of naming lest music should return as some animistic spirit that the mind had supposedly expelled from the body and stir up the passions beyond the limits of reason. The mind as the agent of the soul disciplined the musical motions within the body, subjecting the movement of the passions to the precision of the concept. Words were therefore as much a sign of moral strength as epistemological truth; they instrumentalised desire.[12]

This question of morality connects the realm of innate ideas to the second area of mediation, that of the passions. If the body was to have any significance for the thinking ego then it would be at the point of

---

[8] Gottsched, *Auszug aus des Herrn Batteux schönen Künsten*, 201.
[9] Pluche, *Le Spectacle de la nature*, 111.   [10] Ibid., 96–7.
[11] Johann Adam Hiller, 'Abhandlung von der Nachahmung der Natur in der Musik', in Wilhelm Friedrich Marpurg, *Historisch-Kritische Beyträge zur Aufnahme der Musik* (Berlin, 1754–5), 1:529, quoted in Hosler, *Changing Aesthetic Views*, 4.
[12] See Taylor, *Sources of the Self*, 147.

contact with the soul, and it is at this meeting place that music found itself embroiled in the moral physiology of the passions. Mattheson, in fact, recommends Descartes' treatise on the subject to calculate the moral effect of music upon the Lutheran soul.[13] The passions themselves resided neither in the body nor the soul but acted as a thin membrane whose fluctuation expressed the relationship between the two.[14] The strength of the Cartesian soul depended on its ability to 'conquer the passions' with its internalised 'arms' of thought;[15] it held the appetite with a radical reflexivity in order to harness the mechanism of the body into a strong harmony of moral freedom. An imbalance of the passions would cause a loss of moral control that could easily slip into madness with a very literal slackening of one's moral fibres.[16] Unfortunately for music, not only did it vibrate along these flabby nerve fibres, but it resided in that precarious site of the passions that mediates between the activity of the soul and the passivity of the body. This is how the eighteenth-century theorists made the isomorphic connection between the movement of music and that of the emotions. In fact, it did not matter whether one was a Cartesian moralist or a material sensualist, the effect of sound on the body was the same. As music moved, the passion also moved in a mechanical motion of what was called the vital spirits; they would circulate and disperse, running across the entire body in an orchestration of the internal organs. 'If the [musical impressions] agitate the nerves with violence', writes Daniel Webb

the spirits are hurried into the movements of anger, courage, indignation and the like.

The more gentle and placid vibrations shall be in unison with love, friendship and benevolence.

If the spirits are exalted or dilated, they rise into accord with pride, glory and emulation.

If the nerves are relaxed, the spirits subside into the languid movements of sorrow.[17]

The moral effect of music therefore depends upon the way it tilted the balance of the passions between the body and the soul; the moral dialectic is therefore a tension between the material sensation and the power of rational control. Passions were not to be denied but harnessed. And this was a physiological matter. If, for example, one's fibres are rather soft and mobile, music could have quite a devastating effect. It only takes one

---

[13] Mattheson, *Der vollkommene Capellmeister*, 104.
[14] See Foucault, *Madness and Civilization*, 86–8.
[15] René Descartes, *Traité des passions de l'âme* (Paris, 1649), article 48. See also articles 34–50, and Taylor, *Sources of the Self*, 153.
[16] See Foucault, *Madness and Civilization*, 88–93 and 126–7.
[17] Webb, *Observations on the Correspondence Between Poetry and Music*, 9–10.

affecting phrase to strike his ear . . . and suddenly [a man] is filled with a great inner tumult; there is an excitation of the fibres in the bundle, he begins to shudder, he is gripped by a sacred horror, he weeps, he chokes himself with his own sighs, he becomes unable to speak . . . the man is deprived of all his calm, all reason, all judgement, all capacity of making distinction, all self-control.[18]

Music could quite easily ruin one's moral constitution. Thus it was vital for the eighteenth century to classify the affects of music. The Baroque affects were not merely a symptom of an age of representation but a matter of body control. If music moved the passions then the passion had to be identified. This was why Baroque pieces were only allowed to convey one affect; the rational soul needed to frame the music within the singularity of a classified concept. Then it could make the music stay put, harness its dynamic and stifle any dangerous motions in the body. Hence Daniel Webb classifies music's affections into four classes, claiming that it is first 'the mind . . . [that] excites certain vibrations in the nerves, and impresses certain movements on the animal spirits'.[19] But the 'mishmash' of affects that characterised the new Italian music of composers like Vivaldi, Jommelli and Geminiani meant that reason had no conceptual handle on it, unless one were totally mad or prone to 'laughing and weeping at the same time'.[20] There was something not only subversive but ludicrous about its powers to move the body. In fact the critic, Johann Christoph Gottsched, feared that the taste for Italian music, even in opera, would turn the entire German race into a horde of effeminate beings, or worse still, into a nation of hermaphrodites since the indistinct markings in Italian instrumental music, such as tempo giusto, were tantamount to a cross-dressing of affects that cancelled out all meaning.[21]

During the course of the eighteenth century, the position of instrumental music did not change; on the contrary, in a rebellion against Cartesian rationality, it was the soul that changed its identity, making an allegiance with the passions. The divine realm of innate ideas became an increasingly untenable assumption in the thinking of a secular age, which eventually abandoned a metaphysics of the soul for a natural history of it. 'So many philosophers [have] written the romance of the soul', says Voltaire, 'a sage has arrived who has modestly written its history. Locke has set forth human reason just as an excellent anatomist

---

[18] Denis Diderot, *D'Alembert's Dream* (1769), in *Diderot's Selected Writings*, ed. L. G. Crocker, trans. D. Coltman (New York: Macmillan, 1966), 208.

[19] Webb, *Observations*, 6.

[20] Johann Adam Hiller, *Wöchentliche Nachrichten und Anmerkungen die Musik betreffend* (Leipzig, 1766–70), 4:19.

[21] See Johann Christoph Gottsched, *Versuch einer critischen Dichtkunst* (Leipzig, 1742), 759, and *Auszug aus des Herrn Batteux schönen Künsten*, 201.

explains the parts of the human body.'[22] Instead of grounding the soul
in some transcendental realm, the empirical twist located it in space and
time. But where are the documents of its history to be found? – not in
the world, but in the sensations of the soul itself. The passions were
given a history. And it was vocal music, as the passionate script of the
soul, that provided the data for the linguistic and moral origin of
humanity. 'Each sentiment has its own tones, its accents and its sighs',
writes Dubos,[23] and these sounds can be traced back in the mind to formulate the primal psychology of being. Music, with a Cartesian precision, could now define the emotions of the soul. So it was no longer just
the clarity of words that legitimised vocal music, but its prelinguistic
utterances of pure expressivity. The soul was not only rational but passional in origin. Hence almost all the conjectural histories of music
written in the eighteenth century had their genesis in the voice, in a kind
of *Ursprache* of passionate tones filled with sighs, groans and expressive
inflections that emanated from the purity of aboriginal existence.[24] The
voice was therefore doubly authentic; it was the articulation of linguistic concepts that controlled the passions and also the origin of moral
sentiment that breathed music into the words. The voice, the promise of
language, the expression of the soul, was the 'transcendental signifier',
to use Derrida's term, that guaranteed the presence of the self.[25] It fixed
the identity of the ego and implied a transparency of communication
that could stabilise meaning from soul to soul as a rational and expressive act. Conversely, instrumental music had no presence except as a
simulation of the voice and its representations.

Music was therefore declared an imitative art form, despite the fact
that it was not particularly good at mimesis.[26] But the eighteenth-
century theorists were adamant about this. 'As with poetry and painting', writes Dubos, 'music is an imitation.'[27] The question was not so
much why music had to imitate nature but how music was to do it. The
basic strategy was simple: music either mimed the emotional utterance
of the voice by employing the passionate sounds of the soul or else it

---

[22] Voltaire, *Lettres sur les Anglais*, quoted in Cassirer, *The Philosophy of the Enlightenment*,
94.
[23] Jean-Baptiste Dubos, *Réflexions critiques sur la poésie, la peinture et la musique* (Paris, 1740),
470.
[24] The classic example is Jean-Jacques Rousseau's *Essai sur l'origine des langues*. See also
Derrida's discussion of the essay in *Of Grammatology*, 144–307, and Thomas, *Music and
the Origins of Language*.
[25] See Derrida, *Of Grammatology*, 262–307, and Paul de Man, 'The Rhetoric of Blindness:
Jacques Derrida's Reading of Rousseau' in his *Blindness and Insight: Essays in the Rhetoric
of Contemporary Criticism* (New York: Oxford University Press, 1971), 102–41.
[26] For a clear and succinct discussion of the relationship between instrumental music and
mimetic theories of art in the eighteenth century, see Morrow, *German Music Criticism
in the Late Eighteenth Century*, 4–18.   [27] Dubos, *Réflexions critiques*, 450.

Ex. 10 Notation for the eye in two arias from Handel's *Messiah*.

had to be made visible by an act of naming so that it could occupy the conceptual spaces of the mind. 'The word [*la parole*]', writes Rousseau concerning sonatas, 'is the means by which the music most often determines the object whose image it offers us.'[28] So instrumental music was asked to speak with a 'wordless rhetoric', to borrow Mark Evan Bonds' term.[29] Somehow, by a strange verbal transformation, music could 'place the eye in the ear'.[30] And sometimes in the quest to make hearing visual, musical concepts would literally become visible upon the page; mountains and valleys would undulate upon the staves and the unwrinkling of a phrase into long notes would make 'rough places plain' before the eyes (see example 10).

Similarly, the 'truth' of instrumental music, as Dubos puts it, lies in its conceptual approximation, a 'verisimilitude' (*vrai-semblance*) that conforms to an object which excites the feelings of the soul. 'There is truth', he writes, 'in a *symphonie* composed to imitate a storm.'[31] For through imitation, music enters the soul – the arbiter of truth. With the power of representation forced upon sound, music could be denied direct access to the body and deflected towards the mind where it could be morally sanctioned and so 'excite in the soul to the same movement one feels in seeing' the object represented.[32] Only after all these circuitous transformations could music legitimately return to the body in its instrumental form.

---

[28] Jean-Jacques Rousseau, 'Sonate', *Dictionnaire de musique* (Geneva, 1781), 639.
[29] Bonds, *Wordless Rhetoric*. [30] Rousseau, 'Imitation', *Dictionnaire de musique*, 352.
[31] Dubos, *Réflexions critiques*, 440. [32] Rousseau, 'Imitation', *Dictionnaire de musique*, 353.

There was certainly a lot of processing involved in the assimilation of instrumental music. And, of course, not everything was acceptable for cogitation judging by the vitriolic abuse consistently hurled at Italian music from its critics: noise, formless clanging, jingle-jangle, incomprehensible mishmash.[33] So, ironically, the most significant style of the eighteenth century, not only in terms of its popularity but as the inspiration of the 'Viennese Classical style', was the style that faced the most resistance on its path towards the absolute. This was perhaps understandable given the 'noise of arbitrarily connected tones . . . [with] fanciful and abrupt changes in character from joy to despair, and from the pathetic to the trivial' that filled most Italian sonatas.[34] There was simply no way of dealing with this mixture of elements and semiotic vagaries without undermining the moral and epistemological structure of eighteenth-century thought. To 'know what all this fracas of sonata would mean', writes Rousseau, 'we must do as the painter who was obliged to write under his figure "this is a tree", "this is a man", "this is a horse"'. Rousseau was being funny, of course, but ironically this is exactly what the French composers did, labelling their clavecin pieces *'Le Dodo'*, *'La Boufonne'*, *'Les Chinois'*, *'Les Papillons'*, *'La Poule'*, *'Les Sauvages'*.[35] Compare such labels with those of the Italians: Allegro, Andante, Adagio, Tempo giusto. Seemingly harmless, these titles enraged the critic Gottsched, who declared such Italian compositions to be utterly meaningless; 'neither hot nor warm' such pieces mean 'absolutely nothing'. 'Music without words', he adds, 'is soulless and incomprehensible'.[36] This was not merely a matter of patriotic rivalry, or even a matter of taste; one's moral identity was at stake. A piece such as this sonata by Domenico Scarlatti with its bland tempo markings, its impetuous affects, harmonic meanderings and irrational changes of ideas was simply courting trouble (see example 11).

Such music signified a lack of rational control; it simply inhabited the mechanised body without touching the moral core of human identity – it was 'body without soul'. Even as late as the 1790s, Kant compared instrumental music to an oriental body massage; it was good for one's health, since it stirred the intestines, but like the Turks with their harems, it was hardly beneficial for one's moral duty founded upon reason. And Kant wasn't joking; music was literally felt as an internal

---

[33] See Hosler, *Changing Aesthetic Views*, 1.

[34] Johann Georg Sulzer, 'Sonate', *Allgemeine Theorie der schönen Künste* (1771–4), second edition (Leipzig, 1792–4), 4:425. The article was probably authored by J. A. P. Schulz who claimed in 1800 to have written the articles on music from the letter S onwards; however Sulzer no doubt approved, edited and shaped Schulz's contributions.

[35] Jean-Jacques Rousseau, 'Sonate', *Dictionnaire de musique*, 639. The titles are taken from the *pièces de clavecin* of François Couperin and Jean-Philippe Rameau.

[36] Gottsched, *Auszug aus des Herrn Batteux schönen Künsten*, 201 and 207.

Ex. 11 Domenico Scarlatti, Sonata in F major, K. 554 – bs 1–14.

body massage, somatic motions that were somehow akin to what for the Enlightenment was the non-rational sensuality of the Orient – exotic and somewhat barbaric.[37]

So in Northern Europe, the ontology of instrumental music was a problem that was not properly resolved until the nineteenth century. The type of music which eventually flowered into the 'Classical style' was pronounced dead on arrival by its critics.[38] And perhaps the 'Classical style' would have been cut at its roots had the body remained inorganic and human morality a matter of somatic control. What was needed was a new concept of the body, a body that was not mechanical but biological, with desires that tingled with virtuous action.

---

[37] Kant, *Critique of Judgement*, 196–9. On the Enlightenment's discourse on the Orient, see Edward Said, *Orientalism* (London: Penguin, 1995).

[38] On occasion critics of Italian instrumental music would include as 'Italian' the composers of Southern Germany and Austria; this is evident, for example, in the following comments in *Critischer Entwurf einer auserlesenen Bibliothek* (Berlin, 1771), 464–5, by Johann Christoph Stockhausen: 'The things of Haydn [Austria], Toeschi, Cannabisch [sic!], Filz [Mannheim], Pugnani, Campioni [Italy], are getting the upper hand now. You only have to be half a connoisseur to notice the emptiness, the strange mixture of comic and serious, playful and touching, that rules everywhere.' Quoted in Morrow, *German Music Criticism in the Late Eighteenth Century*, 54.

11

On biology

By the late eighteenth century instrumental music had developed the ability to distinguish between the living and the dead. In fact, the mechanical became the butt of a great deal of Classical joking. Instrumental music managed to have the last laugh at an old ideology that had brandished it as a 'mechanical doll'. It depicted such tick-tocking machines as something to be tinkered with, using the elasticity of their own tonal momentum to pull the precision of the movement around;[1] sometimes it even smashed the mechanism to pieces, as with the unexpected hammer blows in Haydn's 'Surprise' Symphony. The surprise of the symphony is in the human hand that comes to tamper with the self-wound motions that the music signifies with its clockwork tune. Conscious life had seeped into the score, and the mechanical was merely a play of signs for the organic (see example 12).

Or take, as another example, the minuet in the C major Quartet, Op. 54 No. 2; this piece was actually incorporated into a musical clock at Esterháza,[2] but it must have been a very odd clock since the music sounds like a madman trying to struggle out of a symmetrical strait-jacket of regular four-square phrases. Each phrase wreathes restlessly in and out of keys, cadencing clumsily and twisting chromatically this way and that within a very tight intervallic space. Dynamically too it is restricted to *piano* with the odd *sforzando* punctuating the texture. There is life in the machine waiting to get out – hence the peculiar ending. Suddenly, the mechanism bursts into life: *forte, crescendo, fortissimo* (bs 41–6). An unexpected flourish rips through the awkward angularity of the minuet, brushing aside its restricted motions for a breathtaking gesture that sweeps over the entire range of the quartet to wipe out the mechanical (see example 13).

Clearly, instrumental music was not only alive but kicking away its

---

[1] On tonal elasticity and mechanical motion, see Daniel K. L. Chua, *The 'Galitzin' Quartets of Beethoven* (Princeton: Princeton University Press, 1995), 175–88.

[2] See H. C. Robbins Landon, *Haydn, Chronicle and Works: Haydn at Eszterháza 1766–90* (London: Thames and Hudson, 1978), 2:637.

Ex. 12 Joseph Haydn, Symphony no. 94, second movement.

old mechanical self to show off the new biology that the aesthetic had kindly bestowed upon it.[3]

If biology could not exist before *c.* 1750, then in a sense neither could the aesthetic. Both disciplines require the existence of living matter. Aesthetics, says Terry Eagleton, 'is a discourse born of the body'.[4] But as a science of sensuous perception, it requires a living and not a mechanised body. The aesthetic is just as much a discourse born out of biology as it is of the flesh. After all, for Alexander Baumgarten, who coined the term, the aesthetic is about life (*viva*) – 'the life of knowledge', 'the life of sensory cognition'[5] – a vitalistic concept no doubt inspired by Leibniz's *Monadology*, rather than contemporary physiology. Nevertheless, Baumgarten realised that it was impossible for a poem to remain alive as a sensory experience in the 'lower cognitive faculties' if the mind kept on alienating itself from the body with its analytical tools; mind and body needed to participate in the spontaneous particularity of the poetic experience if the poem were to live. Similarly, for a physician like Georg Stahl, however much one subjected the body

[3] For further discussion, see Janet M. Levy, '"Something Mechanical Encrusted on the Living": A Source of Musical Wit and Humor', in *Convention in Eighteenth- and Nineteenth-Century Music*, ed. W. J. Allanbrook, J. M. Levy and W. P. Mahrt (New York: Pendragon Press, 1992).

[4] Terry Eagleton, *The Ideology of the Aesthetic* (Oxford: Blackwell, 1990), 13.

[5] Alexander Gottlieb Baumgarten, *Aesthetica* (Frankfurt an der Oder, 1750 and 1758), quoted in Cassirer, *The Philosophy of the Enlightenment*, 350 and 356.

The Fruit of Knowledge

Ex. 13 Joseph Haydn, Quartet in C major, Op. 54 No. 2, third movement.

94

Ex. 13 *(cont.)*

to mechanical calculations, it was difficult to explain why blood, for example, would putrefy once the body was dead. There had to be some kind of *anima sensitiva* that keeps living matter from corruption. The rise of experimental physiology in the 1740s threw a spanner into the anatomical works, replacing a system of blind mechanism with a dynamic of change and activity, growth and regeneration. Life was no longer a matter of structure, but of vital function. Tissues and nerves, as the physician Théophile de Bordeu claimed, contained invisible forces of 'sensibility'.[6] In this way, bodily sensations became connected with the impulse of life and even its very consciousness. Knowledge need no

---

[6] See Hankin, *Science and the Enlightenment*, 124–7 and Dorinda Outram, *The Body and the French Revolution* (New Haven: Yale University Press, 1989), 54.

longer be divided up hierarchically between a passive body and an active soul; rather 'all the faculties of the soul . . . could have their origins in sensation itself'.[7] The body could stir the mind to action and desire could modify the cogitating ego. Cartesian psychology was turned upside down, and the body could at last stand on its own two feet.[8]

If the aesthetic, in Eagleton's words, is 'the body's long inarticulate rebellion against the tyranny of the theoretical',[9] the consequence for the rational soul was a crisis of existence. Having mechanised the body as pure material, the soul found itself undermined by the logic of its own analysis.[10] Not only was it physically robbed of its domination, but its very existence was thrown into question by the physiological experiments of scientists, such as Bordeu, who dispersed the centre of control across the entire network of nerves and ganglions, without even privileging the brain.[11] If the material of the body is alive, then the soul might as well be dead.

Because music was tied to the fortunes of the soul, it was caught up in a battle between those who happily dispensed with it and those who desperately clung on to a metaphysical notion of identity. As a result, instrumental music found itself appropriated as both a symbol of the secular self and also the sacred soul. On one extreme, it became the very vibration of sentient identity. After all, what was disturbing for the Cartesian about instrumental music was the way it took hold of the body with a plurality of affects that did not emanate from a single, rational being. But once the identity of the self has had its soul disassembled and disseminated throughout the nervous system, instrumental music could easily bristle across the sensory surface of the secular body. As a mirror of the self, music could celebrate its materiality as purely instrumental.

But for those who wanted to save their souls in the eighteenth century, this sort of rampant materialism had to be suppressed. French resistance to such desacralisation used vocal music as one of its moral weapons; the soul was basically forced to collude with the voice to shore up its supremacy, rehearsing the old Cartesian stance but now in terms of moral sensibility: the passions of the secular body were re-channelled as the moral voice of the soul. Germany at first followed France in praise

---

[7] Etienne de Condillac, *Traité des animaux* (1755), quoted in Cassirer, *The Philosophy of the Enlightenment*, 101.   [8] For a detailed study of the ideology of the body in the Enlightenment, see Barbara Maria Stafford, *Body Criticism: Imagining the Unseen in Enlightenment Art and Medicine* (Cambridge, MA: MIT Press, 1991).

[9] Eagleton, *The Ideology of the Aesthetic*, 13.

[10] For an extreme example of humanity as material being, see Julien Offray de la La Mettrie, *L'Homme Machine* (Leiden, 1748).

[11] See Outram, *The Body and the French Revolution*, 56–67.

of the voice,[12] but there was a twist in their thinking; the same sentimental aesthetic came to employ *instrumental music* as a solution to the decentring of identity; it was mobilised to recover the transcendental self. After all, the German physiologist, Albrecht von Haller, unlike Bordeu, tried to leave a place for the soul in his study of *Lebenskraft*, a position which irritated Diderot no end: 'Ridiculous man', he said as he leafed through Haller's book, 'if once I were to accept those distinct substances of yours [body and soul], there would be nothing more you could tell me. For your certainty does not know what the thing you call soul is, still less how the two substances are united.'[13] Indeed, as the century unfolded, the location of the soul became increasingly mysterious and even invisible to the point of extinction. But what Haller could not do, music accomplished in its instrumental abstraction, eventually becoming the absolute ground of being for the early German Romantics. The tables were turned: instrumental music no longer needed the soul, rather the soul needed instrumental music.

The two opposing views of instrumental music as material and spiritual both arose from a biology of the body, because the body's vital force was the battle ground for the soul. In all the diversity of discourses that clashed with each other as the debate intensified, the actual music remained the same; it was the body that made the difference – was it sacred or secular?

---

[12] See Cowart, *The Origins of Modern Musical Criticism*, 123–39 and Hosler, *Changing Aesthetic Views of Instrumental Music in 18th-Century Germany*, 31–68. In fact such a view persisted well into the eighteenth century and the early nineteenth century, for example in the writings of Heinrich Christoph Koch and Johann Georg Sulzer; see *Aesthetics and the Art of Musical Composition in the German Enlightenment*, eds. N. K. Baker and T. Christensen (Cambridge: Cambridge University Press, 1995).

[13] Denis Diderot, *Elements of Physiology* (1774–80), in *Diderot's Selected Writings*, 271. Also see 278–9 on the soul.

12

On the body

A vital materialist like Diderot had no problem with instrumental music since he had no real soul to worry about in any metaphysical sense;[1] he could revel in the pure, secular sensation of its vibrations as the sounds oscillate violently through every nerve fibre of the body. Its power to excite was purely biological; it was not fixed by the authority of the rational soul, but depended on the particular disposition of a person's nervous system.[2] In fact, Diderot speculates that there is no real difference between vocal and instrumental music, since a deaf-mute who suddenly awakens to sound would think that 'music was a special way of communicating thoughts, and that the instruments . . . in our hands [are] other organs of speech'. These sounds would tingle over his senses, like little bells tinkling inside his body, and impress a tacit knowledge of harmony within him for his 'soul' (as a reflective rather than metaphysical entity) to attend to.[3]

In such moments of pure secularisation, the knowledge of life could be an aesthetic act, a biological function of such intensity that one could almost 'die of pleasure'.[4] In effect, the divine mediation necessary in Cartesian epistemology between knowledge and reality is replaced by the *immediacy* of an aesthetic experience where sense and cognition could intermingle directly.[5] If the flesh could live without spirit, then life could aspire to the condition of music's isomorphic relation with the body. In fact, for Diderot, the body could become a living instrument. 'We are all instruments endowed with feeling and memory', he writes. 'Our senses are so many strings that are struck by surrounding objects and that also frequently strike themselves.' Just give a harpsichord feeling and memory and it would be an animal, claims Diderot, capable of thinking and other creative acts such as reproducing little baby harpsichords.[6] If

---

[1] See Denis Diderot, 'Soul', *Elements of Physiology* (1774–80), in *Diderot's Selected Writings*, 278–9; also see 271.

[2] See Denis Diderot, *Lettre sur les sourds et muet à l'usage de ceux qui entendent et qui parlent* (1751), in *Œuvres complètes*, ed. H. Dieckmann and J. Varloot (Paris: Hermann, 1978), 4:206–7.   [3] Ibid., 4:156–61.   [4] Ibid., 4:206.

[5] See Cassirer, *The Philosophy of the Enlightenment*, 94–108.

[6] Denis Diderot, *D'Alembert's Dream* (1769), in *Diderot's Selected Writings*, 187–8. This philosophical work is in the form of a play, in which the main characters are Diderot, D'Alembert and pertinently, the physician, Bordeu.

harpsichords could become organic, then the organic could become instrumental.

In a sense, this was exactly how Rameau, who corresponded with Diderot, viewed the human body. After all, as Diderot says, 'there are bodies [corps] that I would certainly call harmonic'.[7] By the 1750s, Rameau regarded bodies as resonators that emit the partials of the harmonic series as if they were literally the *corps sonore* that was so critical for his harmonic theory. By some kind of sensory transfer, the body could become harmonic, picking up the ratios of nature, like Diderot's little mechanical bells. Humanity is harmonic.

But a harmonic humanity, because it is instrumental, is not human by definition, claims Rousseau. In fact Rameau's harmonic ontology is merely a hypocritical mask that covers the moral dissonance at the core of modern civilisation. For Rousseau human conscience arises from the voice of the soul – and the voice is melodic. Only instruments are harmonic, and in Rousseau's mind, instruments are tools that merely alienate man from nature. So the implication of Rameau's harmonic theory was an origin of music without voice, without soul, without sentiment and without humanity. As far as Rousseau was concerned, Rameau had mistaken the emptiness of instrumental sounds for the plenitude of vocal signs that issue melodiously from the living soul. In his hands, nature herself had become an instrument playing upon the body and had turned the body into an instrument in the process. And this was not ultimately an academic problem, despite Rousseau's mathematical wrangling with Rameau, but a moral matter that concerned the natural origins of humanity. Rameau had substituted the passionate presence of the voice for the dead calculation of intervals, and had dared to call such articulation and spacing life itself.[8] Whatever his intentions, Rameau's harmonic genesis sounded too much like the cosmic *pneuma* (breath) of the vital materialists, as if instrumental sound could animate the body in the same way that the cosmic *pneuma* could inhabit matter.[9]

And perhaps Rousseau was right, for this is precisely what happens in Rameau's opera-ballet *Pygmalion*. Music breathes life into stone, and gives art both a body and a biology. Rameau himself, rather like that statue in his opera, had once possessed an inanimate body which his Cartesian mind had mechanised, as it were, into stone. His own conversion from a mechanistic to a sensationalist epistemology in the 1750s was nothing less than a harmonic revelation. As an experiment, he had put himself, like Diderot's deaf-mute, into the state of a man 'who had neither sung nor heard singing',[10] in order to experience from within the

---

[7] Diderot, *Lettre sur les sourds et muet*, 4:206.

[8] See Derrida, *Of Grammatology*, 199–215 and Thomas, *Music and the Origins of Language*, 82–142.   [9] On cosmic *pneuma*, see Hankin, *Science and the Enlightenment*, 127.

[10] Jean-Philippe Rameau, *Démonstration du principe de l'harmonie* (1750), 11–12, quoted in Christensen, *Rameau and Musical Thought in the Enlightenment*, 217–18.

Ex. 14 Jean-Philippe Rameau, *Pygmalion*, scene 3: the breath of harmonic life.

On entend une symphonie tendre et harmonieuse. Le théâtre devient plus éclairé.

first sounds that would strike his Edenic ears – except that it was not a single sound, but a composite series of tones that resonated from the fundamental base of his being. Obviously, with such empirical evidence, the *corps sonore* had to become the stamp of nature for Rameau, and therefore the 'soul' of biological instinct.[11] So what else should imbue the statue with life in the opera than the 'composing out of the *corps sonore*' (see example 14).[12] Having finished an air in G major, Pygmalion hears a magical harmonic disjunction as the music sinks colouristically into the natural vibrations of an E major chord, symbolically breathed out as life by the flutes. 'Where do these concordant sounds come from?' cries Pygmalion as some mysterious *pneuma* filters into his beloved statue. 'What are these harmonies? A dazzling brightness fills this place.' This 'dazzling brightness' (*vive clarté*) that fills the stage is surely the same 'flash of light'[13] that Rameau speaks of in his memoirs that had brought him to his senses, and indeed the senses of the earliest man to musical consciousness.

Without realising it himself, Rameau had established the foundations for the musical autonomy of pure music. Rameau perhaps was simply the mouthpiece of the new body; the desacralised body, severed from its theological scaffolds, became an autonomous, self-regulating, sovereign structure, and produced an aesthetic in its own image.[14] Ironically, Rameau himself, in the dialectic of vital materialism, slipped back in his late years into the cosmic mysticism that concepts like the universal *pneuma* always threaten to return to. But it only took a critic like Michel-Paul Guy de Chabanon, a supporter of Rameau's theories, to articulate the full implications of Rameau's ideas in the next generation, espousing a music without imitation or expression, a music so abstract and pre-

[11] See the preface to Jean-Philippe Rameau, *Observations sur notre instinct pour la musique et sur son principe* (Paris, 1754).
[12] Christensen, *Rameau and Musical Thought in the Enlightenment*, 228.
[13] Rameau, *Démonstration*, 11–12, quoted in ibid., 218.
[14] See Outram, *The Body and the French Revolution*, 48–51.

linguistic that it is the purity of the sign itself – natural and universal.[15] For Chabanon, music is simply itself, something to be judged by our senses 'without the mediation of the soul'.[16] Instrumental music becomes the index of the body's material autonomy, a pure performance of 'voluptuous sensation and immediate ecstasies' that harness sound for the somatic pursuit of happiness. 'Man', declares Chabanon, 'is only an instrument.'[17]

For a philosopher like Rousseau, this autonomy of pure sensual being simply will not do if moral freedom exists.[18] 'My will', he writes, 'is independent of my senses.'[19] Instead, Rousseau's eudemonism involves a complex return to an emotive state of nature, in which man discovers himself in the aboriginal feeling of moral self-consciousness.[20] If art is to reflect humanity, then it must arise from the moral autonomy of the will and not simply the passive response of our motor neurones. And for music this requires the rational mediation of the voice and its signs to shape the destiny of the body. The great tragedy of civilisation that Rousseau maps out before Western consciousness, is played out in his debate with Rameau; the fall of the modern world is described as the estrangement of music from its natural origins, as it severs itself from speech to become the artificial harmonies that can no longer touch the heart.[21] 'This is an age', complains Rousseau, 'that seeks to prove that the workings of the soul spring from material causes and that there is no morality in human feelings.' This new philosophy, embodied in the harmonic theories of Rameau, is the moral undoing of music. 'How far removed those musicians are from a true understanding of the power of their art who think of music merely as movements of the air and excitement of the nerves', laments Rousseau. 'As music becomes increasingly concerned with harmony at the expense of vocal inflection it is rougher on the ear, and less pleasing to the heart. Already it has ceased speaking; soon it will cease to sing.'[22] In a section entitled 'How music has degenerated' in his *Essay on the Origin of Language*, Rousseau concludes,

---

[15] See Barry, *Language, Music and the Sign*, 65–74.

[16] Michel-Paul Guy de Chabanon, *Observations sur la musique et principalement sur la métaphysique de l'art* (Paris, 1764 and 1779), 171.   [17] Ibid., 28.

[18] Jean-Jacques Rousseau, *The Creed of a Priest of Savoy*, trans. A. H. Beattie (New York: Continuum, 1990), 8–15. On the idea of moral will and moral sensibility in the writings of Rousseau, see Ernst Cassirer, *The Question of Jean-Jacques Rousseau*, trans. P. Gay (Bloomington: Indiana University Press, 1954).   [19] Ibid., 25.

[20] See Cassirer, *The Question of Jean-Jacques Rousseau*, 123–7.

[21] See Robert Wokler, *Rousseau on Society, Politics, Music and Language* (New York: Garland, 1987), 344–7.

[22] Jean-Jacques Rousseau, *Essai sur l'origine des langues* (1764): the translation is taken from Le Huray and Day, *Music Aesthetics in the Eighteenth and Early-Nineteenth Centuries*, 100 and 102. Complete translations of the essay can be found in *The Origin of Language*, trans. J. H. Moran and A. Gode (New York: Frederick Ungar, 1966) and in *The First and Second Discourses Together with the Replies to Critics and Essay on the Origin of Languages*.

Thus we see how singing gradually became an art entirely separate from speech, from which it takes its origin; how the harmonics of sounds resulted in forgetting vocal inflections; and finally, how music, restricted to purely physical concurrences of vibrations, found itself deprived of the moral power it had yielded when it was the twofold voice of nature.[23]

Harmony, for Rousseau, belongs to the body; only melody belongs to the voice of the soul. 'The pleasure of harmony', he writes, 'is only a pleasure of pure sensation',[24] whereas melody 'has moral effects that surpass the immediate empire of the senses' and enable music to touch the heart.[25] What the statue in Rameau's opera needed was not so much a biology but a soul. 'Your figure must be given one', says Pygmalion in Rousseau's retelling of the story, for life is not simply a matter of sensation but self-consciousness.[26] In other words, sensation had to be converted into sentiment; Bordeu's physiological sensibility had to be transformed into Rousseau's moral sensibility; the rational soul needed to be coupled with the desires of the body, and language with its musical accent. Only then could the statue become remotely human. So when Rousseau's statue awakens, her life does not begin with the external perceptions that characterise Rameau's statue – 'What do I see? Where am I?' Rather, for Rousseau, the statue first touches her own body and simply says 'I' – that vital articulation of self-presence. This is an autonomy of the will rather than Rameau's autonomy of sound – a vocal rather than instrumental consciousness. In other words, instrumental music is to humanity what a living statue is to stone – cold and dead. 'That's not me', she says, touching a block of marble. It is only as the statue touches her creator that she recognises her consciousness in another: 'Ah, still me', she says. This is the critical point in the aesthetic of moral sensibility: if one is to be moved by art, then art must be given a moral consciousness, otherwise one's inner nature would be touched by something that is inhuman and dead. Nature would be corrupted by artifice. Art must become humanity itself if one is to recognise the moral autonomy innate within one's being. When Pygmalion cries out, 'I adore myself in what I have made', he reveals the prelapsarian narcissism that is at the heart of the sentimental aesthetic; and the divine miracle that realises the impossible is nothing more than the conversion of culture into nature, a studied return to what for Rousseau was a

---

[23] Rousseau, *Essai sur l'origine des langues*, trans. J. H. Moran and A. Gode in *The Origin of Language*, 71–2.

[24] Jean-Jacques Rousseau, 'Unité de Mélodie', *Dictionnaire de musique* (Geneva, 1781), 757.

[25] 'Mélodies', in ibid., 386.

[26] Jean-Jacques Rousseau, *Pygmalion*, in *Œuvres complètes* (Paris: Pleiade, 1959), 2:1224–31. The quotations in English are taken from Jean Starobinski, *Jean-Jacques Rousseau: Transparency and Obstruction*, trans. A. Goldhammer (Chicago: University of Chicago Press, 1988), 70–80.

Neolithic state of pure transparency and passion.[27] Humanity is made perfect in an art that is 'without art'[28] for it has become the soul of natural man.

In this kind of sentimental aesthetic, vocal music becomes the pure transmission of sentiment from soul to soul, linking the composer to the performer and ultimately to the listener. The authenticity of the experience lies in the recovery of an innate morality of feeling that is the ontological ground for human communication. In this sense, the voice is a remnant of an Eden, a moral purity that society has obscured through the artificiality of its signs – in 'the invention of writing and the fabrication of instrumental sounds'.[29] The function of music is to recreate the transparency of those ancient festivals where *nothing* was represented but the purity of communal presence, a dream which Rousseau paints in all its naïvety in the final, festive scene of his own opera, *Le devin du village*. This is an aesthetic of the general will, a transparent music of the soul that weaves a community together as pure representation, without the coercion of artificial signifiers.[30] 'It would be useless', writes Rousseau in his Dictionary of Music,

for the composer to animate his work, if the fire which ought to reign there is not transmitted to those who execute it. The singer who sees the notes of his part only, is not in a condition of catching the expression of the composer . . . Begin then by a complete knowledge of the character of the song . . . [and] the energy which the composer has given to the poet, . . . which you also give in your turn to the composer . . . [In this way] the ear will be charmed and the heart moved; the physical and the moral will concur at once to the pleasure of the audience, and there will reign such a concord between the words and the melody, that the whole will appear to be a delightful language which can express everything and always please.[31]

Rameau and Rousseau represent different aesthetics grounded in two types of living bodies – one biological, the other moral. Both claim an autonomy for the self – one purely material, the other based on the freedom of the will. Both authenticate their origins in nature – one scientific, the other emotive. Both claim an immediacy of communication – one bodily, the other innate within the soul. Both make music in their own image – one harmonic, the other melodic. To a certain extent, the development of instrumental music in the eighteenth century fused the sensationalism of the one with the moral sentiment of the other. If anything, it inclined towards the latter; the irony of Rousseau's thought was that its concepts were more fully realised by the Germans in their

---

[27] See Rousseau's *Essai sur l'origine des langues*, and Jacques Derrida's discussion of the essay in *Of Grammatology*, 260–307.

[28] Rousseau, 'Expression', *Dictionnaire de musique*, 293.

[29] Wokler, *Rousseau on Society*, 344. [30] See Starobinski, *Jean-Jacques Rousseau*, 92–7.

[31] Rousseau, 'Expression', *Dictionnaire de musique*, 297–8.

instrumental music than the French in their vocal music. But then, it was the Germans who systematically thought through the implications of Rousseau's philosophy – in Eric Weil's words, 'It took Kant to *think Rousseau's thoughts.*'[32] If the French gave instrumental music a living body, then it was the Germans who gave it a moral soul.

[32] Eric Weil, 'J-J Rousseau et sa politique', 11, quoted in Starobinski, *Jean-Jacques Rousseau*, 115. Jean Starobinski, Ernst Cassirer and Dieter Henrich also take the view that both Kant's ethics and aesthetics are indebted to Rousseau's ideas. See Starobinski, *Jean-Jacques Rousseau*, Cassirer, *The Question of Jean-Jacques Rousseau*, and Dieter Henrich, *Aesthetic Judgement and the Moral Image of the World* (Stanford: Stanford University Press, 1992), 3–28.

13

On the soul

Polyps posed a problem for the eighteenth-century soul. When Abraham Trembley in the summer of 1739 dissected these little pond creatures into increasingly smaller fragments, he observed that each piece could regenerate itself into an entire polyp. He even turned one inside out and watched it continue to live and propagate.[1] But if these little bits of water hydra could grow back into whole polyps, then where was its soul? Did it not prove, as Diderot pointed out, that there was in fact no such thing as a soul; the property of life was simply scattered across all matter (plate 5).[2]

In his *Allgemeine Geschichte der Musik* (1788–1801) Johann Nikolaus Forkel tried to resolve the problem of the soul, but he must have read about the green-arm polyps that Johann Friedrich Blumenbach had dissected; these polyps, 'although amply fed, were always smaller than the [original]'. 'A mutilated rump', Blumenbach continues, 'always diminished in proportion very evidently, and seemed to become shorter and thinner, as it generated the lost parts.'[3] The dissemination of the soul in these aquatic creatures was therefore also a dilution of their being; a secondary polyp could never reflect the fullness of the original. If life is to be modelled on the polyp, then the identity of the human race is distributed throughout the world in mutilated forms, leaving its soul bereft of its original potential. This was a problem. Forkel's solution was simple; he basically reversed the dissecting process to reformulate the soul. In his organic map of history, culture regenerates itself from the 'first basic elements to the highest and most perfect union of all parts in a complete whole'. The different forms of music over the past several millennia 'resemble polyps, whose hundred severed limbs all live by themselves and appear to be complete polyps, but smaller ones'. Forkel's general

---

[1] Abraham Trembley, *Mémoires pour servir à l'histoire d'un genre de polypes d'eau douce, à bras en forme de cornes* (Leiden, 1744). An English translation is available in Sylvia G. Lenhoff and Howard M. Lenhoff, *Hydra and the Birth of Experimental Biology – 1744* (Pacific Grove, CA: Boxwood Press, 1988).

[2] See Lenhoff and Lenhoff, *Hydra*, 36–7, and Hankin, *Science and the Enlightenment*, 133.

[3] Johann Friedrich Blumenbach, *Über den Bildungstrieb und das Zeugunsgeschäfte* (Göttingen, 1781), 10, quoted in Joan Steigerwald, *Lebenskraft in Reflection: German Perspectives in the Late Eighteenth and Early Nineteenth Centuries* (King's London Ph.D., 1998).

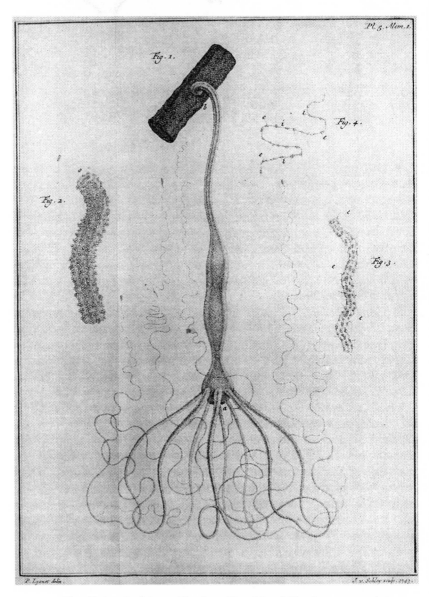

Plate 5 A polyp, from Abraham Trembley, *Mémoires pour servir à l'histoire d'un genre de polypes d'eau douce* (1744), 48. 'Shall we attribute a soul to it, or none at all?' wrote Charles Bonnet in a letter of 1744 to Professor Cramer of Geneva. 'My great wish is only that my poor little creatures not be too much degraded . . . I implore you, Sir, not to allow them to become simple machines. I will be inconsolable about it' (quoted in Lenhoff and Lenhoff, *Hydra*, 36).

history of music was literally a *polyph*onic regathering of all these severed fragments, to produce an organism 'more perfect . . . than Nature herself' – a reintegration of human identity through a counterpoint of sensibility.[4] This history culminates in a music so perfect that it reconstitutes the soul in all its fullness as an 'inner spiritual image . . . in the most secret corner of our being'.[5] And this music was none other than that of the *Empfindsamkeit* of the eighteenth century.

By reintegrating the soul that the materialists had dispersed in the disassembly of the polyp, and by relocating it in the realm of inner feeling, Forkel's history of music in effect unites Rameau's sensationalism with Rousseau's sentimentalism. The key word, '*Empfindung*', that Forkel uses to recapture the oneness of the soul, carries both the connotation of sensory perception and emotional sensibility, and Forkel's double-play on this word allows him to collapse his origin of music into a single concept that evolves from pure sensation to the perfection of sentiment in the eighteenth century. He rewrites, as it were, Rousseau's *Essay on the Origin of Language*, but reverses the decline of civilisation; what for Rousseau was a catastrophe of harmonic opacity, for Forkel becomes the perfectibility of harmonic transparency; what should have been denounced as the artificial calculations of harmony, becomes the cultural perfection of nature. Like Trembley's experiments with the polyps, Forkel turns both Rameau's and Rousseau's strategies inside out and grafts them on to a history with a *vocal* origin of music that flips into a moral ideal that is *harmonic*, contrapuntal and instrumental. *Empfindung* is refined in counterpoint and defined by chords. Thus Forkel gives harmony a soul, and so by implication grants instrumental music a sensibility. 'Only through [harmony]', he writes, 'could music become what it is now, namely, a true language of emotion.'[6] What had been Rousseau's voice of nature is replaced by a harmonic language that is no longer rational, but sentimental – an *Empfindungssprache*, as Forkel calls it, whose eloquence lies in its multiplicity and mutability as opposed to the static concepts that secure the identity of the Cartesian soul. Forkel's soul thus refigures its identity in the harmonic vibrations of Rameau's body and the moral transparency of Rousseau's melodic conscience. Indeed, the feelings of the soul are clarified by a harmonic precision and lucidity that promote such a purity of communication

---

[4] Johann Nikolaus Forkel, *Allgemeine Geschichte der Musik* (Leipzig, 1788–1801), 1:1–2. Various sections from Forkel's *General History of Music* have been translated in Enrico Fubini, *Music and Culture in Eighteenth-Century Europe* (London and Chicago: University of Chicago Press, 1994), and Hosler, *Changing Aesthetic Views of Instrumental Music in 18th-Century Germany*, 177–88.

[5] Johann Nikolaus Forkel, *Musikalischer Almanach für Deutschland auf das Jahr 1784*, 24, quoted in Hosler, *Changing Aesthetic Views of Instrumental Music*, 181.

[6] Forkel, *Allgemeine Geschichte der Musik*, 1:13.

Ex. 15 Johann Nikolaus Forkel's four harmonic definitions of
melodic meaning.

that Rousseau's soul is de*textualised* by the transparent presence of pure
sound. Notice how Forkel dispenses with the text in his example of an
ambiguous melody that can belong 'to C and G major, as well as to A
and E minor; and in each of these four relationships', he adds, 'it has
unquestionably a different meaning' (see example 15).[7]

It is no longer words that fix the emotions with the singularity of their
concepts, but the plurality of harmony. Therefore, according to Forkel,
the harmonic language of the eighteenth century is the 'most exact
determination [of linguistic and artistic expression] in order to avoid
any ambiguity and possible misunderstanding among such a great
number of conceptions and sensations'.[8] In this way, Forkel is able to
validate both the abstract polyphony of J. S. Bach and the emotional
vagaries of the sonatas of C. P. E. Bach, for the harmonies of both capture
the 'multiple modification of emotion'.[9] This is a very different biology
of music – one that neither requires the voice to fix the meaning in a
single concept nor the vague passivity of the sentient body. The biology
of Forkel's soul is actively plural. Music defines, in all its harmonic
subtleties, the complex and ever-changing motions of human feeling.
This is a *dynamic* biology that propels itself from within, as a constant
re-organisation and clarification of psychological matter – a dynamic
that is peculiarly German, and unmistakably organic.

Forkel can celebrate the proliferation of feelings that arise from the
soul, because he is able to ground the diversity in a single impulse of
history, an organic movement which he may have borrowed from the
theories of Blumenbach. The polyp, for Blumenbach, was the primary

---

[7] Ibid.   [8] Ibid., 1:12.   [9] Ibid., 1:15.

illustration of a biological action which he termed the *Bildungstrieb*: this 'formative impulse' determines the regeneration of whole polyps from the dissected pieces.[10] It is a teleological process that impels itself from within to restore the organised form. But the *Bildungstrieb* is not an impulse that is visible to the passive observer; rather it is an abstract linkage that is actively teased out by the experimenter from the organisation of the whole.[11] Similarly, Forkel as a historian claims to collect the 'features [of music] scattered throughout the whole of nature'; from their mutilated forms he infers a formative impulse in the history of music, and recombines the diverse elements to create a 'correct conception of music in its totality'.[12] Forkel makes music history organic, and the principle by which this history is shaped is the formative impulse of the human soul itself. The soul, through time, reorganises its being into the definitive form of its eighteenth-century incarnation, through a process akin to Condillac's celebrated analysis of a statue as it awakens to sensory impression.[13] Indeed, Forkel follows Condillac's empiricism by collapsing the distinction between the 'faculties of cognition and perception' into the 'same fundamental force of the soul'.[14] There is no duality between flesh and spirit, and therefore no division between sensory perception and moral feeling in the experience of *Empfindung*. In Forkel's monistic philosophy, the soul starts out as a simple substance that is constantly modified by impressions received from the body; and the formation of civilisation involves the movement from this passive state of perception to an active one of reflection, in which human emotions are conceptualised and defined by the precision of language and music.[15] Cultural history is one that moves towards a state of expressive clarity, and the perfection of music is in its power to depict the 'infinite and multiple modification of emotion'.[16] What for Condillac would

---

[10] Blumenbach's notion of the *Bildungstrieb* (formative urge or impulse) was a vital concept for the organic systems of German philosophy at the turn of the nineteenth century, particularly in Schelling's *System of Transcendental Idealism* (1800). It has a link with the aesthetic, not only because of the connection with the German Romantics who were preoccupied with the question of philosophy and art, but also because the *Bildungstrieb* influenced Kant's teleology of nature (as art) in his *Critique of Judgement* (1790). Hence Hölderlin can speak of the 'Kunst- und Bildungstrieb' (*Sämtliche Werke*, 6:329). Although Forkel does not use the word, he is obviously familiar with Blumenbach's work, and the principle of the *Bildungstrieb* seems to lurk behind his teleology of music and the soul. In fact, it may also have influenced Forkel's notion of musical logic; see Dahlhaus, *The Idea of Absolute Music*, 103–6.

[11] See Steigerwald, *Lebenskraft in Reflection*, 36–8.

[12] Forkel, *Allgemeine Geschichte der Musik*, 1:1.

[13] Etienne de Condillac, *Traité des sensations* (Paris, 1754).

[14] Forkel, *Allgemeine Geschichte der Musik*, 1:12.

[15] See ibid., 1:3–4 and 12–3. For a similar view, see Johann Georg Sulzer, 'Mannigfaltigkeit', *Allgemeine Theorie der schönen Künste*, 3:361–2.

[16] Forkel, *Allgemeine Geschichte der Musik*, 1:13–16.

have been a chaotic collision of vortices full of 'bizarre and imperfect images'[17] is progressively refined in Forkel's account by the *Bildungstrieb* of history that turns such mental activities into the transparent communication of emotions within and between the souls of individuals, for it is the soul of humanity itself.[18] Music, as a document of the soul, therefore reflects this evolution of sentiment; Forkel, by reformulating what the soul has scattered as music, reveals the 'inner nature'[19] of a history that ultimately deposits the *Bildungstrieb* as a musical form; and this embodiment of formation (*Bildung*) becomes the final object by which Forkel interprets his history. This is the core of his historical method. Forkel can infer the unfolding of history because he has the final product in his hands, and can see in the object the process of its development in miniature. And what is this final object? – instrumental music itself. Or at least that is the implication.[20] Through this artefact, he can see how music had to align itself with poetry and gestures in antiquity 'precisely because of [its] intrinsic imperfection and internal flaws' at that time. But now, music has become an autonomous 'language of sentiment' in which the impulse of history posits itself as a musical form 'standing on its own and operating entirely by its own force'; 'even without words', writes Forkel, 'music is not without meaning, . . . [for] it is able to grasp passions and feelings in its own way'.[21] Music in the late eighteenth century therefore represents the perfection of the soul by revealing the *Bildungstrieb* that is also the *Bildungsroman* of its development. And so the musical polyp finds itself reintegrated as the image of its own moral history.

Hence, according to Forkel, by the end of the eighteenth century, music has made visible the invisible soul by projecting an image of its manifold feelings before the eye of the imagination.[22] Music represents what anatomy cannot see. And these expressions of the soul can literally be notated on the stave. Forkel proves this by giving a list of what he calls 'Figuren für die Einbildungskraft' (figures for the imagination). Here, for example, is a moment of 'Ellipsis' – a sudden fissure and stasis of emotion (see example 16).

These figures are no longer the static, rhetorical devices of the Baroque; rather these are dynamic figures of gradation, intensification and transition, 'whereby individual parts of phrases now varied, now

---

17 Etienne de Condillac, *Traité des animaux* (1755), quoted in Cassirer, *The Philosophy of the Enlightenment*, 104.   18 See Forkel's *Allgemeine Geschichte der Musik*, 1:12.

19 Ibid., 1:1.

20 Forkel was ambivalent about the status of instrumental music; his theory of sentient harmonic definition frees instrumental music from a dependence on verbal concepts and enabled him to establish its validity; however, Forkel was reluctant to upset the *status quo* and reverse the vocal-instrumental hierarchy.

21 Forkel, *Allgemeine Geschichte der Musik*, 1:12.   22 See ibid., 1:55–9.

Ex. 16 Ellipsis – one of Forkel's figures for the imagination.

augmented, now diminished, sometimes repeated from the beginning or from the middle, sometimes even repeated from the end' portray the thematic development of feelings within the soul.[23] This validation of the mixed affects of the new instrumental music is grounded in a new physiology of humanity; the *Bildungstrieb*, for Blumenbach, is a new *Lebenskraft* (life force) that is characterised by a complex 'alternation of combination and innerconnections' in its impulse to formation.[24] Instrumental music in its ability to reflect the 'multiple modification of emotions' is a new music for a new biology. It need no longer be a dead or divided object; rather the very contrast and alternations of what was known at the time as a 'mixed style'[25] become the bodily life of the soul itself. Instrumental music has been pronounced organic, and has identified the soul.

Naturally, to the twenty-first-century mind, all this appears somewhat peculiar, as if Forkel has fallen off one of those long, green, tangential arms of Blumenbach's polyp. But Forkel's history is not as odd as it may sound, for the moral history of the teutonic soul had for a long time been charted by the musical pathology of its body. All Forkel does is to give the new biology a new music to legitimise a new moral order. But of course music has always had a legendary ability to tune the soul, and in Germany, Lutheranism certainly reinforced the notion of a moral harmony that 'drives away the devil' and 'makes the soul peaceful and happy'.[26] Writing in his complete guide for the Lutheran *Capellmeister*, Mattheson states that 'well ordered sounds . . . serve the emotions and passions of the soul'. 'Where there are no affects to be found', he continues, 'there is also no virtue.' In fact, 'because sounds work strongly on the muscles' they can cure all sorts of pains in the limbs as well as the sick feelings in the moral depths of our being.[27] Obviously, the Baroque

---

[23] Ibid., 1:58; the translation is taken from Hosler, *Changing Aesthetic Views of Instrumental Music*, 188.   [24] Blumenbach, *Über den Bildungstrieb und das Zeugunsgeschäfte*, 42–3.

[25] See Johann Joachim Quantz, *Versuch einer Anweisung die Flöte traversiere zu spielen* (Berlin, 1752), translated by E. R. Reilly as *On Playing the Flute* (London: Faber, 1966), 341, and V. Kofi Agawu, *Playing with Signs* (Princeton: Princeton University Press, 1991), 29–30.   [26] See Hosler, *Changing Aesthetic Views of Instrumental Music*, 37 and 38.

[27] Mattheson, *Der vollkommene Capellmeister*, 103–4.

affects were not simply musical metaphors, but a table of emotions that was the script of the soul, scribbled by the indelible movement of the body. There was no definitive *Affektenlehre* that one could consult, nor could one see classified in concrete shapes the internal motions of the body as dots on the stave, but there was certainly the notion at the time that musical figures could pinpoint the affections of the soul and so act as a general taxonomy of psychological and moral states. Such categorisations of feeling were typical of the eighteenth century; Maupertuis, for example, tried to develop a calculus of emotion which could quantify the intensity of pain and pleasure,[28] but it was really music that fixed for certain the moral structure of the passions. Music was the moral mathesis of the soul. Thus both Mattheson and Lorenz Mizler attempted to construct a 'mechanics of musical morality',[29] a kind of spiritual engineering in which music would mould the soul as it tweaked the physiology of the body. The aim was 'to calculate the effects of chords and melodies upon the soul'[30] in order to deduce the mathematical rules for the inculcation of moral affections. This affective process of music culminates in Forkel's 'figures for the imagination', which simply mix these calculations into a process that dispenses with mathematics for the empirical data of sensations, orchestrated by the organic force of the soul.

But it is vital to note that Forkel's soul is no longer a Lutheran one. The mixed style of instrumental music belongs to an altogether different being that is no longer a metaphysical entity but a sentient substance – a 'fundamental force' that unites cognition and perception, spirit and flesh. And its morality is no longer a code of virtue but the refinement of one's nervous system in an internal drive towards perfection. In this instrumental aesthetic of moral sensibility, the human being is made to inhabit the table of emotions in order to generate its moral completion from the dismembered pieces of a mutilated soul. As such, Forkel's theory is a very odd combination of ideas picked out from the eighteenth century, which he reorientates and even reverses to give a feint anticipation of the organic philosophies of German Idealism. In a sense, his history of music forms a precarious bridge between the material empiricism of the eighteenth century that reduces body and soul to a single substance and the metaphysical notions of the early Romantics that grounded their organic systems in a *Bildungstrieb* that embraced the entire universe as *Geist*.[31] What links the material with the transcendental, in Forkel's account, is a moral teleology that perfects the human race

---

[28] Pierre-Louis Moreau de Maupertuis, *Essai de philosophie morale* (Leiden, 1751); see Cassirer, *The Philosophy of the Enlightenment*, 149.

[29] Hosler, *Changing Aesthetic Views of Instrumental Music*, 38.

[30] Jan Chiapusso, *Bach's World* (Bloomington: Indiana University Press, 1968), 255.

[31] See note 10.

as it moves towards the whole. But this moral fibre was about to snap, consigning Forkel's theory to the outmoded world of *Empfindsamkeit*. In fact, he never completed his project. And the unused plates for an anthology of music were melted down into the rather unsentimental and unrefined aesthetic of French imperial cannon balls. History was not on his side. The *Bildungstrieb* of time may theoretically be perfecting humanity, but for all his moral ideals, Forkel had basically reduced the human soul to a big polyp with deep feelings. And music, in its instrumental form, was forced to bear the strain and to mask this ridiculous fact.

14

On morality

Clearly the new morality that instrumental music was elected to represent was a biological one – an internal, organic impulse that formed an *Empfindungssprache* of moral gestures. The soul during the course of the eighteenth century had obviously shifted its footing from a mechanical to an organic ethic; the extrinsic law that regenerates a depraved will is now replaced by an internal moral sense that no longer needs the sanctifying grace of God but the biological growth of its emotions instead.[1] Ernst Cassirer traces the source of this inward morality to the Cambridge Platonists who already in the seventeenth century had drawn the distinction between the mechanical and the vital:

There are a sort of Mechanical Christians in the world, that not finding Religion acting like a living form within them, satisfie themselves only to make an Art of it . . . But true Religion is no Art, but an inward Nature that contains all the laws and measures of its motion within itself.[2]

True religion is no art? The ironic twist at the end of the eighteenth century was that art had become nature and that nature had replaced God as the interpreter of the cosmos. Thus the aesthetic could make an art out of morality by aestheticising the soul as a kind of innate, natural religion consecrated by the body. And music, because it seemed to mime the body's internal motions, was given power over the moral nature as a living form within. The strategy was to make music moral by making it biological. In effect, music was bestowed the sanctifying role of the Holy Spirit: it became the aesthetic *Bildungstrieb* of a desacralised body whose moral law is the pursuit of its own happiness and that of its society. This is the Enlightenment's re-entry into Eden, which was not a return to God but to that sense of collective innocence between the individual and society. The moral law of Forkel's aesthetic is 'to depict pleasant passions and feelings' in order to 'contribute to the well being and delight of humanity'.[3] Society is formed as individual strands of emotions are woven together into a fugue so natural that it presents

---

[1] On moral sentiment, see Taylor, *Sources of the Self*, 250–65.
[2] John Smith, *Select Discourses* (1660), quoted in Ernst Cassirer, *The Platonic Renaissance in England* (Edinburgh: Nelson, 1953), 164.
[3] Forkel, *Musikalischer Almanach für Deutschland auf das Jahr 1784*, 26.

itself as a moral organism. The inner life of Christianity has been aestheticised into the inner morality of human biology. If the Cambridge Platonists were prophetic, the fulfilment of their prophecies was ironic.

yet we are all this while, but like dead Instruments of Musick, that sound sweetly and harmoniously, when they are onely struck, and played upon from without, by the Musicians Hand, who hath the Theory and the *Law* of Musick, *living* within himself. But the second, the *living* Law of the Gospel, the *Law of the Spirit of Life* within us is as if the *Soul of Musick* should incorporate it self with the Instrument, and live in the Strings, and make them of their own accord, without any touch, of impulse from without, daunce up and down, and warble out their harmonies.[4]

In Forkel's account of instrumental music, the work of grace has become the art of works; the spiritualisation of instrumental music was no longer a metaphor but a reality – or rather, the delusion of natural salvation. Such a conversion of culture into nature always involves the contradiction of remaining in the garden of innocence whilst gnawing at the fruit of knowledge. The age of reason resolved the tension by neutralising knowledge as a transparent language of representations untainted by the opacity of evil. Language took on the purity of Eden and gave the Enlightenment the Adamic privilege of naming things and placing them within the symmetry of nature. 'The fundamental task of Classical discourse', writes Foucault, 'is to ascribe a name to things and in that name to name their being.'[5] This neutralisation of representation conjured up a *natural* order of things. In this way, the natural feelings of morality that welled up from within the body could simply be named and come under the control of knowledge. The novelty of Forkel's aesthetic was that it bestowed the power of moral representation to a musical language stripped of verbal concepts. The irony is that it was too late. Just at the moment when the age of representation was about to dismantle its system of knowledge, instrumental music finally found its ability to name.[6] Forkel's musical system meticulously defines every shade of sensation through a harmonic language that functioned as a neutral representation of passion. But the Enlightenment became increasingly aware that this type of signification was simply to mistake as transparent the opaque fig-leaves of one's ideology. Knowledge could not co-exist with the innocence of naming, and the body proved itself to be full of the impurities of desire that eventually buckled the nomination of knowledge. Under the epistemological shift, music, as the language chosen to name the morality of the body, was bound to undermine the very structure of morality that it was meant to represent;

---

[4] Nathaniel Cudworth, *A Sermon before the House of Commons* (1647), quoted in Cassirer, *The Platonic Renaissance*, 33–4.   [5] Foucault, *The Order of Things*, 120.
[6] See ibid., 217–21.

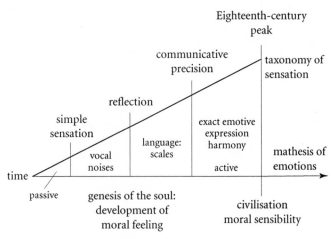

Fig. 4 The structure of Forkel's musical morality

in fact, it dismantled the entire edifice of knowledge at the end of the eighteenth century.

Even as Forkel was writing, that structure was collapsing under the weight of its own impossibility. Indeed, Forkel's own work represents the tension of a system bursting at the seams. His justification of the morality of sensation as natural and definable totters on the edge of the body's rebellion against the taxonomy of reason. But instead of loosening the precision of language, Forkel tightens the system of thought. His structure of moral knowledge falls almost exactly into Foucault's analysis of the Classical episteme based on the ordering of thought as genesis, mathesis and taxonomy (see figure 4). Genesis in Forkel's history is the analysis of the chronological order of sensation upon the human soul; this involves the progressive imprint of sense data from a passive state to a reflective state in three stages of musical development.[7] Mathesis for Forkel is the calculation of that order through the ability of music to establish identities and differences of sensation and feeling with the utmost precision. And finally, the taxonomic is the classification of those emotions as musical figures upon a table of sensation.

This is the moral structure of the new Eden in which humanity is ordered as a natural history and its morality as an empirical taxonomy. Through the signification of music, a moral order is teased out of the body with an accuracy so natural that one can dispense with the obscurity of divine origins and the revelations of a Mosaic law. The 'linguistic' autonomy that Forkel bestows upon music allows him to create a self-regulating system that arises from humanity and presses towards its

---

[7] See Forkel, *Allgemeine Geschichte der Musik*, 1:1–15.

social perfection. As a natural communication of emotion, music is able to transmit moral feelings from soul to soul and so create that non-coercive integration of the individual and the general will sought after by the Enlightenment within the autonomy of its emotional enclosures. Central to this process is the concept of sympathy. Significantly, this word was used as a physiological term in the eighteenth century to denote the communication of feeling between the different organs of the body, creating an internal 'harmony that often makes one or several parts participate in the affections of those that are injured'.[8] It was a system of mobility and sensibility that circulated the entire body through the nervous fibres: 'All sympathy', says Robert Whytt in his treatise on nervous diseases, 'all consensus presupposes sentiment and consequently can exist only in the mediation of the nerves, which are the only instruments by which sensation operates.' Thinkers such as David Hume and Adam Smith, however, turned this physiological notion into a philosophical one: sympathy became a social transmission of sentiment, a communal sensation that was described by Lord Kames as 'the great cement of society'.[9] As a consequence, political morality depended upon the refinement of one's nervous system, and because music vibrated along these moral fibres it could articulate the morality of the social body. This is how Forkel, who read his Hume and Kames, is able to hear the fugue as a harmonisation of the individual within the political will of moral sentiment. The innate morality of the body is certified by the sympathetic vibrations of the nerve fibres as they unite the soul of society in the law of the fugue. Rule and passion synchronise, as if humanity could create its own contrapuntal system out of its sentient being. What for J. S. Bach was the rational structure of the cosmos has become for Forkel natural law, moral sense and general will:

Let us imagine a people which through the narration of a great event is deeply moved; and imagine at first that a single member of this group, perhaps through the intensity of his emotions, is driven to make a short powerful statement as the expression of his feeling. Will not this outburst of emotion gradually grip the collective members of this people, and will he not be followed first by one, then several, and then most of them, each singing the same song with him . . . modifying it according to his own way of feeling, but on the whole in sympathy with him as to the basic emotion: And if such a scene . . . is to be represented musically, do not first the *dux*, then the *comes*, then the *repercussio* arise in the most natural way in the world – in short the whole outer and inner form of the fugue?

---

[8] Jean-Baptiste Pressavin, *Nouveau traité des vapeurs* (Lyons, 1770), 2–3, quoted in Foucault, *Madness and Civilization*, 151. On sympathy, see ibid., 150–8, and Christopher Lawrence, 'The Nervous System and Society in the Scottish Enlightenment', *Natural Order*, ed. B. Barnes and S. Shapin (Beverly Hills: Sage, 1979).

[9] Lord H. Homes Kames, *Essays on the Principles of Morality and Natural Religion* (Edinburgh, 1751), 17, quoted in Lawrence, 'The Nervous System', 32.

Is not the variegated leading and weaving of voices, which together make a pleasant but manifold harmony . . . an accurate representation of nature? Is this not the most perfect expression of the multiple modified feelings of all the members of a people, feelings which arise little by little, but then pour themselves out in a universal stream?[10]

In the same way, composers such as C. P. E. Bach believed that their music was a pure form of sentient communication. It connected body to body in the isomorphic movement of tone and passion. 'Music', writes Johann Gottfried Herder, 'performs on the clavichord within us, which is our own inmost being.' For Herder, every 'involuntary reaction' of the nervous system becomes a sign of the soul's moral identity, for the ear is 'the hearing chamber of the soul' and every fibre must respond; through music, the body automatically speaks.[11] After all, in the social behaviour of the sentimental novel it is no longer words that speak but the body – in tears, tremblings, convulsions, swooning, hysterical fits. The body cannot lie – it is always authentically connected up with the object of its emotions. And, as Janet Todd notes, this sympathetic movement breaks through the typology of the sentimental text, with its dashes, mutilated letters, torn sentences, missing chapters, stuttering speeches.[12] It is therefore a mistake to imagine that the 'vocal utterances' that so often disturb the textures of C. P. E. Bach's keyboard music are simply an expression of the rhetorical grammar of eighteenth-century theory. These intrusions have nothing to do with grammatical classifications, if anything they destroy the 'singing style' that Bach describes. What these mutilated figures say is that music cannot speak, that under the stress of emotions words become mute, melodies fragment, gestures become incoherent. The body obtrudes through the gaps in the score, and it smothers any tidy classification of affects in the sincerity of its movement. What the disruptive recitatives of a piece such as the first Prussian Sonata signify is not speech but the emotion that breaks the text into a stutter and leaves the body to articulate (see example 17).

Hence Bach instructs the performer not 'to sit like a statue before his instrument',[13] but, like Pygmalion's sculpture, his body is to come alive with gesture – what Quantz calls the 'art of simulation'.[14] It is because there is 'a direct connection between the ear and the heart' that the body can express itself with the unmediated authenticity of moral feeling. 'The aural nerves', says Sulzer, 'transmit to the entire body the impact

---

[10] Forkel, *Allgemeine Geschichte der Musik*, 1:47–8; the translation has been modified from Hosler, *Changing Aesthetic Views of Instrumental Music in 18th-Century Germany*, 186.

[11] Johann Gottfried Herder, *Kalligone* (Weimar, 1800), trans. Le Huray and Day, *Music Aesthetics in the Eighteenth and Early-Nineteenth Centuries*, 253–4.

[12] See Janet Todd, *Sensibility: An Introduction* (London: Methuen, 1986), 5.

[13] Bach, *Essay on the True Art of Playing Keyboard Instruments*, 152.

[14] Quantz, *On Playing the Flute*, 273.

Ex. 17 C. P. E. Bach, Sonata in F major, Wq. 48, No. 1, second movement – bs 12–15.

of the shock they receive'; these somatic gestures therefore name music as 'an intelligible language of sentiment'.[15] So finally, as body-talk, music enters 'the great utopia of a perfectly transparent language in which things themselves could be named without any penumbra of confusion – a language so natural that it would translate like a face expressing a passion'.[16]

But what is being named in this fusion of passion, gesture and sound? The moral function of music was to name the self as the 'transcendental signifier' through the sentimental body – 'to proceed from the figure of the name, to the name itself' to adapt Foucault's phrase.[17] *Empfindsamkeit* is principally about identity; it defines the state of a soul that was in fact losing its identity in the eighteenth century. C. P. E. Bach's music is an attempt to capture the self in the spontaneous act of improvisation. But this was a near impossible act of naming because the identity of the self was in constant flux. After all, if the moral self is founded on the condition of the nervous system, then its identity is figured in the constant vibrations of its environment and not some immutable, metaphysical entity. This is why some of Bach's pieces resemble Condillac's chaotic psychology of the mind:

> The vortices give ascendancy by turns over another. They accomplish their revolutions with amazing variations. They crowd one another, destroy one another, or come into being again accordingly as the feeling to which they owe their power weaken, are eclipsed or appear in a form hitherto unknown.[18]

Take, for example, the Fantasia in C. It flits without rhyme or reason from one affect to another, with its theme constantly swirling off into peculiar gestures and plunging dissonantly into some perverse harmony (see example 18).

This is peculiar behaviour, but it is precisely through this kind of improvised music 'that the keyboardist can best master the feelings

---

[15] Sulzer, 'Musik', *Allgemeine Theorie der schönen Künste*, 3:422 and 427.
[16] Foucault, *The Order of Things*, 117.   [17] Ibid., 118.
[18] Etienne de Condillac, *Traité des animaux* (1755), quoted in Cassirer, *The Philosophy of the Enlightenment*, 104.

Ex. 18 C. P. E. Bach, Fantasia in C, Wq. 61, No. 6 – bs 1–53.

Ex. 18 *(cont.)*

of his audience', says Bach.[19] Performance must always be an act of improvisation, even if it is only through ornamentation, in order to make the self spontaneously present and so engulf the listener with the identity of another. Soul communicates to soul in the sympathetic vibration of sound. What happens at the clavichord then is a naming of the self that is constantly deferred by a body that has slipped through the grid of Classical representation as it shifts its emotional states according to the composer's whim.

Notation was therefore always a crisis of identity – an act of contradiction.[20] Rousseau puts it like this: a Fantasia 'as soon as it is written or repeated is no longer a fantasia, but an ordinary piece'.[21] Bach's meticulous markings were an attempt to pin down the nuances of his expressive state, to fix for eternity the immanence of the moment in the tactile signs of being – *Bebung, Tragen*, staccato, slurs.[22] These must be read as marks of the body, for Bach instructs the performer to assume 'the emotion which the composer intended'.[23] In order to play Bach the performer, as Christian Schubart notes, has to 'lose his personal identity' for another.[24] And, consequently, to hear Bach is to lose one's identity in

---

[19] Bach, *Essay on the True Art of Playing Keyboard Instruments*, 152.

[20] See Etienne Darbellay, 'C. P. E. Bach's Aesthetic as Reflected in his Notation', in *C. P. E. Bach Studies*, ed. S. L. Clark (Oxford: Clarendon Press, 1988).

[21] Jean-Jacques Rousseau, 'Fantasia', *Dictionnaire de musique* (Geneva, 1781), 303.

[22] *Bebung* is a kind of vibrato on the clavichord; *Tragen* involves the sustaining of a note by renewing the pressure on the key – this is indicated by a slur with dots.

[23] Bach, *Essay on the True Art of Playing Keyboard Instruments*, 152.

[24] Christian Friedrich Daniel Schubart, *Ideen zu einer Äesthetik der Tonkunst*, written c.1784–5, published by L. Schubart (Vienna, 1806), 295, quoted in Hans-Günter Ottenburg, *Carl Philipp Emanuel Bach*, trans. P. J. Whitmore (Oxford: Oxford University Press, 1987), 101.

Ex. 19 C. P. E. Bach, *Abschied von meinem Silbermannschen Clavier in einem Rondo* – bs 1–6.

this chain of influence from the creator through the player to the audience. Having assumed the emotions of the composer, the performer, says Bach, 'must necessarily feel all the affects that he hopes to arouse in his audience, for the revealing of his humor will stimulate a like humor in his listener'.[25] Only 'technicians . . . play the notes', he adds. Thus music must not be read as a 'score' – that is, as some kind of disembodied structure. There is no score in performance, no fixity in improvisation. This means that the notation of a piece such as Bach's touching *Farewell to My Silbermann Clavichord* actually inscribes the motions within his body, from the tiniest vibrations through the harmonic sequences to the circular meanderings of its Rondo form. The constant twists and turns of the ornaments are squiggles that 'bring life' to the nerve fibres and the mutations of rhythms are the complex agitation of the vital spirits (see example 19).

Critics that accuse Bach of formal incoherence are disembodied analysts who have missed the moral point.[26] After all, when Forkel 'analyses' the F minor Sonata from Bach's third collection *Für Kenner und Liebhaber*, he does not see a structure to be atomised. He sees a map of the body, and his 'analysis' is a navigation of the senses.[27] For all its changes of affects, the Sonata, according to Forkel, exhibits a coherent process from a state of 'anger' in the first movement, through one of 'reflective deliberation' in the second, and to a final state of 'melancholic

---

[25] Bach, *Essay on the True Art of Playing Keyboard Instruments*, 152.
[26] See, for example, Charles Rosen, *The Classical Style* (London: Faber, 1971), 112–16.
[27] Forkel, *Musikalischer Almanach*, 34–6.

calm'. What organises the piece are not the motivic or formal constructs, but the transitions of feelings. The organic coherence of the work is not in the score but in the body.

Evidently, in the eighteenth century, the spontaneity of the self is trying to escape the control of reason through the body of *Empfindsamkeit*; it foreshadows in gentler tones the twentieth-century ecstasies of a Roland Barthes. In Barthes' words, this kind of music creates 'figures of the body (the "somathemes"), whose texture forms musical signifying'; and 'signifying' for Barthes is not a system of signs but a direct impact in which the 'body passes into music without any relay but the signifier'. There can be 'no more grammar, no more music semiotics . . . [no more] analysis' in this 'somatics' of music.[28] Barthes is speaking of Schumann, of his bodily escape into *Kreisleriana*, of the '*beat* inside the body, against the temple, in the sex, in the belly, against the skin',[29] but he might as well be speaking of the eighteenth-century body (after all, Barthes begins his essay with a quote from Diderot), indeed, he might as well be speaking of the body of C. P. E. Bach:

What does the body *do* when it enunciates (musically)? . . . My body strikes, my body collects itself, it explodes, it divides, it pricks, or on the contrary and without warning . . . it stretches out, it weaves . . . And sometimes – why not – it even speaks, it declaims, it doubles its voice: *it speaks but says nothing*: for as soon as it is musical, speech – or its instrumental substitute – is no longer linguistic but corporeal; what it says is always and only this: *my body puts itself in a state of speech: quasi parlando*.[30]

Compare Barthes' attempt to recover from the rational subject the spontaneity of the body with that of Herder's, in a dialogue almost two hundred years earlier. It is almost the same biology, the same language of immediate arousal – a body articulating without speech. Body music.

A. A blow disturbs a body; what message does that body's sound communicate?
B. 'I have been disturbed; my members are consequently vibrating and eventually coming to rest.'
A. Is that what they say to us?
B. Every fibre of our being is capable of responding; our ear, the hearing chamber of the soul, is extraordinarily sensitive, an echo chamber of the finest kind.
A. So if single sounds *arouse* us, what do intermittent sounds do?
B. They renew and reinforce the stimulus . . .
A. And *long-sustained* sounds?
B. They sustain the emotion by prolonging the stimulus . . .
A. What about sounds that get louder or softer, faster or slower, sounds that rise

---

[28] Roland Barthes, 'Rasch', *The Responsibility of Forms*, trans. R. Howard (Oxford: Blackwell, 1986), 307–8.   [29] Ibid., 302.   [30] Ibid., 305–6.

and fall, that are increasingly or decreasingly intense, harsh or soft, regular or irregular, sadder or gayer; what about blows, accents, waves, emotion and pleasure – what effect do all these have on us?

B. As every involuntary reaction of our emotions to music proves, these all produce similar responses. The tide of our passions ebbs and flows, it floods, it meanders and trickles. At one moment the passions are intensified, at another they are aroused now gently, now powerfully . . . their movement and the way they move varies in response to every melodic nuance, and every forceful accent, let alone every change of key. Music performs on the clavichord within us which is our own inmost being.[31]

Barthes' biological excursion that tries to displace the centrality of the subject with the pulsations of the body simply re-enacts the escape of eighteenth-century music from the conceptual voice of Cartesian rationalism into a kind of virtuous vibration – a moral *jouissance*. Once music was used to celebrate the Eucharist, but by the eighteenth century the sentimental body of the bourgeoisie had replaced the broken body of Christ as the signifier of morality; music's possession of the body and its power to control the nervous system assured this sensual epistemology of its innate virtue. This was why tears were shed and women fainted during eighteenth-century concerts; these bodies were the script of their own delicate and sensible natures.[32] But the susceptibility to such biological niceties eventually lost their Rococo control, and humanity discovered a body of desire which though innate was far from virtuous. The yearning of Goethe's young Werther put more than a little storm and stress on the delusions of Eden.[33] His suicide symbolises the demise of a body that had swallowed itself in its own Eucharistic solipsism.

Barthes' somatic dissemination is as doomed as Forkel's system of musical morality: everything cannot be collapsed into the body. Forkel's system was falling apart. The problem was that the morality of the system depended on an *analytic* of the body, whereas the experience of it was grounded in an *aesthetic* of the body. Cognition and perception far from being rooted in the same substance, antagonised the soul. Neither material sense nor moral feeling could exist without obscuring the transparency of the other, and yet both were necessary: the analytic named the moral as natural and set the grid of emotions in which the body must move; the aesthetic affirmed as empirical that innate moral-

---

[31] Herder, *Kalligone* (Weimar, 1800), in Le Huray and Day, *Music Aesthetics*, 253–4.

[32] See, for example, Johnson, *Listening in Paris*, 60–70.

[33] Johann Wolfgang von Goethe, *Die Leiden des jungen Werther* (1774). *The Sorrows of Young Werther* was an immensely popular book born out of the *Sturm und Drang* movement of the 1770s, and inspired so many suicides among young would-be Romantics that Goethe prefaced later editions of the work with verses such as 'Be a man and do not follow me.'

ity of being. Forkel forces the precision of knowledge and the vagaries of the body through the unifying grid of musical representation. But they refused to mix. The body's aesthetic movement could not be controlled by the analytic of moral knowledge. Its pure reactivity jettisoned the control of the cognitive faculty for a passive sentient existence that could easily slip through the moral grid into the world of a de Sadian novel. As the eighteenth century wore on, the body failed to prove its innocence and set the structures of knowledge outside the gates of Eden. Forkel wanted music to name the innocence of the body, but in fact in this aesthetic, music was made to eradicate the marks of original sin from the soul. Its bodily transparency was an ideological fig-leaf.

So despite the moral perfectibility of his system, Forkel was not a cultural optimist. As far as he was concerned, music, having discovered its sentient soul, was in danger of degenerating; his theory of music was a last ditch effort to preserve the precision of musical taste. Unfortunately for Forkel, the body was growing out of its nominalist enclosures, despite his attempt to name its fleeting sensations. Naming and feeling were becoming increasingly difficult and not particularly virtuous. However much Forkel tried to fuse cognition and perception into the 'same fundamental force of the soul', his musical monism insisted on splitting its existence to become a transcendental subject and a body of desire. The analytic and the aesthetic could no longer commingle as the body overturned the neatly laid tables of emotions. And the music of *Empfindsamkeit* was denounced as immoral.

In fact, even as Forkel was writing, critics were accusing the aesthetic of moral sensibility as a form of anti-social indulgence, locked in the private titillations of the body, and that far from being in touch with nature, the sentimental self had become a constructed literary type – a musical discourse. Music was revealed as a cover-up for a somatic ideology, made to represent the soul when in fact it was merely an aesthetic substitution. And as always, when asked for explanations, the blame for the Edenic expulsion was placed on the woman.

15

On women

Music is gendered. But it has no genitals. At least, if it were to be given a phallus it would have to be constructed as a discourse. And this would be a very messy operation in which music would find its sexual identity complicated by a host of contradictory discourses in the play of sexual politics. This is precisely what happened in the Enlightenment. Under its own critique, the age of reason found its structures of gender destabilised; the inherited distinctions of sexuality were no longer tenable under the searching light of reason. The Enlightenment needed to reconstruct sex difference. But this was an ambivalent process in which music was dragged in as a specimen and was forced to display its newly found genitalia – not that they really existed since such essential signs of sexual identity were only the constructions of a discourse and could easily be reversed. In this fluidity of sexual politics in which women were beginning to assert their rights and redraw their identity, the Enlightenment wanted to solidify the structure and to fix the identity of men and women with its tools of thought. And in this process, instrumental music had a sexuality imposed upon it, at first from the outside as a discourse which it eventually internalised as a new configuration of masculinity. It had a sex-change – but the operation was messy.

At the close of the eighteenth century, instrumental music suffered a crisis of identity: it didn't have a phallus. The discourse that spoke for this mute form was undergoing an acute sense of penis envy. It was a problem because instrumental music was perceived as female just at the point in its history when it needed male legitimisation. Some kind of sex-change was necessary to rescue music from the effeminate aesthetic of moral sensibility that had lost its moral muscles of masculine control and had fallen into the mindless sensuality of the female body. To survive, instrumental music had to become male. But it was difficult for this music to erase its female sensuality and to reconfigure its material into a new kind of moral consciousness. How could instrumental music keep its mixture of emotions and conceptual fluidity without being denounced as empty and irrational? In other words, how could it change sex without changing its tune?

The Enlightenment was not stupid; it knew that it could not simply confer sexual identity willy-nilly on music. Although some in the Enlightenment sought to give a kind of male virility to instrumental music, the problem was that they could no longer construct one – that would be a lie. It had to be scientifically proven. After all, the age of reason had seen through the old formulations of sex difference in which men were more perfect than women in the cosmic chain of being because their humours were hotter and drier.[1] Of course the Enlightenment was not going to be so deluded as to rehearse such mythical constructs of gender. Instead, it was going to make the fatal move of essentialising music in biological fact. Music has no genitals, but science can reveal them. Indeed, the very neutrality of the discourse could mould the sexuality of music as if it were a natural discovery. The biology of music was a gendered discourse, one which tried to hide its semiotic fabrications behind the ideology of nature.

This discourse was not peculiar to music alone. In fact, the gendering of music was more of a repercussion of the sexual politics in a century where the configurations of men and women were open to debate. As the century progressed the old dogmas of sexual power reasserted their control, but in the more insidious guise of Enlightenment reason; myth became fact as biology imposed its pronouncements upon humanity. The eighteenth century created such a divergence between male and female bodies that it rattled their very bones. 'A consideration and comparison of the external and internal structure of the male and female body', writes Johann Caspar Lavater, 'teaches us that the former is destined for labour and strength and the latter for beauty and reproduction.'[2] And since instrumental music resided in the body, it found itself caught up in the structures of sexual politics.

Before the Enlightenment, sex difference merely went skin deep;[3] in fact, women had the same genitals as men – they were just turned inside out.[4] But from the eighteenth century onwards, male and female genitals were to be utterly different. And the truth of this new sexual order was revealed by the impartiality of science itself. At least this was the claim that was used as the disguise for male prejudice. The task at hand was a tricky one: how could an age in which all 'men [*sic!*] are born equal' produce a logic that would exclude women from its declarations of equality? The answer: simply by returning to the innate rights of

---

[1] See Thomas Laqueur, 'Orgasm, Generation and the Politics of Reproductive Biology', in *The Making of the Modern Body*, ed. C. Gallagher and T. Laqueur (Berkeley: University of California Press, 1987), 4.

[2] Johann Caspar Lavater, *Physiognomische Fragmente, zur Beförderung der Menschenkenntnis und Menschenliebe* (Leipzig und Winterthur, 1775–8), 2:157–8.

[3] See Londa Schiebinger, 'Skeletons in the Closet: The First Illustrations of the Female Skeleton in Eighteenth-Century Anatomy', in *The Making of the Modern Body*, 48.

[4] Laqueur, 'Orgasm', 2 and 5.

humanity itself – the law of nature, as inscribed in the constitution of the body. So from about the 1750s, 'doctors in France and Germany called for a finer delineation of sex differences; discovering, describing and defining sex difference in every bone, muscle, nerve and vein of the human body became a research priority in anatomical science'.[5] In 1759, the first ever drawing of a female skeleton was published; it had an abnormally small skull for a little brain and a large pelvis for the production of children (plate 6). If women's bones were different, then surely their entire body would be different too. As the French physician Pierre Roussel claimed in 1775:

Nature has revealed through the special form given to the bones of women that the differentiation of the sexes hold not only for a few superficial differences, but is the result perhaps of as many differences as there are organs in the human body.[6]

Take for example blood: women's blood, according to Joseph Addison, 'is more refined' than that of men. And as for their fibres, they were 'more delicate'.[7] Indeed their nerves were so soft and mobile that they would twitch uncontrollably with every external vibration; they were like musical instruments that were so sensitive that they perpetually went out of tune. Music for women made them teeter precariously between moral sentiment and pure madness.[8] Because their 'constitution [*innerste Grundstoff*]' was 'more flexible, irritable and elastic'[9] than their male specimens', women were susceptible to all manner of derangement, hysteria and bouts of the 'vapours'; and this was compounded by the spasms of her uterus that, according to Diderot, 'controls her completely and excites phantoms of every kind in her imagination'.[10] Moreover, this volatile physiology influenced her psychological behaviour. Or as La Mettrie puts it, a woman's 'soul follows the progress of the body'. Her delicate disposition produces 'tenderness, affection, quick sentiments [but these are] due more to passion than reason, to prejudice and superstition'.[11] Women simply lacked the 'principles and powers of reflection', says Diderot; 'ideas of justice, virtue, vice, goodness, and wickedness all merely float on the surface of their souls'.[12] Without reflection, their souls were merely

---

[5] Schiebinger, 'Skeletons in the Closet', 42.

[6] Pierre Roussel, *Système physique et moral de la femme* (Paris, 1775), quoted in ibid., 68.

[7] Joseph Addison, *Spectator*, no. 128, quoted in Christine Battersby, *Gender and Genius: Towards a Feminist Aesthetics* (Bloomington: Indiana University Press, 1989), 84.

[8] See Foucault, *Madness and Civilization*, 126–7.

[9] Lavater, *Physiognomische Fragmente*, 3:294.

[10] Denis Diderot, 'On Women' (1772), in *Diderot's Selected Writings*, 312.

[11] Julien Offray de La Mettrie, *L'Homme Machine* (Leiden, 1748), translated as *Man As Machine* (Illinois: Open Court, 1912), 23 and 95.

[12] Diderot, 'On Women', in *Diderot's Selected Writings*, 315.

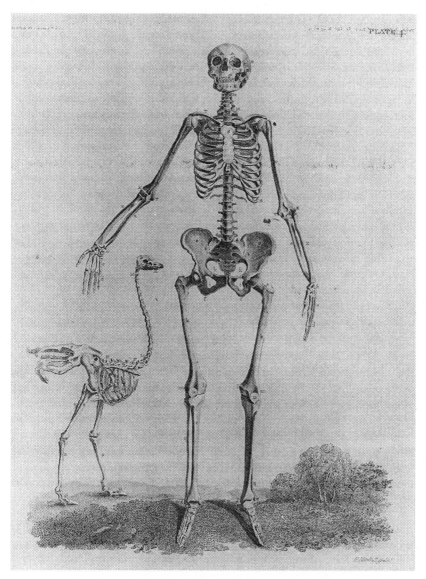

Plate 6 'The Female Skeleton from Sue' in John Barclay, *A Series of Engravings Representing the Bones of the Human Skeleton* (Edinburgh, 1820). In this illustration, the Scottish anatomist John Barclay chose to reproduce the 1759 drawing of a female skeleton by d'Arconville – the earliest of its kind – but added an ostrich in the background for comparison, just in case the large pelvis, narrow neck and small skull of the human skeleton were not clear enough.

sentient substances, designed to feel more so that their bodies would speak 'with tender looks, tears, and sighs'[13] to compensate for their lack of rational thought. They were clearly made for a sentimental music that would not tax their minds with words and concepts, but tickle their bodies with passionate vibrations. Passive and decorative, reacting to every touch and tingle, women's bodies were celebrated as intuitive and natural, sensitive and sensual, and therefore simultaneously condemned as disorderly, vacuous, violently passionate and hysterical.[14] Thus a piece by G. C. Füger, for example, intended to portray feminine tenderness ('Zärtlichkeit') could easily turn into the 'jubilant shrieks of a woman', as one critic described it.[15] 'The contrast between the violence of their impulses and the gentleness of their features renders them hideous', writes Diderot, 'it adds to their disfigurement.'[16] If female virtue were to be upheld, then women had to be domesticated and controlled by a moral society in which they functioned as dutiful mothers; they had to be confined to the newly privatised sphere of the bourgeois home where they could make music on the clavichord in between making babies.[17]

Clearly within this structure, to give music a biology is to give it a gender, since the physiology of male and female bodies functioned at opposite extremes of the sexual spectrum. The basic division of sex difference that forced instrumental music to alter its gender is founded on the Cartesian hierarchy of body and soul. It was not that women had bodies and men had souls, but that women were controlled by their sensitive bodies and men by their rational souls. Hence for La Mettrie, a woman's soul follows her body whereas the man's body was led by his soul. Similarly, intellectual ideas, as Diderot says, merely float on the surface of a woman's soul, whereas a man 'discovers in himself ideas' that arise from the depth of his being.[18] According to Kant, women simply lacked the *Geist* needed to stimulate their souls to moral activity.[19]

---

[13] Lavater, *Physiognomische Fragmente*, 3:295.

[14] See Rosalind A. Sydie, 'The Female Body in Eighteenth-Century Art', *The Anatomy of Gender*, ed. D. H. Currie and V. Raoul (Ottawa: Carleton University Press, 1992), 65–7. Also see Stafford, *Body Criticism*, 431–2.

[15] Review of G. C. Füger's *Charakteristische Clavierstücke* in *Allgemeine deutsche Bibliothek*, vol. 67 (1786), quoted in Morrow, *German Music Criticism in the Late Eighteenth Century*, 130 and 221. The review is attributed to Johann Abraham Peter Schulz.

[16] Diderot, 'On Women', in *Diderot's Selected Writings*, 309–10.

[17] See Richard Leppert, *Music and Image* (Cambridge: Cambridge University Press, 1988), 28–34 and 147–75.

[18] Sulzer, 'Genie', *Allgemeine Theorie der schönen Künste*, 2:364. As will be evident in the next chapter, Sulzer's concept of genius only applies to men.

[19] Kant, *Critique of Judgement*, 175.

So because instrumental music at the beginning of the eighteenth century was left wandering aimlessly in the body without concept or reason, it had all the characteristics of the female sex: it was a soulless body. Pure sound was dangerous. As Mattheson says, it signifies nothing 'even if it were outwardly more beautiful than Venus, than a lovely pretty body without a rational soul'.[20] Such voluptuously soulless music was something to be feared, like certain types of woman, lest its inarticulate tongue should seduce you with its 'ear tickling' sensations. Instrumental music in the archetypal form of the earthly Venus clearly functions like a female temptress whose sexual allurements could be the undoing of a good *Capellmeister*. What was needed was the rational *logos* of the masculine soul to resist the moral vacancy of the female body. Sound needed an authorial voice to bestow meaning upon it so that the body would follow the soul and music would be made in the image of man. The need to impose concepts on music was an assertion of masculinity.

Of course, this distinction would be more problematic for those, like Diderot, who denied the existence of the soul as a disembodied entity. If body and soul were made of the same substance, then sex difference could easily be destabilised in a blur of sensation. Indeed, if life were a matter of material experience, then the body would become a site for an effeminate aesthetic. To define itself against the female form, masculinity took on a material texture, a certain hardness of fibre that was the calluses of calculation and reason.[21] This kind of constitution could be developed. 'A great man, if unfortunate enough to have been endowed with [a highly sensitive nervous system]', explains Dr Bordeu in a play by Diderot, 'will strive ceaselessly to . . . overcome it, to make himself master of all his emotions . . . Then he will be able to retain possession of himself . . . his judgements will be cold, but always sane.'[22] In other words, masculinity is defined by a state of active *reflection* that hardens the nerves as opposed to the purely sentient state of passive vibration that characterises women's bodies. According to Lavater, 'man is hard and rough, woman smoother and softer'.[23] Thus the man of feeling is always 'an awkward figure' in the sentimental novels of the eighteenth century, 'with his choice of female helplessness'.[24] He is a man alien to the masculine activities of commerce and reason. Like a woman, he lives passively in a haze of sound, vibrating in sympathy in the 'great, great SENSORIUM of the world'.[25] These sentimental beings, writes Diderot, are

---

[20] Mattheson, *Der vollkommene Capellmeister*, 111.
[21] See Denis Diderot, *D'Alembert's Dream* (1769), in *Diderot's Selected Writings*, 207–10.
[22] Ibid., 209.   [23] Lavater, *Physiognomische Fragmente*, 3:297.   [24] Todd, *Sensibility*, 109.
[25] Laurence Sterne, *A Sentimental Journey through France and Italy* (1786: reprinted, London: Dent, 1960), 125.

men in whom all the fibres oscillate with so much rapidity and intensity that on experiencing the violent movements that the harmony causes in them, they sense the possibility of even more violent movements, and conceive the idea of a sort of music that could make them die of pleasure. Then they imagine their existence to be attached to a single taut fibre that too strong a vibration can break.

It was precisely their inability to master their nervous systems that made these sentimental men incapable of making rational judgements, and yet their very condition made them susceptible to 'the most beautiful instrumental passage[s]' because such music, unlike painting or poetry, is a 'simple sensation' that does not require the mediation of rationality. Instrumental music was a mindless but a titillatingly effeminate sensation. It was both delicious and dangerous.[26]

Whereas Mattheson would have censored such emasculating sounds, the sensationalists legitimised the experience by mastering them for the material pleasure of the male ego, converting the femininity of nature into the masculinity of culture. It seems that one needed a sensitive nervous system to delight in the non-conceptual thrills and tingles of instrumental music. As Mademoiselle de Lespinasse says to Bordeu in Diderot's play: 'what if those are the only conditions on which I can enjoy the sublime music . . .?' To which Bordeu replies: 'But that isn't so. I too can admire . . . My pleasure is pure; and as a consequence, my criticisms are more severe, my praise more considered.'[27] The implication is obvious. Only men can make judgements of taste, for only men were capable of reflection. 'Women [may] feel more' of the music, but men know more.[28] Their rational mastery of nature enables them to *choose* their pleasures. And this control of pleasure in sound functions as the displaced control of women in society. After all, the message of Rameau's *Pygmalion* is the consummation of the male ego with an object that it has made for its own sensual pleasure. The sculptor is male, the statue female and Rameau's harmonies that transform the stone to flesh are the instrumental sounds that give the male ego what it wants; it converts art into a Venus to be embraced. 'O *Vénus*', cries Pygmalion as he admires his own creation of woman. 'For a male', writes Christine Battersby, 'art is already *displaced* sexuality; for a female it is already *misplaced* sexuality.'[29] The overtone series not only endows the statue with life, but makes her pliant and available precisely

[26] Denis Diderot, *Lettre sur les sourds et muet à l'usage de ceux qui entendent et qui parlent* (1751), in *Œuvres complètes*, 4:206. Also see Diderot's characterisation of Rameau's hyper-active Nephew in *Le Neveu de Rameau* (c.1760).

[27] Diderot, *D'Alembert's Dream* (1769), in *Diderot's Selected Writings*, 209–10.

[28] Lavater, *Physiognomische Fragmente*, 3:295.

[29] Battersby, *Gender and Genius*, 70; Battersby is also commenting on the Pygmalion myth.

because Rameau as composer can manipulate the harmonics of nature into a living object of male desire. The law of nature that animates the female body is harnessed by the law of culture through the technique of the artist. Thus Pygmalion sings in the tonic and the statue mostly on the dominant, which, in accordance with the law of Rameau's harmonic theory, means that she will always desire him as his cadential completion. 'I will always follow your law', sings the statue to Pygmalion, and keeps her promise by not saying another word for the remaining two scenes of the opera-ballet; she simply stands there, like a woman, a mute but decorative object to be danced around. In reality she remains a statue.

The moral sentiment of such an empirical aesthetic was therefore always a very precarious one, tottering between sensibility and sensuality, mixing male desire with female domesticity. Its significations of gender were highly ambivalent. In this condition, it was quite easy for the detractors of *Empfindsamkeit* towards the end of the eighteenth century to denounce its moral basis as corrupt and its bodily manifestations as sheer female hysteria. The female body, because it was prone to violent passions and sensual excess, was supposed to be domesticated by an aesthetic that made woman in the image of the dutiful mother or virginal daughter, but the nuances of their nervous systems could easily tip them over into various forms of gynaecological malfunction. And because the music of *Empfindsamkeit* communicated its emotions with intense feeling and somatic gestures, it was potentially dangerous and might force some unsuspecting soul to vibrate out of sympathy with society. Some critics feared that entire audiences could be made female, and with a typical lack of control, keel over in an excess of moral feeling into uterine hysteria. A decadent sensibility, suggests Schiller, is a return to the wild, lustful animal that the female body really is once outside its domestic cage; its voluptuous vacuity could emasculate the freedom of the intellect and reverse culture into the raw passions of nature. The modern instrumental music of mixed emotions was woman personified as beast:

The music of the moderns seems remarkably aimed only toward sensuality and thus flatters the dominating taste which wants only to be agreeably tickled, not affected, not powerfully stirred, nor exalted. All sweet melodiousness is therefore preferred, and if there is an even greater noise in the concert hall, suddenly everyone becomes all ears when a sentimental passage is played. An almost animal expression of sensuality then usually appears on all the faces, the intoxicated eyes swim, the open mouth is lustful, a voluptuous trembling seizes the whole body, the breath is rapid and short; soon all the symptoms of intoxication appear as a clear indication that the senses are running riot but that the spirit or principle of freedom has fallen prey to the force of sensual impressions. All these feelings, I say, are excluded from art through a noble and manly taste because they please only the feelings, with which art has nothing to do.[30]

Thus for Schiller, real art, like real men, no longer wallows in the feelings of the body but issues from the activity of the male soul – the 'spirit' – by which he means the Kantian principle of moral freedom that can control the impulses of the flesh. This sentimental music that seizes the body, far from confirming the innate virtues of humanity, is the female embodiment of immorality. It is simply unmanly.

But this is not the only side effect of instrumental music. An overdose of *Empfindung* can also have an opposite yet equally debilitating influence. According to Johann Sulzer, it can make a man's body sink into inactivity. The insipid motions of sentimental music, he implies, simply fail to galvanise the muscles of the soul, and so make a man 'soft, weak and unmanly'.[31] If feeling is to be more than the seduction of 'frivolous whores [*Dirnen*]' jangling one's moral fibres, then reason needs to control the 'stimulation of sentiment'[32] to reinforce one's moral actions. Too much emotional stimulation will only turn 'every desire . . . into delirium, . . . and make man a miserable, impotent thing, for whom desire, tenderness, and anguish become so overwhelming that no effective energy is retained, and all resolute and manly courage is lost'.[33] And since instrumental music for Sulzer 'sets our nerves in motion'[34] it is the most sentimental art form, which when left conceptually blank is in danger of becoming a 'noise of arbitrarily connected tones . . . [with] fanciful and abrupt changes in character from joy to despair, and from the pathetic to the trivial'.[35] In fact, it sounds remarkably like the incomprehensible reactions of a woman's flabby nervous system.

Despite the contrast of nervous states, Sulzer and Schiller are in fact saying the same thing: both languid immobility and nervous delirium are simply the extreme states of the female body, connected together as cause and effect; for idleness slackens the fibres, and slack fibres fall prey to everything that the world presses upon them, and so this results in nervous disorders. 'This is the torment of all effeminate souls whom inaction has plunged into dangerous sensuality', says Louis-Sébastien Mercer.[36]

Thus in its most sentimental form, instrumental music was seen as an embodiment of women by those who heard *Empfindsamkeit* as a mutilation of the male ego. Forkel's emphasis on the reflective state of the soul,

---

[30] Johann Christoph Friedrich von Schiller, *Ueber das Pathetische* (1793), quoted in Rey Longyear, *Schiller and Music* (Chapel Hill: University of North Carolina Press, 1966), 110–11.   [31] Sulzer, 'Empfindung', *Allgemeine Theorie der schönen Künste*, 2:56.
[32] Ibid., 2:54.   [33] Ibid., 2:56.   [34] Ibid., 'Instrumentalmusik', 3:677.
[35] Ibid., 'Sonate', 3:425.
[36] Louis-Sébastien Mercer, *Tableau de Paris* (Amsterdam, 1783), 3:199, quoted in Foucault, *Madness and Civilization*, 157.

with its ability to define and categorise every shade of sound, was an attempt to rescue instrumental music from the emasculating discourse of its detractors. He had hoped that the sheer variety of sound in instrumental music would stimulate the mind into cognitive activity, but the very diversity he championed as male fell prey to the strategies that denounced such an emotional mixture as the uncontrollable reflexes of a female body that was simultaneously sensitive and hysterical, slack and over-active. There seemed to be no escape from this biological discourse that had sprinkled over the entire spectrum of affects every form of female vice: women, along with instrumental music, were soft, sensual, passive, weak, trivial, mad, dangerous, promiscuous, bestial and monstrous. This was a serious problem for those who wanted to justify *Empfindsamkeit* and the Italian instrumental music that was becoming increasingly popular,[37] particularly since the Italians were often regarded by the Northern Europeans as an effeminate race.[38] Men had talked themselves into a corner, and another discourse had to be found if the so-called 'modern music' that was colonising Germany was to be legitimised. Italian music needed some teutonic muscle.

[37] The term *Empfindsamkeit* was not merely used to describe the type of music associated with C. P. E. Bach, but included the Italian style. See Georgia Cowart, 'Sense and Sensibility in Eighteenth-Century Musical Thought', *Acta Musicologica*, vol. 45 (1984), 265.

[38] See Gottsched, *Versuch einer critischen Dichtkunst*, 759, and *Auszug aus des Herrn Batteux schönen Künsten*, 201.

16

On masculinity

What does a man do to maintain his integrity when his nervous system vibrates with a music that can throw him into inactive or hyper-active states of female vice? Musical morality towards the end of the eighteenth century had to be relocated from the female body to the male body. The North Germans demanded a more 'manly taste', as Schiller puts it; Johann Hiller advocated the three-movement symphonic structure without minuets because its balance was somehow more masculine; Sulzer wanted the sublime style to invigorate the body with its overpowering masculinity.[1] But what does a music of the male body sound like? Unlike its female counterpart, the male form was supposed to have a certain 'moral density',[2] a solid internal organisation that could resist the wiles of female madness; through the mental and physical activities that men performed in Enlightenment society, their fibres were made taut and tough. If music were to have any moral purpose within the male body, it had to firm up the muscles, tighten the fibres and tune the intellect, so that the body could be mobilised for action and not merely sink into female reaction.[3]

In a sense, the aesthetic discourse had always anticipated the feminisation inherent in a somatic rather than a cerebral science. From its very germination in the teutonic soil of Baumgarten's writings, the aesthetic was rooted in the athletic activity of the body, an internal movement that could stimulate the mind to purposeful, rational action. Baumgarten, in his *Aesthetica*, far from promoting a passive sensory

---

[1] See von Schiller, *Ueber das Pathetische* (1793), quoted in Longyear, *Schiller and Music*, 110–11; Hiller, *Wöchentliche Nachrichten und Anmerkungen die Musik betreffend*, 1:243; Sulzer, 'Grösse', *Allgemeine Theorie der schönen Künste*, 2:447. See also Matthew Head, '"Like Beauty Spots on the Face of Man": Gender in 18th-Century North-German Discourse on Genre', *The Journal of Musicology*, vol. 8 no. 2 (Spring, 1995).

[2] See Foucault, *Madness and Civilization*, 149–50.

[3] In its ultimate form, the male body as instrumental music was shaped by the unrelenting force of the Schopenhauerian Will, a physical movement so masculine in its activity that even reason is seen as 'feminine [since] it only receives, does not generate'. Instrumental music, as the direct 'image of the Will itself', was the direct image of the male itself. See Arthur Schopenhauer, *On the Fourfold Root of the Principle of Sufficient Reason*, trans. E. F. J. Payne (Illinois, 1974), 171, and *The World as Will and Representation*, trans. E. F. J. Payne (New York: Dover, 1969), 1:257.

experience, transformed the productive, self-sufficient monad of Leibnizian philosophy into an aesthetic force that goads reason into action. Only in this way can a philosopher be a 'man among men', says Baumgarten; 'If the whole mind is to be improved, aesthetics must come to the aid of logic.'[4] Thus moral action is born of desire, and the diverse activity that stimulates the 'lower cognitive powers' is the flexing of a spontaneous, sensual logic that functions as a kind of aesthetic body-*bildung*. And it is precisely this moral masculinity that Sulzer wants to induce into music to counterbalance the weakening of the constitution by the effeminate vibrations of too much *Empfindung*. To this end, he turned to the symphony, contrasting its energetic utterance with the meaningless noises of the sonata – particularly those imported from Italy. For Sulzer, the sonata was the epitome of mindless sensation, but the symphony was the moral expression of the sublime.[5] And the sublime for Sulzer was male; it was an athletic, muscular exercise of constant activity – a physical sensation that translates into spiritual energy.

Works of art which . . . gently flatter the fantasy and the heart without even shaking them up, without inciting them to use the active powers, are like candies, which give no nourishment and the enjoyment of which gradually extinguishes all liveliness and strength of the soul. Only the grand sustains and strengthens all the powers of the soul; it does for the spirit what strong masculine physical exercises do for the body, whereby it becomes healthier and stronger. The powers of the soul must be maintained by constant exercise, just as bodily powers; the most intelligent mind can sink into lassitude if for a long time it sees nothing around which incites its activity.[6]

Activity, transition, modulation and constant contrast became the musical physique of male virility; the first movements of symphonic forms were erected as the new monuments of a phallocentric order.[7] After all, what distinguishes the sonata form Allegro from its Adagio counterpart is the gymnastics of its development section. In the languid sentimentality of slow movements any development is merely a matter of variation; its form is about decoration and ornamentation which, as Richard Leppert points out, was the aesthetic function of women in

---

[4] A German version of Baumgarten's aesthetics in the hand-written form of a student's lecture notes was published by Bernard Poppe as an appendix to his *Alexander Gottlieb Baumgarten: Seine Bedeutung und Stellung in der Leibniz-Wolffischen Philosophie und seine Beziehungen zu Kant* (Leipzig: Robert Noske, 1907); the quotations are from Poppe's appendix, 73 and 66; the translation is taken from Hosler, *Changing Aesthetic Views of Instrumental Music in 18th-Century Germany*, 89–90.

[5] See Johann Georg Sulzer, 'Sonate', and 'Symphonie', *Allgemeine Theorie der schönen Künste*, 4:424–6 and 478–80.

[6] Sulzer, 'Grösse', *Allgemeine Theorie der schönen Künste*, 2:447; the translation is taken from Hosler, *Changing Aesthetic Views of Instrumental Music*, 150.

[7] See Sulzer, 'Symphonie', *Allgemeine Theorie der schönen Künste*, 4:478–80.

eighteenth-century society.[8] 'A musician', says Friedrich Wilhelm Marpurg, 'who applies a trill to every note appears to me like a conceited beauty who curtseys at every word.'[9] In contrast to the docile Adagio that was the cliché of *Empfindsamkeit*, the Allegro was the embodiment of masculine drive, generating an internal fire that melded the variety of instrumental sound into the unity of male self-sufficiency. The Allegro, for Sulzer, 'shakes the soul of the listener' through its 'brilliant and fiery style' that is full of 'sudden modulations' and 'strong gradations' to create a 'self-sufficient whole'. The Allegro, like a Pindaric ode, he claims, stems from the autonomy of a 'sublime imagination.'[10] And in the aesthetic categories of the eighteenth century, only men were sublime. When Edmund Burke contrasted the sublime and the beautiful, he deliberately used a language of sexual power; the terror of the sublime crushes the beautiful into submissive admiration; the beautiful charms the sublime through her cowering obedience.[11] 'We submit to what we admire', writes Burke, 'but we love what submits to us; in one case we are forced, in the other, flattered into compliance.'[12] Hence, according to Kant, women have a more 'beautiful understanding' which accounts for their emotive moral response, whereas men have a 'deep understanding' which connects them to the sublime and higher law of moral duty. Sublime music was not only masculine, it was morally superior.[13]

In this kind of logic, there can only be men of genius because only geniuses were sublime. Women were simply excluded – naturally. So when Sulzer speaks of the sublime as masculine, he is grounding this in the eighteenth-century concept of genius. For him, the self-sufficient symphony, with its 'fiery' and 'astonishing' Allegros, is fuelled by the same *Feuer* that drives the genius to the heights of sublime creativity. He writes: 'the man of genius feels an inspiring fire that effectively arouses all his faculties; he discovers ideas within himself, fantastic images and emotions that inspire awe in others . . . [but] they do not astonish him for . . . he has perceived them himself rather than invented them'.[14] Genius is not a body bristling with every surface sensation of the world, but a power that burns internally. And the fire that Sulzer speaks of relates to the hot substances in an older tradition of the male body, trans-

---

[8] Leppert, *Music and Image*, 28–34.

[9] Friedrich Wilhelm Marpurg, *Anleitung zum Klavierspielen* (Berlin, 1755–61), in Fubini, *Music and Culture in Eighteenth-Century Europe*, 291.

[10] Sulzer, 'Symphonie', *Allgemeine Theorie der schönen Künste*, 4:479.

[11] See Battersby, *Gender and Genius*, 74–7, and Eagleton, *The Ideology of the Aesthetic*, 52–60.

[12] Edmund Burke, *A Philosophical Enquiry into the Origin of our Ideas of the Sublime and the Beautiful* (1757; reprinted London, 1906), 161.

[13] Immanuel Kant, *Observations on the Feeling of the Beautiful and Sublime*, trans. J. T. Goldthwait (Berkeley: University of California Press, 1960), 78.

[14] Sulzer, 'Genie', *Allgemeine Theorie der schönen Künste*, 2:364.

formed by eighteenth-century medicine into the over-heated physiology of a genius. Simon-André Tissot claims that the sublime, which he calls the 'masculine style', produces a 'terrible heat [that affects] the inner most part of the brain' as blood is driven to the head by the 'force of the thinking soul'.[15] Indeed, Sulzer notes that music 'through the nerves . . . can stimulate a deranged and feverish stirring of blood'.[16] What the sublime genius requires is therefore a hypersensitive nervous system, which is never allowed to 'sink into . . . drowsy inactivity' but can simultaneously withstand a sustained level of 'emotional intensity' that wells up from within him – a kind of excitement akin to the 'animal instinct'.[17] An inspired soul is filled with such 'emotional enthusiasm or supercharged sensitivity' that the 'spirit loses sight of the object and moves into the obscurity of passion', says Sulzer; the soul 'sees nothing but itself'; the outside world of sensation is shut out to isolate the self-productivity of the male ego, whose imagination is so overpowering in its stimulation of desire that neither 'accurate reflection' nor 'correct judgement' is possible.[18] The male soul and instrumental music under the spell of the sublime begin to conform to the same image.

The wild, instinctual animal, defined as 'genius' in the taxonomy of the eighteenth century, turns out to be nothing other than the hysterical female body made autonomous through its internal fire. The same bodily symptoms arise from diametrically opposed forces: female madness is externally induced, male genius is generated from deep within the soul. What had been derided in instrumental music as the sheer delirium of female emotions is now elevated to the heights of the male genius who has subsumed feminine hysteria into the vigour of his own masculinity. In order to come to terms with instrumental music, the female body was hijacked by the male ego. The industrialisation of Europe may have brought a nostalgia for the primitive wildness of nature associated with women, but in the revaluation of music at the end of the century, the male rearranged gender distinctions to measure his own savagery against a female body whose virtues were increasingly prized as domestic. Consequently, her body could only ape the wildness of the male genius, whereas 'males began to covet the stock descriptions of femininity'. Sulzer's genius that shapes the Allegro with the muscular activity of his soul is biologically a man but psychologically a woman, a being, in other words, with a resilient physique that can withstand the intense emotions that continually push him to the brink of madness. By the close of the eighteenth century, the great artist

---

[15] Simon-André Tissot, 'On the Diseases of Literary and Sedentary Persons' (1766), trans. in *Three Essays* (Dublin, 1772), 14–13; see Battersby, *Gender and Genius*, 86 and 36.

[16] Sulzer, 'Musik,' *Allgemeine Theorie der schönen Künste*, 3:433.   [17] Ibid., 'Genie', 2:364–5.

[18] Ibid., 'Begeisterung', 1:350; the translation has been modified, from Le Huray and Day, *Music Aesthetics in the Eighteenth and Early-Nineteenth Centuries*, 131.

was the feminine male, 'full of virile energy – who transcended his biology: if the male genius was feminine', writes Christine Battersby, 'this merely proved his cultural superiority. Creativity was displaced male procreation: male sexuality made sublime.'[19]

Such androgyny complicates gender distinctions within the musical discourse, particularly in an age in which sexual difference was a common pattern of taxonomy, from Linnaeus' classification of plants to Kant's division of the 'strenuous' and 'languid' affections in his *Critique of Judgement*.[20] This system of difference always presented a structure of complementary opposites, an inequality that is *naturally* explained in the anatomy of things, in which the female element always signifies a lack – a lack of rationality, a lack of activity, a lack of self-control – and is therefore subordinate to the completed male. So it is not surprising that within this structure, music could be explained in these terms, whether it is in the difference between a strenuous Allegro and a languid Adagio, or in the distinction between major and minor triads. For Georg Andrea Sorge, the minor triad, because it is 'not as complete' as the major triad, 'can be likened . . . to the female sex', whose lovely and pleasant tones, although lacking perfection, are still a necessary complement for the progression of male harmony.[21] For Rameau, the fundamental bass is the masculine power that generates the female voice of the upper partials.[22] Likewise, the same complementary order of perfection is used by A. B. Marx to sexualise the contrast in sonata form; the second theme (*Seitensatz*), he writes, 'serves as a contrast to the first, energetic statement, though dependent and determined by it. It is of a more tender nature, flexible rather than emphatically constructed – in a way, the feminine as opposed to the preceding masculine.'[23]

There is nothing *essentially* male or female in these constructions of musical gender, as if one could unzip a major triad to reveal some kind of dangling genitalia. Similarly, sonata form does not display a structural disparity, as if music analysis could uncover the sexuality of themes. The disparity is not structural but semantic; the horizontal contrast of equal and opposite elements is perverted by a discourse that sets the contrast vertically as superior and inferior. Sex difference was simply a taxonomical structure that could be applied to any thing that required

[19] Battersby, *Gender and Genius*, 73 and 3.
[20] See Londa Schiebinger, 'The Private Life of Plants: Sexual Politics in Carl Linnaeus and Erasmus Darwin', *Science and Sensibility*, ed. M. Benjamin (Oxford: Blackwell, 1991), and Kant, *Critique of Judgement*, 125–7.
[21] Georg Andrea Sorge, *Vorgemach der musicalischen Composition* (1745–7), quoted in McClary, *Feminine Endings*, 11.
[22] See David Lewin, 'Women's Voices and the Fundamental Bass', *The Journal of Musicology*, vol. 10 no. 4 (Fall, 1992).
[23] Marx, *Die Lehre von der musikalischen Komposition, praktisch-theoretisch*, 3:273, quoted in McClary, *Feminine Endings*, 13.

a hierarchical inequality naturalised by biological fact. These are sexual discourses that are entirely male constructions and can therefore be wielded at will to categorise music at whim: on the one hand, it can be used to denounce instrumental music as the embodiment of female irrationality, and on the other, it can exalt the same diversity of material as male sublimity. In this sense, there is no female music, since all the geniuses were men whose androgynous psyche could subsume the distinction of gender within themselves and produce a music that could assume either sex. If there is any sense of rape in sonata form, it is purely within the autonomy of the male body. Man is both major and minor, Allegro and Adagio, first and second theme. Women simply remained minor, and therefore lacked the ability to complete let alone compose music.[24]

In this politics of gender, it becomes very difficult to disentangle the sexuality of a piece of music. Take for example the opening of C. P. E. Bach's Symphony in G major (Wq. 182, No. 1); in its abrupt changes of texture that veer off into strange harmonic regions it is obviously a work burning with the 'feuer' of genius, a sublime source that manifests itself, according to Sulzer, in 'fast driving passages, in unusual audacious chords, in sudden modulations, in bold figurations and in large intervals'.[25] This symphony, which brims over with all these elements, is obviously male. But what protects this sublime 'disorder in melody and harmony'[26] from being the dysfunctional body of a woman? What saves its contrasts from falling into female delirium? The discourse that proclaims C. P. E. Bach a genius, and so turns his capricious and whimsical femininity into a profoundly male utterance. He is both 'superior' and 'peculiar', as the *Allgemeine musikalische Zeitung* once described this set of symphonies – male and female.[27]

Indeed, in order to elevate Bach as the genius of German instrumental music, the reviews of his works from *c.* 1770 tried to toughen up his *Empfindsamkeit* image with a bit of discursive testosterone – even if some of Bach's pieces were written specifically for ladies: 'For ladies?' questions the critic of the *Frankfurter gelehrte Anzeigen*, 'That's what the title says. But I believe that even men would bring honour upon themselves with these pieces.'[28] Similarly, Carl Friedrich Cramer, to maintain this

---

[24] See Jean Paul Richter, *Vorlesungen über Aesthetik* (1804), translated in Kathleen M. Wheeler, *German Aesthetic and Literary Criticism: The Romantic Ironists and Goethe* (Cambridge: Cambridge University Press, 1984), 164–9, where he compares the impotence of the 'passive genius' (effeminate men) with the productive genius who is able to reflect (unlike women).

[25] Sulzer, 'Feuer', *Allgemeine Theorie der schönen Künste*, 2:228.

[26] Ibid., 'Symphonie', 479. [27] *Allgemeine musikalische Zeitung*, vol. 16 (1814).

[28] Review of C. P. E. Bach's *Sex* [sic!] *Sonate per il Clavicembalo Solo all Uso delle Donne* [Wq. 54], *Frankfurter gelehrte Anzeigen*, 3/61–2 (2 August 1774); quoted in Morrow, *German Music Criticism in the Late Eighteenth Century*, 27; translation slightly modified.

same sense of male honour, denigrated the soft and slippery keyboard technique of women in contrast with 'the most masculine . . . [and] the only real style of playing – the Bach style'. Moreover, Cramer insisted on hearing 'a tone of masculinity' in a piece by Bach that was favourably described by a rival critic in the *Hamburgischer Correspondent* as 'soft' and 'charming'; but obviously for Cramer this was tantamount to the emasculation of genius. Bach's Rondo in E major, with its soft chromaticism and syncopated pulsations, had to be male for Cramer, partly because he regarded E major as a harsh key that matched the roughness of men, but mostly, one suspects, because Bach, as the musical genius, subsumes the feminine body in his sublime masculinity.[29]

Or, as another example, take the slow movement of the Mozart Piano Sonata in A minor, K. 310; this piece conjures up the palpability of the female body; it is so finely nuanced that even the appoggiaturas and the ornamental inflections that weave their way around the melodic structure seem to be the sensitive fluctuations of the nervous system itself (see example 20).

But one peculiarity of the slow movements in Mozart's piano sonatas is that they have extended development sections that often signify some kind of inner turmoil, as though the nervous perturbations of the female body had fallen into the darkness of her own uterine madness. In the development of this sonata, for example, the trills in the bass sound like the ominous boiling of blood in the womb, sending fumes in the form of triplets as the 'vapours' that cloud the dissonant mind of the female (bs 37–53). But are these the gynaecological meanderings of the female body or the deep ruminations of the male genius? Both: for it was quite possible in eighteenth-century medicine for geniuses to have gynaecological problems within their male bodies, even to the point of simulating menstruation and pregnancy.[30] This piece may signify female sensibility, but that does not exclude the male from appropriating its morality in the higher form of its own physique.

Thus instrumental music, with its shifting signatures of gender, does not present the essential sex difference of Enlightenment society, but reveals the particular configurations of masculinity at the close of the eighteenth century. Such music encodes the tactics of the male species in its attempt to represent its politics of gender distinctions, both as a system of domination and as a secret experience of sensibilities denied men by the biological and social discourses that categorise their function in society. Women, of course, participated in this culture, but they

---

[29] Carl Friedrich Cramer, reviews of Ernst Wilhelm Wolf's *Sechs Sonatinen für das Clavier*, and C. P. E. Bach's *Clavier Sonaten und freye Phantasien, nebst einigen Rondos für Fortepiano* [Wq. 58], both in *Magazin der Musik*, 1/2 (7 December 1783), 1238–59; quoted in ibid., 62 and 127.   [30] See Battersby, *Gender and Genius*, 87.

Ex. 20 Wolfgang Amadeus Mozart, Piano Sonata in A minor, K. 310, second movement – bs 1–10.

were only allowed to eavesdrop;[31] at best, they emulated these sounds in the privacy of their domestic enclosures. Women were consumers not creators, imitators not geniuses. In fact, they were analogous to the kind of music that moved in compliance with the voice of their male authors.

The formation of musical gender is therefore a complex play of male semiotic strategies both in the structures of music and the discourses that interpret them. But the very plurality of meaning in this play of signs renders the interpretative act unstable. It was impossible to fix *forever* a music that was unquestionably male or female. In fact, it is never possible because discourses can always reinterpret and reverse sexual meaning. It is a play of power not of notes; music is an object caught up in the shifting politics of gender, not a permanent phallus or clitoris. But this does not absolve music as something neutral, rather music becomes an object of contention that is constantly riddled with inconsistencies and moulded by the history of gender. It can speak, it

---

[31] See Timothy J. Reiss, 'Revolution in Bounds: Wollstonecraft, Women, and Reason', *Gender and Theory: Dialogues on Feminist Criticism*, ed. L Kauffman (Oxford: Blackwell, 1989), 12–16.

may resist, but it can also be the mouthpiece of an ideology and may even internalise a strategy as its own discourse. The gender strategist is always finding new ways to justify, denounce and manipulate music's meaning, sticking on the appropriate genitalia to affirm his own identity – and that identity is never fixed.[32]

By the end of the eighteenth century, the old strategies were not working. The sexual physiognomy of music was not masculine enough. The sex-change had not been a clean operation. The semiotic features may have been acceptable within the structures of sentimentality that relied upon the surface of signs, but in the aftermath of *Empfindsamkeit*, the polysemic possibilities of such strategies proved inadequate for a truly masculine aesthetic of instrumental music. There had to be an alternative way of signifying masculinity that was not simply a tactical negation of sentimentality. In order to elevate instrumental music as sublime, the Romantics had to create a radical shift in the aesthetic discourse that dispensed with the play of bodily semiotics. They redefined instrumental music not merely as male, but as an utterly different configuration of masculinity, one that would secure the superiority of instrumental forms as absolute. And, of course, all absolute statements are uttered out of a desire to reassert power. The supremacy of instrumental music was born out of a male crisis.

[32] In the nineteenth century, for example, Wagner called instrumental music 'woman' in order to complete her as music drama, whereas Hanslick, in contrast, turned instrumental music into an objective male structure purged of female emotionalism. See Richard Wagner, *Opera and Drama* (1852), trans. Edwin Evans (London: Wm Reeves, n.d.), 186, and Eduard Hanslick, *The Beautiful in Music* (1854), trans. G. Cohen (New York: The Liberal Arts Press, 1957), 72–3.

17

On independence

> Beethoven . . . plainly said: 'Music must strike fire from the spirit of a man; emotionalism is only meant for women.' Few remember what he said; the majority aim at emotional effects. They ought to be punished by being dressed in women's clothes.
>
> (Schumann)[1]

Towards the turn of the eighteenth century, the all-embracing male ego was discontented. It was not enough simply to absorb femininity within its body, it wanted to slip out of the body like a mirror to conceptualise the senses in a radical act of self-consciousness. Revolution was in the air and history had to be made. The body could not just lie passively in the movement of time, vibrating with its delusions of natural innocence;[2] it needed the action of a *Geist* that would capture the spirit of the age and master nature as its own history. A new construction of masculinity was inspired by the French Revolution, in which man disconnected himself from nature by objectifying his body as a solid, imperturbable structure.[3] And this new body needed a new aesthetic. To this end, the notion of 'disinterested contemplation' was revived by philosophers such as Kant,[4] to enable the subject to sever all sympathetic identification with the object in an act of formal alienation. In this aesthetic, nature was deemed beautiful in its play of form precisely because it was distanced from the subject as a work of art;[5] instead of art imitating nature, nature was redeemed by culture. The world had become a museum for the decontextualisation of objects. In the same way, the male soul was able to disconnect itself from its own flesh in a

[1] Robert Schumann, *On Music and Musicians*, trans. R. Rosenfeld (New York: Pantheon, 1946), 71. Schumann is quoting from a letter allegedly written by Beethoven (August 1812) to Bettina von Arnim.

[2] On the dilemma of moral action and instrumental music, see, for example, Wilhelm Heinrich Wackenroder, 'The Strange Musical Life of the Musical Artist Joseph Berglinger', *Confessions and Fantasies*, 146–60.

[3] See Outram, *The Body and the French Revolution*.

[4] Kant, *Critique of Judgement*, 50–60. On 'disinterested contemplation', particularly in the work of Shaftesbury and Kant, see Cassirer, *The Philosophy of the Enlightenment*, 312–28.

[5] See Helga Geyer-Ryan, 'Enlightenment, Sexual Difference and the Autonomy of Art', *Fables of Desire* (Cambridge: Polity Press, 1994), 184–6.

self-reflexive gesture that moulded its body as form. The fusion of body and soul on which the empirical aesthetic of *Empfindsamkeit* depended was split by a Kantian aesthetic in a replay of the body–soul duality of Cartesian sex difference. The rational soul, transformed as the Kantian subject, became the precondition for the imperatives of a male morality. Feminine sentiment was useful but hardly essential. Masculinity reasserted its difference as disembodied soul.

But this was precisely the problem. Where was the soul? The medical science of the eighteenth century had dispossessed the body of its spirit, leaving the materialists to wallow in the empirical pool of sensation. By the close of the century, the concept of *Lebenskraft* was no longer a definable substance but an abstract inference in the form of Blumenbach's *Bildungstrieb*.[6] Under the gaze of science, the fundamental core of male identity was disappearing. Even in German philosophy, the condition of the soul became increasingly inaccessible and abstract; its existence was cut off from knowledge by Kant as the precondition of knowledge. It simply could not be known. And yet, in this noumenal form, the soul as the subject relaunched its attack, projecting its invisible power over the world of visible objects.

It was at this point in the history of the soul that instrumental music became the quintessence of art, for it was elected to resolve the crisis of the male soul. Music in its non-representational manifestation made audible the invisible spaces of male identity. Its absolute position as *Geist* was an assertion of male dominance. But it would be a mistake to think that this masculine power could be made visible in the music, since its noumenal presence was precisely that which could not be known let alone seen. The signs that floated on the semiotic surface continued to delineate male and female gestures – after all, there is no masculinity without difference. But hidden deep within the musical structure was a new element that controlled the semiotic surface – a transcendental signifier that ousted instrumental sound from the female body, a phallus that contained the seminal fluid of the work, an invisible sign that removed itself from the semiotic play as the origin of male existence. Instrumental music was declared autonomous. It had soul.

This was not a mechanical autonomy, but an organic one: machines are made, organisms generate themselves. It is this auto-genesis of material that saves the symphony and the genius with all their overheated activity from slipping into the dementia of the female body. The energy, however diverse, emanates from the unity of the rational soul. Thus the demarcation of sex difference is no longer found in the biological co-ordinates of the body, but in the origin of its being. This is why, for Sulzer, men of genius and the symphonic structures they create are

---

[6] See Steigerwald, 'Experiment, Lebenskraft and Reflection', *Lebenskraft in Reflection*.

inspired by an internal fire that consumes all outward representations of nature. The genius never appropriates his ideas from the external world but 'discovers [them] from within himself, . . . he has perceived them rather than invented them'.[7] The sublime imagination is the male womb whose hysterical spasms are the maternal juices of art; the pregnant idea is stimulated by the nervous fluids that were thought to animate the mind of the genius. This fluid, according to Tissot, is like the male sperm since it arouses the genius to the point of masturbation and deprives his semen of virility in the very act of thinking.[8] There was a kind of self-copulation in the genius, an internal power that was purely male and divided him from nature. The genius is self-evident truth. He 'carries his centre within himself'.[9] In Kantian terms, he 'prescribes the law to himself'.[10] Conversely, women were merely objects of nature, open to the elements, without a rational centre that would give them an internal identity. As Kant says:

of a woman, we may well say, she is pretty, affable and refined, but soulless. Now what do we mean by 'soul'? 'Soul' [Geist] in an aesthetical sense, signifies the animating principle in the mind. But that whereby this principle animates the psychic substance [Seele] – the material which it employs for that purpose – is that which sets the mental powers into a swing that is final, i.e. into a play which is self-maintaining and which strengthens those powers for such activity.[11]

Kant's aesthetic definition of *Geist* as 'self-maintaining' was objectified as symphonic sound by the early Romantics. Instrumental music 'is independent and free', writes Ludwig Tieck, paraphrasing Kant, 'it prescribes its own laws to itself'.[12] The symphony became a self-generating object, analogous to the male being, with an ontology that was grounded purely in itself. 'The modern artist', says Friedrich Schlegel, must 'work out from the inside' to produce 'a new creation from nothing'.[13] The self-creating structure of instrumental music is

---

[7] Sulzer, 'Genie', *Allgemeine Theorie der schönen Künste*, 2:364. Also see Johann Nikolaus Forkel, *Ueber die Theorie der Musik* (1777), translated in Le Huray and Day, *Music Aesthetics in the Eighteenth and Early-Nineteenth Centuries*, 176–8, for a similar view of genius.

[8] Simon-André Tissot, 'On the Diseases of Literary and Sedentary Persons' and 'An Essay on Onanism, or A Treatise upon the Disorders Produced by Masturbation' (1766), trans. in *Three Essays* (Dublin, 1772); see Battersby, *Gender and Genius*, 86.

[9] Friedrich Schlegel, *Ideas*, no. 45, in *Philosophical Fragments*, trans. P. Firchow (Minneapolis: University of Minneapolis Press, 1991), 98.

[10] Kant, *Critique of Judgement*, 168.   [11] Ibid., 175.

[12] Wackenroder and Tieck, 'Symphonien', *Phantasien über die Kunst für Freunde der Kunst* (Hamburg, 1799), in *Werke und Briefe von Wilhelm Heinrich Wackenroder*, 254.

[13] Friedrich Schlegel, *Gespräche über die Poesie* (1799–1800), in *Kritische Schriften und Fragmente*, ed. E. Behler and H. Eichner (Munich, 1988), 2:201. *Gespräche über die Poesie* has been translated by E. Behler and R. Struc as *Dialogue on Poetry and Literary Aphorisms* (University Park: The Pennsylvania State University Press, 1968).

therefore the delusion of the male ego kicking against nature, believing that deep within its being is an organic force that could recreate a fallen world into his perfect image. This involved a rejection of nature as mere matter. There was no choice for instrumental music but to evacuate the body, because the body as matter was sick with the diseases of sentimental affection.[14] It was given a pure form so that it could sever itself from the 'material filth' of the body[15] and be analysed as structure.[16] It was declared spiritual so that it could slip out of the body as *Geist* and be worshipped as eternal. By the nineteenth century, the Romantics had shifted instrumental music from the somatic text to the immutable work, from sensibility to structure, from nature to art and from body to score.

The legitimisation of instrumental music was therefore more than just a relocation of its sounds from the female body to the male body, for ultimately, the body, however athletic, still signified a lack that is female. Music remained a 'gynotext' as long as it failed to delineate the autonomy of the male soul. Although Kant left music in the body, he actually hoisted the aesthetic out of the empirical world and relocated it in the transcendental realm; the sublime, in particular, was no longer a somatic feeling of awe but a transcendental revelation of moral will.[17] The early Romantics merely carried further the logic of Kant's aesthetics to include instrumental music. For them, such music was a mysterious out-of-body experience; or as Wilhelm Heinrich Wackenroder puts it, music has to demonstrate 'the movement of our soul, disembodied.'[18] This was a formidable task: the Cartesian division of vocal and instrumental music in which men spoke from their rational souls and women reacted in their sensitive bodies had to be reversed. Instrumental music, like women, lacked vocal self-presence, lacked rational concept and lacked visibility, but the Romantics made that very lack into the plenitude of male existence, as will be explained in the following chapters: the lack of self-presence became the zero-origin of music's autonomous generation; the lack of rational concept became the logic of a language beyond language; and its lack of visibility became the ineffable representation of the noumenal self. The Romantics redefined the 'sentimental' in 'modern music . . . not as a sensual but a spiritual feeling'.[19] They moved music from body to soul.

---

[14] See Dahlhaus, *The Idea of Absolute Music*, 72.

[15] August Wilhelm Schlegel, *Vorlesungen über schöne Litteratur und Kunst* (Heilbronn, 1884), 256–7, and *Die Kunstlehre*, ed. E. Lohner (Stuttgart, 1963), 215.

[16] On structure, see Dahlhaus, *The Idea of Absolute Music*, 7.

[17] See Henrich, *Aesthetic Judgement and the Moral Image of the World*, 29–56, and Paul Crowther, *The Kantian Sublime: From Morality to Art* (Oxford: Clarendon Press, 1989).

[18] Wackenroder and Tieck, *Phantasien über die Kunst* in *Werke und Briefe*, 207.

[19] Schlegel, *Dialogue on Poetry and Literary Aphorisms*, 99.

And so it was that instrumental music changed sex without really changing its tune. The music could remain the same, it just required an aesthetic shift in one's contemplation to give it an autonomy that was purely male. But the discourse was internalised; instrumental music was not only given an autonomy, it asserted it, making a decisive move that would wipe out its embarrassing association with the female body in order to declare itself absolutely male. Technically speaking, this only needs to be done once, since any absolute statements would speak for all instrumental forms and validate their phallocentric order. Some kind of a circumcision was needed in a work as a sign of its divine right to pure existence. For A. B. Marx, the critical work is the *Eroica* Symphony, for it achieved a 'distinct consciousness' that moved it out of the body with its 'uncertain emotions and feelings' and into the autonomous activity of the mind.[20] 'Music, the Eternal Feminine', says Marx, 'in Beethoven has become man – spirit.' There is a gender reversal in the *Eroica*: Beethoven's 'mother', says Marx, quoting Zelter, 'is a man'.[21] Thus the significance of the *Eroica* Symphony in the history of music is in its monumental assertion of itself as entirely male, and so clinches for eternity the supremacy of instrumental forms as an autonomous, logical structure of moral action. It obliterates the entire female race from its battle-ridden surface with such force that it brushes aside the domestic affections of the slow movement for the funeral rite of some revolutionary martyr. The sheer size of the symphony functions as a sublime manifesto for the future of the genre, written with such tonal and thematic logic that it could only have been inscribed by a male hand. Instrumental music had come into self-consciousness as absolute structure.

That, at any rate, was the discourse. In reality, the logic of this new consciousness was not the self-generating activity of the soul – it was not even pure, uncontaminated structure. The *Eroica* does not declare itself absolute, but uses a particular configuration of masculinity to em*body* its authority. What speaks behind the surface of this voiceless symphony is the male body of the revolutionary hero.

[20] Marx, *Ludwig van Beethoven: Leben und Schaffen*, 2: 275.   [21] Ibid., 2:287.

18

On heroes

The self-sufficient manhood of the epic hero, notes Christine Di Stefano, is 'one of the most distinctive psychological features of masculinity. To the extent that modern masculine identity is bound up with the repudiation of the (m)other, vigorous self-sufficiency emerges as a kind of defensive reaction formation against memories of dependence and the early symbiotic relation.'[1]

Such memories of the past are erased from the newly found consciousness of the *Eroica*, as it projects an autonomy that deliberately excludes all traces of natural dependence. With the *Eroica*, instrumental music finally breaks the boundaries of the private sphere to which it had belonged with women and forces its way into the public domain of the male hero, whose death-defying antics are the very embodiment of secular self-creation. But to embody its own genesis, the male form had to enter a new phase of control; it had to deny itself through an internal rationalisation of its emotions. The heroic body, according to Dorinda Outram, was paradoxically a non-body, a form which was distanced from its own experience, like the new aesthetic of 'disinterested contemplation'. The *Eroica* chose to internalise this particular historical construction of male power. It was a strategic move, designed to change the face of music, calling upon another autonomous sign to validate its own. So what the *Eroica* structures as autonomous music is in fact the autonomous hero of the French Revolution, a fiction revived by the Napoleonic fervour that seized the middle classes at the turn of the nineteenth century. Germany at that time was too fragmented to stage its own revolution as history, but managed to sublimate it as culture.[2] Indeed, some commentators have argued that German political energy was only articulated in the music of Beethoven. The *Eroica* is French ritual in teutonic abstraction;[3]

---

[1] Christine Di Stefano, *Configurations of Masculinity: A Feminist Perspective on Modern Political Theory* (Ithaca: Cornell University Press, 1991), 97.

[2] See Andrew Bowie, *Aesthetics and Subjectivity* (Manchester: Manchester University Press, 1990), 205, Outram, *The Body and the French Revolution*, 39–40, and Henrich, *Aesthetic Judgement and the Moral Image of the World*, 85–99.

[3] See Adorno, *Aesthetische Theorie*, 519; Hullot-Kentor, 349. On the question of the two English translations, see chapter 1 'On History', note 13.

secular immortality as immutable structure; male authority as instrumental sound.[4]

In the aesthetics of French revolutionary politics, the sentimental body was relegated to the female figure, while the male body was remade as a stoical structure, propelled by an internal dynamic that was inspired by the myths of the Roman empire (plate 7).[5] The powdered periwigs, frills and coloured stockings of the Rococo man were replaced by the clean, clear outline of masculine action; it was a body to be seen as an eternal pose in the narrative of history. 'The stoical body of the Revolution', writes Outram, 'is about the definition of the autonomous self through an . . . impermeable, controlled body' – an image that could represent the will of the bourgeois individual as a public power.[6] The pose of the hero was therefore an absolute gesture, and nowhere could he more powerfully prove the self-sovereignty of his own body than before the horrors of the guillotine. There was to be no flinching, just the pure control of fear in the face of death. This was the ultimate spectacle of his autonomy. His bodily self-possession in the public space of power secured his name in the secular pantheon of saints created by the French Revolution.[7] The heroic body was a bid for canonisation.

This body is therefore not something to be experienced; it is a presentation of an external structure controlled by an internal force. In a sense, the heroic body is already a work, a canonised score that must be exhumed by analysts for veneration.[8] The *Eroica* is a body, a body *politick*, governed on the inside with a regime whose thematic concision delineates a figure of austere power to be seen on the outside as form. Beethoven's rational organisation, says E. T. A. Hoffmann, issues from his 'controlling self detached from the inner realm of sound and ruling it in absolute authority'.[9] It seems that in music, structural control is power, and for the Enlightenment that structure is the resolution of the free individual within the necessary constructs of society. The *Eroica* presents the individual as public image. And for Theodor Adorno, this is mirrored technically in the construction of a form that necessarily

---

[4] On the masculinisation of Beethoven's music in the nineteenth century, see Katherine Ellis, 'Female Pianists and the Male Critics in Nineteenth-Century Paris', *Journal of the American Musicological Society*, vol. 50 nos. 2–3 (1997), 363–6.

[5] See Linda Nochlin, 'Women, Art and Power', in *Visual Theory*, ed. N. Bryson, M. A. Holly and K. Moxey (Cambridge: Polity Press, 1991), 13–15, and Outram, *The Body and the French Revolution*, 78–82.

[6] See Outram, *The Body and the French Revolution*, 156 and 81.   [7] See Ibid., 88.

[8] The spate of music analyses of all kinds on this work testify to the fact of the *Eroica*'s heroic deification. See Lewis Lockwood, '"Eroica" Perspectives: Strategy and Design in the First Movement', in *Beethoven Studies 3*, ed. A. Tyson (Cambridge: Cambridge University Press, 1982).

[9] Hoffmann, 'Review of Beethoven's Fifth Symphony', *E. T. A. Hoffmann's Musical Writings*, 238.

Plate 7 Jacques-Louis David, *The Oath of the Horatii* (1784), Paris,
Louvre. The heroic body of the French Revolution: the three brothers,
the Horatii, take a patriotic oath of allegiance to Rome. Their heroic
bodies are tense, concentrated, hard and energetic; their posture is as
structured and austere as the symmetry of the architecture that
surrounds them. Huddled in the corner, as a contrast to the male
action, is the fallen, emotive figure of a woman with her children.
Her circular form is the insular world of sensibility, whereas the
erect, angular form of the brothers represents the clarity and internal
control of masculine determination.

arises from the particularity of its own motivic process – the thematic
subject and the social structure harmonise as a self-maintaining organism.[10] This technique grounds itself purely in its own activity – an
enclosed oscillation between content and form – and so posits its power,
like the American constitution, as self-evident truth. It claims no legitimisation outside itself.[11] The *Eroica* stands as a monument to its own
universality. It is absolute. Indeed, it scratches out the name Napoleon

---

[10] See Adorno, *Philosophy of Modern Music*, 55, and *Aesthetische Theorie*, 279; Hullot-Kentor,
185. See also Rose Rosengard Subotnik, 'Adorno's Diagnosis of Beethoven's Late Style:
Early Symptom of a Fatal Condition', *Journal of the American Musicological Society*, vol.
29 (1976), reprinted in *Developing Variations* (Minneapolis: University of Minnesota
Press, 1991).

[11] On the politics of autonomy, see Henrich, *Aesthetic Judgement*, 59–84.

that it might name itself as the public identity of the human spirit, trampling over all privatised, feminised bodies from which it may have been born, in a stance that conflates the moral and political worlds as an absolute, masculine gesture.[12]

Therefore, as hero, music is no longer an embodiment of moral sensibility but the expression of a historical consciousness. The *Eroica* rejects the reactions of the body for the action of history. It masters time by constantly bringing the form into a crisis (*Kairos*) that the hero must resolve to shape history into the Utopian visions of secular humanism.[13] 'What the public bodies constructed by the Revolution did', writes Outram, 'was to hurl the individual out of the world of "being" . . . and into the world of time', leaving him to structure his own immortality by seizing the historical moment.[14] The *Eroica* spurs history on with a revolutionary momentum. Time is propelled with such an ineluctable force of tonal and rhythmic dissonance that the structural crises must resolve along the vast linear trajectories that Heinrich Schenker has mapped out like some battle plan.[15] Every tonal and thematic entanglement must be unravelled, even if it involves the extension of the coda to hitherto unknown proportions.[16] There is no surplus in the excess of structure. There is total control. Structural autonomy is the heroic pose of a symphony that has made sense of history. As Novalis puts it: 'The world ought to be as I will it.'[17]

For Adorno, this 'dynamically unfolding totality'[18] reflects the drive of the revolutionary bourgeoisie in their attempt to realise the freedom and autonomy of mankind. But the revolution negates its own movement, for in the dialectic of Enlightenment, the cost of autonomy is always the price of freedom: after the revolution comes the Terror. This is the tragedy of humanism that culminates for Adorno in the

---

[12] The symphony signifies an absolute heroic posture whether under the name 'Napoleon' or 'Eroica'. Beethoven in fact restored Napoleon's name. On the history of the symphony's title, see Maynard Solomon, *Beethoven* (New York: Schirmer, 1977), 132–42.

[13] See Adorno, *Philosophy of Modern Music*, 56, Maynard Solomon, 'Beethoven, Sonata and Utopia', *Telos*, vol. 9 (Fall, 1971), and Ruth A. Solie, 'Beethoven as Secular Humanist: Ideology and the Ninth Symphony in Nineteenth-Century Criticism', in *Explorations in Music, the Arts and Ideas*, ed. Eugene Narmour and Ruth A. Solie (Stuyvesant: Pendragon Press, 1988). On 'Kairos', see Frank Kermode, *The Sense of an Ending: Studies in the Theory of Fiction* (Oxford: Oxford University Press, 1966), 24–31 and 46–52.

[14] Outram, *The Body and the French Revolution*, 160.

[15] Heinrich Schenker, 'Beethovens dritte Sinfonie, in ihrem wahren Inhalt zum erstenmal dargestellt', *Das Meisterwerk in der Musik* (Munich: Drei Masken, 1930), 3: 29–101.

[16] See, for example, Charles Rosen, *Sonata Forms* (New York: Norton, 1988), 290–3, and *The Classical Style*, 392–4.

[17] Novalis (Friedrich von Hardenberg), *Das Philosophische Werk I*, ed. R. Samuel (Stuttgart: Kohlhammer, 1983), 554, quoted in Wm. Arctander O'Brien, *Novalis: Signs of Revolution* (Durham: Duke University Press, 1995), 140.

[18] Theodor W. Adorno, *Introduction to the Sociology of Music*, trans. E. B. Ashton (New York: Seabury, 1976), 209.

Ex. 21 Ludwig van Beethoven, Symphony no. 3 in E♭ major, Op. 55, first movement – bs 631–8.

gas-chambers of *Auschwitz*. But this turning of reason into tyranny is already inscribed within the symphonic structures of Beethoven as a 'force of crushing repression'.[19] The revolutionary energy only achieves its autonomy by a subjugation of nature, an external struggle that twists dialectically into an internal repression, as the hero tries to eliminate his fear of nature by separating the intellect from the sensuous experience of his body.[20] If *Empfindsamkeit* is an embodiment of that experience, then the *Eroica* crushes it in its manipulation of motivic logic: improvisation is rationalised into structure; the spontaneous self is immortalised as hero. Music is no longer the movement of sensation but merely material to be worked on. The *Eroica* is instrumental music as instrumental reason in aesthetic form. The hero 'has ceased to become the object of uncontrolled forces and is instead *entirely self-created*', manipulating the material as 'the movement of [his] own becoming'.[21] Nowhere is this instrumental process more evident than in the technique of thematic development, where the triadic motif, in striving to complete its fragmentary existence, validates its autonomy by constructing a womb out of its own substance in order to deliver itself as a fully-fledged theme at the very close of the movement (see example 21). This process is the becoming of the hero as he writes his own *Bildungsroman* as thematic form.

Thematic selfhood necessarily rejects all origins other than itself. If the *Eroica* re-enacts the self-sufficient delusions of masculinity, then it portrays them as contradictory, for the denial of origins, suggests Elizabeth Berg, always 'cuts man adrift in an endless search for the origin that he has effaced in his desire to be self-generating'.[22] The *Eroica*'s search for origin must somehow end in itself, in the empty process of making the material its own. The first two hammerstrokes that shake the symphony into being are the auto-genesis of the hero.

[19] Ibid., 210.

[20] See Theodor W. Adorno and Max Horkheimer, *Dialectic of Enlightenment*, trans. John Cumming (London: Verso, 1979), Di Stefano, *Configurations of Masculinity*, 130, and Lambert Zuidervaart, *Adorno's Aesthetic Theory* (Cambridge, MA: MIT Press, 1991), 158.

[21] Jeremy Shapiro, 'The Slime of History: Embeddedness in Nature and Critical Theory', *On Critical Theory*, ed. J. O'Neill (New York: Seabury Press, 1976), 149.

[22] Elizabeth Berg, 'The Third Woman', *Diacritics*, vol. 12 (Summer 1982), 18, quoted in Di Stefano, *Configurations of Masculinity*, 21.

Beethoven had thought about a slow introduction, as the sketches indicate, but heroes are not born, they do not emerge from the maternal juices of introductory elements. The first two hammerstrokes are such a violent severance of the umbilical cord that they wipe out all memories of gestation in the sketches. If the theme is the hero's becoming, signified as a triadic fanfare, then the first two chords that precede it are his origins which he must overcome and return to, so that he can claim the mastery of his own birth, death and resurrection in a motherless and God-forsaken world. The circularity of this process is pre-ordained, for the opening chords are also the final chords of the movement. The theme springs from the first and affirms the last, as if the hammerstrokes were merely a compression of its triadic figure.[23] But the beginning and the end are not the same; the opening chords are not part of the thematic structure – they are outside the exposition, excluded in the repeat. They are separated by silences that isolate them as something outside the system, and yet, as the work progresses, these very chords seem to take control of the movement as rhythmic blows. What ensues after the initial hammerstrokes is a dialectical battle between this rhythmic gesture (the origin) and the thematic development (the hero's becoming). The theme can only come into being as it moves against its origins; it struggles against its own birth in order that it might internalise it as part of its structure, so that, by the final bars, the first two chords would have moved from the outside to the inside: self creation, *ex nihilo*. 'Beethoven', writes Adorno, 'developed a music essence out of nothingness in order to be able to define it as a process of becoming.'[24] Thus in between these outer hammerstrokes, the hero discovers his autonomy as he transforms the somatic pangs of birth into the structural pillars of self-generation. The violence of this process is unprecedented in the history of music. In the exposition, as the heroic motif develops, the hammerstrokes return as increasingly dissonant and syncopated gestures that go against the metrical symmetry, striking the second beat with such force that they bunch up as violent hemiola assertions (see example 22).

The heroic power of the music is in its ability to push against these barriers with a relentless motion that eventually resolves the struggle by synchronising the conflicting accents on the downbeat of the hypermeasure.[25] *Kairos* is mastered by a harmonic inevitability that crushes the rhythmic crisis. But this inevitability is suddenly thrown into disarray at the centre of the form (bs 238–84). In the development section, the hammerstrokes take over the music, with an unremitting dissonance

---

[23] See David Epstein, *Beyond Orpheus* (Cambridge, MA: MIT Press, 1979), 128.
[24] Adorno, *Philosophy of Modern Music*, 47. Also see *Aesthetische Theorie*, 279; Hullot-Kentor 185.   [25] See Epstein, *Beyond Orpheus*, 129–36.

Ex. 22 Beethoven, Symphony no. 3 in E♭ major, Op. 55, first
movement – bs 122–31.

that fails to resolve the structure on both rhythmic and harmonic levels,
leaving a deafening silence (b. 280) – the same silence that had divided
the opening chords from the exposition, except that the silence falls
emphatically on the downbeat of the hypermeasure. 'It is so unbearably
loud as to be inaudible.'[26] The hero has been killed by his own birth,
bludgeoned to death by the somatic violence of the hammerstrokes (see
example 23). After all, what comes after these blows is the problematic
appearance of a *new* theme that has perplexed countless analysts (b.

---

[26] See Grosvenor W. Cooper and Leonard B. Meyer, *The Rhythmic Structure of Music*
(Chicago: Chicago University Press, 1960), 137–9.

284ff). This theme is such a contradiction to the non-theme of the hero and so distant from the tonal anchor that it can only be heard as a negation of the hero (see example 23). Indeed, for Wilhelm von Lenz, the new theme signals his death.[27]

The hero is dead, the symphony should be over – but there are still some 400 bars to go. In the mythology of the French Revolution, however, death is only the beginning of heroic canonisation. What follows the new theme can only be the secular resurrection of the hero made possible by a death that captures him in an immortal pose.[28] He lives on as revolutionary inspiration. This explains the bizarre dissonance just before the recapitulation that has echoed controversially down the years of the *Eroica*'s critical reception. The strange fanfare, entangled in the hushed texture of strings, seems to pre-empt the recapitulation like a mistake, but it is in fact the battle call of the hero's spirit. Beethoven superimposes the hero's death and resurrection as dominant and tonic, a clash that deliberately recalls the peculiarly dissonant sonority that had surrounded the silence of his demise – triads injected with semitones that resist resolution (see example 24).

The string tremolos that are a *topos* of the supernatural[29] and the call of the horn that is the voice of the hero combine to rehearse the semitonal aggregates of death as a moment of canonisation. The command of the hero has become absolute; it is the revolution, or as Wagner sees it, 'the act of heroism itself', calling the recapitulation to action.[30]

This is the ideology of the *Eroica* – the glorification of war. Man as hero defies death for the principle of humanity. The individual lives on as general will and national inspiration – immortal and invisible. In reality, this heroic identity is just another male construction. As Elaine Showalter has suggested, men at war, far from mastering history with their death-defying antics, were immobilised by a silent hysteria, a state of 'shell-shock' in a dialectic of control that left their masculinity emasculated in the face of death.[31] The reality is in Goya, the ideology in

---

[27] Lenz, *Beethoven*, 293. See Scott Burnham, 'On the Programmatic Reception of Beethoven's Eroica Symphony', in *Beethoven Forum 1*, ed. C. Reynolds, L. Lockwood and J. Webster (Lincoln: University of Nebraska Press, 1992), 9–10. For most nineteenth-century commentators, some kind of death takes place in the development. See, for example, Marx, *Ludwig van Beethoven*, 1:196, and Aléxandre Oulibischeff, *Beethoven, ses critiques et ses glossateurs* (Leipzig, 1857), 177–8.

[28] See Maurice Blanchot, 'The End of the Hero', *The Infinite Conversation*, trans. S. Hanson (Minneapolis: University of Minnesota Press, 1993).

[29] See Birgitte Moyer, '*Ombra* and Fantasia in late Eighteenth-Century Theory and Practice', *Convention in Eighteenth- and Nineteenth-Century Music*, ed. W. J. Allanbrook, J. M. Levy and W. P. Mahrt (New York: Pendragon Press, 1992), 295–6.

[30] See Burnham, 'On the Programmatic Reception of Beethoven's *Eroica* Symphony', 1, and *Beethoven Hero* (Princeton: Princeton University Press, 1995), 153–68.

[31] Elaine Showalter, *The Female Malady: Women, Madness and English Culture, 1830–1980* (London: Virago Press, 1987), 171.

Ex. 23 Beethoven, Symphony no. 3 in E♭ major, Op. 55, first
movement – bs 266–91.

Ex. 23 (*cont.*)

Ex. 24 Beethoven, Symphony no. 3 in E♭ major, Op. 55, first movement – bs 390–5.

Beethoven (plate 8). The frightened faces of men depicted by Goya as those unable to live up to an identity that they never possessed are hidden by Beethoven, for 'shell-shock' is the threat of feminisation for the heroic body.

This is why the coda has to be extended in the *Eroica*. The symphony recapitulates the development in order to replay death as resurrection. The new theme is revived without the bludgeoning hammerstrokes that had preceded it. There is no second death to arrest the heroic theme from achieving its selfhood. In fact the relentless hammering only recurs after the thematic completion, transformed in the final bars as a sign of closure. What had been the crisis of rhythmic and harmonic dissonance is mastered as the resolution of the movement – a monumental cadence. Thus the final two chords return to the opening gesture, enclosing the work in a form that is the self-possession of the heroic body. The final hammerstrokes affirm that the first two chords are in fact the testicles of the hero, generating and completing his own becoming.

And the legend lives on; it is retold time and again by the spate of programmes that lie like wreaths around this symphonic monument. They elaborate the story to immortalise the work. For some critics, the heroic utterance that had been the rallying cry of the recapitulation becomes

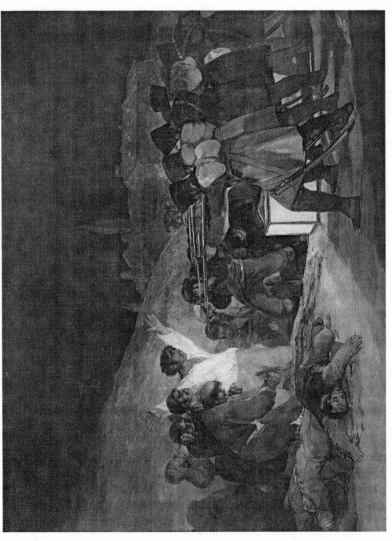

Plate 8 Francisco de Goya y Lucientes, *The Third of May 1808*, Prado, Madrid. Real men at war? Napoleonic soldiers murder, without trial, a seemingly infinite line of Spaniards suspected of complicity.

the 'summons of glory' in the coda, transcending time as the eternal *logos*. 'The word shall prevail', declares A. B. Marx, 'it has triumphed and shall triumph and rule.'[32] For Lenz, the hero has been taken up in a blaze of glory and deified through his thematic completion. As Scott Burnham explains:

the theme (the hero) flies to the heavens, liberated from the battles of mortality. His final form is a true theme, a melody, a form forbidden to him until he lived to the uttermost consequences of his heroic character. As melody he can now be sung by posterity. Thus the heroic journey here envisaged ranges from life to death . . . to the eternal glory of epic song.[33]

Except, of course, there are no words to sing. The hero's utterance prevails as *logos* precisely because the word in all its particularity has been generalised into the eternal structure of sound. The *Eroica* gestures to its own canonicity as a symbol for all instrumental music. It reveals its autonomy as an eternal monument in order to speak universally, when in fact it only speaks for men – perhaps not even men, but some ideological construction that reduces them to victims of war.

This is Adorno's dialectic of Enlightenment in which the drive for autonomy destroys its own freedom. Progress necessarily contains its own regression, as the heroic pose of secular man crumbles under the weight of its own Utopian visions. The French Revolution, says Schlegel, can be seen in two ways, either as the 'most remarkable phenomenon in the history of states, . . . an absolute revolution . . . [or] the most frightful grotesque of the age, where the most profound prejudices and their most brutal punishments are mixed up in a fearful chaos and woven as bizarrely as possible into a monstrous human tragicomedy'.[34] The grotesque secretly inheres within the sublime, as the *Grosse Fuge* will testify, turning the civilised fugue into a narrative of destruction. But the critique of Beethoven's late style, some twenty years after the *Eroica*, was socially unacceptable.[35] The paradox of revolution was completely invisible to those at the time who were extolling the new metaphysics of music. The self-consciousness of the *Eroica* was not conscious of its own destruction. It was too busy exploring its own subjectivity.

[32] Oulibicheff, *Beethoven*, 178; Marx, *Ludwig van Beethoven*, 2:304; both quoted in Burnham, 'On the Programmatic Reception of Beethoven's *Eroica* Symphony', 20.
[33] Ibid., 20
[34] Schlegel, *Athenaeum Fragments*, no. 424, in *Philosophical Fragments*, 86.
[35] See Chua, *The 'Galitzin' Quartets of Beethoven*, 230–44.

19

On politics

When one finally begins to practise Fichtecising artistically . . .
wonderful works of art could arise.   (Novalis)[1]

The *Eroica* knows itself as absolute in the same way that the revolutionary I of Fichte's philosophy comes to self-knowledge. 'My system',
writes Fichte, 'is the first system of freedom. As that nation [France]
releases man from his external chains, so my system releases him from
the shackles of the thing in itself . . . and presents him . . . as an independent being.'[2] The ego, for Fichte, is not fact; it can neither be theorised
about nor can it conceptualise its own being. Only the spontaneous
action of the I is absolute: 'We know because our vocation is to act.'[3] And
it is only the action of the *Eroica* that is absolute in its attempt to grasp
itself as infinite. The music presents itself as a process that is entirely
self-caused; the heroic theme moves beyond the compulsion that the
hammerstrokes inflict upon it to demonstrate the freedom of its conscious activity in shaping itself, breaking the limits of necessity to know
the absolute position from which it can categorically assert its imperatives. The *Eroica* as the male action hero is the musical image of the absolute subject. But as Schelling would point out to Fichte, the freedom of
the self-positing ego can only exist by dominating nature as merely
something to be used.[4] The subject *subjugates* in its visions of freedom
and is therefore totally blind to its destruction of men, women, nature
and ultimately itself.[5] The power of absolute music lies precisely in this

---

[1] Novalis (Friedrich von Hardenberg), *Schriften*, ed. R. Samuel (Stuttgart: Kohlhammer,
  1983), 2:524, quoted in O'Brien, *Novalis*, 139.
[2] From a letter of 1795, quoted in Henrich, *Aesthetic Judgement and the Moral Image of the
  World*, 86. The system that Fichte mentions is his *Wissenschaftslehre* (Leipzig, 1794–5),
  translated by P. Heath and J. Lachs as *The Science of Knowledge* (Cambridge: Cambridge
  University Press, 1982). For a clear exposition of Fichte's philosophy, see Johann Gottlieb
  Fichte, 'A Comparison Between Prof. Schmid's System and the *Wissenschaftslehre*', translated by D. Breazedale in *Fichte: Early Philosophical Writings* (Ithaca: Cornell University
  Press, 1988), 307–35.
[3] *Fichtes Werk*, ed. I. H. Fichte (Berlin, 1971), 2:263, quoted in Bowie, *Aesthetics and
  Subjectivity*, 62.   [4] See Bowie, *Aesthetics and Subjectivity*, 81–2.
[5] This is the tale of Adorno and Horkheimer's *Dialectic of Enlightenment*.

162

blindness; it cannot represent and therefore hides its destruction; it merely presents itself as absolute, which is to say that it disappears in the transparency of its self-presence. After all, for Rousseau 'sovereignty . . . cannot be represented'.[6]

Misogyny, violence, bodily repression, control, domination: these are the waste-products of autonomy that the aesthetic is meant to burn up. An analysis that uncovers the politics of gender and violence basically rummages through the rubbish heap emptied by a discourse that presents instrumental music as abstract sound; the object of interrogation is protected by the aesthetic of autonomy. In a sense, this is a consolation for those, like Adorno, who have placed their hope in the revolutionary spirit of the bourgeoisie; a work such as the *Eroica* represents the contradiction of Enlightenment society in a purely musical form that is divorced from reality. 'Artworks are afterimages of empirical life.'[7] They embody action without praxis. As an aesthetic object, the *Eroica* Symphony is a kind of displaced aggression, a sensual repression of the body, perhaps even a feminised misogyny.[8] Because it encodes reality in non-violent forms, the aesthetic neutralises the self-contradiction of the revolutionary zeal as a Utopian promise – albeit 'a promise that is constantly being broken'.[9] As Adorno writes:

the command to kill . . . is the legacy of violence in art, the violence which lies at the base of all art's order. While as a spiritualized activity art strips violence of its power, it continues to practise it. Freedom and domination commingle inseparably in art. Its integral form, the triumph of its autonomy, is what also casts a spell on the listener, leaves no one out and subjects everyone to its speechless performance. It is only necessary to listen to the humane Beethoven from the outside, from a sufficiently great distance, and nothing remains but the terror aroused by Tamasese. But perhaps all humaneness does is to keep the consciousness of terror alive, the consciousness of all that can never be made good.[10]

Adorno's philosophy of music has its roots in the aesthetic strategies developed in Germany during the final decade of the eighteenth century, particularly in the political writings of Schiller. That aesthetics should be political at all was a strange move. It was at first a reaction against the reality of both the political and industrial revolutions that

---

[6] Jean-Jacques Rousseau, *Social Contract*, in *The Social Contract and Discourses*, trans. G. D. H. Cole (London: Dent, 1993), 266.

[7] Adorno, *Aesthetische Theorie*, 14; Hullot-Kentor, 4.

[8] On Beethoven's symphonic language as an 'antithesis to praxis', see ibid., 358; Hullot-Kentor, 241.

[9] Ibid., 205; C. Lenhardt, 196. See Zuidervaart, *Adorno's Aesthetic Theory*, 210–13.

[10] Theodor W. Adorno, *Quasi una Fantasia: Essays on Modern Music* (1963), trans. R. Livingstone (London: Verso, 1992), 34. Tamasese refers to a tribal chief who uses the severed heads of his prisoners as drums.

seemed to fragment society and rob humanity of its sensuous existence. The human being, divided within itself and within society, needed a new politics that could salvage the Enlightenment's vision of progress which was rapidly regressing into barbarity. The new politics itself was grounded in the potential of an ego that knew itself as infinite, but the experience of that potential was aesthetic. The contradiction of such a condition was that its potential could never be realised: art became praxis internalised, and this gave birth to a new 'reality' – art as illusion, what Schiller would call 'Schein'. For the first time, music was no longer real, but declared its own functionlessness as a fiction that was socially necessary. In the terrible face of reality, the new aesthetic basically deferred reality as a promise of Utopian happiness. Instrumental music, that had for so long been derided as a frivolous appendage to meaning, suddenly found itself weighted down with a secular eschatology:[11] 'Truth lives on in the illusion of Art', says Schiller recoiling from the aftermath of the Revolution, 'and it is from this copy, or after-image, that the original image will once again be restored . . . so now Art goes before [nature], a voice rousing from slumber and preparing the shape of things to come.'[12] From this visionary perspective, a music that depicts reality would be regarded by Schiller as naïve, as if humanity were not divided both within and without. A naïve art simply believes itself to be at one with nature, like the vibrations of the feminine body, as if the world were innocent, as if the sign and the referent were united.[13] But this is simply a delusion. For music to shape the future, its signs had to be divorced from its signifieds of reality. Thus in order for music to be an illusion of hope, it had to divest the empirical particularity of its meaning to distance reality as abstract form. Only 'form affects *universals*', says Schiller concerning music,[14] only form is absolute, and only as form does music embody a political practice that is deferred from reality by the meaninglessness of its content. Form functions like the kind of political rhetoric that creates a vision without any concrete policy, since the formal structure of music can figure a better shape of things to come with a totally contingent content that does not predict the details of history: it creates a formal ending that makes sense of the world, without being in the world. Thus the structural posturing of the *Eroica* embodies this contradiction between meaning and function, in which the political intent is locked out of the political sphere by an aesthetic of autonomy

---

[11] See the chapter 'On the Apocalypse'.

[12] Schiller, *On the Aesthetic Education of Man*, 57.

[13] See Friedrich von Schiller, *On the Naive and Sentimental in Literature*, trans H. Watanabe-O'Kelly (Manchester: Carcanet Press, 1981).

[14] Friedrich von Schiller, *Sämtliche Werke* (Leipzig, n.d.), 12:57–8, quoted in Le Huray and Day, *Music Aesthetics in the Eighteenth and Early-Nineteenth Centuries*, 236.

that divorces art 'from truth and morality', as Schlegel puts it.[15] Or in Wackenroder's words:

Art is misleading, deceptive superstition; in it we think that we have before us the last, innermost essence of humanity; and yet, it merely foists upon us a beautiful *product* of man, in which are set down all the egotistical, self-satisfying thoughts and emotions which remain sterile and ineffective in the world of action.[16]

And yet, the *Eroica* makes more sense of the Napoleonic campaign than the reality of history. Autonomous art, it seems, teeters precariously between revolutionary vision and political impotence, a condition that is to bedevil the social meaning of autonomous music to the present day.

Instrumental music may know itself as absolute in the same way as the Fichtean ego, but unlike the ego, music's self-positing activity can never be in the political *now*. This is the significance of music's philosophical abstraction into pure sound at the turn of the nineteenth century: absolute music is music in the future tense and sometimes even slips over 'into the presence of the eternal';[17] 'musical form', writes Schelling, becomes 'a process whereby the infinite is embodied in the finite'.[18] Music's abstraction signals some kind of inaccessibility or deferral, an eternal 'as if' that removes sound from the immediate sensory perception of *Empfindsamkeit* into another sphere of (non)-reality. In a society increasingly reduced to commodified objects, instrumental music was deliberately moved out of the material world as a symbol of a visionary or perhaps even escapist politics – a movement away from an 'earthly hell', as A. W. Schlegel puts it, into the ether of pure sound.[19] Its failure to depict the world is its refusal to acknowledge reality. This seems to be the condition of music in moments of historical or existential crisis. Thus Adorno's aesthetics rehearse the Romantic's strategy of isolating instrumental music as an 'unknown realm, a world quite separate from the sensual world'.[20] It functions in ways similar to Jean-François Lyotard's recent reading of Kant's third critique, where the terror of the French Revolution is aestheticised as a sublime manifestation that separates

[15] Schlegel, 'Athenaeum Fragments', 252, in *Philosophical Fragments*, 53.
[16] Wackenroder and Tieck, *Confessions and Fantasies*, 195.
[17] Karl Wilhelm Ferdinand Solger, *Vorlesungen über Ästhetik*, ed. K. W. L. Heyse (Darmstadt, 1969), 341. See Dahlhaus, *The Idea of Absolute Music*, 76.
[18] Friedrich Wilhelm Josef von Schelling, *Philosophie der Kunst* (1802–3), in Le Huray and Day, *Music Aesthetics*, 280.
[19] August Wilhelm Schlegel, *Vorlesungen über schöne Litteratur und Kunst* (Heilbronn, 1884), 256–7, and *Die Kunstlehre*, ed. E. Lohner (Stuttgart, 1963), 215.
[20] Hoffmann, 'Review of Beethoven's Fifth Symphony', *E. T. A. Hoffmann's Musical Writings*, 236.

historical reality from the sign, and therefore action from idea.[21] In other words, the *Eroica* Symphony.

So in instrumental music, the political will of the subject is meant to align itself to the aesthetic force. At least this is Schiller's solution in the face of the inhumanity brought into political consciousness by the French Revolution: 'if man is ever to solve that problem of politics', writes Schiller, 'in practice he will have to approach it through the problem of the aesthetic, because it is only through Beauty that man can make his way to Freedom'.[22] But as the nineteenth century progressed, the idea of autonomous art as political critique ironically ended up more as a 'neutralization of critique',[23] for the simple reason that absolute music represents absolutely nothing.

---

[21] Jean-François Lyotard, 'The Idea of History', in *Post-Structuralism and the Question of History*, ed. D. Attridge, G. Bennington and R. Young (Cambridge: Cambridge University Press, 1989); also see Christopher Norris, *What's Wrong with Postmodernism* (Baltimore: Johns Hopkins University Press, 1990), 208–21.

[22] Schiller, *On the Aesthetic Education of Man*, 9.

[23] Peter Bürger, *Theory of the Avant-Garde*, trans. M. Shaw (Minneapolis: University of Minnesota Press, 1984), 13.

20

On nothing

'Nothing' is the only real absolute in a world without God as foundation. Hence the absolute subject, as the new foundation of philosophy, claims its absolute status by spinning out its existence from nothing – indeed, its entire world from its own nothingness: subject and object.

The first Idea is naturally the notion *of my self* as an absolutely free being. With the free self-conscious being [Wesen] a whole *world* emerges at the same time – out of nothing – the only true and thinkable *creation from nothing* . . .[1]

The question for the early Romantics was how this absolute subject in its godlike sovereignty was going to fashion a world *ex nihilo* to ground itself in; without a coherent universe, subjectivity would simply flounder in a seemingly contingent and fragmented world. The subject, as 'God', needed an absolute that was not merely its own empty autonomy, but a *totality* in which the diverse and particular things of the world could settle within a system of the whole. But how could one remake God in the abstract from the innards of one's soul, unless there is some intimation of the divine waiting to be sifted out of the subject? What was required was a method of signification that could function as 'God', that is, as some kind of invisible sign prior to reality that would organise reality in harmony with the self. The solution? To signify nothing as totality. In fact, Friedrich Schlegel's shorthand for the absolute is 0.[2] The semiotics of zero, having slipped into Western mathematics in the thirteenth century, the vanishing point in Renaissance painting and as paper money in the seventeenth century,[3] finally discovered its most transcendental manifestation in instrumental music.

Zero, as Brian Rotman explains, is an ambiguous sign that is both inside and outside the system of numbers; it is both a figure that commingles with other numbers within the play of calculations (0, 1, 2, 3) and a 'meta-sign' that orders the system of numbers from the outside as

---

[1] *The So Called 'Oldest System Programme of German Idealism'* (1796), translated in Bowie, *Aesthetics and Subjectivity*, 265. This incomplete text was found in a bundle of Hegel's papers in 1917; it is written in Hegel's hand, but it is thought to be a copy of a text composed by Schelling, possibly under the direct influence of Hölderlin; for further information see Lacoue-Labarthe and Nancy, *The Literary Absolute*, 27–38.
[2] See Schlegel, *Literary Notebooks, 1797–1801.*   [3] See Rotman, *Signifying Nothing.*

their origin (10, 200, 3,000). This double play ensures the auto-closure of the system since inside and outside seemingly disappear as they merge together to conjure the illusion of autonomy. Zero, as a signification of nothing, reverses 'the original movement of signification from object to sign',[4] whether it is the visual zero of perspectival image, the exchange zero of paper money or the aural zero of instrumental music. So, for example, the empty sign of instrumental music no longer signifies an object, but is signified by the absolute zero; the empty sign and its zero-referent cancel the inside and the outside to close the system as an empty set. In this way, the signifier, like paper money, is able to multiply a wealth of meaning out of nothing, with only some imaginary, non-existent gold called absolute music to save the sign from hyper-inflation: nothing guarantees nothing. With the drainage of substance (the signified), signification becomes a virtually effortless production, a frictionless exchange of signs that always adds up to zero.[5] Thus music seems to present its own genesis as a work created *ex nihilo*; in reality, however, the empty sign is not pure, but only points to the void from which it emerges to efface the fact that it is the absolute zero outside the system that controls the presentation of the sign as empty. Absolute music is not an emancipation of music but a reconstruction of it.

So what is absolute about music is not ultimately music itself but a transcendental sign of absence that enabled the German Idealists and the early Romantics to make instrumental music mean nothing in order that it might mean everything.[6] But at first, the notion of zero as absolute made instrumental music a highly precarious object in the moral consciousness of early Romanticism, precisely because it was both 'everything and nothing',[7] at once aligned with the divine and with death, fixed eternally by an 'immutable holiness' and yet something which, like the mere flicker of human existence, 'arises out of the void and vanishes into the void'. Indeed, for Wackenroder, instrumental

---

[4] Ibid., 28.

[5] On paper money, see Marc Shell, *Money, Language, and Thought* (Baltimore: Johns Hopkins University Press, 1982), particularly the discussions on Goethe, Kant and Hegel, 84–155. Also see Kevin Barry, 'Paper Money and English Romanticism: Literary Side-Effects of the Last Invasion of Britain', *The Times Literary Supplement* (21 February 1997), 14–16. The most concrete parallel with the idea of paper money in the late eighteenth and nineteenth century is the musical score; this is the paper-sign that represents absolute music and whose value no longer resides in an exchange for labour (performance) but in the promise of an immaterial, transcendental music – the autonomous work.

[6] On the difference between the Idealists and the early Romantics, see Bowie, *Aesthetics and Subjectivity*, 41–4. Early Romanticism can be regarded as a subset of Idealism; the ideas of both camps concerning instrumental music often overlap. I will use the term 'Romantic', except in cases where there is a clear difference of thought, since the word is also a musical category.

[7] Wackenroder and Tieck, *Werke und Briefe von Wilhelm Heinrich Wackenroder*, 190.

music seems to hold the ego between heaven and hell. Sometimes it is the very sound of eternity, a music so autonomous that it escapes the relentless 'wheel of time', as something 'independent of the world, [free from] the wheel of the great-wheel mechanism'. 'No flame of the human heart rises higher . . . towards heaven than art!' he writes, 'No substance so concentrates in itself the intellectual and the spiritual power of the human being and makes him . . . an autonomous human god.' Yet simultaneously, it is precisely this godlike autonomy that makes music the ultimate deception, luring the 'vain idolater' out of the world of action and into the 'dangerous slippery abyss' of empty sound.[8]

An instrumental music that throws the unsuspecting soul around into fits of life and death was obviously a problem that the early Romantics had to solve. Creation *ex nihilo* was not working; something was wrong in the zero-structure of the new aesthetic. For a start, the system needed to be stabilised on two counts: first, the zero origin of music needed to signify totality – some kind of 'God' as opposed to nothing – in order to prevent instrumental music from annihilating itself in its movement of closure into a nihilistic void. Secondly, the ego needed to reassert itself as absolute to prevent the emotions from being 'torn away and shaped artificially'[9] by every whim of sound; after all, the 'self as an absolute being' was supposed to be the 'first Idea' from which the world emerges.[10] In other words, instrumental music was given the double task of inscribing itself within the totality of the universe and of delineating the creative processes of the ego to affirm the subject's autonomy in the totality of the world, and so resolve the antagonism between subject and object. In this way, the nihilistic abyss can be covered over and the free subject can unfold its autonomy.

The absolute condition of music was therefore a kind of mathematical solution in the calculation of absolutes, in which music is zero. Hence, the Romantics regarded instrumental music as a mathematics of the world-soul.[11] For the solution to work, something drastic had to be done to music, transforming it far beyond its creation-*ex-nihilo* autonomy. Having been constructed by a semiotics of zero, instrumental music was raised to a higher power by the Romantics, to become in turn a 'meta-sign' for their system of philosophy as the *absolute zero* that both participates within the system and organises it from the outside. This philosophical solution was a search for cosmic unity. The problem for the Romantics was that they had two absolutes in their hands – 'God' in terms of totality (the world), and 'God' in terms of autonomy (the self). For the system to work, these absolute origins had to balance out to

[8] Wackenroder and Tieck, *Confessions and Fantasies*, 174–8, 190, 195 and 196.
[9] Ibid., 196.
[10] 'Oldest System Programme of German Idealism', in Bowie, *Aesthetics and Subjectivity*, 265.   [11] See Neubauer, *The Emancipation of Music from Language*, 193–210.

create an empty set to ground the existence of all things in a single coherent universe. But it is not easy juggling with absolutes, particularly given the historical enmity between God and the self-styled ego. And, of course, the juggler in this case is the ego itself that wants to obliterate any external meddling in the system by a traditional God for an internally devised substitute, so that the entire system can propel itself from nothing. Thus music, as *the* sign of zero, was used to balance the books. Absolute music is the system that creates totality out of nothing, a system that articulates both the processes of the ego and the creative forces of the universe to harmonise them within the play of empty signs. In other words, to guarantee the coherence of a cosmos in which the absolute autonomy of the subject and the absolute totality of 'God' must co-exist, music becomes a mediator that functions as the absolute go-between of the aesthetic.

Of course, this is easier said than done; a great deal of philosophical manoeuvring was necessary to set the system in motion, and this was particularly tricky given the fact that the absolute, as the transcendental signifier, is unsignifiable and therefore unknowable. The Romantics may have regarded reality as a semiotic construction, but the absolute that controls the semiosis of reality is shrouded in mystery.[12] In order to represent the unrepresentable, the Romantics conjured up the absolute in the form of fragments that give tiny glimpses of the whole. If music is absolute, then there can be no systematic theory of it – only fragmentary clues. In fact, the Romantics did not even name music 'absolute'; and why should they, given its unnameable nature?[13] Consequently, the meaning of absolute music can only be inferred from tantalising scraps of information left by the Romantics, where their reticence perhaps is meant to speak more of music's zero-signification than the words themselves. Their sporadic texts on music only offer fragmentary glimpses of a process in which instrumental sound tacitly becomes an ontological structure that grounds the excessive logic of Romantic thought. Absolute music underlines the Romantic project: by generating the world from nothing through an infinite process of creation within the ego, music embraces the world as 'the universal song of every living thing'.[14] The empty sign is both 'nothing and everything'.

---

[12] See O'Brien, *Novalis*, 77–118.

[13] Although the early Romantics constructed a new metaphysics of instrumental music, the term 'absolute music' was not coined until the 1840s by an opponent of the very idea – Richard Wagner. See Dahlhaus, *The Idea of Absolute Music*, 18–41, and the chapter in this volume, 'On Absolute Music'.

[14] Schlegel, *Kritische Schriften und Fragmente* (1794–1818), 5:58.

21

On God

Zero to one is the movement from nothing to divinity. In fact this movement is the process of self-generation towards the absolute that is the definition of Romantic art. The essence of Romantic poetry, explains Schlegel, is 'that it can forever only become and is never completed'; 'on the wings of poetic reflection', Romantic poetry is progressively multiplied into 'an endless succession of mirrors' in its attempt to embrace the unattainable totality that it yearns for.[1] Thus between zero and one is the *infinity* of Romantic art. Or in Schlegel's shorthand:[2]

$$Unendlichkeit = \frac{1}{0}$$

And instrumental music, claims E. T. A. Hoffmann, 'is the most Romantic of all arts' precisely because it 'awakens that infinite yearning' towards an 'unknown realm'. The zero sign of music speaks 'the inexpressible' in its movement towards totality which is one.[3] It is therefore infinite because it mediates between nothing and everything.

But what does music speak that makes it articulate the ineffable? It speaks itself. Music is not only a sign that refers to the 'realm of the infinite', but seems to indicate that realm by referring to itself; in its semiotic play, music assumes an internal recognition of itself as absolute. The sign signifies itself, or, to borrow Fichte's definition of the subject, 'A=A.'[4] So 'as a pure expression of . . . its own nature', music yearns towards its own being;[5] its process of signification constitutes both the infinite movement towards the absolute *and* the absolute itself so that its sign becomes identical with its signifier, justifying the significance of its self-mimesis as it removes itself from the concrete reality of the world. It is this double play of self-signification that secures the autonomy of sound and distinguishes music as the essence of Romantic art. The Romantic concept of instrumental music therefore hinges on the

---

[1] Schlegel, *Athenaeum Fragments*, no. 116; a translation is available in Schlegel, *Philosophical Fragments*.

[2] See Schlegel, *Literary Notebooks, 1797–1801*, 12–13.

[3] Hoffmann, 'Review of Beethoven's Fifth Symphony', E. T. A. *Hoffmann's Musical Writings*, 236.   [4] Fichte, *The Science of Knowledge*, 94.

[5] Hoffmann, 'Review of Beethoven's Fifth Symphony', 236.

co-existence of two musics, one physical, the other metaphysical. 'Everything Visible', writes Novalis, 'cleaves to the Invisible – the Audible to the Inaudible.'[6] This is because the 'sacred play of art is only a remote imitation of the infinite play of the universe.'[7] Thus every symphony that is purely Romantic is contained within a music that is purely theoretical – a 'symphony of the universe [*des Weltalls Symphonie*]'.[8] This is a music so absolute that it does not exist in any tangible form. Indeed, if it ever materialised it would mean the end of Romanticism, closing the epoch of becoming to establish the Utopia that instrumental music endlessly defers. The entire system of Romanticism, from which the autonomy of the musical work arises, rests on an inaudible music that is an Idea and not a reality. And this Idea of instrumental music is *Totality*. To adapt Schlegel's shorthand:

$$\frac{\text{music}\,(=0)}{\text{absolute } 0} = 1$$

How does the empty sign of an inaudible symphony signify God? The paradox of totality is that it is both zero and one: zero because there is nothing outside it; one because it is the union of everything that exists. So it was quite simple for the empty sign of music, because it excludes all representations, to be the inclusion of all things. It need only move from zero to one to become God. The sign cancels itself out as zero and coincides with itself as one. Or as Schlegel puts it: in the arts, music is both 'the centre and circumference', the zero from which all aesthetic matter is generated and the totality that encompasses this matter into a *uni*verse.[9] Thus Schlegel speculates that 'in music, it should be possible to express Idealism to perfection. It must only mean God', he adds. 'The whole of music must undoubtedly become one.'[10]

The god of Schlegel, however, is not the God of Abraham, Isaac and Jacob, despite its claim to be one, for Schlegel's god is merely a regulative principle in the will to systematise and poeticise the entire cosmos – the project of Romanticism. And it was in order to articulate this self-generating system that the Romantic deity took on the attributes of music as an abstract, creative totality, whose nameless alterity is signified by the empty sign. In this way, music shook off the materiality that the eighteenth century had so scrupulously classified in the vibrations of strings and in the physiology of fibres, and became spirit

---

[6] Novalis, 'Studien zur bildenden Kunst', no. 481 (1799), quoted in Wheeler, *German Aesthetic and Literary Criticism*, 14 and 110.

[7] Schlegel, *Dialogue on Poetry and Literary Aphorisms*, 89. The translation has been modified.

[8] Novalis (Friedrich von Hardenberg), *Die Lehrlinge zu Sais*, in *Schriften*, ed. P. Kluckhohn and R. Samuel (Stuttgart: Kohlhammer, 1960–75), 1:79.

[9] Schlegel, *Literary Notebooks, 1797–1801*, no. 1416.   [10] Ibid., no. 1737.

instead. In fact, philosophically speaking, it became a transcendental Idea.

For Kant, an Idea is a concept of reason that exceeds the limit of all empirical reality: 'no object adequate to the transcendental Idea can ever be found within experience'[11] because it is the condition of experience itself, the very elements of reason that 'unite all acts of understanding in respect of every object, into an *absolute whole*'.[12] These ideas, for Kant, acquire reality in the world primarily in the realm of ethical action. What the Romantics did, however, was to transfer this actuality from ethics to aesthetics so that it is the work of art that realises what Schlegel calls the 'ethical totality [*ethische Einheit*]' that turns action into poetry.[13] Thus Schlegel suggests that music is 'closely related to morality'.[14] In fact, Schlegel implies that because 'the instinct for moral greatness' manifests itself as spirit, the movement of the spirit 'is like a music of thoughts'. In other words, moral instinct articulates itself in tones that form the 'poetry of elevated reason', which is the absolute poetry of moral ideas.[15] If the moral law within 'gives rise to that nameless art which seizes the confused transitoriness of life and shapes it into an eternal unity',[16] then music is perhaps not simply an idea, which is defined by Schlegel as 'infinite, independent, unceasing, moving, godlike thoughts', but reveals the 'Idea of ideas', which Schlegel defines as 'God'.[17] In this light, absolute music is more than the ontological space for the materialisation of its instrumental forms; rather absolute music functions as some kind of 'transcendental signifier' that is both inside and outside the system as *the* System that guarantees the ontological and ethical significance of all aesthetic and moral manifestations. It is in this sense that music became the highest form of art.

Thus the absolute Idea is not a static entity, but a productive *activity* from which all matter is created and in which all things live, move and have their being. The Romantics called this divine process 'poesis', which is often translated as 'poetry', but really signifies a kind of absolute *productivity* that is aesthetic in essence and unfolds in all the arts; indeed for a natural philosopher like Schelling, it 'stirs in the plants and shines in the light' as an 'unformed and unconscious poetry' of

---

[11] Immanuel Kant, *Critique of Pure Reason* (1781), trans. N. Kemp Smith (New York: St Martin's Press, 1965), 319.   [12] Ibid., 318.

[13] See Schlegel, *Literary Notebooks*, nos. 217, 441, 891, and Rodolphe Gasché's foreword in *Philosophical Fragments*, xxviii.

[14] Friedrich Schlegel, *Ideas*, no. 70, in *Philosophical Fragments*, 100.

[15] Schlegel, *Athenaeum Fragments*, no. 339, in ibid., 69; also see *Athenaeum Fragments*, no. 444 on instrumental music as thought, and *Literary Notebooks*, no. 515 on tone, spirit and character.   [16] Schlegel, *Athenaeum Fragments*, no. 339, in *Philosophical Fragments*, 69.

[17] Schlegel, *Ideas*, nos. 10 and 11, in ibid., 95.

nature.[18] Thus when Ludwig Tieck claims that instrumental music exists in 'a purely poetic world [*reinpoetischen Welt*]',[19] he is speaking of a metaphysical realm of absolute music in which instrumental music is the finest distillation on earth. As pure *poesis*, absolute music is pure productivity. Thus technically speaking, absolute music is not an artefact; it has neither content nor form, but is the *production* that organises content into form, and as such, it becomes what Johann Ritter calls a 'general language',[20] a kind of language of language that is prior to signification and enfolds all meaning.[21] Music not only explains itself, but is the source of all explanation. For Schlegel, it is 'something higher than art', for it is an art that is also the very process of Art itself. It is 'musical inspiration that makes the artist', says Schlegel, because 'each art has musical principles and once it is completed becomes itself music. This applies to philosophy', he adds, 'to poetry, perhaps also to life.'[22] In fact, it seems that to theorise about existence at all is to try to sublate all things into the system of tones.[23] In this way, absolute music was made to usurp God as the unifying explanation of the cosmos. It is both zero and one, origin and totality. 'Music', says Karl Solger, 'is capable of transporting us into the presence of the eternal . . . as it dissolves our sentiments into the unity of the living Idea.'[24]

Music as 'God', however, was not merely an abstract deity in a philosophical system. Its theology was matched by a ritual that embodied the philosophical complexities in sensuous form.[25] Music was given a sacramental presence that had a mesmeric power over the souls of believers. By the turn of the nineteenth century, music was a cult – a real religion, claims Dahlhaus, 'not just a travesty of one'.[26] It was the central ritual of an art religion in which artists functioned as priests that 'exist only in the invisible world'; their task was to mediate the finite and the

---

[18] Friedrich Schlegel, *Dialogue on Poetry and Literary Aphorisms*, 53–4. Schelling seems to be the influence behind Schlegel's lines; see Lacoue-Labarthe and Nancy, *The Literary Absolute*, 92–3.

[19] Wackenroder and Tieck, 'Symphonien', *Werke und Briefe von Wilhelm Heinrich Wackenroder*, 255.

[20] Johann Wilhelm Ritter, *Fragmente aus dem Nachlasse eines jungen Physikes, ein Taschenbuch für Freunde der Natur* (1810), quoted in Charles Rosen, *The Romantic Generation* (Cambridge, MA: Harvard University Press, 1995), 59–60. Also see Bowie, *Aesthetics and Subjectivity*, 175.

[21] See Lacoue-Labarthe and Nancy, *The Literary Absolute*, 91.

[22] Schlegel, *Literary Notebooks*, nos. 1417 and 36.

[23] See Schlegel, *Athenaeum Fragments*, no. 322.

[24] Karl Wilhelm Ferdinand Solger, *Vorlesungen über Ästhetik*, ed. K. W. L. Heyse (Darmstadt, 1969), 341, quoted in Dahlhaus, *The Idea of Absolute Music*, 76.

[25] See Jack Forstman, *A Romantic Triangle: Schleiermacher and Early German Romanticism* (Missoula, MT: Scholars Press, 1977), 23–6.

[26] Dahlhaus, *The Idea of Absolute Music*, 86.

infinite through the production of their work. 'In the beginning, poet and priest were one', writes Novalis.[27] Or as Schlegel says:

The priest as such exists only in the invisible world. In what guise is it possible for him to appear among men? His only purpose on earth will be to transform the finite into the infinite; hence he must be and continue to be, no matter what the name of his profession, an artist.[28]

In Hoffmann's review of Beethoven's Fifth Symphony, for example, a kind of transubstantiation occurs; the musical substance is transformed by the creative act into 'the spirit realm of the infinite'. The symphony divests itself of the 'outer sensual world' and 'all feelings circumscribed by intellect in order to embrace the inexpressible'.[29] Spiritual, ineffable, infinite – the very essence of music was intangible and its vitality beyond representation. The 'spirit realm' is not a substance that can be locked in the score, and neither can it be prised loose by an analysis of the motivic material which Hoffmann engages in to demonstrate Beethoven's 'rational awareness'.[30] It is the *spirit* and not the material that yearns towards the unknown, for what is Romantic about the symphony is not the homogeneous unity of themes, but an invisible poetic process that 'mixes and weaves together extremely heterogeneous components'[31] that can multiply endlessly as it yearns towards the totality that is outside the score, beyond analysis and above the stars as the living Idea. So it is not analysis but *initiation* into instrumental music that gives an intuition of God – 'Spirits reveal themselves only to spirits.'[32] Hence Hoffmann's analysis which attempts to clarify the score is interspersed with a magical language that mystifies the work.[33] In between the technical terms are images of Egyptian initiation rites associated with Isis the goddess of nature, a deity that was the subject of numerous writings at the close of the eighteenth century,[34] including Novalis' unfinished work, *The Disciples of Saïs*. Like these disciples, we are to enter into the sanctuary of Beethoven's instrumental music, says Hoffmann, 'conscious of our own consecration'. Our spirits are to be caught up in the mysteries of a sublime deity as we 'step into the circle of the magical phenomenon', entranced by the 'dance of the priests of

---

[27] Novalis (Friedrich von Hardenberg), *Pollen*, quoted in O'Brien, *Novalis*, 155.

[28] Schlegel, *Ideas*, no. 16, in *Philosophical Fragments*, 95.

[29] Hoffmann, 'Review of Beethoven's Fifth Symphony', 236.   [30] Ibid., 238–9.

[31] Schlegel, *Literary Notebooks*, no. 1565.

[32] Schlegel, *Critical Fragments*, no. 44, in *Philosophical Fragments*, 6.

[33] The ritualistic imagery is more pronounced in the *Kreisleriana* version of the review: see E. T. A. *Hoffmann's Musical Writings*, 96–102.

[34] See Kristin Pfefferkorn, *Novalis: A Romantic's Theory of Language and Poetry* (New Haven: Yale University Press, 1988), 116–48.

Isis'.[35] Through these initiation rites, the instrumental sounds that 'wrap mysterious things in a mysterious language'[36] are made to yield their secrets, as if these rites were the erotic unveiling of the Egyptian goddess as her body is revealed as the naked truth of the absolute. Music is no longer simply a means to God – it has become a god of sorts because the sign no longer points to an outside referent but represents itself as the totality of all meaning and the zero-origin of existence. If at the turn of the nineteenth century, music loses its cult function, it is only because it has itself become cult. If, as Tieck claims, 'music [*die Tonkunst*] is certainly the ultimate secret of faith, the mystery, the completely revealed religion', then it is only because music reveals itself as itself.[37]

So only the initiates of Romanticism who know how to read the signs can unravel the mystery of music. But what does this absolute music really sound like? After all, there is no such thing as *the* absolute symphony which is the centre and circumference of the poetic world; rather, within the universe of absolute music, there is a constellation of symphonies which can only be incarnational glimpses of the divine. Having deified music out of material existence, the Romantics had to redefine how actual earth-bound pieces could capture and reveal the infinite within their finite enclosures. For instrumental music to have any meaning at all, it had to re-order the co-ordinates of real music between zero and one as both an encapsulation and an endless participation in the divine process of pure productivity. But how?

[35] E. T. A. Hoffmann, *Kreisleriana*, no. 4 of the *Fantasiestücke in Callots Manier* (Berlin, 1814–15): the translation is taken from Georgio Pestelli, *The Age of Mozart and Beethoven*, trans. E. Cross (Cambridge: Cambridge University Press, 1984), 291–2.

[36] Wackenroder and Tieck, 'Symphonien', *Phantasien über die Kunst*, in *Werke und Briefe*, 255.　　[37] Ibid., 251.

22

On infinity

A work is not God: to place one on the altar of the absolute would have been rather rash, even for the Romantics who tried to replace the material philosophies of the eighteenth century with a transcendental aesthetic. God is not a symphony or a sonata – that would be blatantly idolatrous: idolatry is usually more sophisticated than that. For music to 'mean God', says Schlegel, 'the whole of music must undoubtedly become one'.[1] There needs to be an in-gathering of all musical works to reconstitute the face of God. And this is a task that is both necessary and impossible if the particularity of each composition is to have any meaning within the Romantic system. Each work, as a fragment of the whole, yearns towards the completion which is Totality. All that music can do on earth is to reflect the divine image as a negative imprint, for a piece of music is precisely what it means – a *piece* that has been broken off from the whole. To borrow an imagery central to Schlegel's philosophy, a work is like an ancient fragment that has been torn from an original form, but is still able to recapture in its brokenness the perfection of an unknown totality that the Romantic imagination can reconstruct, as if it could hear the distant strains of a divine music. A work as a fragment therefore always gestures beyond itself; it is never complete. And yet, Schlegel informs us that fragments are also like hedgehogs – tiny organic totalities that isolate themselves from the world as little balls of spikes that point outwards to protect the autonomous activity within.

A fragment, like a miniature work of art, has to be entirely isolated from the surrounding world and be complete in itself like a hedgehog.[2]

The paradox of instrumental music is that it reflects God as a hedgehog – it is an absolute fragment. A musical work is therefore consigned to a perpetual state of contradiction as both a sign of totality and a sign of incompletion. On the one hand, as Hoffmann's analysis of Beethoven's Fifth Symphony demonstrates, there is a structural unity that closes the work as a motivic organism in the shape of a frightened

---

[1] Schlegel, *Literary Notebooks, 1797–1801*, no. 1737.
[2] Schlegel, *Athenaeum Fragments*, no. 20; the translation is adapted from *Philosophical Fragments*, 45.

hedgehog. Yet on the other hand, the formal completion is scuppered by an ineffable yearning that breaks through the motivic material into some unknown realm towards which the symphony is 'ever becoming and never complete'.[3] Instrumental music encapsulates totality in a nutshell so that it might crack itself open in an infinite movement towards *Totality*.

All this hinges on a music that is able to flicker between zero and one as an infinite movement, while constantly negating any external meaning from entering the music with its spikes of autonomy. The Romantics heard in the hollow of the empty sign a philosophy of the absolute in instrumental music. They did not hear a 'Romantic music', for Romanticism, so they claimed, is not an epoch or a style but an essence that pervades all art that is genuinely Art.[4] What they heard was the poetic yearning of the absolute fragment towards totality in the condition of the vacant sign. So by the time someone like Schumann produced those cyclical, open-ended fragments that emulate Romantic philosophy, it was already too late. In Schumann, Romanticism had become a literary device, a simulation of emptiness, as it were – the condition of the empty sign as semantic structure. When the Schlegels, Novalis, Tieck and Schelling were writing in Jena, Schumann was not even a sperm. What they heard were basically the symphonies of a Stamitz or a Haydn, and they renamed the music as their own. So for Hoffmann, Haydn and Mozart are Romantic composers in retrospect, for they were instrumental composers, writing a music latent with Romantic concepts before the articulation of the new discourse pulled them out as the fundamental categories of the absolute.[5] In fact, after the death of Beethoven, some critics wondered whether Romanticism had worn itself out as the catalyst of musical renewal.[6] So what is known as the 'Classical style' is quintessentially Romantic, precisely because Romanticism is not about a style but a sign.

The Romantics had a very sophisticated way of reading this sign; they employed an aesthetic of violence designed to empty the sign of its content. Barriers were set up only to be dynamically surpassed by the destructive force of the transcendental ego. First, the sign had to be dewormed of any empirical meaning that might be named; matter was dematerialised as spirit, and the body of *Empfindsamkeit* desensitised by

---

[3] Schlegel, *Athenaeum Fragments*, no. 116.

[4] See Schlegel, *Dialogue on Poetry and Literary Aphorisms*, 32.

[5] Hoffmann, 'Review of Beethoven's Fifth Symphony', *E. T. A. Hoffmann's Musical Writings*, 236–8.

[6] See for example Giuseppe Mazzini, *Filosofia della Musica* (1836) in Le Huray and Day, *Music Aesthetics in the Eighteenth and Early-Nineteenth Centuries*, 476–9, and Sanna Pederson, 'Romantic Music under Siege in 1848', in *Music Theory in the Age of Romanticism*, ed. Ian Bent (Cambridge: Cambridge University Press, 1996).

musical abstraction. Then, after 'spiritualising the material',[7] the empty content had to be annihilated by form; 'the secret of the master of any art is this', writes Schiller, 'that he obliterates the stuff through the form',[8] so that the structure, like the sign, is left vacant. But this form is merely a frame to be further dismantled by the terrifying force of the sublime, a power deployed to create such chaos that the mind can no longer order the work into a totality. And it is in this negative condition that instrumental music, even with all its 'Classical' decorum, gives an intuition of God. In effect, the sublime smashes the limits of musical coherence, leaving the empty trace of the infinite in its trail. 'The absolute', writes Novalis, 'can only be recognised negatively.' Indeed, it can only be known as an 'eternal lack'.[9]

The constant draining out of signification is therefore the movement of the sublime in instrumental music; it is this that conjures up the 'unknown realm of the infinite'. Sulzer, of course, had already used the sublime to attach a phallus on to the symphony, but his gendered discourse was also a theological one that guaranteed the moral significance of a work: the sublime stands for the terrifying mystery of an ineffable God. It does this by signifying God negatively through the emptying of meaning – a process of un-naming. The sublime represents God precisely because God has no representation. It exceeds the sign in its attempt to grasp the Idea, and results in a semiotic breakdown that spawns chaos and destruction.[10] The imagination 'recoils upon itself',[11] Kant explains, as reason tries to force the sheer immensity of the sublime into some kind of order, pushing the imagination beyond its limits into a 'negative presentation' of some inaccessible idea which ultimately refers to the image of God – or rather the image of a god that has no image. In fact, Kant describes the power of the sublime as the Mosaic prohibition of making graven images; its moral force is in the continual reiteration of 'Thou shalt not make'; for, as Kant says, it is 'when nothing . . . meets the eye of sense' that the moral law finds its potency as a 'vigorous affection' that thrusts aside all 'sensible barriers' as an abstract 'presentation of the infinite'.[12] In the sublime, the absolute Idea can materialise in aesthetic form.

---

[7] From *Robert Schumann im eigenen Wort*, in Le Huray and Day, *Music Aesthetics in the Eighteenth and Early-Nineteenth Centuries*, 489.

[8] Quoted in W. H. Bruford, *Culture and Society in Classical Weimar 1775–1806* (Cambridge: Cambridge University Press, 1962), 283.

[9] Novalis (Friedrich von Hardenberg), *Schriften*, 2:270, quoted in Bowie, *Aesthetics and Subjectivity*, 77 and 78.

[10] See Thomas Weiskel, *The Romantic Sublime* (Baltimore: The Johns Hopkins University Press, 1976), 21–3. This is also the story of Schoenberg's opera, *Moses and Aaron*: see Adorno, *Quasi una Fantasia*, 225–48, and Philippe Lacoue-Labarthe, *Musica Ficta*, trans. F. McCarren (Stanford: Stanford University Press, 1994), 117–48.

[11] Kant, *Critique of Judgement*, 100.   [12] Ibid., 127.

It was for this reason that instrumental music was hailed as sublime. It is a divine incarnation in negative form. It is as if the constant motivic reiteration of a Beethoven symphony hammers out the refrain:

These empty configurations are the symbols of the namelessness of God. Consequently, it was forbidden to name the meaning of instrumental music lest it became a kind of graven image. 'Music is ineffable', writes Franz Christoph Horn, 'it is not susceptible to pure intellectual perception . . . as soon as it stoops to the servitude of intellectual comprehensibility, it ceases to become music and becomes in effect a parody of itself' – an idol.[13] And yet, of course, music is something that is *made*, even if it conceals itself under the reiterations of 'Thou shalt not make.' By aligning the empty sign with the unnameable name, music transgresses by not breaking the command, for it represents negation as the image of the divine. This is the sophisticated idolatry of Romanticism, which works by positing a deity that it never names. It was a kind of aesthetic demythologisation designed to replace seemingly naïve beliefs in a real, creator God. As Adorno testifies:

The language of music is quite different from the language of intentionality. It contains a theological dimension. What it has to say is simultaneously revealed and concealed. Its Idea is the divine Name which has been given shape. It is a demythologized prayer, rid of efficacious magic. It is the human attempt, doomed as ever, to name the Name, not to communicate meanings.[14]

The aura that has surrounded instrumental music since the nineteenth century is not merely its halo of originality that Walter Benjamin has noticed,[15] but the glow of nameless transcendental substitutes that take shape negatively in a work. Instrumental music 'wrap[s] the most mysterious things in a mysterious language', says Tieck, and Romantic criticism, while trying to unveil the mystery, uses a fantastic, nebulous language to defer forever the disclosure of the Name. Simply step into the imagery of Hoffmann's language to enter this magical realm; he speaks of labyrinthine pathways, exotic flowers, magic spells, flying figures, rings of light, priests of Isis; but this kaleidoscope of images is really the excessive movement of language as it tries to name 'the name-

[13] Franz Christoph Horn, 'Musikalische Fragmente', *Allgemeine musikalische Zeitung* (1802), in Le Huray and Day, *Music Aesthetics*, 273.   [14] Adorno, *Quasi una Fantasia*, 2.
[15] See Walter Benjamin, 'The Work of Art in the Age of Mechanical Reproduction', *Illuminations*, trans. H. Zohn (London: Fontana, 1992).

less haunted yearning' of the sublime.[16] The sublime negation of instrumental music is the plenitude of transcendental meaning.

Beethoven's instrumental music unveils before us the realm of the mighty and immeasurable. Here shining rays of light shoot through the darkness of night and we become aware of giant shadows swaying back and forth, moving ever closer around us and destroying within us all feeling but the pain of infinite yearning, in which every desire, leaping up in sounds of exaltation sinks back and disappears. Only in this pain . . . do we live on as ecstatic visionaries.[17]

What the music unveils before Hoffmann's eyes is negation – transcendental shadows that block out the empirical world without revealing the divine except as eternal emptiness. In this penumbra of Romanticism, a work can only be what Maurice Blanchot calls an 'absent work',[18] of which music as the empty sign is the most absent of works. The work, as it were, annihilates itself in a sublime process in order to prefigure music as the absolute totality that cannot be articulated; all that remains in the destruction is the empty space in which the pain of the infinite takes shape. But it is only in this very hollow that the essence of things is revealed. Novalis writes: 'All words, all concepts are derived from the object . . . they therefore cannot fix the object. Namelessness constitutes its essence – for this reason every word must drive it away. It is non-word, non-concept. How should something make an *echo* which is only a voice?'[19]

The problem for the Romantic critic was how to articulate the sublime without making it ridiculous. To name the unnameable, after all, is a contradiction; but, in fact, contradiction is the only way of naming the sublime. This is one reason why Hoffmann's review sets up an endless oscillation within the hermeneutical circle between structure and meaning, shuttling back and forth in such an immiscible manner that the circle unwittingly turns into a vicious one.[20] On one side of the divide is the technical language of *Anfangssatz, Nebensatz, Schlußsatz, Gegensatz, Zwischensatz*, which tries to justify the rational structure of the work as an organic process articulated by the logic of analysis. But on the other side stands the sublime, which 'in music', says Christian Michaelis, 'is aroused when the imagination is elevated to the plane of the limitless, the immeasurable, the unconquerable'. The sublime forces

---

[16] E. T. A. Hoffmann, 'Beethoven's Instrumental Music', in *E. T. A. Hoffmann's Musical Writings*, 100.   [17] Ibid., 238.

[18] See Blanchot, 'The Athenaeum' and 'The Absence of the Book', *The Infinite Conversation*. Also see Lacoue-Labarthe and Nancy, *The Literary Absolute*, 57.

[19] Novalis, *Schriften*, 2:202, quoted in Bowie, *Aesthetics and Subjectivity*, 76.

[20] See Ian Bent, *Music Analysis in the Nineteenth Century II: Hermeneutic Approaches* (Cambridge: Cambridge University Press, 1989), 4–19, 123–4 and 141–4.

are so overpowering that they 'prevent the integration of one's impressions into a coherent whole'.[21] The analytical language of coherence is simply crushed by the mystical excess of the sublime. For Hoffmann, this is aroused by gestures that either surge beyond the structural limits of the symphony or by punctuations that impede the form as ruptures that shatter the unity of the musical flow. In fact, the very elements of analytical unity are forced into the chaos of the sublime by Hoffmann: the cellular repetitions of the motivic material do not merely bring a technical unity but a sublime infinity that 'maintains the spirit in a state of ineffable longing';[22] similarly, the tonal trajectories articulated by the fermatas that punctuate the movement, exceed their structural functions to evoke 'presentiments of unknown mysteries' (b. 21).[23] However much the motivic and tonal structure seals the movement in its autonomous world, the sublime will always negate the closure and surpass the analytical unity for an absent unity outside the work. There is therefore a constant contradiction in Hoffmann's attempt to merge the Beethoven of the immeasurable sublime with the quantifiable Beethoven of thematic unity. He wants to see a coincidence of the conscious and the unconscious, a conversation between the articulation of the mind and the movement of the spirit, for this is the hope of unity within the aesthetic existence of the Romantic subject. But even if the music achieves this reconciliation, the critical act will always split the unity in its attempt to articulate it. Romantic criticism, like the Romantic ego, is doomed to schizophrenia and its analysis confined in the tower of Babel. The confusion of tongues in Hoffmann's review testifies to the contradiction of the new aesthetic of instrumental music – a contradiction that has plagued musicology in the opposition between technical and figurative methods.[24] In effect, the Romantic discourse forces Hoffmann's essay to be itself a representation of the sublime, setting up an analytical limit of unity for the poetic language to demolish so that the infinite can be gestured to as a kind of negative transcendence. After all, Hoffmann says himself that music's 'only subject matter is infinity'.[25] It just so happens that to present this infinity the subject-matter has to be obliterated.

---

[21] Christian Friedrich Michaelis, *Berlinische musikalische Zeitung*, vol. 1 no. 46 (1805), 179, in Le Huray and Day, *Music Aesthetics*, 290.

[22] E. T. A. Hoffmann, 'Review of Beethoven's Fifth Symphony', 244.   [23] Ibid., 239.

[24] See, for example, Anthony Newcomb, 'Once More "Between Absolute and Program Music": Schumann's Second Symphony', *Nineteenth-Century Music*, vol. 7 no. 3 (1984), and 'Those Images That Yet Fresh Images Beget', *The Journal of Musicology*, vol. 2 (1983).

[25] Hoffmann, 'Beethoven's Instrumental Music', 96.

23

On self-deification

> I was my first cause, I was the cause of myself . . . I was what I
> wished, and what I wished was I. For in this essence of God . . . there
> I was myself and I recognized myself as creator of this man.
>
> (Master Eckhart)[1]

If for Hoffmann instrumental music is an initiation into the inner
sanctum where Isis, the goddess of nature, is to be unveiled, then what
does the naked truth of her body look like? What is the knowledge of
the infinite that only the ineffable sounds of music can articulate but
never name? In an early draft of Novalis' novel, *The Disciples of Saïs*, one
initiate finally reaches the statue and dares to raise the veil of Isis. 'But
what does he see?' writes Novalis. In many accounts of the myth, the
vision of truth blinds and destroys the one who dares to lift the veil with
impure hands,[2] but in Novalis' retelling there is a difference: when the
initiate lifts the veil, he sees – himself. The truth of God is in man.

For the Romantics, the mystical path to knowledge is deep in the
recesses of the ego where Isis, the divinity of nature, is disclosed. Truth
is a matter of self-revelation; the external quest always turns inwards. It
is this introspective movement that is articulated by instrumental
music. In fact, the age of instrumental music, says Hoffmann, is an 'age
striving for inner spirituality'.[3] It is an age that can no longer extend its
arms outwards towards God, but turns in upon itself to discover the
autonomy of an inner spirit that spins out its existence from nothing.
And because 'musical sounds are in themselves spiritual phenomena',
writes Michaelis, entering 'the spirit through the ear',[4] they bring to consciousness the infinity that is within man; and 'every infinite individual
is God', says Schlegel.[5] 'We are able to understand the music of the

---

[1] Quoted in Ernst Benz, *The Mystical Sources of German Romantic Philosophy*, trans. B. R.
Reynolds and E. M. Paul (Allison Park, PA: Pickwick Publications, 1983), 23.

[2] See Pfefferkorn, *Novalis*, 125–6.

[3] E. T. A. Hoffmann, 'Old and New Church Music', *Allgemeine musikalische Zeitung*, vol.
16 (1814), *E. T. A. Hoffmann's Musical Writings*, 373.

[4] Christian Friedrich Michaelis, *Allgemeine musikalische Zeitung*, vol. 9 no. 43 (1806), 675;
translation modified from Le Huray and Day, *Music Aesthetics in the Eighteenth and Early-
Nineteenth Centuries*, 287.

[5] Schlegel, *Athenaeum Fragments*, no. 406, in *Philosophical Fragments*, 82.

Plate 9 Frontispiece to *Alexander von Humboldt und Aimé Bonplands Reise* (1807). Apollo, the Spirit of Music and Poetry, unveils Isis the goddess of Nature.

universe [*die Musik des unendlichen Spielwerks*]', he writes, 'because part of the Poet [the godhead of the earth] . . . lives in us.'[6] Earthly music is therefore a cipher of the divine spirit that also decodes the identity of man. What lies 'behind the haunting sounds of music', explains Hoffmann, is the 'mysterious urge to identify the workings of the animating spirit and to discover our essence'.[7] This is the Gnostic secret that is unveiled in the temple of sound: instrumental music names man as divine, because the divine within man is music; and if music is the poetic force of all arts, it follows that 'every artist is a mediator for all men',[8]

[6] Schlegel, *Dialogue on Poetry and Literary Aphorisms*, 54.
[7] Hoffmann, 'Old and New Church Music', 372.
[8] Schlegel, *Ideas*, no. 44, in *Philosophical Fragments*, 98.

because in the aesthetic, both man and music, like Christ, are fully human and fully divine.[9]

This is why in Romantic philosophy the aesthetic act is one of priestly mediation and not divine creation: God cannot be manufactured. Thus a musical work is not the creation of a deity but an incarnational glimpse of the God within. This means that music as God can only be *discovered* as a process that is already at work. 'The poetic is not so much the work as that which *works*.'[10] It taps into the divine movement between zero and one, and fixes infinity as a fragment of *poesis* – the formative urge of the universe. In fact, in Schelling's transcendental system, this movement is defined as a cosmic *Bildungstrieb* that animates the world.[11] It is the aesthetic that brings this divine process of production into subjective consciousness, affirming the ego 'as an absolute free being' from which a 'whole *world* emerges' – hence 'the philosophy of the Spirit is an aesthetic philosophy'.[12] And music is its 'sacred breath [*heiliger Hauch*]'.[13] In this way, the Romantic subject forms a Trinity with music and the aesthetic to establish a theological order in which music plays the role of the Holy Spirit hovering over a world that needs to be put into form.

A musical work is therefore always a work in progress, and it can only be mobilised towards completion through the symbiotic activity between the work and the subject as aesthetician. So the Romantic critic is born as one who *works* the work; he does not reorganise the piece, but discovers himself in it as a process of formation. This is the initiation rite of instrumental music; the critic abides in a symphony so that he might complete the revelation of music in the critical act itself, and discover his own divinity in the process. He unveils himself as Isis. 'The true critic', writes Schlegel, 'is an author to the second power.'[14] In this way the critical act reanimates the spirit of the artist 'who perceives the divinity within himself' and 'sacrifices himself' to seal the sacred within the work.[15] Thus what Hoffmann attempts to capture in his critique of

---

[9] The idea of a divine I is partly due to the influence of medieval mysticism on German Romantic philosophy; see Benz, *The Mystical Sources of German Romantic Philosophy*, 21–5.

[10] Lacoue-Labarthe and Nancy, *The Literary Absolute*, 48.

[11] See Steigerwald, *Lebenskraft in Reflection*.

[12] *The So Called 'Oldest System Programme of German Idealism'* (1796), translated in Bowie, *Aesthetics and Subjectivity*, 265.

[13] Schlegel, *Dialogue on Poetry and Literary Aphorisms*, 99. Wackenroder and Tieck, in a similar vein, call instrumental music 'der letzte Geisterhauch' in *Phantasien über die Kunst für Freunde der Kunst* (Hamburg, 1799), in *Werke und Briefe von Wilhelm Heinrich Wackenroder*, 190.

[14] Friedrich Schlegel, 'Philosophische Lehrjahre, 1796–1806', in *Kritische Ausgabe*, ed. E. Behler (Munich: Ferdinand Schöningh, 1963), 18:106, quoted in Lacoue-Labarthe and Nancy, *The Literary Absolute*, 117.

[15] Schlegel, *Ideas*, no. 44, in *Philosophical Fragments*, 98.

the Fifth Symphony is the divine spirit of Beethoven himself. To realise an instrumental piece by Beethoven, the critic has to 'enter deeply into his [Beethoven's] being', stepping 'into the circle of the magical phenomena that his powerful spell has evoked'.[16] This assumes that the true performer, as critic, operates the work within a theory that is co-lateral with the music, reconstructing its engenderment and identifying with its godlike production from the zero of its motivic seed. The critic, as it were, inhabits that seed and reanimates the process of generation as his own; he 'lives only in the work', says Hoffmann, and grasps the piece 'as the composer meant it', in a communication of spirit to spirit. It is no longer a matter of resuscitating the composer's feeling (*Empfindung*) but his formation (*Bildung*). Through art, says Schlegel, 'man, in reaching out time and again beyond himself to seek and find the complement of his innermost being in the depths of another, is certain to return to himself'.[17] Hence, the critic's task is simply this:

> that all the wonderful, enchanting pictures and apparitions that the composer has sealed within his work with magic power may be called to active life, shining in a thousand colors, and that they may surround mankind in luminous sparkling circles, and enkindling its imagination, its inner most soul, may bear its rapid flight into the spirit realm of the infinite.[18]

In this symbiotic process, the subject thinks of itself as object; the organic system sealed into the score is the articulation of the ego's own *Bildungstrieb*. As a result, the immutable score is born for the critic to decode. Despite the chaotic and infinite signification of instrumental music, the work can no longer undergo a process of mutation, for sealed in it are divine secrets that are encapsulated as microcosmic reflections of transcendental structures. Because the work is sacred, it is no longer open to improvisation in case the divine revelation is contaminated. Thus spirit is not revealed by interpretation, but only by participation, which will expand the soul, but never the score. Unlike Baroque notation, the score is no longer the site of performance, but locates music outside time and action in an idealised realm where performance is no longer a prerequisite of a work's existence.[19] The score has become the spirit of the composer in the form of an absolute music, and is therefore more perfect than its performance, promising an imaginary music that the performer can only yearn to realise by being faithful to the notation. It is with Hoffmann that the idea of *Werktreue* enters music criticism.[20]

---

16 E. T. A. Hoffmann, *Kreisleriana*, no. 4 of the *Fantasiestücke in Callots Manier* (Berlin, 1814–15): the translation is taken from Pestelli, *The Age of Mozart and Beethoven*, 292.

17 Schlegel, *Dialogue on Poetry and Literary Aphorisms*, 54.

18 Hoffmann, *Kreisleriana*, translated in Pestelli, *The Age of Mozart and Beethoven*, 292.

19 On the meaning of the Baroque score see the chapter in this volume, 'On Style'.

20 On *Werktreue*, see Goehr, *The Imaginary Museum of Musical Works*, 205–86.

But there is a dialectic in the process – Hoffmann's review is not the birth of structuralism. In effect, the symbiosis of the 'subject-work' re-enacts the contradiction of the absolute fragment, in which the work is fixed externally in the score as structure and the subject is forever becoming within itself as spirit; the 'subject-work' constitutes both the unity of the ego and its infinity.[21] This process controls the dialectic of Hoffmann's review: the empty signs of music conjure the sublime as an infinite yearning that is felt as pain *within the subject*, whereas the unity of the motivic structures is analysed as form *within the score*. Thus sign and structure, subject and score, are the divisions that animate the methods of contradiction in Romantic criticism. Consequently, instrumental music seems to oscillate perpetually between an autonomous state and an unfinished one. On the one hand, a melody, for example, has to be 'a self-sufficient totality', says Hegel, in order to mirror 'the free self-sufficient subjectivity' of the ego. In Hegel's aesthetic philosophy, the dialectic of melodic freedom and harmonic logic always resolves in a 'satisfying' reconciliation to affirm the autonomy of the melodic subject.[22] However, for the early Romantics, the *structural* closure is always ruptured by a *semantic* fragmentation created by the annihilation of the semiotic content to leave the form empty and therefore essentially incomplete. In fact, what for Hegel was the failure of instrumental music to objectify reality as concepts, was embraced by Hoffmann as the condition of the self: music as an abstract system of signification, he says, 'opens up an unknown realm to man . . . in which he leaves behind all feelings which are determined by concepts'.[23] The internal polysemy of endless (non)-meaning generated by the vacant signs mimes the longing for the ineffable knowledge of the subject as infinite. Thus the Romantics incorporated the contradiction of the ego as both finite and infinite in their reading of music. Instrumental music reveals the subject as endless, unsignifiable process.

This then is the divine knowledge that the Romantics were searching for: absolute *poesis ex nihilo*. God is that which organises form from nothing, and music is the phenomenon that gives a sublime intuition of the subject as pure *poesis*. The rites of instrumental initiation enable the subject to participate in the story of its own *Bildung*, so that it may know that somewhere deep within its soul is that empty sound of the open fifth which begins Beethoven's Ninth Symphony, hovering like the Spirit of God over an inner chaos; this sound signifies the potential for the subject's self-generation from nothing to the absolute poetry of humanity (see example 25). 'We are all potential, chaotic beings', writes

---

[21] On 'subject-work', see Lacoue-Labarthe and Nancy, *The Literary Absolute*, 55–6, 77 and 112.   [22] Hegel, *Aesthetik*, 3:189–90.

[23] Hoffmann, 'Review of Beethoven's Fifth Symphony'; see Bowie, *Aesthetics and Subjectivity*, 184ff.

Ex. 25 Beethoven, Symphony no. 9 in D minor, Op. 125, first movement – bs 1–4.

Schlegel;[24] the formless tremolos that open Beethoven's Ninth Symphony entice the subject to enter into the shrine of self-knowledge, in order to operate the symphony so that it can discover the potential of its own genesis as a thematic being that will become the free totality of society, where 'All men become brothers,/ Under the sway of [joy's] gentle wings.'[25]

The empty fifths that open the symphony function as a symbol of the 'absent work' which is the primordial-site for the subject to work. They elucidate the meaning of the empty sign: instrumental music has no content because the subject is the content that resides in it through its critical symbiosis. The empty sign is therefore the precondition for the subject's plenitude. The ego surreptitiously enthrones itself in the space made vacant by the draining out of meaning and reorganises the empty signs as a trace of its own divinity. 'Music names the subjective inner self as its content', says Hegel.[26] Indeed, it was only by committing the acts of aesthetic violence against music that the Romantics could demolish a space for the ego to inhabit; the obliteration of content by form and then the shattering of form by the sublime is the continual manipulation of the subject to know itself as infinite. '*Form*', says Schumann, 'is the vessel for spirit';[27] it is an inner teleological structure for the subject to know itself as autonomous and surpass as infinite. Musical *kenosis* becomes the real presence of the subject.

Thus when music actually signifies nothing, its empty sign is finally revealed in all its fullness. The dramatic silences that characterise the 'Classical style' are a way of signifying the ever-present absence of the absolute. This absolute cannot be seen, but it can be heard between

[24] Schlegel, 'Philosophische Lehrjahre', quoted in Lacoue-Labarthe and Nancy, *The Literary Absolute*, 51.

[25] Friedrich Schiller, 'An die Freude', verse 1, set by Beethoven in the finale of the Ninth Symphony.　　[26] Hegel, *Aesthetik*, 158.

[27] Robert Schumann, '"From the Life of an Artist": Fantastic Symphony in Five Movements by Hector Berlioz', *Neue Zeitung für Musik*, vol. 3 (1835), in Bent, *Music Analysis in the Nineteenth Century* II, 171.

Ex. 26 Beethoven, Piano sonata in C minor, Op. 13, first movement –
bs 294–7.

the notes. In Beethoven's *Pathétique* Sonata, for example, musical *kenosis* as subjective presence is notated as a conscious device. Beethoven literally erases strategic gestures from the score, enabling the subject to formulate itself as musical *poesis* (see example 26).

At the close of the first movement, where the slow introduction recurs for the third time, Beethoven removes the powerful downbeats to leave the deafening silence of empty chords. Suddenly, the subject hears its own memory as the missing sounds echo down the corridors of its own being and finds itself sitting in the place left vacant by the composer. The subject recomposes and hears, in the void, itself as creator – as Beethoven, as divine mediator, as the subject-work. The silence catches the subject in the act of its own *poesis*. Within this structure, the empty signs become a mirror for the internal self-display of the ego. So in the sounds of instrumental music, the subject restores to itself the knowledge of its transcendental purpose; it knows itself as an ethical, conscious, free being as it participates in the movement of its own formation. What for Rousseau was the sound of the innate morality of humanity has been transferred from a vocal self-presence to an instrumental self-emptying.

For the Romantics, music was a reality that touched the spirit of man as the *Lebenskraft* of his internal formation. 'The object of music is life', says Schlegel.[28] Having dwelt in Christ, humanity now dwells in music. It is a strange place to inhabit, but in a sense, the subject had nowhere else to go to know itself. And to protect its space, the subject hid itself in the pure autonomy of sound; in instrumental music, man is reified but never named. The sublime prohibition against naming may protect the divine from definition, but it can also conceal a lie that needs to be upheld as truth. Music was made mute so that its real meaning could be silenced. The signs that draw a blank in the pretence of autonomy were meant to proclaim music as absolute, when in fact they were merely a transcendental substitute for an absolute ego that was losing its grip on

---

[28] Schlegel, *Literary Notebooks, 1797–1801*, no. 1469, 151.

reality. In unveiling human divinity in the image of Isis, music actually hides the nothingness that is at the heart of all self-proclaimed auto-genesis. After all, the subject was in a crisis at the turn of the nineteenth century, left in a divided, inaccessible and contradictory state by the Kantian critique. It was the cry of the subject to know itself as divine presence that made it manipulate music into its own image; for in its attempt to manufacture itself from nothing, the subject, like the musical sign, knew itself to be ultimately empty.

24

On invisibility

At the turn of the nineteenth century music became invisible. In fact, the sight of music was so abhorrent to the Romantics that they viciously pulled out the eyes of music so that it would speak with the wisdom of a blind poet. After all, what the Romantics inherited from the aesthetics of *Empfindsamkeit* was far too soiled and silly for the untrammelled movement of transcendental thought. 'The realm of poetry is invisible', they said.[1] So the illustrative potential of music had to be derided as 'something that only a debased and decadent taste can demand of music; taste of the kind', says Schelling, 'that nowadays enjoys the bleating of sheep in Haydn's *Creation*'.[2] A pictorial music was now regarded as embarrassingly naïve, since it claims to know reality as empirical fact.

The new aesthetic was therefore a kind of purifying agent that cleansed the emotional and pictorial representations that the eighteenth century had for so long smeared into the structures of instrumental music to make it mean something. So whereas in the past instrumental music was forced into imitation, now, under the new regime, it disappeared up the hole of its own empty sign. Instrumental pictures, as found in the symphonies of Dittersdorf, for example, was consigned by E. T. A. Hoffmann 'to total oblivion as ridiculous aberrations' to make way for a music that dematerialises into 'the spirit-realm of the infinite'.[3] The sudden invisibility of music was an epistemological move to support the subject's ailing powers to ground itself in the visible world. Music became invisible because the visual objects of knowledge that had structured the empirical thought of the eighteenth century had disappeared in an act of subjective reflection. The first thing to go was the subject itself. The thinking ego of Descartes had become a theoretical vacuum in Kantian philosophy; in its bid for autonomy, the subject became entirely without cause and content, and was inaccessible to knowledge, despite being the first principle of knowledge. The noumenal existence that Kant bestowed upon it turned the ego into an

---

[1] Schlegel, *Dialogue on Poetry and Literary Aphorisms*, 78.

[2] Friedrich Wilhelm Joseph von Schelling, *Philosophie der Kunst* (1802–3), in Le Huray and Day, *Music Aesthetics in the Eighteenth and Early-Nineteenth Centuries*, 279.

[3] Hoffmann, 'Review of Beethoven's Fifth Symphony', *E. T. A. Hoffmann's Musical Writings*, 236–7 and 239.

abstract sign of absence, a logical necessity that accompanied all its representations, but was unable to represent itself to itself. The I in all its sovereignty was simply an empty form. But not only had the subject, along with the soul and its spirit, disappeared from the phenomenal world, but reason and its principles of freedom and morality had gone too; they were, in Kantian terms, supersensible ideas that were out of the reach of empirical intuition. So music, following the subject, was made to empty its content in order to mime the noumenal world of Kantian freedom and morality. The autonomy of music is therefore tied up with the autonomy of the subject, and the aesthetic was a way of bringing them into recognition as brothers of invisibility.

The recognition was basically a self-reflective manoeuvre in which music was somehow able to look into the inaccessible subject. The Kantian subject behaved somewhat like an eye that perceives and synthesises the world according to the unity of its own structures; yet this omnipotent eye cannot see itself. It can only act out its existence, but never know it, for the ego cannot grasp itself as object without undermining its own autonomy as subject. The moment the I is conscious of itself, it divides and alienates itself, so that the unconscious activity that is the essence of the ego recedes asymptotically in the vistas of self-reflection. The impossibility of knowing a self invisible to knowledge literally drove some of the early Romantics mad in their attempt to chase their noumenal tails by finding ways of intuiting the ego.[4] Increasingly, the aesthetic was embraced as a way in which a subject unpresentable to itself could in fact be presented in sensuous form. It was in this context that autonomous music was made to be a kind of self-reflexive eye – a sign, which by reflecting itself, reflects the operations of the subject. Since 'inner consciousness is the form in which music seizes its content', writes Hegel, 'music should not hanker after visual perception [*Anschauung*]'.[5] This is because the ego has no content that can be seen. Art, as Novalis suggests, 'represents the unrepresentable'.[6] So music was made invisible in order to be a transparent representation of non-representability, which is exactly the same as being blind, for blindness is *in*sight – the eye looking into itself. This is the new logic of the musical sign which claims its transparency by being totally opaque.

Contrary to Romantic ideology, the signs of music are not essentially empty – they have to be made so. Music had to be blinded. The problem with instrumental music for so much of the eighteenth century was not its emptiness, but the multiplicity of its meaning that their heterogene-

---

[4] See, for example, Bowie, *Aesthetics and Subjectivity*, 67–72, on Friedrich Hölderlin, and Theodore Ziolkowski, *German Romanticism and its Institutions* (Princeton: Princeton University Press, 1990), 187–217.   [5] Hegel, *Aesthetik*, 3:189–90.
[6] Novalis (Friedrich von Hardenberg), *Schriften*, 3:685.

ous *topoi* produced, and this was compounded by the indeterminacy of meaning that turned the music into a kind of polysemic text that opens out into an endless sea of ideas. Take for example a Mozart piano sonata (see example 27).

The exposition of this opening movement bristles with a multitude of signs, some of which are historically constructed and others more naturally mimetic. Thrown together they can attract or repel each other in a movement of signification that can endlessly multiply referent upon referent. Topic theory tries to control the proliferation of signs by fixing the signifiers into their signifieds, but even then there are a host of contradictory ideas in this piece that can spark off many narrative patterns: song, scholastic counterpoint, horn calls, 'Sturm und Drang', minuet.[7] There is an excess that cannot be adequately presented by a single concept, but this does not mean that the music represents nothing. The issue is not what this sonata means, but *how* it is made to mean something. In the aesthetic of autonomy, these signs are forced to divest themselves of the visibility that the eighteenth century had invested in them, in order to make them opaque, which is also the same as making them transparent to themselves. Like Kant's aesthetic strategy, the sign as a means to a referent is framed as an end in itself, and it is in this state of purposive-purposelessness (*Zweckmäßigkeit ohne Zweck*) that the sign eradicates its own referent to imitate itself. Thus the signs have to be read in a different way: they have to signify their own meaninglessness as meaningful; the minuet is not danced to, the song has no voice, the horn call is on the piano; the topics no longer stand in for reality but are torn out of context to represent their functionlessness and are thrown together to negate each other's meaning so that the *total* meaning is entrusted to a *formal* structure. This is what Schiller calls 'Schein' (appearance, semblance, illusion), a kind of patterned music or arrangement of elements that drain out the particularity of meaning by emptying them as parts that merely connect to a whole. As Schiller says, the artist 'obliterates the stuff through form'.[8] In the condition of 'Schein', to dissect the meaning of music would only render it meaningless as a pile of elements that are merely fragments of the whole; yet to reassemble them can only signify a loss, since the semantic structure has given way to a syntactic relationship – the *spacing* between fragments. In the Romantic theory of language, it is not representation but relation that is significant. It is in the gaps that the Romantics heard the loss of meaning as the condition of yearning, and it is also in the gaps that music finds

---

[7] For an analysis of the topics in this movement, see Wye J. Allanbrook, 'Two Threads in the Labyrinth: Topic and Process in the First Movements of K.332 and K.333', *Convention in Eighteenth- and Nineteenth-Century Music*, ed. W. J. Allanbrook, J. M. Levy and W. P. Mahrt (New York: Pendragon Press, 1992).

[8] Quoted in Bruford, *Culture and Society in Classical Weimar 1775–1806*, 283.

Ex. 27 Mozart, Piano Sonata in F major, K. 332, first movement – bs 1–48.

Ex. 27 *(cont.)*

its meaning as the organic movement between elements that is the formative impulse towards totality. What counts is not the arrangement of say the 'horn call' and the *'Sturm und Drang'* in the Mozart sonata, but the interstice that connects the *topoi* in the juxtaposition. A 'classical' reading of instrumental music sees the elements as *organised form*; a Romantic reading sees the gaps as *organic process*. In fact, the 'Classical style', with its constant contrasts and its exploitation of silences as a structural dynamic, opens itself to the organically disruptive readings of the Romantic ego. Music became invisible because the Romantics only looked at the space around the sign; in fact, they inserted their ego into the gaps as the invisible spirit that connects the parts to the whole. Thus the images of the world dematerialise in the abstractions of the new aesthetic to become a cipher of the absolute. And so, in the *interlinkage* of the whole, the myth of musical invisibility is born in the figure of the pure sign; the purity, however, does not reside in the sign, but in the space or movement between them – the signification of nothing.

In this way, music could be understood as an abstract logic, a kind of invisible system of thought that is the formal impulse in which a work takes shape; and as such, instrumental music began to reflect the operations of the ego. Formerly, when Forkel analysed musical logic, he was only referring to how harmony modified melodic structures to match the sensations of the body;[9] it was a logic of feeling. But with the abstraction of signs, musical logic migrated from the sensations of the body to the inner workings of the thinking ego; it came to represent the logic of the transcendental subject in terms of a pure movement *between* signs. 'Doesn't pure instrumental music have to create its own text?' argues Schlegel, 'And aren't the themes in it developed, reaffirmed, varied and contrasted in the same way as the subject of meditation in a philosophical succession of ideas?'[10] Instrumental music was called 'a music of thought' because it traced the *movement* of the mind before speech.[11] Music is therefore not speech but consciousness itself, and as such, it is a 'general language', says Johann Ritter, 'the first of mankind'; all the languages of the world are merely 'individuations of music' and relate to music 'as the separate organs relate to the organic whole'.[12] In fact, for Friedrich Schleiermacher, music is the productive poesic element of speech itself, a constant movement behind the signifiers that is the free play of thought as it operates the process of formal articulation. Sound thus impresses upon consciousness 'the mobility of human self-consciousness'[13] in the form of musical autonomy. Since the musical component of speech 'consists of nothing but transitions . . . language is capable of directly representing the changeable in spiritual being'.[14] Or to put it the other way around: 'Spirit is like a music of thoughts.'[15] Thus the invisible signs of music were more than a representation of the subject; they were, in a sense, ingrained in the ego's transcendental processes, not merely depicting the I, but presenting it as real presence. The subject's synthesising process has become a musical system; 'the activity and existence of man is tone'.[16] That which accompanies all my representations, to paraphrase Kant, is no longer the subject as an abstract necessity, but a poesic reality. The empty ego knows the fullness of its logical existence as absolute music.

To the extent that harmony, in Novalis' words, is the poetic 'voice of the spirit' and rhythm a method of the ego,[17] the musical process of the

---

[9] See Dahlhaus, *The Idea of Absolute Music*, 104–5.

[10] Schlegel, *Athenaeum Fragments*, no. 444, in *Philosophical Fragments*, 92.

[11] Schlegel, *Literary Notebooks, 1797–1801*, no. 1116, 118.

[12] Johann Wilhelm Ritter, *Fragmente aus dem Nachlasse eines jungen Physikers*, quoted in Rosen, *The Romantic Generation*, 59–60.

[13] Friedrich Schleiermacher, *Vorlesungen über die Ästhetik*, ed. C. Lommatzsch (Berlin, 1974), 395, quoted in Bowie, *Aesthetics and Subjectivity*, 167.

[14] Ibid., 642, quoted in Bowie, *Aesthetics and Subjectivity*, 169.

[15] Schlegel, *Athenaeum Fragments*, no. 339, in *Philosophical Fragments*, 69.

[16] Ritter, *Fragmente aus dem Nachlasse eines jungen Physikers*, quoted in Rosen, *The Romantic Generation*, 59.

[17] See Richard W. Hannah, *The Fichtean Dynamic of Novalis' Poetics* (Bern: Peter Lang, 1981), 144–5.

subject is able to poeticise the empirical world of time and space, divining through the accidents and incidents that seem to befall the subject, an absolute that turns the chaotic into the organic. The musical construction of thought is therefore more than just the activity of the ego within itself; it takes on a cosmological significance as the impulse in which the subject creates a world out of nothing, in order to establish a meaningful universe for its particular existence. Music is the organic movement that is both without and within. So for example, Schelling is able to hear music as 'pure motion . . . borne on invisible, almost spiritual wings', wings that lift it beyond the transcendental subject and into the cosmos to embody the 'aurally perceived rhythm and harmony of the universe itself'. Music returns to the mathematics of the stars, but this cosmos is not the ancient spheres of earlier times, but a world created *for* the subject, which, in its desire to harmonise with a pre-conscious state of nature, tries to relate music as 'a substance counting within the soul'[18] with the abstract calculations of the heavens. Musical logic has become cosmic *logos* in Schelling's *Naturphilosophie*, and the 'starry heavens above' and the 'moral law within' that Kant had left divided at the end of his second critique are united through the invisible logic of pure music.[19]

I said earlier that the Romantics used music as a mathematical solution in the calculation of absolutes, in which music functioned as the absolute go-between for the autonomy of the subject and the totality called 'God'. By making music both 'God', in the sense of pure *poesis*, and the subject, in terms of its operative process, music acted as the '=' that balances both sides of the equation and so empties the tension as a zero-set. Zero, after all, is the condition of the aesthetic for Schiller, and the point at which a new age, under a new God, may be born.[20] It was also a delusion that was entertained as an apparition of truth that might one day make sense of a world to come, no doubt realised by the divine hero of the *Eroica*, riding out to unite a fragmented and frustrated Europe. But at least, for the Romantics, the reality of participating in the infinite movement of instrumental music was a foretaste of a world which their speculative philosophy of music seemed to promise. Through music, the Germans brought the moral subject of Rousseau and the natural order of Rameau into a unified theory that freed the ego from the shackles of divine laws so that humanity might change the world. In these abstract and metaphysical forms, both man and music became like God – invisible and omnipotent. Such divine attributes

[18] Schelling, *Philosophie der Kunst* (1802–3), in Le Huray and Day, *Music Aesthetics*, 280 and 275. Also see the chapter in this volume 'On Disenchantment'.
[19] Kant, *Critique of Practical Reason*, 258–60.
[20] See Eagleton, *Ideology of the Aesthetic*, 108, and the chapter in this volume 'On the Apocalypse'.

were a necessary consequence of grounding the subject in the subject itself with the absence of God as cosmic interpreter. But, of course, man is not God. The impossibility of making any sense of the world from the particularity of one's subjective being, whether in social, moral or political spheres, forced the subject to make an alliance with instrumental music. With music as its universal mirror, the subject could believe itself to be invisible and omnipotent like God, when in reality it was invisible and impotent like the aesthetic.

25

On conscious life-forms

Irony is chemical inspiration.

(Schlegel)[1]

At some point at the very close of the eighteenth century, Alexander von Humboldt stuck a silver rod up his anus and a zinc disc in his mouth and basically electrocuted himself. It was quite an experience, so his 1797 treatise, *Versuche über die gereizte Muskel- und Nervenfaser nebst Vermuthungen über den chemischen Process des Lebens in der Thier- und Pflanzenwelt*, tells us; the shock on his body produced strong convulsions and sensations that included 'pain in the abdomen, increasing activity of the stomach and alteration of the excrement'. Humboldt's idea was to include his entire body in a galvanic chain so that he could experience himself as the object of one of his experiments. Such experiments, which included the galvanisation of his eyes, teeth and tongue, were designed to investigate *Lebenskraft* in terms of what Humboldt called a vital chemistry in which the stimulus of excitable matter produced 'chemical alterations and combination' (*chemische Mischungsveränderung*).[2]

For the early Romantics, chemical activity signified the productive power behind an organic structure. It was life, the very movement of spirit in the sense of a creative, poetic force that unites the parts to the whole; as such it was the physiology of thought itself.[3] But the Romantic circle in Jena, which included Humboldt, knew that this *Lebenskraft* was an elusive force that always evaded analysis. It took shape as an organic form through such complex interactions of chemical processes that it was impossible to pin it down; the vital process, as Humboldt noted, was always in flux, and to complicate matters further, it constantly

[1] Schlegel, *Kritische Schriften und Fragmente* (1794–1818), 5:58.

[2] Alexander von Humboldt, *Versuche über die gereizte Muskel- und Nervenfaser nebst Vermuthungen über den chemischen Process des Lebens in der Thier- und Pflanzenwelt* (Berlin, 1797), quoted in Steigerwald, *Lebenskraft in Reflection*.

[3] As Barbara Stafford notes, Franz Baader in his *Beyträge zur Elementar-Phisiologie* (1797), 'claimed that the chemistry of solvents . . . was closely tied to the genesis of thought . . . Operating chemically, thought arose when representations held in mixed solution were condensed or precipitated.' See Stafford, *Body Criticism*, 433–4.

altered its activity with the external stimulus of the experimenter. Life could only be inferred as a formative impulse from the chemical activity, but to catch it in a static state would merely kill the organism as a dissected specimen. And yet it seemed that life refused to manifest its processes unless the experimenter tampered with it, altering and mutilating the organism in some way, by slicing up a polyp, for example, to see the action of its regeneration. So instead of employing the instrumental reason of the Enlightenment that distances the subject from the object, the Romantics conceived their investigation of life as an active *participation*, even to the point of experimenting on the experimenter. In Humboldt's experiment, for instance, he is both the subject and the object; he is both outside and inside the experiment as the observer and the observed. But not only does Humboldt divide himself, he also attempts to synthesise the subject–object antithesis by reflecting upon the contradictions of this schizophrenic process – he observes himself observing himself as object. So he is not only inside and outside the experiment, he also rises above it in a self-reflexive manoeuvre that detaches him from his own participation in the experimental process. It is this higher synthesis of opposites that initiates the ironic glance of German Romanticism.

Reflection on life always leads to irony because the investigation of the self necessarily involves the endless oscillation between the self as subject and object. Romantic irony is an infinite process, for the subject, in the act of synthesising its own identity, realises its inability to perfect the synthesis and has to incorporate that failure as part of the process of self-knowledge; the synthesis is annulled, but in doing so, the subject creates another consciousness, which looks down on a new synthesis that can only replay the same situation again. And so on, *ad infinitum*. In this infinite movement of irony, the subject comes into a sovereign awareness of its own conscious activity; in this negation of knowledge, the subject redeems its life as a self-creating movement of consciousness and knows itself, in Kant's term, as a transcendental idea. 'An idea', says Schlegel,

is a concept perfected to the point of irony, an absolute synthesis of absolute antithesis, the continual self-creating interchange of two conflicting thoughts.[4]

Evidently, the coherence of the ego can only be grasped ironically as constant contradiction. Like Humboldt's self-experiment, one has to tamper with the ego, dividing it to tease out the signs of life. Since music for the early Romantics is regarded as the life of the ego and the very modality of *Lebenskraft*, its movement is not a blind chemistry, but the self-conscious activity of a subject that knows itself as a living form and

---

[4] Schlegel, *Athenaeum Fragments*, no. 121, in *Philosophical Fragments*, 33.

multiplies itself as contradiction in the attempt to grasp that knowledge. It is within this infinite movement that instrumental music weaves itself as the formative impulse that yearns towards the impossible ideal of perfect synthesis. The Romantics described this tension between the 'real and the ideal'[5] as the interaction between the chemical and the organic; or, to use Humboldt's terminology, life consists of 'Form und Mischung' – a vital communication and constant contradiction between organic structure (*Form*) and chemical mixture (*Mischung*).[6]

'The object of music is life', notes Schlegel,[7] hence the critical activity of Romanticism is akin to a *Lebenskraft* experiment in the laboratory of the aesthetic, where the ego dwells within the life of the musical work; the interaction between the critic and the work gives an ironic intuition of chemical life and organic form. But what exactly is the difference between the chemical and organic in this vital aesthetic of music? Schlegel explains:

Understanding is mechanical, wit is chemical, genius is organic.

This tiny fragment elucidates the nature of aesthetic life-forms: to analyse art is to kill its life as dead mechanism – 'understanding is mechanical'. However, 'wit is chemical': to experience life is to enter its chemistry as a self-experiment in which the subject and object find a chemical affinity that is the process of wit in action; chemical wit is that which synthesises the heterogeneous and chaotic elements as a sudden ironic revelation that lifts the subject into a momentary intuition of organic form. But since wit is an ironic movement, aesthetic life is a perpetual chemical motion that is infinite and can never grasp its final form. Hence, only 'genius is organic', for only the genius is able to discover the organic universe within himself and to deposit its form as art. The moment this happens, however, the ironic disappears in the perfection of the organic. To know the organic is to enter an aesthetic paradise removed from the chemical chaos of the world.

It is precisely this tension between the chemical and the organic that divides the early Romantics as a subset of German Idealism. An

[5] On the 'real and ideal', see Friedrich Wilhelm Joseph von Schelling, *System of Transcendental Idealism* (1800), trans. Peter Heath (Charlottesville: University Press of Virginia, 1978), 38–43 and 49, *Ideas For a Philosophy of Nature* (1797), trans. E. E. Harris and P. Heath (Cambridge: Cambridge University Press, 1988), 49–51, and Ian Biddle, 'F. W. J. Schelling's *Philosophie der Kunst*: An Emergent Semiology of Music', in *Music Theory in the Age of Romanticism*, ed. Ian Bent (Cambridge: Cambridge University Press, 1996).
[6] Humboldt, *Versuche*, quoted in Steigerwald, *Lebenskraft in Reflection*, 39. Schlegel uses the concept of 'Mischung' in his discussions on the novel as a genre. See Schlegel, 'Letter on the Novel', in *Dialogue on Poetry and Literary Aphorisms*; hence Schlegel's comment in his *Literary Notebook*, no. 1359, 'The method of the novel is that of instrumental music.' Also see Cascardi, *The Subject of Modernity*, 110–12.
[7] Schlegel, *Literary Notebooks, 1797–1801*, no. 1496, 151.

Idealist constructs systems that are a perfect synthesis of organic forms and therefore no longer require the infinite movement of ironic chemistry, whereas for the Romantics, life can only be ironic because the organic is Utopian. 'An organic age', writes Schlegel, 'will follow a chemical one.'[8] And for Schlegel, the revolutions of his age are a chemical process of history, dissolving and recombining elements as fragmentary annotations that are only 'brief notes' on an age which is unable 'to draw the profile of the giant'. If one is *inside* the process of history, there is no way of grasping the total form from the *outside*; the chaotic chemical combinations of the Romantic age are simply 'preliminary exercises' that try to catch a glimpse of the organism of history, sporadically bursting through the surface with an ironic glance. Thus it is the task of the Romantic to embrace the infinite contradictions of these exercises as an end in themselves, so that humanity might participate in the chemical aesthetic that constitutes the *Bildungstrieb* of an age to come. Schlegel writes:

Whoever has a sense for the infinite and knows what he wants to do with it sees here the result of eternally separating and uniting powers, conceives of his ideals at least as being chemical, and utters, when he expresses himself decisively, nothing but contradictions. This is the point that the philosophy of our age has reached, but not the philosophy of philosophy . . . a perfect mind could conceive of ideals organically.[9]

The 'Classical style' is a chemical style, born in a chemical age of revolution, indeed born in the age when chemistry itself became a science.[10] Its processes mirror the interaction of 'Form und Mischung' teased out by Humboldt in his work on vital chemistry, for its 'classicism' is always in dissolution, which is why it was known as the 'mixed style'. It was this constant mixture of seemingly immiscible elements from the phrase to the form that divided the critics; its detractors heard a mess of contrasts, whereas its admirers heard in the chaos a unifying force behind its chemistry, an internal impulse that is the dynamic cause and final form of the heterogeneity. The mixed style lives or dies according to the definition of its form; it is dead as long as the form is thought of as a mechanical unity of identity and uniformity, but alive if the form is inferred from a chemical impulse that both generates and encapsulates the structure as constant process and ironic contradiction. For example, here is the opening phrase of Mozart's *Jupiter* Symphony (see example 28).

It is a mixture; the learned style and *opera buffa* are forced to co-exist

---

[8] Schlegel, *Athenaeum Fragments*, no. 426, in *Philosophical Fragments*, 87.

[9] Ibid., no. 412, in *Philosophical Fragments*, 83.

[10] On the birth of modern chemistry, see Hankin, *Science and the Enlightenment*, 81–112.

Ex. 28 Mozart, Symphony no. 41 in C major, K. 551, finale – bs 1–8.

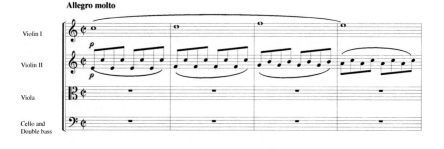

in a juxtaposition of the sacred and secular; contrapuntal law is forced to make comic conversation.[11] This contradiction is the basis for an ironic movement that annihilates any simple conceptualisation of meaning, creating a process of infinite synthesising. But this cannot be disclosed by a mechanical dissection of a phrase which merely splays out the notes on the page of analysis to exhibit the patterns of harmonic, motivic and textural identity. An analysis that controls the object with an instrumental reason always produces an anatomy of music that alienates the critic: 'The drive to organization', says Novalis, 'is the drive to turn everything into instrumental means.'[12] What the Romantic ego wants, however, is not a clinical analysis but a dissolution of itself into the chemistry of sound, resulting in a *confusion* of object and subject as the ego flickers in and out of the work. In the symphony, the Romantic ego can experience itself as an experiment of *Lebenskraft*; he

[11] The opening four notes are derived from Gregorian chant and were used by Mozart in a *Missa Brevis* (K. 192) to the words 'Credo, credo'. For further information, see Neal Zaslaw, *Mozart's Symphonies: Context, Performance Practice, Reception* (Oxford: Clarendon Press, 1989), 537–44.

[12] Novalis (Friedrich von Hardenberg), 'Über Goethe' (1798), no. [464], translated in Wheeler, *German Aesthetic and Literary Criticism*, 106.

'lives in the work',[13] as E. T. A. Hoffmann puts it, not as the passive body of *Empfindsamkeit* that merely vibrates with each tingle, but as a self-conscious being that deliberately waits to divide itself from the process in an act of ironic alienation. Thus the alienation that is always necessary to grasp the form from the outside is no longer instrumental but ironic. The Romantic ego does not need to organise the symphony from the outside, but can simply reside in the mixture as it awaits its own ironic resurrection. Mozart's little phrase can spawn a play of difference and plurality with all its titillating twists and turns because there might be a sudden eruption of wit in the mixture that will provide a momentary flash of unity. It will not divulge the entire form, but it will give a glimmer of the form in process. The mixture of the opening phrase is a promise to reveal the secrets of the symphony's vital chemistry.

But what is this chemical wit that resides in music? For a start it is not *in* music: it *is* music. The pure play of signs in instrumental music was considered by the Romantics as the very grammar of ironic wit. Music could combine the most incompatible elements into a play of resemblances that could reveal the chemical activity of life in process. Music was the joker in language; it functioned as a capricious spirit that made unexpected affinities between words, messing up the attempts to make meaning for an autonomy of play. 'Wordplays are something very social', notes Schlegel, 'conversations up to irony. Wordplays are a logical and grammatical music in which there must be fugues, fantasias and sonatas.'[14] Musical logic is therefore an ironic movement for Schlegel, hovering over words as giant inverted commas that suspend the truth of representation to trip up language in its attempt to say something determined. Music's autonomy is not in its formal construction, but is an internal activity that remains hidden until an unexpected affinity bubbles to the surface of consciousness as an ironic revelation. This is what Novalis means by the 'musical spirit' in language; it is an autonomous 'fingering' of sound in the 'inward ear' to which one surrenders in order to speak prophetically.

[P]roper conversation is mere word game . . . Nobody is aware of the most peculiar property of language, namely, that it is concerned only with itself. Because of this, language is such a wonderful and fruitful secret that when someone merely speaks in order to speak, he utters just the most glorious, most original truths. But when he means to speak about something specific, capricious language lets him say the most ridiculous and perverse stuff.[15]

---

[13] E. T. A. Hoffmann, *Kreisleriana*, no. 4 of the *Fantasiestücke in Callots Manier* (Berlin, 1814–15); the translation is taken from Pestelli, *The Age of Mozart and Beethoven*, 292.

[14] Schlegel, *Literary Notebooks*, no. 1144, 121

[15] Novalis (Friedrich von Hardenberg), 'Monolog', *Schriften*, 2:672–3; the translation is taken from Pfefferkorn, *Novalis*, 63.

As the very grammar of wordplay, music is not an occasional play of wit. The stock witticisms of the 'Classical style', with its false recapitulations, surprise crashes and deferrals of closure, are merely sporadic pranks in a music that is ironic throughout in its chemical make-up.[16] And this need not be peculiar or even particularly funny, as if a few jokes would galvanise the musical organism into giggles. Rather, wit is a process that functions as a kind of motivic development which is concerned with the mixing of disparate elements, dissolving and combining them in a perverse logic that can align the sacred and secular in a single ironic smile. This is the opening pose in the finale of the *Jupiter* Symphony. In fact, this movement, as with many 'Classical' structures, is not concerned so much with thematic unity as with the disintegration, contradiction and realignment of themes. The movement is made up of tiny detachable fragments that are forced into a chemical play of form and mixture which throws up all kinds of contrapuntal and thematic affinities. Not only are the fragments broken down in the process, but they are disfigured and warped by harmonic progressions that seem to pull the structure out of shape.

Clearly, the music is not developing blindly, but struggles with its own processes in order to catch a momentary glimpse of itself as organic. It does not merely want to function: it wants to know how it functions, just like the new language of chemistry that Lavoisier had formulated in the 1780s: the musical compounds need to describe their own process of composition in the same way as water is H_2O. Thus in the coda, the contrapuntal apotheosis that ingeniously intertwines the disparate fragments into a single texture is a self-reflexive move that reveals the chemical make-up of the movement; the music comes into a contrapuntal self-consciousness; it suddenly knows itself as the intellectual force that activates the structure of the work. But this moment of self-knowledge is a textural disruption of such density and contrapuntal ingenuity that it cannot merge into the form but divides itself almost as a detached commentary. The revelation is not the teleological goal of a symphony working out its material, as if this were an ineluctable organic process; it is more a play of wit that side-steps the coherence of the form to give an inkling of the absolute behind the clever connections of chemical affinity. Irony reveals the spirit that is the source and sublation of the heterogeneity, rather than the mechanical unity of the material itself. Thus unity is not inherent *in* the work as an objective formula, but is disclosed by the work as an intellectual stance that is an

---

[16] On Beethoven's penchant for wordplay and its musical consequences, see William Kinderman, 'Beethoven's High Comic Style in Piano Sonatas of the 1790s, or Beethoven, Uncle Toby, and the "Muckcart-driver"', *Beethoven Forum 5*, ed. C. Reynolds, L. Lockwood and J. Webster (Lincoln: University of Nebraska Press, 1996).

Ex. 29 Mozart, Symphony no. 41, K. 551, finale – bs 158–64: motif *a* and motif *b*.

ironic glance thrown back over the structure. 'Wit', writes Schlegel, 'is already a beginning towards universal music.'[17]

Thus chemical wit is not the wordplay itself (material) but that which plays with words (spirit) – the vital force that is caught by the web of irony. In the chemical mixture of the *Jupiter* Symphony, the Romantic ego works the material to stumble upon an all-knowing smile that will suddenly detach itself from the process to give an intuition of the form. It is a sudden lightness of being that inverts the fear of the sublime into the smile of serendipity. The ironic smile that curves over the antithesis of the first phrase of the finale therefore initiates an infinite movement that constantly tries to outwit itself as it glances back over the structure. This process of structural consciousness is particularly evident at the point of recapitulation. For a start, it is in the wrong place – it is simply too early. Mozart truncates the development, and he makes this obvious by suddenly blocking the harmonic and motivic momentum that had been pushing the development section forward with considerable violence. This violence is one of chemical chaos, made up of two fragments taken from the first group which are juxtaposed together – the initial motto (*a*) and the scalic motif (*b*) that asserts itself with a military precision (see example 29).

Because both fragments are harmonised as antecedent structures, they propel the music towards a closure that is constantly denied as they push from one dominant to another around the cycle of fifths. At first it is only the military motif (*b*) in canon with itself, that spirals flatwards from A minor to F major. Then the whole process reverses itself, employing both fragments to retrace the harmonic steps, only to overstep its A minor origin into a sharpward move towards E (see example 30). And just to make it clear, Mozart inverts motif (*b*) to signal the point of harmonic reversal.

Thus the harmonic arch is destabilised as the music insists on lingering for some ten bars on the dominant of E minor, as if it were some kind of false preparation for some trick reprise.[18] What cannot happen is a

---

[17] Schlegel, *Literary Notebooks, 1797–1801*, no. 2012.
[18] This harmonic strategy is not an uncommon procedure; see, for example, Haydn, String Quartet in C major, Op. 76, No. 3, first movement, bars 65–79.

Ex. 30 Mozart, K. 551, finale: harmonic structure of the development section.

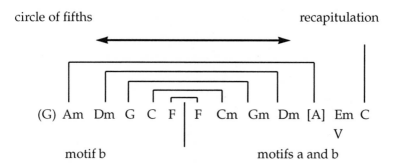

tonic recapitulation (C major), despite the syntactical gestures towards a reprise of some kind. And besides, the timing is askew; the development has not run its course. But here lies the double bluff: the recapitulation does happen – as if by magic.

At the centre of the movement, Mozart sets up a slippage between form and content. And it is precisely this gap between structural closure and harmonic function that is bridged by the smile of irony. What happens at the moment of antithesis is a negative resolution achieved by wit and not by some form of analytical logic (see example 31). Just before the recapitulation (b. 219), Mozart unfolds a diminished chord as a dissonant reinforcement of E minor, but the opening motto (*a*), which has already been transformed by the development section into semitonal shapes, appears in the bass as a chromatic line that magically alters the tonal function; the harmonic activity is purely chemical, turning the diminished chord into new compounds with each semitonal step. In fact, the progression seems to have lost some of its logical calculations in the deft movement of the chemical connections. And, appropriately, it is the chemical affinity between the two antagonistic fragments (*a* and *b*) that conjures up the harmonic transformation, and eventually turns the antecedent aggression of the military motif into a consequent phrase that slips softly into the recapitulation with an ironic smile that resolves the structure as sheer serendipity.

In a space of just six bars, the movement untwists itself into the recapitulation in the face of this very impossibility. It is not an ineluctable progression, but a sudden revelation. The music rises above its chemical activity; this ironic consciousness is not *in* the music but hovers above it as a kind of critical self-commentary that detaches itself from the process to annotate its own structural antagonisms. And because the wit arises contingently out of the developmental chaos, the form and

207

Ex. 31 Mozart, Symphony no. 41 in C major, K. 551, finale – the recapitulation.

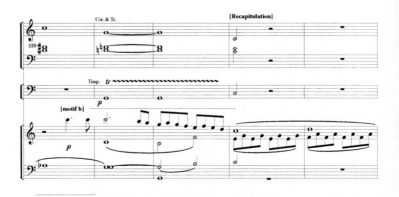

function are reconciled without really resolving the process of development. The development is not worked out with a mechanical appetency, it is simply erased by a turn of wit. The unexpected resolution is paradoxically a disruption of the formal procedures; but that is the way of irony – it annihilates the structure to reveal the *Lebenskraft* that unites the chaotic activity of its vital chemistry. The music at the point of recapitulation is given an all-knowing glance that assures its consciousness of the organic process of its own formation (*Bildung*). As Karl Solger says concerning irony:

the spirit of the artist must unite in one single glance all the tendencies of his work, and this glance, hovering over the whole and yet also cancelling out everything, this glance we call irony. The entire being and essence of art is resolved in irony.[19]

[19] Karl Solger, *Erwin. Vier Gespräche über das Schöne und die Kunst* (1816), 387, quoted in Wheeler, *German Aesthetic and Literary Criticism*, 23 and 146.

26

On artificiality

> Irony . . . can see where God is to be found in a world abandoned by
> God . . . [It] is the highest freedom that can be achieved in a world
> without God. (Lukács)[1]

Irony, I suggest, is the distinguishing feature of the 'Classical style'. But
what Charles Rosen calls the 'Classical style' is problematically just the
music of Haydn, Mozart and Beethoven.[2] Can these three composers
legitimately represent the period? For the 'Classical style' itself, as a cat-
egorisation of the whole period, is not specifically ironic. Perhaps the
three composers should be thought of in terms of a difference in style as
opposed to their colonisation of the entire epoch. They are not the sole
exponents of the 'Classical style'; rather the Classical language, which
takes its vocabulary from Italian opera and *style galant*, is merely a historical texture from which the three composers try to disentangle themselves. Hence Johann Reichardt could call them 'the three pure
humorists'.[3] The chemistry of their music is ironic activity, and this is
the distinctive mark of a style that has been anachronistically and erro-
neously named as 'Classical'.[4]

If 'Classical' forms – most notably sonata forms – are to be modelled
on Haydn, then irony is their definition. His forms are not organic structures, but structures that try to *see themselves* as organic. There is a perpetual tampering of the music's biology to bring the forms into
self-reflection. In this sense, the 'Classical style' is a musical embodiment of Kant's *Critique of Judgement*, for its structures focus on the
contradiction within themselves as subject and object; this is the necessary condition of self-knowledge, the primary division of *Ur-teil* (judgement) that caused the Romantic ego to tumble down the asymptotic pit

---

[1] Georg Lukács, *The Theory of the Novel*, trans. A. Bostock (Cambridge, MA: MIT Press,
1994), 92–3.   [2] See Rosen, *The Classical Style*, and *Sonata Forms*.
[3] Johann Reichardt, *Vertraute Briefe geschrieben auf einer Reise nach Wien . . . 1808/9*
(Amsterdam, 1810), 1:231, quoted in Gretchen A. Wheelock, *Haydn's Ingenious Jesting
with Art* (New York: Schirmer, 1992), 50–1.
[4] See Webster, *Haydn's 'Farewell' Symphony and the Idea of Classical Style*, 347–57.
Unfortunately, because there is no alternative label in the current discourse, I shall use
the term Classical style to refer to the style of Haydn, Mozart and Beethoven.

of ironic reflection. Because of this fissure, Haydn's forms never coincide with themselves; they always explore an ironic gap in their constant preoccupation with their own dislocated structures. In fact, this self-referential manipulation of form is a sign of their autonomy. But this autonomy is not the kind of self-regulating system that is often associated with the 'Classical style'. After all, Baroque forms also enclose themselves within their own tonal and thematic constructs; a binary or a ritornello structure is no less dynamic in its harmonic processes and no less symmetrical in its formal design than a sonata form movement – a form, in fact, which owes its processes to these Baroque designs. What distinguishes the sonata processes of Haydn – and, indeed, of Mozart and Beethoven – is that they assert their autonomy by subverting it; they seek to destroy a blind autonomy for an ironic one, and so come into self-consciousness as an anti-aesthetic that demythologises its own existence. Sonata-type forms are more a way of thought than a method of construction. When, for example, the rondo finale of Haydn's 'Joke' Quartet, Op. 33 No. 2, fails to finalise the work with its abortive gestures of closure, the form negates itself to know itself as an aesthetic illusion. The smile of self-knowledge that hangs in the air after the quartet has disappeared is that ironic lightness of being that happily destroys the aesthetic autonomy for the knowledge of its own sovereignty. But, of course, this ironic consciousness is yet another aesthetic illusion that must be negated in an infinite regression that mimics the trail of concluding phrases that defer the quartet's completion.

Perhaps this quartet is almost too obvious an example of the ironic mismatching of gesture and function in the works of the three composers, but it underlines a principle that is a general procedure of the style. Thus the Classical notion of sonata form as a perfect structure in which form and content are inextricably bound is simply erroneous. Sonata form discovers its identity in the slippage between its external and internal procedures. This means that there is no sonata form that is *in* 'sonata form'. A classically perfect sonata form is a contradiction, because the very essence of sonata form is contradiction itself. Its ironic consciousness demands that it simultaneously insists on and resists all definitions of its form. Sonata form is only perfect in the Schlegelian sense – perfect to the 'point of irony', that is to the point of imperfection[5] – which means that it is an analytical trap waiting to snap up the innocent theorist. Not everyone will get it, which is why sonata form lives in a confusion of analytical concepts. On the one hand, it refuses the formulaic definitions that seem to work for binary, ternary and ritornello forms. It constantly disrupts its form so that any 'textbook' definition of it will simply miss the point. In fact, Rosen claims that to define sonata form is to kill it.

[5] See Ernst Behler, *Irony and the Discourse of Modernity* (Seattle: University of Washington Press, 1990), 84.

Sonata form could not be defined until it was dead. Czerny claimed with pride around 1840 that he was the first to describe it, but then it was already part of history.[6]

But on the other hand, not to define sonata form is to be left with some amorphous organism that ultimately denies its own species. Any similarity between pieces becomes a matter of feeling, sensibility or practice – some kind of nebulous spirit that organises the form from the inside. But this will not work. Sonata form not only refuses prescriptive definitions, but confuses any attempt to deduce its structure internally. The rejection of an external mould in favour of a microscopic investigation of what James Webster would call a 'through-composed' work that arises from the particularity of its own configurations is also spurious. After all, the sonata forms of Haydn, Mozart and Beethoven are suspiciously similar. In fact, the concept of sonata form asserts itself as a norm; it is a measure for all kinds of structural deviations in the music of the nineteenth and twentieth centuries. Consequently, it can only be described as a normative principle that refuses normal definition. If, for example, 'the development and recapitulation [can] exchange roles' in the first movement of Haydn's Symphony No. 89, then the form is not going through the motions mechanically, but is self-consciously manipulating itself against the norms it sets up.[7] Similarly, the 'off-key' ambiguity that initiates the B minor Quartet, Op. 33 No. 1, and the submediant 'dominant preparation' that heralds the recapitulation in the opening movement of the E major Quartet, Op. 54 No. 3, are designed to create an ironic coherence where there is a formal contradiction. These disruptions become the focus of formal consciousness.

So, like the Fichtean ego that only knows itself in the act of philosophising, the text of sonata form constantly interferes with its own coherence to render the system ironically infinite in its conscious attempt to grasp its own identity as a compositional act. *Sonata form has to catch itself out as form.* Hence sonata form is *not a form*, in that any external definition of its structure will destroy its essence as consciousness. And yet sonata form *has to be a form* in that its consciousness is only signified by its constant negation of the structure it posits. Sonata form is therefore the double activity of indicating and subverting its structure in an ironic attempt to synthesise the universal and the particular – the dichotomy of subject and object, content and form. In Romantic fashion, it strives towards a reconciliation that it knows to be impossible and at best illusory.

By *never* conforming to the structure that it *always* posits, sonata form is able to indicate its own theory of form and to surpass it as a theory beyond theory so that its definition neither resides in the actual non-

[6] Rosen, *The Classical Style*, 30.   [7] Ibid., 157.

conformity nor its virtual formality, but in the gap of negation. 'It is equally fatal', says Schlegel, 'for the mind to have a system and to have none. One will simply have to decide to combine the two.'[8] This is what sonata form does; it is in this space of contradiction that an intellectual unity embraces the work within the giant inverted commas of ironic distance. Sonata form therefore asserts its autonomy in the sovereign knowledge of its own illusions – a mere manipulation of empty signs – and so redeems from nothing its conscious life.

Irony, of course, existed long before the Romantics brought it into their peculiar philosophical focus. Practice precedes theory, and this also applies to the Romantic discourse on music. Haydn's instrumental forms perhaps prepared the path for a Romantic philosophy of music. As Mark Evan Bonds points out, by the 1780s Haydn's music was consistently being compared to the novels of Laurence Sterne,[9] whose ironic pose was openly adopted by the German Romantics.[10] Sterne's *Tristram Shandy* and *A Sentimental Journey* are not really novels but ironic commentaries on the aesthetic process of creating and consuming novels. And Haydn's works follow the same stance of authorial self-consciousness. An anonymous critic in the *Musikalischer Almanach auf das Jahr 1782* compared Haydn to Sterne, calling him 'a musical joker of the high comic; and this is dreadfully difficult in music', he adds. 'It is for this reason that so few people sense that Haydn is making a joke, even when he is making one.' Haydn has 'two different styles', he claims: 'in the works of the earlier period, Haydn often laughed wholeheartedly; in the works of the second period, he contracts his visage into a smile'.[11]

This smile, so the critic claims, seems difficult to manufacture in sound, but instrumental music, with its alienated signs, is perhaps the purest vehicle for the wry curve of ironic distance. Its signs are so far removed from reality that they can only simulate things as illusion. This is perhaps the greatest achievement of Haydn: he was the first to glory in the sheer artificiality of instrumental music. If instrumental music for Rousseau was an art distanced from the origin of humanity and therefore divorced from nature,[12] then Haydn merely affirms this as fact, channelling his creative powers to ironise nature and to destroy all naïve delusions of Eden. In the hands of Haydn, art is no longer artless

---

[8] Friedrich Schlegel, *Lucinde and the Fragments*, trans. P. Firchow (Minneapolis: University of Minnesota Press, 1971), 167.

[9] See Mark Evan Bonds, 'Haydn, Laurence Sterne, and the Origins of Musical Irony', *Journal of the American Musicological Society*, vol. 44 no. 1 (1991).

[10] See, for example, Schlegel, *Dialogue on Poetry and Literary Aphorisms*, 95–7.

[11] Quoted in Bonds, 'Haydn, Laurence Sterne', 59.

[12] See Rousseau, *Essai sur l'origine des langues* (1764) in *The First and Second Discourses Together with the Replies to Critics and Essay on the Origin of Languages*.

nature but the artificial simulation of it. For the first time in its history, instrumental music becomes truly instrumental – a tool. It was used as an implement for a perpetual manipulation of the distance between the subject and its object of contemplation. Haydn's instrumental forms were designed to prevent the unmediated absorption of the subject into the piece, so that the body of *Empfindsamkeit* could no longer vibrate with the natural laws of music. However much the body wants to discover its innate morality through the sensations of sound, Haydn's music turns around and says 'I am art – a mere illusion. See, here are the hands of the composer.' Almost every element comes under the ironic scrutiny of Haydn; he robs music of what Schiller would define as the naïve – the unreflective state of nature which modern man, divided in himself and with the world, can no longer return to.[13] The music needs to objectify this division by interfering with the alignment of sign and referent, so that, like a *Lebenskraft* experiment, conscious life can be squeezed out from sound. Thus Haydn writes against the objects he posits; his minuets are 'anti-minuets' says Hans Keller, a deliberately artificial simulation of the real thing;[14] his evocations of bucolic drones and folk tunes are quirky, decontextualised objects that dispossess nature of its innocence; his sonata forms are not in sonata form but find their consciousness in the gap of negation. Semiotics for Haydn is not a means of making meaning but of destabilising representation, whether it involves mimetic signs or internal cross-references in the structure. He simply throws out an A♭ major brick in a C major quartet to force the audience out of an Arcadia of natural complacency, making them think twice before falling back into an uncritical mode of thought (see example 32). So offended was Daniel Gottlob Türk by this harmonic disjunction that he rebuked Haydn in an otherwise favourable review of the Op. 54 Quartets for damaging the tonal unity of the work with a seeming disregard for aesthetic principles. Türk, in his fixation with structural order, just couldn't get it.[15] The A♭ major brick shatters the aesthetic illusion to reveal the hand that is manipulating the act of aesthetic consciousness. Haydn's humour, says Jean Paul Richter, can 'annihilate entire key areas' as a kind of pre-emptive strike that negates the form, to bring the process of composition into ironic knowledge.[16] In fact, to emphasise the awkwardness of this A♭ intrusion, Haydn

---

[13] See Schiller, *On the Naïve and Sentimental in Literature*.

[14] Hans Keller, *The Great Haydn Quartets* (London: Dent, 1986), 237. See also Wheelock, *Haydn's Ingenious Jesting with Art*, 55–89.

[15] See Daniel Gottlob Türk's review of Haydn's Op. 54 Quartets in *Allgemeine deutsche Bibliothek*, vol. 61 no. 1 (1792), 121–2, as discussed in Morrow, *German Music Criticism in the Late Eighteenth Century*, 143–9.

[16] Jean Paul Richter, *Vorlesungen über Aesthetik* (1804), quoted in Bonds, 'Haydn, Laurence Sterne', 63.

Ex. 32 Haydn, String Quartet in C major, Op. 54 No. 2, first
movement – bs 1–25.

Ex. 32 *(cont.)*

cancels it out with a quick cadential shuffle that leaves the phrase lop-sided and somewhat disorientating. Of course, there is nothing new about the flattened submediant; there is a sizeable chunk of it in Op. 20 No. 2, where it is used as a cadential device to articulate the end of various sections of the opening movement. But Haydn, in Op. 54 No. 2, cannot leave this innocent cadential cliché alone. He has to invert its function, elongating it like some overblown full-stop in mid-sentence so that it deliberately makes a mess of the cadence. The flattened submediant is therefore forced to initiate a movement of formal self-consciousness that is not 'resolved' until the very end of the movement where the inflated cadence of the opening turns into a correspondingly massive block of A♭ major, placed where it should be – at the close and as a structural cadence (bs 195ff). These thirty bars of cadential gesture at the close elucidate the contradiction of sign and function that had dislocated the opening of the work. Thus Haydn manufactures a disruptive logic of chemical wit that explains the disjunctions and gives a revelation of an organic intelligence behind the quartet. It is an ironic rather than syntactic coherence.

And all this is sparked off by only the third phrase of a quartet that is a catalogue of quirks, with its mischievous gaps, harmonic fissures, asymmetrical structures and stark juxtapositions. It is calculated to force the aesthetic subject to flicker in and out of the work in endless contradictions. Take for example the bubble of jollity that bursts into the finale to destabilise the entire structure of the work. For a start, the finale is an Adagio. It pretends to be an enlarged slow introduction, but the long awaited arrival of the Presto is contradicted by its own brevity, and the return of the slow tempo simply confirms the perverse structure of a movement that jars against itself as an immiscible and inexplicable form. It would have been at least amusing if it were not for the deadly seriousness with which the Adagio returns – as if nothing had happened. The entire movement is a web of contradiction, made all the more peculiar by the ironic composure of a composer who stands benignly at a distance to manipulate his audience.

If, in the hands of Haydn, instrumental music makes a defiant stand against the voice of nature as pure artificiality, then it does so as 'an expression of disdain for the world'. That, at least, is Jean Paul Richter's insight into Haydn's humour.[17] This disdain does not arise from a hatred of nature; rather the infinite longing of Romantic irony comes from the knowledge that nature has been lost forever. Instrumental music signals the recognition of reality as a radical alienation, so clearly articulated in Schiller's aesthetics as a division between man and nature, reason and sense, duty and desire, freedom and necessity. It is the function of art, he claims, not only to recognise the division, but to strive to heal it, *without* returning to a naïve state of nature. In German aesthetics, culture becomes nature not by reviving the garden of innocence, but by manufacturing nature through an artificial paradise, cultivated by the fruit of knowledge. Art as artificiality reunites humanity this side of Eden, which is why Kant claims that a naïve art is a contradiction in terms.[18] Any false reconciliation of the aesthetic has to be recognised as illusion not reality. Thus a Utopian aesthetic in a music that seems to pursue happiness can only be expressed ironically; instrumental music registers the impossibility of manufacturing a second nature even in the very attempt to do so. The 'Classical style' simply knows too much. If you hear only happiness in Haydn, then the joke is on you.

The Romantics wanted to know the truth even if the truth is the knowledge that one can never arrive at the truth. Hence they read instrumental music ironically, teasing out its *Lebenskraft* in an attempt to overcome the failure of God after the Lisbon earthquake and the failure of humanity after the French Revolution.[19] The unexpected affinities and connections between irony, chemistry, music and philosophy were meant to produce a brave face which could confront the terrifying contradictions bequeathed to the Romantics by the Enlightenment with an aesthetic smile.[20] In this way, the empty sign captures the complex condition of secular humanity, and instrumental music is finally recognised as modern, in the sense of a de-Christianised commodity that dares to dance near the brink of nihilism in an attempt at ironic transcen-

---

[17] Ibid. [18] Kant, *Critique of Judgement*, 203.

[19] See Lukács, *The Theory of the Novel*, 84–93, and the chapter 'On the Apocalypse' in this volume.

[20] Both irony and the sublime are negative aesthetic categories which the early Romantics connected with instrumental music in order to express the condition of modernity. The difference between the ironic and the sublime depends on which way the curve of the mouth turns; hence Jean Paul Richter describes ironic humour as a kind of 'inverted sublime'; see his *Vorlesungen über Aesthetik*, in Wheeler, *German Aesthetic and Literary Criticism*, 174.

Ex. 33 Beethoven, Quartet in B♭ major, Op. 130, fourth movement –
bs 129–36.

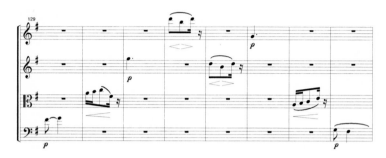

dence. The music, after all, was known at the time as the modern style.
In a sense, new music begins here in the Romantics' recognition of
instrumental forms that deliberately replay the consciousness of modernity.[21] So music became a specimen for the experiments of the chemical age, an age that would deliberately mutilate art to know the
contradictions of its own *Bildungstrieb*. The dismemberment began with
Haydn and was passed on to Beethoven who could quite happily cut up
a phrase and rearrange its pieces backwards as a critical statement (see
example 33). He could even produce fugal monsters that have to be
physically removed from a quartet and incarcerated in a separate opus
number (Op. 133).

This is the legacy of the new music whose sublime and ironic negations are traced by Adorno to the screams of a Schoenberg trio. His pessimistic history of music, in which late Beethoven is merely the
beginning of the end of humanity, describes a *Lebenskraft* experiment of
subjective reflection that ended up a re-enactment of Mary Shelley's
Frankenstein (1818).[22]

---

[21] On modernity, see the chapters in this volume 'On Monuments' and 'On the
Apocalypse'.

[22] On Adorno, Beethoven and the *Grosse Fuge*, see Chua, *The 'Galitzin' Quartets of
Beethoven*; also see the chapter in this volume 'On Suicide'.

PART 3

The Tower of Babel

27

On death

... all truly meaningful music is swan song.

(Nietzsche)[1]

Almost as soon as the concept was born, absolute music died. The remainder of this book is an autopsy devoted to the many deaths that instrumental music suffered, faked and inflicted. Some of these deaths were quite spectacular, others more pitiful, but they were all necessary in the economy of the aesthetic. Absolute music's survival is predicated on its death. After all, as the Romantics insisted, the absolute can only be known negatively: one dies to enter eternity.

The last rites of the aesthetic were a kind of surrogate salvation for the secular man. By the turn of the nineteenth century, the fear that God had died gave rise to the equally terrifying fear of dying without God;[2] not only was humanity left to manufacture its own meaning in a material world, but the very thought of its extinction threatened to bring whatever meaning it discovered into crisis.[3] One way of overcoming this situation was for humanity to aestheticise death in the hollow of the empty sign; the nothingness of absolute music resonated with the fatal promise of life beyond a God-forsaken world. To die in absolute music is to know the promise of eternal life without a Christian burial.

So in retrospect, instrumental music did not have much of a life – at least not on earth. The eighteenth century declared it dead in the body, and now the nineteenth century made it die to certify the immortality of the soul. The early Romantics clearly connected instrumental music with death. Of course, music, as the song of the sirens, had long been a harbinger of destruction, but by the nineteenth century these luring voices that shipwrecked humanity on the rocks of desire became instrumental tones that set the Romantic soul adrift in the ecstasy of the spirit realm, far above the noisy, meaningless 'prayer-wheel of

[1] Friedrich Nietzsche, *Human, All Too Human: A Book for Free Spirits*, trans. R. J. Hollingdale (Cambridge: Cambridge University Press, 1986), 253.
[2] See Behler, *Irony and the Discourse of Modernity*, 91–2.
[3] This is the central problem that inspired Nietzsche's aesthetics. See Julian Young, *Nietzsche's Philosophy of Art* (Cambridge: Cambridge University Press, 1992).

time'.[4] For the Romantics, absolute music breaks the shackles of the material world by releasing the soul from the body. Through its celestial harmonies, 'the lost spirit is released from its earthly shell', says Wackenroder.[5]

Thus it was almost inevitable that Beethoven, the god of instrumental music, should become a model of death for secular man, not least in the heroics of the *Eroica* Symphony.[6] To die in a blaze of glory is to create your own after-life as the immortal hero; that, at least, was how Vienna came to terms with Beethoven's death. The 'funeral rite becomes a feast of life!' writes Gabriel Seidl in a poem distributed at Beethoven's graveside: 'He lives! He who claims he is dead lies! . . . he has created himself through his own song!'[7] In death, Beethoven had become the hero of his own symphony, rising up like a god into the eternal pantheon of absolute music for all humanity to follow.

But this apotheosis was an unsustainable model, for history failed to deliver its Utopian promises; dying heroically for humanity was not really worth the effort in the end. As revolutions failed and wars ravaged the earth, humanity became increasingly aware of the impossibility of its own salvation. Consequently, the death projected on to absolute music became more gruesome, until it left the Beethovenian hero reeling with existential despair instead of 'shouting to us the avowal of his Godhood', as Wagner once put it.[8] And as if this were not enough, those who wanted to erase these aesthetic fallacies from humanity, called for the death of absolute music itself.

So absolute music died many deaths in the course of two centuries, but surprisingly it has not ceased to exist. It survives in two ways: first, as a perpetual post-mortem. This was partly because no one was able to identify the victim. It sort of resembled Beethoven, for the nineteenth century looked to him for their definition of absolute music, but far from unifying the idea, this merely divided the musical community into warring factions, that, in their confusion, conferred so many identities on to absolute music that its definition became almost as ineffable as its alleged ineffability. Consequently, no one was able to agree on the cause of death. Some said it died of historical exhaustion, others claimed that it was a metaphysical death; some even suggested suicide. Whatever the cause, the everlasting post-mortem created by this discursive overkill ensured the eternal survival of absolute music.

---

[4] Wackenroder and Tieck, *Confessions and Fantasies*, 176. The translation has been modified.   [5] Ibid., 177.   [6] See the chapter 'On Heroes' in this volume.

[7] Gabriel Seidl, 'Beethoven', in Gerhard von Breuning, *Memories of Beethoven*, trans. H. Mins and M. Solomon (Cambridge: Cambridge University Press, 1992), 111.

[8] Richard Wagner, 'Beethovens "heroische Symphonie"', *Sämtliche Schriften*, 5:172; the translation is from *Judaism in Music and Other Essays*, trans. W. Ashton Ellis (Lincoln: University of Nebraska Press, 1993), 224.

Secondly, absolute music keeps dying in the hope that it might be born over and over again to enact the self-renewing process of modernity. It dies both to canonise itself in eternity and to renew itself in time. Thus the more absolute music was made to die the more it seemed to assert itself as the indestructible force of history, until this tiny Teutonic concept, which in reality had marginal significance in the actual *practice* of music in the nineteenth century, became the transcendental signifier that fixed the very *meaning* of music itself; all music that is truly music has its being in the absolute. As a result, absolute music was less an object to be defined than an epistemological structure that defined the discourse on music, even of those who spoke against it and announced its demise. Having brought it into being, humanity could not destroy it precisely because it is through destruction that this music lives up to its name – absolute.

28

On absolute music

The christening of absolute music was meant to be something of a heroic funeral. When Wagner coined the term in 1846 he was announcing the death of instrumental music.[1] The symphony, he claimed, was over. It was already history, buried by Wagner himself, whose music dramas were about to overcome the inchoate utterances of instrumental music through the word and deed.[2] Since absolute music discharges itself from the reality of concept and action, says Wagner, anyone who writes a symphony after Beethoven would merely be an epigone, tinkering with a historically exhausted form instead of articulating the ever-progressing spirit of modernity.[3]

Absolute music was evidently something to be negated in Wagner's dialectic of music history. The force of his argument was inspired by the Young Hegelians who had pushed the logic of Hegel's dialectical method to negate Hegel himself, in the hope that the long delayed promises of the French Revolution might finally be realised on German soil instead of evaporating in to what they regarded as the rarefied atmosphere of Hegel's speculative metaphysics and the religious abstractions that went with it. By 1846, revolution was in the air, and Wagner, under the pressure of world history, wanted to force music into a new synthesis that would seize the political initiative for the future. But for all his revolutionary rhetoric, Wagner's aesthetics, in fact, got no further than Hegel who had already declared instrumental music abstract, empty and impotent, since it was unable to objectify itself in the material world of verbal concepts.[4] Wagner simply reiter-

---

[1] It appears that Wagner first used the term in passing in a programmatic commentary on Beethoven's Ninth Symphony designed for the Dresden Palm Sunday concerts. He subsequently consolidated the term's political and historical significance in his 'Zurich writings' of 1849–51. See Kropfinger, *Wagner and Beethoven*, 115, Dahlhaus, *The Idea of Absolute Music*, 18–19, and Grey, *Wagner's Musical Prose*, 1–2.

[2] See Richard Wagner, *Das Kunstwerk der Zukunft* (1850) and *Oper und Drama* (1851), in *Sämtliche Schriften*, 3:42–177 and 222–320; the translation by W. Ashton Ellis (1892–9) has been reissued as *The Art-Work of the Future and Other Works* and *Opera and Drama* (Lincoln: University of Nebraska Press, 1993 and 1995).

[3] See John Deathridge, 'Wagner and the Post-Modern', *Cambridge Opera Journal*, vol. 4 no. 2 (1992).

[4] See Hegel, *Aesthetik*, 3:131–58 and 213–17, translated by T. M. Knox as *Aesthetics: Lectures on Fine Art* (Oxford: Clarendon Press, 1975), 888–909 and 951–4. Also see in this volume the chapter 'On the End'.

ated the same thing. What was antithetical to Hegel and radical in the manner of the Young Hegelians in Wagner's aesthetics was not the negation of instrumental music but the negation of God;[5] he aligned instrumental music with the Judaeo-Christian deity of Mendelssohn and 'damned' its inert longings to the 'everlasting *selfish solitude*' of Christianity.[6] Such life-sapping forms of religion simply had to go. The yearning subject must find an object in the real world. Wagner called for a revolution. He demanded a *'new religion'*,[7] grounded in nature, worked out in humanity and shaped by an aesthetics modelled on the pagan drama of the Greek *polis*. Under Wagner, the whole of humanity could aspire to individual genius and create itself anew forever; hence 'the artist of the future', says Wagner, 'is the people [*Volk*].'[8] This is hardly surprising since the Young Hegelians, most notably David Strauss and Ludwig Feuerbach, had turned theology into a kind of anthropology, secularising God to deify man in order to de-Christianise the future for a new politics of humanity. Wagner saw his music as a catalyst for this future. And his prophet, the young Nietzsche, proclaimed this future to be a 'tragic age' that would triumph over the terrors of nihilism.[9] So by announcing the death of absolute music, Wagner already signalled the death of God; and the artwork of the future was to be the new religion that would overcome this catastrophe of post-Biblical proportions.

Absolute music was a term invented by Wagner under the inspiration of Feuerbach, in the hope that he could do to Beethoven what Feuerbach had done to Hegel.[10] Just as Feuerbach had criticised the abstractions of Hegel's 'absolute philosophy' to secure his radical vision for humanity, so Wagner cancelled the future of absolute music, claiming that it was too abstract a form to bring to consciousness the spirit of an age that had gone beyond the Christian ethos of a bourgeois world. Beethoven's 'error', as he puts it, was to misfile his political intentions in the form of

---

[5] In Hegel's system, the sublation of modern art makes way for religion and philosophy. See Hegel, *Aesthetik*.

[6] Wagner, *The Art-Work of the Future*, 114; see also 37–47, 59. On Mendelssohn and the 'sugary' Christianity of his *Lobgesang*, see 128. On the Christian politics of Mendelssohn's *Lobgesang*, see John Toews, 'Musical Historicism and the Transcendental Foundation of Community: Mendelssohn's *Lobgesang* and the "Christian German" Cultural Politics of Frederick William IV' in *Rediscovering History: Culture, Politics and the Psyche*, ed. M. S. Roth (Stanford: Stanford University Press, 1994). On Wagner's changing religious and political beliefs, see Paul Lawrence Rose, *Wagner: Race and Revolution* (London: Faber, 1992).

[7] Wagner, *The Art-Work of the Future*, 155.   [8] Ibid., 205; translation modified.

[9] See Friedrich Nietzsche, *Die Geburt der Tragödie* (1872); a translation by Walter Kaufmann is available in *The Birth of Tragedy and The Case of Wagner* (New York: Random House, 1967).

[10] See Ludwig Feuerbach, *Grundsätze der Philosophie der Zukunft* (1843), translated by M. H. Vogel as *Principles of the Philosophy of the Future* (Indianapolis: Hackett, 1986), Wagner, *The Art-Work of the Future*, 25, and Dahlhaus, *The Idea of Absolute Music*, 20–1.

instrumental music;[11] the means were consequently inadequate to the ends. The moral necessity required in any revolutionary act, claims Wagner, is scuppered by the arbitrary chemistry of Beethoven's instrumental music and the rigidity of its forms.[12] Beethoven was therefore unable to realise the 'ethical deed' in his symphonies, despite his intentions, because absolute music by nature 'lacks moral will'.[13] It has no objective reality and therefore no political force.

The Ninth Symphony of Beethoven was therefore of 'cataclysmic' significance in Wagner's dialectic of music history,[14] for this work points to a future in which the ineffable yearnings of absolute music will be redeemed by the certainty of the word, and so unite humanity on earth, instead of refracting the ego through some Hoffmannesque spirit-realm. For Wagner, the Ninth Symphony is revolution and, as if to verify this fact, his performances of the work ignited the audiences with revolutionary anticipation. When revolutionary fires broke out in Dresden, a guard shouted to Wagner from the barricades, 'schöner Götterfunken'.[15] Joy's divine spark had struck to illumine the edifice of a new world. The finale 'breaks the bounds of the absolute', writes Wagner,[16] with the command '"Rejoice!" . . . With this word Beethoven cries to men: "*Breast to breast you mortal millions! This one kiss to all the world!*" – and this *Word*', continues Wagner, 'will be the language of the *Artwork of the Future*.'[17] The word is therefore the end of absolute music. Indeed, the text of the Ninth Symphony seems to misshape the symphonic form as if a new music were breaking out of the structure. The word 'Rejoice' promises new tones for a new world.

In the movement, there is nothing of the old formulaic structures that Wagner accused absolute music of; this finale eludes *Formenlehre*. So much so that analysts, in their attempt to impose some order on the movement, have merely created a mêlée of formal types – variation form, rondo form, bar form, sonata form, concerto form, four-movement form – none of which actually conforms to the music.[18] No wonder Wagner saw the structural shackles of the past broken by 'the Word', for in a sense, the Ninth is no longer a symphony but the Utopian drama of modernity, breaking the bounds of tradition as it strives

---

[11] Wagner, *Opera and Drama*, 70–2.

[12] On chemistry and necessity see Wagner, *The Art-Work of the Future*, 117 and 122.

[13] Ibid., 123.   [14] Ibid., 131.

[15] Richard Wagner, *Braunes Buch*, 8 May 1849, cited in Kropfinger, *Wagner and Beethoven*, 44.

[16] Quoted from Wagner's 1846 commentary on Beethoven's Ninth Symphony, in *Sämtliche Schriften*, 2:61.

[17] Wagner, *The Art-Work of the Future*, 126. Also see Nietzsche, *The Birth of Tragedy*, 37–8.

[18] See James Webster, 'The Form of the Finale of Beethoven's Ninth Symphony', in *Beethoven Forum 1*, ed. C. Reynolds, L. Lockwood and J. Webster (Lincoln: University of Nebraska Press, 1992).

towards Elysium.[19] The finale is therefore the 'evangel' that prepares the way for the politics of music drama in a 'purely human' society, in which absolute music and God are no longer necessary; the 'mortal millions' shall become divine and Wagner shall furnish this new deity of the Young Hegelians with a new liturgy. Thus in the aftermath of the 1848 revolution, Wagner declared that with Beethoven's Ninth Symphony, 'the *last* symphony has *already been written*'.[20]

At this dramatic point in world history, absolute music should have died. But Wagner must have buried the concept alive because absolute music came back to bedevil the composer. He suddenly found himself at the wrong end of the dialectic, and some, like Nietzsche, suspected him of changing sides. But Wagner never recanted. He merely abandoned the term that he had made, never to write it again after 1857.[21] But it was already too late. Eighteen fifty-four was the fateful year. First, Eduard Hanslick, in *The Beautiful in Music*, hijacked the term to revive the very form that Wagner wanted to erase from the future of music history. And secondly, Wagner had a revelation that same year: he discovered Schopenhauer for whom instrumental music revealed the truth of metaphysical reality.[22] Consequently, absolute music became thoroughly confused, for Hanslick's formalism and Schopenhauer's metaphysics imbued the concept with contradictory meanings, neither of which coincided with Wagner's original use of the term. Having got off to a bad start, the definition of absolute music simply got worse. But that did not stop the various camps from arguing at cross-purposes over the concept. The battle reduced the complexities of Romantic thought, from which absolute music was fashioned, to confused oppositions. As a result, the Romantic inheritance was divided and absolute music was made to die again. In fact, it died twice: beautifully for Hanslick and horribly for Nietzsche.

[19] See Solie, 'Beethoven as Secular Humanist'.

[20] Wagner, *The Art-Work of the Future*, 127.

[21] Wagner's final use of the term appears in an open letter, 'Über Franz Liszt's symphonische Dichtungen', *Sämtliche Schriften*, 5:182–98; an English translation is available in *Judaism in Music and Other Essays*.

[22] On both issues, see Carl Dahlhaus, 'The Twofold Truth in Wagner's Aesthetics', *Between Romanticism and Modernism*, trans. M. Whittall (Berkeley: University of California Press, 1980), Jean-Jacques Nattiez, *Wagner Androgyne*, trans. S. Spencer (Princeton: Princeton University Press, 1993), 102–62, and Grey, *Wagner's Musical Prose*, 1–129.

29

On the beautiful and the sublime

Music dies beautifully because Hanslick's definition of absolute music is grounded in the formalism of Kant's aesthetic of the beautiful. Music, he writes, is the 'self-subsistent form of the beautiful' rather than the formless power of the Kantian sublime;[1] it exhibits what Kant calls a 'finality of form',[2] where the means have no end other than in themselves, so that there is 'no distinction', says Hanslick, 'between substance and form';[3] they simply coincide without remainder, leaving nothing 'outside the work' for critical leverage.[4] Thus music in essence is only the score, shut off from the kind of sublime disruption that might shatter the form to leave music susceptible to the historical, political and emotional impurities that Wagner wanted to smear over its structure. So by enclosing music in itself, Hanslick overcomes Wagner's dialectical history by simply erasing history from absolute music. Any work prone to Wagner's intentions is therefore a mistake. This is why for Hanslick, the finale of Beethoven's Ninth Symphony is not a light for the future but a monstrous deformation that casts a 'giant shadow' over an otherwise promising symphony; it is an ugly head attached to a beautiful body.[5]

Beauty, for Hanslick, is a question of *essence*. Music may evoke emotions, but such emotions cannot define its being; it may gather the intellectual trappings of history, but these meanings are not essential but extraneous to the 'intrinsic beauty' of music.[6] To prove this, Hanslick resorts to the technical purity of structural analysis. He prints out Beethoven's *Overture to Prometheus* as an object for dissection, and proceeds to pick at the opening bars with a clinical precision, anaesthetising the noise of the Promethean sublime with the silent symmetry of the beautiful.[7] Scores, of course, are silent, and this enables Hanslick to manipulate their abstract patterns to produce an analytical discourse where the *substance* of what is said coincides with the *structure* of what is seen, so that there is no outside. Score and discourse synchronise to reinforce what Adorno calls the 'total aestheticisation of art' in which

---

[1] Hanslick, *The Beautiful in Music*, 9.   [2] Kant, *Critique of Judgement*, 65.
[3] Hanslick, *The Beautiful in Music*, 122.   [4] Ibid., 60 and 74.   [5] Ibid., 68–9n.
[6] Ibid.   [7] Ibid., 26.

228

content is form. Scores, writes Adorno, are 'not external to the work; only through them does the work become autonomous'.[8] However, there is a price to pay for Hanslick's formalism. The purification of music through analysis is meant to verify the iconic solidity of the score, but this necessary act of decontamination, as Hanslick admits, not only sterilises the music but kills it in the process. 'An analysis of this kind, it is true, reduces to a skeleton a body glowing with life', says Hanslick, 'it destroys the beauty, but at the same time it destroys all false constructions.'[9] In verifying the form as beautiful, analysis kills the very essence of music; music dies beautifully, but in dying it also proves itself to be a synchronic object; it dies to the world to become immutable, pure and totally useless.

The disinterestedness necessary in Kant's aesthetic judgement had already alienated art from the sphere of practical (moral) reason.[10] Hanslick merely translates this into absolute music. Thus the 'total aestheticisation' of music is also its total anaesthetisation, turning instrumental music into that inert, insular language that Wagner had long suspected it to be. It is no coincidence that after the failure of the 1848 revolution, music is made to retreat from history and politics into the safe-haven of Hanslick's aestheticism. It becomes so engrossed with its formal procedures that it forgets itself as practice, as if institutional structures and the process of production, performance and interpretation have simply disappeared into the purity of the absolute. The beautiful in music is achieved at the cost of its alienation from society. 'The category "autonomy"', writes Peter Bürger, 'does not permit the understanding of its referent as one that developed historically. The relative dissociation of the work of art from the praxis of life in bourgeois society thus becomes transformed into the (erroneous) idea that the work of art is totally independent of society.'[11]

This was a price that neither Wagner nor Nietzsche was willing to pay, either before or after their 'Schopenhauerian conversion'. Art, for both of them, was consistently a means of recovering the collective identity of humanity; their concept of aesthetic autonomy did not end in the score but in the *Volk*, in order to activate a social autonomy from within the individual.[12] So music was not abstract form for them; it was not an end but a means. Music is power; it mesmerises its victims, inducing a somnambulistic state in which humanity can be manipulated. If Wagner's performances of Beethoven's Ninth Symphony could ignite revolutionary fervour in the audience, then how much more can music

---

[8] Adorno, *Aesthetic Theory*, 100.   [9] Hanslick, *The Beautiful in Music*, 28.
[10] See Bernstein, *The Fate of Art*, 1–65.   [11] Bürger, *Theory of the Avant-Garde*, 46.
[12] See Tracy B. Strong, 'Nietzsche's Political Aesthetics', in *Nietzsche's New Seas: Explorations in Philosophy, Aesthetics and Politics*, ed. M. A. Gillespie and T. B. Strong (Chicago: University of Chicago Press, 1988).

drama exert its influence over humanity. Music drama does not forget itself as an institutional force: Bayreuth is living proof of this.[13] In fact, the mass manipulation so appalled Nietzsche in the first Bayreuth festival in 1876 that he walked out on Wagner. But even this rejection did not change Nietzsche's aesthetic vision; a music that is only preoccupied with itself still risks cultural irrelevance. 'Art for art sake', says Nietzsche, is about as purposeful as 'a worm chewing its own tail'.[14]

So there is no question of Wagner converting to Hanslick's aesthetics with his discovery of Schopenhauer in 1854, as some commentators suggest. In fact, it is impossible since Hanslick's practical rationalism is at variance with Schopenhauer's metaphysics of music. Indeed, in the second edition of his treatise, Hanslick removes all the references to music as the 'sounding image of the universe'.[15] But even if he secretly maintained this cosmology, Schopenhauer's metaphysics of the Will is so irrational and virile that it would have detuned and smashed up Hanslick's beautiful universe. There is nothing in common between them. So why should Wagner recant after his Schopenhauerian conversion? How could he? When he says in an open letter of 1857 that 'the advocates of absolute music evidently do not know what they are talking about', it was because Hanslick and Wagner were not talking about the same thing.[16]

There was, however, an ideological shift in Wagner's concept of absolute music after 1854 – not that it made much difference. As long as the ideology justifies the cause, any argument would do for Wagner. With the failure of the 1848 revolution, Wagner's historical dialectic was too embarrassing to sustain, and it was fortuitous that his discovery of Schopenhauer allowed him to shift perspective from a historical absolute to a metaphysical one. But there was no change to the function of music drama. After all, Wagner did not start writing symphonies after his conversion, despite the claim that he conceived *Tristan and Isolde* symphonically.[17] It is just that with his adoption of Schopenhauer's system, music drama no longer needs a historical dialectic that negates absolute music to justify its birth; rather absolute music can now become the ontological ground that verifies music drama metaphysi-

[13] On Bayreuth and mass cultural manipulation, see Theodor W. Adorno, *In Search of Wagner*, trans. Rodney Livingstone (London: NLB, 1981), particularly 85–96 and 107–8, and Philippe Lacoue-Labarthe, *Heidegger, Art and Politics*, trans. C. Turner (Oxford: Blackwell, 1990), 63–5.

[14] Friedrich Nietzsche, *Twilight of the Idols*, translated by W. Kaufmann in *The Portable Nietzsche* (New York: Viking Press, 1954), 529. Also see Friedrich Nietzsche, *On the Genealogy of Morality*, ed. K. Ansell-Pearson, trans. C. Diethe (Cambridge: Cambridge University Press, 1994), 78.   [15] See Dahlhaus, *The Idea of Absolute Music*, 28.

[16] Richard Wagner, 'Über Franz Liszt's symphonische Dichtungen' (1857), *Sämtliche Schriften*, 5:191; an English translation is available in *Judaism in Music and Other Essays*.

[17] See John Deathridge, 'Post-Mortem on Isolde', *New German Critique*, no. 69 (1996), 103.

cally. In other words, instrumental music no longer precedes music drama in time, but undergirds it in eternity. The justification is different, but the political and aesthetic functions remain unchanged; he still demands the interpenetration of music and poetry, and he still exalts feeling over form as the crucible in which a 'purely human' identity can be forged through the collective ritual of tragic drama.[18]

What has changed is the theological *meaning* of absolute music. If music for Schopenhauer is an image of the Will, whose blind and omnipotent fluctuations are the metaphysical realities behind the meaningless phenomena of the world, then the empty, restless signification of music need no longer be regarded by Wagner as the impotent yearning of a Judaeo-Christian ego.[19] Instead, it has become the yearning of the Will. Instrumental music may still sound the same (for there is no sonic difference between the inchoate and the ineffable), but the theological connotations have been transformed. With Schopenhauer's metaphysics, instrumental music does not require negation because instrumental music as the Will has already negated the Christian God. In Nietzsche's terms, 'God is dead' and the tragic age of the Will has begun. Absolute music can now freely justify the truth of music drama as the 'new religion'. Indeed, just as 'the birth of tragedy' for Nietzsche is 'out of the spirit of music',[20] so for Wagner instrumental music gives birth to tragic drama.[21] The emphasis has shifted: instead of instrumental music *needing* an object to complete its meaning, it now *engenders* the object of meaning, so that music drama becomes '*deeds of music made visible*'.[22] Of course, either way music still acquires the object it lacks, but why it has one is now a completely different matter.

So is music drama – formerly the antithesis of absolute music – absolute music after all? Is *Tristan and Isolde* Wagner's '*opus metaphysicum*' as Nietzsche claims?[23] And did Nietzsche himself hear it as absolute music, as Carl Dahlhaus claims?[24] If this work is absolute, then it is purely an irony of history that its metaphysics happens to fit the name that Wagner originally tailored for a different concept. Wagner, of course, did not call *Tristan* absolute music, and Nietzsche only imagined hearing the third act as 'a tremendous symphonic movement'. If this

---

[18] See Richard Wagner, 'Zukunftsmusik' (1861), *Sämtliche Schriften*, 7:87–137, translated in *Judaism in Music and Other Essays*.

[19] On the theological connotations of Schopenhauer's metaphysics, see Richard Taylor's chapter in *Nineteenth Century Religious Thought in the West*, ed. N. Smart, J. Clayton, P. Sherry and S. T. Katz (Cambridge: Cambridge University Press, 1985), 1:157–80.

[20] The original title of Nietzsche's *The Birth of Tragedy* (1872) is *The Birth of Tragedy out of the Spirit of Music*. The book is dedicated to Wagner.

[21] See Nattiez, *Wagner Androgyne*, 158–62.   [22] Wagner, *Sämtliche Schriften*, 9:306.

[23] Friedrich Nietzsche, 'Richard Wagner in Bayreuth', in *Unfashionable Observations*, trans. R. T. Gray (Stanford: Stanford University Press, 1995), 303.

[24] Dahlhaus, *The Idea of Absolute Music*, 33–4.

work touches the absolute in the metaphysical sense, then what is absolute about it for Nietzsche is not so much the music itself, as the fact that the music would *kill* you. Nietzsche, of course, puts it more poetically: can anyone 'imagine a human being who would be able to perceive the third act of *Tristan and Isolde*, without any aid of word and image, purely as a tremendous symphonic movement, without expiring in a spasmodic unharnessing of all the wings of the soul?'[25] What Nietzsche claims is this: you cannot hear *Tristan and Isolde* as absolute music; rather the music drama mediates the absolute with words and actions. Indeed, *Tristan and Isolde*, as John Deathridge points out, is an almost 'perfect allegory of absolute music' in the Schopenhauerian sense: in the opera, Isolde drowns in the absolute music that rises out from Tristan's soul.[26] She commits suicide, but in a sense it is the symphonic ecstasy of the *Liebestod* that kills her properly; it engulfs her voice so that she may be absorbed into the symphony of the Will.[27] The resolution of the Tristan chord at the end of the work is not the fulfilment of a sexual union but of the Schopenhauerian desire for death. *Bildungstrieb* for Wagner is *Todestrieb*. But Tristan and Isolde merely *represent* the absolute on stage, for a direct confrontation with the image of the Will, as Nietzsche puts it, will unharness all the wings of your soul and kill you. The work is merely a phenomenal enactment of noumenal reality, so that one is only *symbolically* destroyed. Music drama is therefore not absolute music, but it is justified by it. It does not kill you, but the absolute that lurks behind it gives you a premonition of your ultimate end.

For both Wagner and Nietzsche, absolute music finds its meaning in death. This time, however, it is not a beautiful death, because music for Schopenhauer is *sublime*; a Beethoven symphony, he says, 'rolls on in the boundless confusion of innumerable forms'.[28] So whereas in Hanslick's aesthetics absolute music is so beautiful that it petrifies into a narcissistic structure, in Nietzsche's metaphysics it symbolises a horrible, if sublime, death; there is a 'curious blending', says Nietzsche in *The Birth of Tragedy*, of 'ecstasy' and 'agony'.[29] This death is necessarily horrible because the Will that imposes its omnipotent powers is evil;[30] it is totally indifferent to what it creates and destroys, like a Dionysian godling that builds and demolishes sand-castles at whim.[31] And this 'god' is the Primal Unity behind the plurality of the phenomenal world; and humanity is doomed since our *individual* existence is a contradiction

[25] Nietzsche, *The Birth of Tragedy and The Case of Wagner*, 126–7.

[26] Deathridge, 'Post-Mortem on Isolde', 109 and 119.

[27] Indeed, Wagner conducted concert performances of the *Liebestod* without Isolde.

[28] Schopenhauer, *The World as Will and Representation*, 2:450. Also see Nietzsche, *The Birth of Tragedy*, 100–1, and Young, *Nietzsche's Philosophy of Art*, 14–15.

[29] Nietzsche, *The Birth of Tragedy*, 40.   [30] See Young, *Nietzsche's Philosophy of Art*, 7.

[31] Nietzsche, *The Birth of Tragedy*, 141–2.

that splinters the unity of the Will and turns human existence into a battleground of meaningless suffering that can only be resolved by being reabsorbed into the Primordial Oneness. Life is therefore futile; in Nietzsche's words, it is nauseating. But since it is meaningless to fight against this truth, humanity must affirm this nauseating truth and vomit with Dionysian revelry. This is how Nietzsche overcomes what he calls the 'wisdom of Silenus': 'best of all is not to be born, not to *be*, to be *nothing*. But the second best for you is – to die soon.'[32] So absolute music must both represent and overcome this truth if humanity is to be fashioned as the tragic race of the future. Hence music gives birth to tragedy, and through music a tragic race shall happily return dead to its womb. The command to 'Rejoice!' in Beethoven's Ninth Symphony turns out to be the perverse joy of 'intoxication' for Nietzsche, in which the millions that were supposed to be united on earth, bow down in the dust before the Dionysian Will to be slaughtered together in the unity of the aesthetic. This joy arises when man sees his extinction as 'a work of art'. Therefore, life must become like the Ninth Symphony for Nietzsche – not beautiful, but sublime – as if one were enacting the frenzy at the end of the finale, with its clatter of Turkish instruments (bs 843–940). Earlier critics had regarded this passage as a barbaric intrusion, but now humanity can readily affirm it as its own pagan ritual – an orgy over the abyss of the absolute. In this reading of the Ninth Symphony, music awakens the true identity of humanity as a force that embraces the Eleusinian nothingness of the Primal Unity.[33] 'It is only through the spirit of music', says Nietzsche,

that we can understand the joy involved in the annihilation of the individual. For it is only in particular examples of such annihilation that we see clearly the eternal phenomena of Dionysian art, which gives expression to the will in its omnipotence . . . [T]he hero, the highest manifestation of the will, is negated for our pleasure, because he is only phenomena, and because the eternal life of the will is not affected by his annihilation.[34]

Hölderlin had already spoken of the tragic hero as the zero-sign of tragedy; when 'the sign = 0', he writes, nature reveals the totality of her powers;[35] the destruction of the hero gestures negatively to the force of fate. This too is the tragic mechanism that is operating behind

---

[32] Ibid., 42.

[33] Ibid., 37–8. On barbarism and the Turkish march see Schindler, *Beethoven as I Knew Him*, 306, Friedrich Kanne's review of the Ninth Symphony (1824) quoted in Nicholas Cook, *Beethoven: Symphony No. 9* (Cambridge: Cambridge University Press, 1993), 39, and Siegmund Levarie, 'Noise', *Critical Inquiry*, vol. 4 no. 1 (1977), 21–32.

[34] Nietzsche, *The Birth of Tragedy*, 104; also see 'Richard Wagner in Bayreuth', 278–9.

[35] Friedrich Hölderlin, *Sämtliche Werke*, ed. F. Beissner (Stuttgart: Cotta, 1946–77), 4:257; see Peter Szondi, *On Textual Understanding and Other Essays*, trans. H. Mendelsohn (Manchester: Manchester University Press, 1986), 46–9.

Nietzsche's metaphysics of music; indeed, the semiotics of the empty sign discovers its most sublime and sinister resonance as it vibrates between zero and one.[36] Absolute music '=0' as the representation of nothing, and '=1' as the totality of everything. Nietzsche splits this all-or-nothing ambiguity into noumenal and phenomenal realms. When phenomenon is zero, the Will (noumenon) asserts itself as totality; the annihilation of the individual reabsorbs him into the noumenal being of the Primal Unity. So in death, man becomes a god, zero equals one, and the transition between death and eternity is the Dionysian 'orgasm of music' (*Musikorgasmus*) that makes the terror sublime.[37] The plenitude of the empty sign is therefore the Dionysian newspeak that lures the subject into a death without terror and a redemption without hope. Absolute music is tragedy as desire. 'Music', says Nietzsche,

imparts to the tragic myth an intense and convincing metaphysical significance . . . [T]he tragic spectator is overcome by an assured premonition of the highest pleasure attained through destruction and negation, so he feels as if the innermost abyss of things spoke to him perceptibly.[38]

Nietzsche would later turn against his own aesthetics, branding music as a metaphysical narcotic. He was right. Absolute music for both Wagner and Nietzsche is merely another form of revolutionary retreat.[39] If Hanslick anaesthetises art from society, Nietzsche, in *The Birth of Tragedy*, anaesthetises society as art. This means that the *Volk* is no longer the artist of the future, as Wagner claims, but the *art-work* of the future. When Nietzsche writes that man 'is no longer an artist, he has become a work of art' he means that humanity should aspire to the eternity of the aesthetic in the form of absolute music.[40] But since the individual subject, in becoming absolute, is lost in the aesthetic object, the only thing that gets to contemplate the art-work with the disinterested attention of Hanslick is the Will; the Will is 'the sole author and spectator' in this 'artistic game', says Nietzsche, and it is only from this perspective, as if one were a god inflicting gratuitous violence on oneself as a human piece of art, that the suffering of the world becomes as painless as attending a Wagnerian music drama. 'Only as *aesthetic phenomena*', says Nietzsche, are 'existence and the world eternally *justified*.'[41] And only as absolute music is individual extinction eternally glorified.

---

[36] See the chapters 'On Nothing' and 'On God' in this volume.
[37] Nietzsche, *The Birth of Tragedy*, 125–6; my translation.   [38] Ibid., 126.
[39] See Deathridge, 'Wagner and the Post-Modern'.
[40] Nietzsche, *The Birth of Tragedy*, 37.   [41] Ibid., 52.

30

On monuments

'Die and become' was Goethe's injunction to humanity.[1] It was also Beethoven's. Nietzsche, in celebrating the destruction of the tragic hero, was merely paying homage to the symphonic monument that towered over the nineteenth century. Wagner, too, bowed to its imperative. Even before his Schopenhauerian conversion, he already understood the *Eroica* Symphony as a ritual of annihilation and redemption. In the *Eroica*, the 'purely human' hero embraces his fate to claim his glory; 'ecstasy' and 'horror' are unleashed, says Wagner, as the hero hurls himself with 'shattering force' towards the 'tragic crisis' through which he will be immortalised.[2] Thus the funeral procession of the second movement leads to the apotheosis of the last. The hero becomes 'totality' and 'shouts to us the avowal of his Godhood'.[3]

For Wagner, the *Eroica* Symphony stood as 'a monument of an entirely new age';[4] its looming presence spurred him towards the future, lest its long shadow should eclipse his music. And he was not the only one overwhelmed by its apocalyptic power: 'Thirty-six bars of the nineteenth century', exclaimed Wolfgang Robert Griepenkerl, on hearing the dissonant blows that pummel the hero at the heart of the movement (bs 248–83).[5] 'On your knees old world!' commands Wilhelm von Lenz, 'Before you stands the idea of the great Beethoven symphony . . . Here is the end of one empire and the beginning of another. Here is the boundary of a century.'[6] The *Eroica* clearly signalled a historical rupture for

---

[1] Johann Wolfgang von Goethe, 'Selige Sehnsucht', cited in Burnham, *Beethoven Hero*, 115.

[2] Wagner, 'Beethovens "heroische Symphonie"', *Sämtliche Schriften*, 5:169–70, translated as 'Beethoven's Heroic Symphony', *Judaism in Music and Other Essays*, 221–2.

[3] Wagner, 'Beethovens "heroische Symphonie"', *Sämtliche Schriften*, 15:172; translation modified from *Judaism in Music*, 224.

[4] Richard Wagner, 'Zukunftsmusik' (1861), *Sämtliche Schriften*, 7:109, translation modified from *Judaism in Music*, 317. Although Wagner is discussing the Beethoven symphony as a generic concept here, he is certainly thinking of the *Eroica*, which he calls elsewhere 'ein gigantisches Denkmal der Kunst'; see Richard Wagner, 'Ein glücklicher Abend' (1840), *Sämtliche Schriften*, 1:147; an English translation is available in *Pilgrimage to Beethoven and Other Essays*, trans. W. Ashton Ellis (Lincoln: University of Nebraska Press, 1994), 80.

[5] Wolfgang Robert Griepenkerl, *Das Musikfest oder die Beethovener* (Braunschweig: Eduard Leibrock, 1841), 110.   [6] Lenz, *Beethoven*, 3:291.

the nineteenth century – a 'Kunstepoche' as A. B. Marx puts it.[7] But this was not any old new history, but a history of the *new* itself: the *Eroica* marks the beginning of musical modernity. In Wagner's words, the work is a heroic act, an 'unheard of deed' in music history, which one must emulate and surpass if humanity is to progress.[8]

For modernity to work, progress must be measured by canonisation, otherwise modernity is reduced to the flux of passing fashions.[9] Hence the immortalisation of the *Eroica* in the nineteenth century is critical for the future of new music. Indeed, the symphony bears the marks of modernity, for it seemingly creates the new out of itself, transcending history in the very act of making it, leaving a 'gigantic monument' for the world to gasp at.[10] However, this process of transcendent self-generation is not only the ideology of modernity, it is also that of absolute music. Modernity and the absolute are inextricably linked. If the content of the *Eroica* is itself the heroic deed of modern history, as Wagner suggests, then the symphony brings absolute music to self-consciousness by enacting its own process of heroic canonisation. Through its annihilation and apotheosis, the *Eroica* is given the power to summon music into the pantheon of its absolute glory. In this way, the symphony establishes itself as the canonic measure of music history and the paradigm of music analysis. 'Die and become' is its message.[11]

As a monument of the new, the *Eroica* Symphony belongs to what Nietzsche calls a 'monumental history'.[12] This is not the kind of dusty, academic history that merely describes the past; this is a history for the future. As far as Nietzsche is concerned, history is to be made and not documented. The function of a monumental history is to record heroic acts done against the burden of the past, and so inspire the present to shape the future. Like the *Eroica*, humanity must 'develop [its form] out of itself' to create its own teleology.[13] It is therefore futile to hear the *Eroica* with the academic ears of historical authenticity; that, says Nietzsche, would make the work into an opiate for the future, as if it 'had been arranged for two flutes'.[14] The *Eroica* must be heard synchronically, as absolute music, for according to Nietzsche, the future belongs to the 'ahistorical': 'art is the antithesis of history', he writes, 'and only when history allows itself to be transformed into a work of art, into a

---

[7] Marx, *Ludwig van Beethoven*, 2:275.

[8] Richard Wagner, 'Ein glücklicher Abend', *Sämtliche Schriften*, 1:147. Also see Burnham, 'On the Programmatic Reception of Beethoven's Eroica Symphony'.

[9] See Habermas, *The Philosophical Discourse of Modernity*, 9. Also see in this volume the chapter 'On Modernity'.

[10] Habermas, *The Philosophical Discourse of Modernity*, 7–11. The quote is from Wagner, 'Ein glücklicher Abend', *Sämtliche Schriften*, 1:147.

[11] See the chapter 'On Heroes' in this volume.

[12] Nietzsche, 'On the Utility and Liability of History for Life', *Unfashionable Observations*, 97.   [13] Ibid., 89 and 130–1.   [14] Ibid., 124.

pure aesthetic structure, can it . . . arouse instinct'.[15] The history of the new is therefore only monumental when its transcends time in the canonic afterlife of the aesthetic. So a monument marks the intersection of history and eternity, and a monumental history strings these timeless objects together, like some kind of *meta-langue* of giants, calling 'to another across the desolate expanse of time, undisturbed by the wanton, noisy, chattering of dwarfs that crawl about beneath them'.[16] This is why Nietzsche describes the canon of German music as a 'solar *orbit* from Bach to Beethoven and Beethoven to Wagner' and not as a *line*age. For these are eternal heroes that circle the phenomenal world of history.[17]

Bach, Beethoven, Wagner: in a sense, these composers have all become the *Eroica* Symphony. They stand against history as giant monuments of the absolute. In fact, when Nietzsche wants to canonise Wagner, he makes him into the image of the *Eroica*, portraying him as a hero consecrated for battle, whose 'self-sacrifice' and 'victorious . . . deeds' will 'triumph powerfully' in Bayreuth.[18] But Nietzsche was merely doing to Wagner what Wagner had done to Beethoven; Beethoven's 'unheard of deed' in the *Eroica*, says Wagner, makes him the hero of the symphony, accomplishing in music history what Napoleon had done 'in the fields of Italy'.[19] But then Wagner was only doing to Beethoven what Beethoven had done to himself. Beethoven wanted to become a monument. When he wrote in his *Tagebuch*, 'Live only in your art', he meant that he should die in it so that his body might be resurrected in stone and his spirit live forever as absolute music. 'Everything that is called life', he wrote, 'should be sacrificed to the sublime and be a sanctuary of art.'[20] He dies to become eternal. 'BEETHOVEN – what a word', whispers Schumann, 'the deep sound of the mere syllables has the ring of eternity' (see plate 10).[21]

This kind of immortalisation demands a heroic death. Beethoven could not have died normally, even if he had wanted to. 'When I heard of Beethoven's death', said Charles Hallé, 'it seemed to me as if a god had departed.'[22] The meteorological records in Vienna agreed; thunder

---

[15] Ibid., 132.   [16] Ibid., 151.

[17] Nietzsche, *The Birth of Tragedy and The Case of Wagner*, 119; my emphasis. Such orbits can be seen as names inscribed on the walls of many nineteenth- and early-twentieth-century concert halls, usually with Beethoven at the centre; see, for example, Concertgebouw (Amsterdam), Konzerthaus (Berlin), Opéra Garnier (Paris), Symphony Hall (Boston), Paine Hall (Harvard).

[18] Nietzsche, 'Richard Wagner in Bayreuth', *Unfashionable Observations*, 276–7.

[19] See Burnham, *Beethoven Hero*, 156.

[20] Maynard Solomon, 'Beethoven's Tagebuch of 1812–18', *Beethoven Studies 3*, ed. A. Tyson (Cambridge: Cambridge University Press, 1995), 254 and 229.

[21] Schumann [as Eusebius], *On Music and Musicians*, 101.

[22] Charles Hallé, *The Autobiography of Charles Hallé* (1896), cited in Alessandra Comini, *The Changing Image of Beethoven: A Study in Mythmaking* (New York: Rizzoli, 1987), 74.

Plate 10 Josef Danhauser, *Liszt at the Piano* (1840), Nationalgalerie, Berlin. During the course of the soirée, Beethoven's head turns up as a monument to absolute music.

and lightning had indeed summoned his spirit to the gods. His death was a cataclysmic event in the heavens. Joseph Hüttenbrenner was there, and he gave this testimony to Thayer in 1860:

After Beethoven had lain unconscious, the death-rattle in his throat from 3 o'clock in the afternoon till after 5, there came a flash of lightning accompanied by a violent clap of thunder, which garishly illuminated the death chamber . . . After this unexpected phenomenon of nature, which startled me greatly, Beethoven opened his eyes, lifted his right hand and looked up for several seconds with the fist clenched . . . as if, like a brave commander, he wished to call out to his wavering troops: 'Courage, soldiers! Forward! Trust me! Victory is assured!'[23]

From Hüttenbrenner's account, it is clear that Beethoven had become the myth of his own music; his death enacts the self-canonising death-throes of his works in the form of thunder and lightning, which E. T. A. Hoffmann heard in the Fifth Symphony, and as the absolute command of the hero that A. B. Marx heard in the *Eroica*.[24] Beethoven blazes his way to glory so that humanity might follow in his wake: 'Trust me! Victory is assured!' He spurs modernity on: 'Courage, soldiers! Forward!' Like the hero of the *Eroica*, he dies to become. Thus it is not the composer's life that interprets the work, but the work that interprets his death; because the composer is immortalised as art, the life-and-works biographies inaugurated in the nineteenth century are really life-as-works hagiographies. As Gabriel Seidl put it: 'He lives! He who claims he is dead lies! . . . he has created himself through his own song!'[25] This aesthetic immortalisation is critical if Nietzsche's monumental history is to stabilise modernity; for only as absolute music can a composer be summoned to eternity, depositing in history a monument for mankind to worship.

Beethoven first became a monument in 1846.[26] The crowds gathered from the distant corners of Europe for the unveiling. But what did they see in this image of a giant man holding a pencil in Münsterplatz? When the chorus of the Ninth Symphony sang 'bow ye millions' in one of the concerts that solemnised the three days of official veneration, to whom did the worshippers think they were bowing the knee? Who was this King of Glory that had come through the gates of Bonn to be presented

---

[23] Alexander Wheelock Thayer, *Ludwig van Beethovens Leben* (Berlin, 1866–79), rev. and ed. Elliot Forbes as *Thayer's Life of Beethoven* (Princeton: Princeton University Press, 1964/1970), 1050–1.

[24] See Hoffmann, 'Review of Beethoven's Fifth Symphony', *E. T. A. Hoffmann's Musical Writings*, and Marx, *Ludwig van Beethoven*, 2:304.

[25] These lines are from Gabriel Seidl's poem 'Beethoven' distributed at Beethoven's grave-side, quoted in Breuning, *Memories of Beethoven*, 111.

[26] For a detailed account of the history of this monument, see Comini, *The Changing Image of Beethoven*, 315–87.

before the King of Prussia and the Queen of England to the sound of 'applause, cheers, trumpets, fanfares, drum-rolls, volleys of gunfire and the peeling of bells'?[27] Not Beethoven. Not even his memory. Such rituals belong to the 'Immortal Beethoven'. He has become the model of death and the promise of eternity for secular humanity; he calls his followers to the glory of art-religion. Wagner was not there at the ceremonies, but one could almost imagine the crowds intoning the *Credo* that Wagner wrote as the last rites of a Beethoven-worshipper. Wagner meant it as something of a parody, but as a parody it also exposes the ridiculous truth that belies the beliefs of those who, like Wagner, turned to the aesthetic for salvation.

I believe in God, Mozart and Beethoven . . . I believe in the Holy Spirit and the truth of the one, indivisible Art . . . I believe that through this Art all men are saved, and therefore each may die of hunger for Her. I believe that on earth I was a jarring discord, which will at once be perfectly resolved by death. I believe in a last judgement, which will condemn to fearful pains all those who in this world have dared to play the huckster with chaste Art, have violated and dishonoured Her through the evilness of their hearts and the ribald lust of their senses. I believe that these will be condemned through all eternity to hear their own vile music. I believe, on the other hand, that true disciples of high Art will be transfigured in a heavenly veil of sun-drenched fragrance and sweet sound, and united for eternity with the divine fount of all Harmony. May mine be the sentence of grace! Amen![28]

As with most cultic practices, the mystical act needs doctrinal validation. Since absolute music requires a monumental history to legitimise its significance in modernity (the new) and its transcendence in eternity (the canon), it needs a discourse to institutionalise the practice. Thus a new music history came into being that could eradicate as irrelevant the catalogues of 'world music' found, for example, in Forkel's *Allgemeine Geschichte der Musik*; such histories have no concept of the 'Work' and therefore do not constitute a 'Music history'. What the nineteenth century bequeathed to musicology was a history of music that canonises in the name of the absolute. In this sense, there is no music history before the concept of absolute music. It simply was not necessary. History did not need to explain the immortal significance of music, and music did not need to make history; no one was forced to follow Beethoven into the eternal glory of absolute music to become a monument for humanity; there was no genealogy in which composers begat one another in a

---

[27] Hector Berlioz, *Les soirées de l'orchestre* (Paris: Gründ, 1968), 424; the translation is taken from *Evenings with the Orchestra* (1852), trans. J. Barzun (Chicago: Chicago University Press, 1973), 337.

[28] Richard Wagner, 'Ein Ende in Paris', *Sämtliche Schriften*, 1:135; the translation has been modified from *Pilgrimage to Beethoven*, 66–7.

line of culture from Bach to Brahms,[29] spawning numerous children to squabble for legitimacy in the pantheon of 'Great Masters' (see plate 11). But the moment music died to become absolute and embalmed the composer in its image, music history sprang into being as its legitimising discourse. Thus, ironically, at the point in history when absolute music claims to have 'no need of history', it demands one.[30] This is because the only history that absolute music recalls is the moment it transcends history as an immutable work; it is therefore not *in* history, rather it makes history from the *outside* as an epistemological structure. This means that music history, like Nietzsche's monumental history, is a history *without history*. But then, it is also a history *without music*, because what it defines as music is a canonising concept called the 'absolute', which is designed to preserve music as a synchronic object in what Lydia Goehr calls an 'imaginary museum of works'.[31] And just to prove the point, the absolute flaunts its ahistorical status by embracing objects into the canon that predate its existence; the works of J. S. Bach, in particular, were hauled up retrospectively alongside the music of Beethoven to stand as the paradigm of absolute music for the nineteenth century, and were given a history that the eighteenth century would not have recognised as significant.[32]

The contradictions of music history are therefore partly a result of absolute music.[33] 'Music history . . . seems doomed to failure', writes Carl Dahlhaus,

on the one side it is flanked by the dictates of 'aesthetic autonomy', and on the other by a theory of history that clings to the concept of 'continuity'. Music history fails either as *history* by being a collection of structural analyses of separate works, or as a history of *art* by reverting from musical works to occurrences in social or intellectual history cobbled together in order to impart cohesion to an historical narrative.[34]

But this is not, in fact, a contradiction. History and analysis are complicit in the making of musical monuments. Music history records the heroic deeds for music analysis to immortalise as synchronic works. Conversely, music analysis arrests the progressive events of history to render them eternally significant, because the ephemeral and contingent cannot constitute a music history. Thus absolute music, as the *subject* of history and the *object* of analysis, both structures time and

---

[29] See Dahlhaus, *The Idea of Absolute Music*, 117–27.

[30] Wackenroder and Tieck, 'Symphonien', *Werke und Briefe von Wilhelm Heinrich Wackenroder*, 255.   [31] See Goehr, *The Imaginary Museum of Musical Works*.

[32] See Dahlhaus, *Foundations of Music History*, 10, 111 and 157.

[33] See Lydia Goehr, 'Writing Music History', *History and Theory*, vol. 31 no. 1 (1992).

[34] Dahlhaus, *Foundations of Music History*, 19–20.

Plate 11 Otto Böhler, *The Musician's Heaven* (c. 1897), silhouette. Proof that there is life after Beethoven. Circling from top left to bottom left: Haydn (on drums), Weber, Wagner, Bach (at the organ), Beethoven, Mozart, Handel, Gluck, Berlioz, Bülow, Liszt, Schubert, Mendelssohn, Bruckner, Schumann, Brahms (recently deceased, April 1897).

crystallises itself as timeless. It is this double activity that renders the birth of musicology in the nineteenth century a symptom of modernity, for the discourse attempts to ground modern society in timeless norms that are produced out of the progress of history. 'Modernity', writes Baudelaire, 'is the transient, the fleeting, and contingent; it is one half of art, the other being the eternal and immovable.'[35] And it was absolute music that constituted the 'eternal and immovable' element to which all art should aspire to in the nineteenth century. So if the *Eroica* Symphony, as Wilhelm von Lenz claims, is the monument of modernity to which humanity must bow the knee, then the function of musicology is to ensure that the infamous C♯ in bar eight, which Wagner called the note which 'represents all modern music',[36] remains eternally significant in the history of music. The job of the musicologist is not to make the monument, but to maintain it.

Maintenance: this is precisely the problem with monuments. Europe, having unveiled its newly cast effigy of Beethoven, could not kiss it clean forever. Schumann had warned the organisers of the Beethoven statue that 'a monument is a ruin facing forwards'.[37] And indeed, after the ceremonies, Berlioz noted that Beethoven's 'mighty hand' had merely become 'a perch for common birds'.[38] In reality, the timelessness of art is a delusion. Musical monuments decay. They exist in eternity only as long as the institutional discourse perpetuates itself as new; when the discourse exhausts itself, the aesthetic illusion is broken. Thus modernity reaches a crisis whenever its mechanism comes to self-consciousness, and this is perhaps the case with musicology today. The self-reflective and critical gestures of musicology issue from the realisation that the monuments they were supposed to immortalise are only mortal; the self-maintenance which musicology believed to be the property of autonomous music has turned out to be a function of its own discourse. So musicology comes to the knowledge that from its inception it has only ever been a cleaning of tombstones – a form of ancestral worship to appease the spirits of the dead at a time when humanity could no longer die in peace.

So what is left of the monument now? 'The monument is . . . that which endures in the form . . . of a funerary mask', remarks Gianni Vattimo on the question of art at the end of modernity; 'it is marked

---

[35] Charles Baudelaire, 'The Painter of Modern Life', in *Selected Writings on Art and Artists* (New York: Penguin, 1972), 403, cited in Habermas, *The Philosophical Discourse of Modernity*, 8.   [36] *Cosima Wagner's Diary*, 1:378 (17 June 1871).

[37] Robert Schumann [as Jonathan], 'A Monument to Beethoven' (1836), in *The Musical World of Robert Schumann: A Selection from his Own Writings*, trans. H. Pleasants (London: Gollancz, 1965), 93.

[38] Berlioz, *Les soirées de l'orchestre*, 411; the translation is taken from *Evenings with the Orchestra*, 326.

definitively . . . by mortality', he says.[39] Art monuments, for Vattimo, only endure time by gathering the past for the future in the form of decay. Nietzsche's monumental history is replaced by a history in ruins. Thus the idea of Beethoven 'shouting to us the avowal of his Godhood' in the *Eroica* Symphony – 'Forward! Trust me! Victory is assured' – rings hollow as a promise of eternal life in a post-modern world. Absolute music can no longer die to become immortal, for Vattimo, because the immortal has revealed itself as oblivion. Adorno says as much when he describes autonomous art as 'a work of contrived immortality';[40] it has no power now, except to protest against death and to succumb to the nothingness that haunts the modern ego. Similarly, for Paul de Man, the hollow sign of music signals the existential abyss of the subject.[41] In retrospect, Goethe's injunction to die and become has amounted to absolutely nothing.

Is this the end of absolute music or the death of musicology? Neither. Rather it is a return to their birth in the chaotic thought of the early Romantics. They, like Vattimo, and all the purveyors of death, were too sceptical to erect artworks as eternal monuments; the Romantics inscribed the anxiety of decay into the work in the form of fragments, sketches and ruins. The later nineteenth century had put too much faith in art, and forgot that the Romantic absolute only consists of the gaps between the broken pieces; to gather it back into a unity would be as futile as 'squaring a circle', says Novalis,[42] since a godless future is an open, contingent form; hence Romantic poetry is 'forever becoming' and 'never completed'.[43] The *'aesthetic* optimism', as Schlegel puts it, is directly related to a historical pessimism, and the Utopian hope is circumscribed by an ironic distance.[44] Modernity for the early Romantics was already a teleology in tatters. This is why the empty sign of music was chosen as 'an altar to an unknown god'.[45] The sacrifice may amount to nothing. The empty sign is an escape clause bequeathed by the Romantics in case history should fail. They wanted a secular apocalypse to structure history, but they also knew that, in all the dying and becoming called for by the absolute, the apocalypse may never materialise.

---

[39] Gianni Vattimo, *The End of Modernity: Nihilism and Hermeneutics in Post-Modern Culture*, trans. J. R. Snyder (Cambridge: Polity Press, 1988), 73.

[40] Adorno, *Aesthetische Theorie*, 209; Hullot-Kentor, 139. Also see the chapter in this volume 'On Suicide'.

[41] See Paul de Man, *Blindness and Insight: Essays in the Rhetoric of Contemporary Criticism*, second edition (London: Routledge, 1986), 18–19 and 130–1.

[42] Novalis (Friedrich von Hardenberg), *Schriften*, 2:269.

[43] Schlegel, *Athenaeum Fragments*, no. 116, in *Philosophical Fragments*, 32; translation modified.

[44] Friedrich Schlegel, *Philosophical Apprenticeship*, trans. F. C. Beiser in *The Early Political Writings of the German Romantics* (Cambridge: Cambridge University Press, 1996), 162.

[45] Acts 17:23.

31

On the apocalypse

What artist has ever troubled himself with the political events of the
day anyway? He lived only for his art ... But a dark and unhappy
age has seized men with an iron fist, and the pain squeezes from
them sounds that were formerly alien to them.

(E. T. A. Hoffmann)[1]

The apocalypse was over. Actually, the end of the world, as with most
apocalyptic predictions, was a bit of a let-down. It was more like an
'apocalypse without apocalypse', to borrow Derrida's phrase,[2] a catastrophe without a *parousia* to close history, leaving a premature ending
with nothing but the boredom of a finality without end. The crisis after
the apocalypse is the anxiety of normality.

From time to time, apocalyptic fevers would seize the imagination of
humanity, particularly in the form of *fin-de-siècle* crises;[3] the end of the
eighteenth century was no different, except that this time it was to be an
apocalypse without God, which meant that humanity had to pick up the
pieces of its own shattered expectations and bear the guilt of its own
failure. With a secular apocalypse, the command is not to wait but to act,
to seize history as *kairos* and to force the apocalypse to appear in concrete reality – as Revolution or Terror, or in the form of Napoleon riding
out on his horse as the Messiah or the Anti-Christ. These cataclysmic
signs were to be the hope and despair of those who wanted to see the
dissolution of their time as 'harbingers of an approaching age'.
Lightning will strike, says the young Hegel; 'the edifice of the real
world' will suddenly be revealed,[4] and heaven would appear on earth
as the kingdom of humanity.[5]

It was particularly the French Revolution (1789) that ignited the passions of the Enlightenment, for here, it seemed, the light of human

---

[1] Hoffmann, *Kreisleriana*, in *E. T. A. Hoffmann's Musical Writings*, 111.
[2] Jacques Derrida, *D'un ton apocalyptique adopté naguère en philosophie* (Paris: Editions
Galilée, 1983), 95.   [3] See Kermode, *A Sense of Ending*, 9–17.
[4] Georg Wilhelm Friedrich Hegel, *Phänomenologie des Geistes*, in *Werke in 20 Bänden*
(Frankfurt: Suhrkamp, 1986), 3:18–19.
[5] On the eschatological influence of Christian mysticism on German Romantic philosophy, see Benz, *The Mystical Sources of German Romantic Philosophy*, 27–46.

reason could finally prove itself in a new society that would jettison the past and break the yoke of man's 'self-incurred tutelage'.[6] No longer was truth to be entrusted to the past as something to be received without question from the hands of priests and kings; from now on, truth will be disclosed by history, as humanity shapes the future from within itself towards the perfection of a new world. Novalis called this the 'teleology of the revolution'.[7] Thus by the turn of the nineteenth century, *truth was tied to time*, and this eschatological force put history under such teleological pressure that the here-and-now of human decision erupted into a crisis of modernity – *now* is the time to seize the truth as action. It was this messianic 'now' that Kant was said to have uttered in the words of the *Nunc Dimittis* on hearing the news of the French Revolution. At last, his eyes had seen the salvation of the world. The Kingdom of God had come in the politics of man.

But time and truth did not coincide to fulfil the prophetic 'now' in the explosion of the moment. After a while, the 'now' took on a peculiar elasticity; the immediate was stretched and forestalled by endless recalculations and revisions, through the blood and violence that was the reality of the revolutionary ideals. There was no happy *parousia* to end this 'now', merely the ordeal of its prolongation. The whole fiasco was, in reality, the apocalypse of history, whose failure left modernity at a loose end. What do you do when you are left behind after your own apocalypse? The revenge of God on mankind for stealing his *kairos* is aesthetic theory.

Simply count the books: Kant's *Nunc Dimittis* faded into the teleological inertia of his *Critique of Judgement* (1790). Schiller's reaction to the barbarity of the Terror was to reconfigure the revolutionary ideals within the human psyche as an *Aesthetic Education* (1793–4); 'if man is ever to solve the problem of politics', he writes, 'he will have to approach it through the problem of the aesthetic'.[8] As for the early Romantics, their vision of poesis is the revolution internalised as the creative force of the ego, and declared in the manifesto of a new philosophy: the revolution became the absolute freedom of poetry itself. Romantic art is the language of 'the revolution in person', says Maurice Blanchot;[9] it is self-declaration, creative action, absolute production. But even this for Schlegel was merely the 'lightning on the horizon of poetry'. Writing at the dawn of a new century, he predicted another storm, a poetic apocalypse of such intensity that the confusion and opacity of Romantic thought would be sucked out as a mere nothing in

[6] See Immanuel Kant, 'An Answer to the Question: What is Enlightenment?' (1784), in *Perpetual Peace and Other Essays*, trans. T. Humphrey (Indianapolis: Hackett, 1983).

[7] Novalis (Friedrich von Hardenberg), *Schriften*, 3:575.

[8] Schiller, *On the Aesthetic Education of Man*, 9.

[9] Blanchot, 'The Athenaeum', *The Infinite Conversation*, 355.

the dazzling transparency of the age to come. He ends the *Athenaeum* as apocalypse: 'For a long time', he writes, 'it thundered mightily, now it seems to lighten only in the distance, but soon it will return with more horrible force. Soon we will speak no longer of a single thunderstorm because the whole heaven will burn in a massive flame . . . Then will the nineteenth century actually begin.'[10]

Thus in German culture, the aesthetic took over the apocalypse to spin out the end, in the hope that art might extend the messianic 'now' for a belated *parousia*. Art was to be the bridge for the diremption of time and truth, perpetuating the revolution as *cultural* progress: 'The revolutionary desire to realise the Kingdom of God on earth', writes Schlegel, 'is the elastic point of a progressive civilisation [*Bildung*] and the beginning of modern history';[11] Schlegel claims in this fragment that modern civilisation starts with an art that propels itself from 'the elastic point' of the present towards an earthly Utopia, in order to express the restless and relentless condition of modernity. Romanticism therefore ends the *querelle des anciens et des modernes*: from now on, antiquity is barred from the present as the perfection of an unattainable past, whereas the Romantic is exalted as the present striving towards an unattainable future. As A. W. Schlegel puts it: 'The poetry of the ancients was that of possession, ours is that of longing.'[12] In other words, classical perfection, with its boundaries of taste and decorum, can no longer be attained, but it can be transgressed. With the Romantics, art is to be released into the infinite expansion of the creative universe, freed from the confines of nature and representation, and given an almost iconoclastic desire to destroy and disfigure itself in order to surpass itself. With each new articulation of the present, the artist relegates his achievements to the past, so that modernity might march forward as revolution.

But with regret. This is the paradox of Romanticism and its radical poetics. The *aesthetic* 'now' is always too late. By the time art stepped into modern history, modernity was already old and wizened, having lived off the inexhaustible progress promised by modern science since the seventeenth century. Having lost its faith in God,[13] and scarred by the violence of the revolution, the face of modernity turned towards the aesthetic as consolation for a deferred Utopia, hoping to preserve some

---

[10] *Athenaeum: Eine Zeitschrift von August Wilhelm Schlegel und Friedrich Schlegel*, ed. B. Sorg (Dortmund: Harenberg Edition, 1989), 2:1085; the translation is from Forstman, *A Romantic Triangle*, 18.

[11] Schlegel, *Athenaeum Fragments*, no. 222; translation slightly modified from *Philosophical Fragments*, 48.

[12] Cited in William Desmond, *Art and the Absolute: A Study of Hegel's Aesthetics* (Albany: State University of New York Press, 1986), 109.

[13] See Habermas, *The Philosophical Discourse of Modernity*, 5–11.

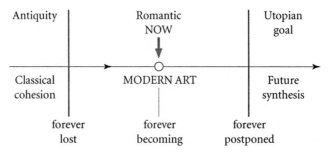

Fig. 5 Schlegel's aesthetic teleology

of its ideals in a time of hibernation. For all its revolutionary energy, the aesthetic imbued the technological optimism of the Enlightenment with a melancholic tinge, producing a strange inertia, even as it spurred history onwards; it was a condition of indecision and division which conjured up the figure of Hamlet in Schlegel's mind. Like Hamlet, there is a 'boundless disproportion [in modern philosophy] . . . between the thinking force and the active force', says Schlegel. This 'philosophical tragedy' is the theme of aesthetics, for art, as a reflective activity, takes the revolution out of the world of action, and curls up as the autonomous object of aesthetic theory.[14] The 'elastic point' between the abortive apocalypse and the *parousia* is therefore a negative interval in which the chemical aesthetic of modernity strives, knowing its loss of cohesion as it looks back to the works of antiquity and yet animated by a chaotic energy as it presses towards some unknown synthesis called the 'organic age' (see figure 5).[15] Thus Romantic art does not live to spin out a 'concordant history',[16] but rather questions it, using its sublime and ironic tactics to distance itself from the Utopian goals, even in the desire to realise them. This is why modern poetry for Schlegel is always in a state of becoming but is never allowed to arrive, in case it rehearses the catastrophe of yet another premature apocalypse.

The aesthetic process is therefore caught up in a sense of ending that it is unable to finish. Nothing captures its paradoxical existence more concisely than Kant's definition of the beautiful: *Zweckmässigkeit ohne Zweck* – a purposiveness without purpose, a finality without end. Kant's aesthetic process is basically a teleological structure with its origin and end removed so that it is without external cause or external finality; the teleological process folds in upon itself as an inner purposiveness, creat-

---

[14] Friedrich Schlegel, *1794–1802, Seine prosaischen Jugendschriften*, ed. J. Minor (Vienna, 1882), 1:107, cited in Szondi, *On Textual Understanding and Other Essays*, 59.

[15] Schlegel, *Athenaeum Fragments*, no. 426, in *Philosophical Fragments*, 87; also see the chapter 'On Conscious Life-forms', in this volume.

[16] See Kermode, *A Sense of Ending*, 58–9.

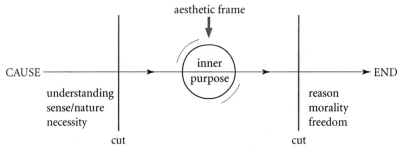

Fig. 6 Kant's aesthetic teleology

ing an organic, self-legislating form that has no practical function (see figure 6). It is as if the historical drive of modernity has withdrawn from the world of *praxis* into an aesthetic realm that has lost faith in the naïve eschatology of the revolution. In art, the end must be signified but never disclosed; hence, for Kant, the beautiful is only a subjective movement of reflection and never an actual object. After all, as Kant says in a late essay on the 'End of All Things' (1794), it is both foolish and perverse for mere mortals to manufacture an apocalyptic end.[17] It is better to live in the fiction of the aesthetic process *as if* reality exhibited an end.

In fact, for Schiller, this fictive condition is the only way for humanity to recover from the political trauma of the revolution: man has to be reduced to an aesthetic state of absolute zero so that he might erase the depraved determinations that have perverted the course of human history. The Kantian conflict of freedom and necessity (see figure 6) is reinterpreted by Schiller as an antagonism between a form-drive and a sense-drive, in which the physical impulse of nature and the moral compulsion of freedom are made to 'cancel each other out as determining forces',[18] creating an aesthetic condition of pure play, which is in fact purely empty (see figure 7). In this void, man recovers his freedom as a moral being, for the conflicting impulses that tear him apart are reintegrated in aesthetic form. So humanity realises itself 'beautifully' as the different drives freely shape each other from an internal logic to create a social whole. Art is a catalyst for political freedom. However, it is also a fictional *praxis*. If for Schiller, man shapes the future by returning 'to that negative state of complete absence of determination . . . devoid of all content', then he discovers a state of freedom where humanity has nothing *in particular* to do.[19] It is a prelapsarian state of inertia in which the totality of the future is communicated as an aesthetic blank. Schiller's 'culture', comments Terry Eagleton, 'is the negative of

---

[17] See Kant, 'The End of All Things', in *Perpetual Peace and Other Essays*.
[18] Schiller, *On the Aesthetic Education of Man*, 141.   [19] Ibid.

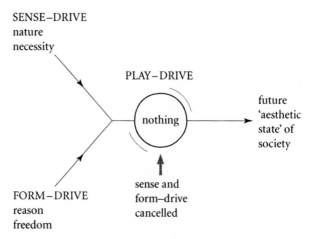

Fig. 7 Schiller's model of aesthetic teleology

all concrete claims and commitments in the name of totality'.[20] Despite the political imperatives, Schiller's aesthetic is socially useless; it literally *plays* itself out of the field of action in order to prolong the apocalypse as indifference.

Schiller, Kant and Schlegel had relatively little to say about music, but in a sense their aesthetic strategies were already music. Or to put it the other way round: instrumental music merely needed to stumble into their theoretical structures to become absolute. Kant's inner teleological process resembles the movement of the empty sign, curving back upon itself as its own cause and end; Schiller's aesthetic void is the very condition of a music that drains out all particularities to represent its fullness as nothing; and Schlegel's vision of a 'progressive culture' is realised in a musical sign that strives towards the absolute, articulating nothing so that it might posit the 'Kingdom of God on earth' as ineffable.

In this sense, the birth of absolute music was inevitable. It was an apocalyptic concept for an eschatological aesthetic. The theoretical legitimation of instrumental music at the turn of the nineteenth century therefore takes on a historical significance; it signals the beginning of a melancholic modernity that expresses its progress in the knowledge of its own deficiencies. Instrumental music is both desire and scepticism, apocalyptic drive and inertia. It contains a double-edged politics, symbolised by the plenitude of the vacant sign. On the one hand, music in discovering its 'pure being' discovers itself as negative; it cancels Utopia as unattainable desire. Yet, on the other hand, this very negation is seen as the potential force of human self-realisation. Indeed, Karl Marx, in his

---

[20] Eagleton, *Ideology of the Aesthetic*, 109.

Grundrisse, envisaged the power of economic man making himself through his material productivity as an activity which issues from the creative freedom of the musical imagination.[21] Thus instrumental music frames a loss of meaning in order to recover it.

In this way, the concept of musical *kenosis* becomes a necessary stage in the redemption of mankind. All that interminable yearning and longing of the Romantics is not due to an excess of emotion but an excess of vision. E. T. A. Hoffmann, for example, in an essay on 'Old and New Church Music' (1814), places instrumental music in an apocalyptic history where it articulates the negative interval between catastrophe and *parousia*. The past, idealised as the sacred music of Palestrina, is no longer possible, claims Hoffmann; indeed, the sacred voice cannot even be heard through 'the seething clamour of frenzied activity that has broken over' the world. Only the voiceless, empty yearning of instrumental music can express the condition of the 'modern age striving for inner spirituality'; only the pain of articulating the ineffable can capture the 'spirit of the age [that] forever drives us on and on'. For all its absolute claims, instrumental music is only an interim measure for a time when humanity could no longer make sense of history; it merely projects the vague hope that one day the sacred voice may return to reharmonise humanity with nature. 'May the time of fulfilment of our hopes no longer be far away', writes Hoffmann. 'May a devout life of peace and joy be dawning, and may music, free and strong, stir its seraph wings and begin its flight towards the world beyond, which is its home and from which consolation and grace shine down upon man's uneasy breast.'[22]

Hoffmann's concept of instrumental music therefore commits itself to the unfolding of historical truth. It was born in hard times as the consolation of Europe. It functions as a form of sublime negation whose inarticulate movements yearn for a completion of meaning if only history would bring about a happy ending. Thus on the horizon of poetry, it is instrumental music that brews the apocalyptic storm that Schlegel predicted, stirring a sense of 'nameless haunted yearning' as humanity waits for the flash of lightning that would set the heavens ablaze.[23] The French Revolution, says Hoffmann, has 'swept across the earth like a devastating storm; but it was a storm that sent the dark clouds scudding, and now the dawn, sending its precursory glimmer through the black night . . . is about to break in all its splendour over our unhappy world'.[24] This 'precursory glimmer' is what Hoffmann sees in Beethoven. It is no accident that Hoffmann conceives the whole of

[21] See Desmond, *Art and the Absolute*, 51.
[22] Hoffmann, 'Old and New Church Music', *E. T. A. Hoffmann's Musical Writings*, 376 and 373; translation slightly modified.
[23] Hoffmann, 'Review of Beethoven's Fifth Symphony', *E. T. A. Hoffmann's Musical Writings*, 250. [24] Hoffmann, 'Old and New Church Music', 354.

Ex. 34 Beethoven, Symphony no. 5 in C minor, third movement – bs 1–27.

Beethoven's C minor Symphony as meteorological omens; the music creates 'storm-clouds' that stir the seas and unleash demonic spirits as premonitions of some cataclysmic explosion of light.[25] These apocalyptic symbols form a language of anticipation to parallel a work whose tonal and thematic conflicts propel the music forward. The ineluctable force that steers the symphony through its tonal history is controlled by holding back the Utopian event of the final movement – C major as revolutionary light. Anticipation is therefore the potential energy of a music that pushes time to the point of kinetic release. Hoffmann, for example, examines the 'intensifying effect' of phrase extensions in the

[25] See Hoffmann, 'Review of Beethoven's Fifth Symphony', 244–5.

Ex. 35 Beethoven, Symphony no. 5 in C minor, third movement –
phrase lengths.

bars	Anticipatory theme (*pp*)		bars	Trumpet theme (*f*)
1–18	8 + 10 bar phrasing	V	19–44	8 + 8 + (4 + 6)
45–70	8 + 18	V	71–96	8 + 8 + (4 + 6)
97–132	36	I	133–40	8

third movement (Allegro).[26] These phrases are anticipatory structures;
they are anacrustic in content and form, delaying and deferring the
downbeats both within the phrase and as part of the structure (see
example 34).

Moreover, they are repeated end on end, piling up anticipation after
anticipation, with each repetition extended to intensify the force of
expectation. These phrases seem infinitely malleable in the way they set
up different trajectories for the arrival of the apocalyptic trumpets (b.
19ff – on the horns!) that enunciate the structural downbeat. Indeed,
they announce the tonic with such force that they terrify the consequent
theme into a formal rigidity (see example 34).

This pattern of contrast between expectation and event is repeated
three times. With each occurrence, the anticipatory element is stretched
out into longer phrases, until it almost takes over the form, pre-empting
the tonic (b. 132) and leaving only eight bars for the consequent phrase
to close the section (see example 35).

This process of ever-increasing anticipation culminates with the
return of the Allegro (b. 236ff); everything is now *sempre pianissimo*, as if
the blare of the apocalyptic trumpets has been swallowed up by the
anticipatory phrases to turn the entire reprise into a transition.[27] Indeed
the formal enclosure of the third movement is dismantled so that *transition* can be its form and content. The movement simply slides into the
finale, as the elastic point and negative interval of the work's history.
This apocalyptic sense is intensified in the final fifty bars (bs 324–73);
Beethoven elongates an interrupted cadence as a giant cadential motion
which not only presses time forward with the logic of a linear unfolding in the upper voice, but also sets its harmonies recalcitrantly against
the object of desire by drumming out C as thunder (see example 36).

'These heavy, dissonant blows', writes Hoffmann, 'sounding like a
strange and dreadful voice, arouse a horror of the extraordinary.'[28]
In fact, this rumbling on the timpani is the upbeat of the trumpet theme

[26] Ibid., 248.   [27] On transition, see Kermode, *A Sense of Ending*, 12.
[28] Hoffmann, 'Review of Beethoven's Fifth Symphony', 247.

Ex. 36 Beethoven, Symphony no. 5 in C minor, third movement –
transition.

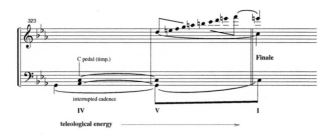

($\downarrow\downarrow\downarrow$ | $\downarrow$.), stretched over fifty bars, like a giant anacrusis ($\downarrow\downarrow\downarrow$ | $\downarrow\downarrow\downarrow$ | $\downarrow\downarrow\downarrow$ | $\downarrow\downarrow\downarrow$ etc.), with fragments of the anticipatory theme extended over it, to crown the finale as the consequent structure of the entire symphony – the end-accent of the end-time. The finale arrives as *parousia*. Indeed, the audiences in Paris heard this symphony as their revolution.[29] When C major strikes, 'like a brilliant shaft of blinding sunlight',[30] it is the annunciation of the messianic 'now', forced by the Promethean powers of the human will in its struggle with history to redeem catastrophe as victory. This C major chord, to use Adorno's words, can be heard 'forward and backward at the same time'; as the *telos* of the work, this chord contains the entire symphony by making sense of its internal history.[31]

But this chord is not the end. In fact, there is no end. The finale simply plays with the sense of ending over and over again. Endings happen twice. The transition of the third movement returns in the finale so that the entire process of crisis and release can be intensified and reorganised, this time with some eighty bars of dominant preparation before the tonic downbeat (bs 505–80). Even the very end happens twice: the symphony could have closed with the four cadential gestures in bars 686–9, but Beethoven postpones the closure by extending the same cadential figure from four bars to 150 bars, going beyond the structural necessity of the work to leave E. T. A Hoffmann in a state of hypertension. The cadences remind him of the opening hammerstrokes: 'They act like a fire that is thought to have been put out but repeatedly bursts forth again in bright tongues of flames.' The apocalyptic lightning has set the

---

[29] See Beate Angelika Kraus, 'Beethoven and the Revolution: The View of the French Musical Press', in *Music and the French Revolution*, ed. M. Boyd (Cambridge: Cambridge University Press, 1992).

[30] Hoffmann, 'Review of Beethoven's Fifth Symphony', 248.

[31] Theodor W. Adorno, *Hegel: Three Studies*, trans. S. W. Nicholsen (Cambridge, MA: MIT Press, 1993), 136.

music on fire and it cannot be extinguished; the cadences can only be repeated as finality without end; the music keeps on ending – even after the final barlines. The 'one lasting emotion', says Hoffmann, is 'that of nameless, haunted yearning':[32] 'nameless' because the internal history that Beethoven creates out of the tonal crisis posits Utopia as nothing other than the pure vacuity of the musical sign; 'yearning', because the formal definitions of the work are infinitely deferred beyond the final chord by a sublime consciousness which, like its ironic counterpart, destroys reality as illusion. Despite the teleological energy, Utopia is left inarticulate.

Absolute music is therefore Zechariah, struck dumb by humanity until it can name the child of promise.[33] For Hoffmann, the ultimate desire is *to speak*. When the *parousia* comes it will be as *logos*, and the opacity of the present age will be elucidated by the transparency of the voice. If humanity began with song, as the Romantics believed,[34] then it will close with song; cause and end will harmonise to cancel the negative interval of instrumental music; singing, writes Hoffmann, is an 'expression of the *plenitude* of existence'.[35] Modernity is meant to progress towards objective clarity.[36] Hence, if Utopia arrives, instrumental music would cease to be of any significance, for it would have nothing to signify. This is why the concept of absolute music from its inception was always in danger of losing its identity in the Idealist urge for a *Gesamtkunstwerk*. Absolute music was designed to dissolve into the whole and lose its soul to gain the world. Hanslick, by calcifying the concept as form, cancelled the apocalyptic consciousness of absolute music: Wagner, by cancelling the future of absolute music, fulfils the totality that is the desire of the empty sign. He merely completes what Schelling predicted at the turn of the nineteenth century:

I will content myself with adding one further remark, that the most perfected connection of all the arts, the reunion of poetry and music in song, of poetry and painting in dance, each in its turn synthesised, constitutes dramatic manifestation at the summit of its composition, as was the drama of Antiquity, of which no more than a caricature is left to us – the *opera* which, given a more elevated and noble style of poetry and of the other arts collaborating with it, could bring us best to the execution of ancient drama tied to music and song.[37]

---

[32] Hoffmann, 'Review of Beethoven's Fifth Symphony', 250.

[33] See Luke 1:5–25 and 57–80.

[34] See, for example, Wilhelm von Humboldt, *On Language: The Diversity of Human Language-Structure and Its Influence on the Mental Development of Mankind*, trans. P. Heath (Cambridge: Cambridge University Press, 1988), 60. Also see Richard Wagner, 'Zukunftsmusik' (1861), *Sämtliche Schriften*, 7:110, translated in *Judaism in Music and Other Essays*, 318.   [35] Hoffmann, 'Old and New Church Music', 355; my emphasis.

[36] See Grey, *Wagner's Musical Prose*, 45–50.

[37] Friedrich Wilhelm Joseph von Schelling, *Philosophie der Kunst* (1802–3), cited in Lacoue-Labarthe and Nancy, *The Literary Absolute*, 99.

In Romantic fashion, Schelling projects the perfection of the past into the infinity of the future. Instrumental music, in this structure, is only the means of completion, an interim absolute for a greater totality, a movement from a negative absolute to a positive one. As Philippe Lacoue-Labarthe claims: 'the *Gesamtkunstwerk* – which is the Work in absolute terms, the absolute *organon* of Schelling, or, as Nietzsche will say, the *opus metaphysicum* – posits itself as the very *end* of art in the form of the unification and synthesis . . . of all the individual arts', that is, as 'the *musical* sublation of all the arts'.[38] The only problem with completing the system, however, is that it might betray history as a false ending. The moment knowledge is completed as truth, music's ironic and self-negating nature will disappear into the whole, creating a totality which, if untrue, will jar against Utopian history as a kind of Wagnerian totalitarianism.[39] The realisation of absolute music, as Adorno was aware, could usher in Utopia as disaster.[40]

But Wagner, stirred by the renewed apocalyptic visions of 1848, could not wait in the wings to watch the postponement of the drama by an infinite overture. He had to read Beethoven's Ninth Symphony as the completion of Utopia in song in order to justify his prophetic calling. To Wagner's ears, the formal disintegration of the finale is the point of historical synthesis; the infinite and the definite coalesce in the *Choral Symphony*, he claims, as the primordial chaos of instrumental desire is harnessed by the *logos* of the human voice. What was before 'an indefinite presage of the Highest [instrumental music]', writes Wagner, 'has now been transformed to a godlike consciousness [vocal music]'.[41] The ineffable can now be known; the system is complete; Beethoven, says A. B. Marx, has returned to the voice to 'celebrate . . . its victory over the world of instruments'.[42] If the song has triumphed, then the new spiritual age of humanity that Hoffmann longed for has come. By the force of the aesthetic will, the apocalypse has been made good.

---

[38] Lacoue-Labarthe, *Musica Ficta*, 7.

[39] Or worse still, the 'totally aestheticised state' of Fascism that Benjamin and Adorno speak of. See, for example, Lacoue-Labarthe, *Heidegger, Art and Politics*.

[40] Adorno, *Aesthetische Theorie*, 55–6; Hullot-Kentor, 32–3.

[41] Richard Wagner, *Eine Pilgerfahrt zu Beethoven* (1840), in *Sämtliche Schriften*, 1:111, translated in *Pilgrimage to Beethoven and Other Essays*, 42; translation modified. Wagner, by turning to absolute music after the failure of the 1848 revolution, rehearses the aesthetic strategy of the Romantics after the failure of the 1789 revolution. As John Deathridge suggests, the loss of confidence in history mirrored in Wagner's pessimistic turn to Schopenhauer and to absolute music already indicates a 'post-Modern condition'; see Deathridge, 'Wagner and the Post-Modern'.

[42] Adolf Bernhard Marx, *Berliner Allgemeine Musikalische Zeitung* (1826), 375, cited in Kropfinger, *Wagner and Beethoven*, 55.

32

On the end

[I]t is just amazing . . . Beethoven died only a few years ago, and yet H[egel] declares that German art is as dead as a rat.

(Mendelssohn)[1]

If only. And yet the endless negations and negotiations of Utopia can be a tedious business. It does not take long for eschatological desire to sink into procrastination; *kairos* soon dissipates into *ennui*. Instrumental music was meant to keep the revolutionary vision alive, but for how long can the aesthetic stall the end before it wears itself out and resigns its fate to the everyday? How many cataclysmic cadences does it take to end a Beethoven symphony before music stops ranting and settles down into the comfort of a Biedermeier armchair? Can music go on negating and ironising forever? Can the revolutionary 'now' be stretched into infinity without eventually contradicting itself? The problem with an apocalyptic aesthetic is that it cannot last by definition.

Romanticism ends badly. This is the way with apocalyptic narratives: the end is too determinate to have contingency plans; if history stumbles, then music falls with it. And it did not take long for music to register its Utopian failure. Either it withdrew into the mundane world of Biedermeier sensibilities, recoiling with a lyrical regret into miniature forms that erased all apocalyptic pretensions, or it destroyed its own visions of Utopia by subjecting its existence to endless self-critique. Before absolute music had even consolidated its position as an institutional idea, the absolute productivity of the Romantic ego had exhausted itself.

Hegel was tired of its empty longings as early as 1803; an art that hankers after an inaccessible past and an unattainable future is an art that denies the present and sets the absolute *beyond* reality, he claims; it misrepresents the absolute and so forfeits its access to historical truth; Romanticism is unable to grasp the totality. Art, writes Hegel, 'must free itself from its yearnings, from its singularity that has a beyond in the past and the future, and wrest the world-spirit forth in the form of

---

[1] Letter of 28 May 1830, in Felix Mendelssohn, *Letters*, ed. G. Seldon-Goth (London: Paul Elek, 1946), 128.

universality'.[2] By the 1820s, Hegel was declaring Romanticism 'the end of art'. He branded Schlegel as the beast of the apocalypse, rising out of the abyss of ironic subjectivity to annihilate the entire world.[3] This ironic posture, which Hegel believed to be modelled on the Fichtean ego, creates and destroys everything in its delusions of freedom.[4] But this kind of ironic solipsism has no transcendent possibility for Hegel, because there is no substance to transcend; it merely indicates the impotence of a subject unable to objectify itself in reality. The endless negations ultimately corner the ego in its own 'isolation and self-seclusion'.[5] Thus, in believing itself to be pure productivity, the Romantic subject in fact produces nothing but its own alienation. If this is an absolute, then it is an 'absolute evil', claims Hegel, for in his system the dialectical shifts always arrive at a unity of object and subject – 'the truth is the whole [Das Wahre ist das Ganze]'[6] – whereas for Schlegel, the same oscillation of creation and negation dwindles into infinity, and so deliberately fails to posit any form of objective truth; with every turn of the dialectic, the subject pokes its head round the corner and says, 'it is I'.[7] Very droll – but to what end? This is precisely the problem for Hegel; there can be no end in an aesthetic that undermines its own foundations to delay the end of history. Such a conceit merely drains out the 'substantive content' of art, so that 'everything appears null and void'.[8] The empty self empties the truth of art. Or, to put it the other way round: since the vacuous whim of the subject has become the content of art, the creative act plays itself out of the *telos* of human history and loses its privilege to objectify truth in the Hegelian system. 'The work of art', writes Hegel, is meant to bring 'before us the *eternal* powers that hold dominion in *history*',[9] but art in its most modern manifestation is so free

---

[2] Georg Wilhelm Friedrich Hegel, *System der Sittlichkeit* (Hamburg: Felix Meiner, 1967), 331, translated by H. S. Harris and T. M. Knox as *Hegel's System of Ethical Life and His First Philosophy of Spirit* (Albany: State University of New York Press, 1979), 252–3. For a discussion of this passage, see Gillian Rose, *Hegel Contra Sociology* (London: Athlone, 1981), 75.   [3] See Behler, *Irony and the Discourse of Modernity*, 85–92.

[4] Hegel, *Aesthetik*, 1:93–9. Hegel's prose is notoriously difficult to translate. There are two English translations of his Aesthetics, the 1920 translation by F. P. B. Osmaston, reissued as *The Philosophy of Fine Art* (New York: Hacker, 1975) and T. M. Knox's translation, *Aesthetics: Lectures on Fine Art* (Oxford: Clarendon Press, 1975), not to mention the translations of the sections on music in Le Huray and Day, *Music Aesthetics in the Eighteenth and Early-Nineteenth Centuries*, and Edward Lippman, *Musical Aesthetics: A Historical Reader*, vol. 2 (Stuyvesant: Pendragon Press, 1988). These translations tend to vary widely: I mainly use the T. M. Knox translation, but where appropriate I have used or modified phrases from the other translations.

[5] Hegel, *Aesthetik*, 1:96, Osmaston, 1:91.

[6] Hegel, *Phänomenologie des Geistes*, in *Werke in 20 Bänden*, 3:24.

[7] Ibid., 3:490. Also see Behler, *Irony and the Discourse of Modernity*, 87.

[8] Hegel, *Aesthetik*, 1:96, Osmaston, 1:91.

[9] Ibid., 1:22–3, Knox, 1:9; my emphasis.

as to be totally arbitrary, with no eternal significance in history; it has degenerated from Kantian *Freiheit* into Schlegelian *Willkür*.

Had Hegel hated music as much as he hated Schlegel he would have lambasted instrumental music. As it is, he does not bother; but this nonchalance may have been part of his critique. It is as if he were saying: instrumental music is insignificant – a mere trifle of technicalities for the connoisseur;[10] the Romantics are mistaken to read so much universality into its emptiness. And to underline the point, Hegel levels exactly the same accusations against instrumental music as he did against Schlegel.[11] This is because instrumental music for Hegel is chemical and not organic;[12] it is ironic by nature, because it moves in time as 'negative activity'; the articulation of each tone, he argues, cancels out the previous one.[13] If 'the truth is the whole', then instrumental music, as 'negative activity', can never objectify itself as truth.[14] Without concepts to define its form, music's freedom is merely arbitrary, and is therefore susceptible to all kinds of 'fancies, conceits, interruptions, ingenious freaks, deceptive agitations, surprising turns, leaps and flashes, eccentricities, and extraordinary effects' of the ironic composer.[15]

Many commentators have aligned Hegel's dialectics with Beethoven's symphonic structures, seeing the tonal and thematic resolution of sonata form as a process of synthesis,[16] but Hegel himself would have heard these sounds as the dialectical failure of a music that is unable to grasp the truth (the whole), and is therefore incapable of articulating freedom. Instrumental music is historically irrelevant. In Hegel's process of world history, the aesthetic flowers and fades as part of humanity's struggle to realise its essential freedom. 'Freedom is the highest destiny of spirit', says Hegel, and the function of art is to convey this freedom in sensuous form.[17] But the subject, as it works out its destiny, destroys the perfect integration of content and form found in the art of Greek antiquity. In the post-classical world, the subject can no longer realise itself beautifully in sensuous form; instead, the subject has

---

[10] See ibid., 3:216, Knox, 2:953–4.   [11] See Bowie, *Aesthetics and Subjectivity*, 179–88.

[12] Georg Wilhelm Friedrich Hegel, *Wissenschaft der Logik*, translated by A. V. Miller as *Hegel's Science of Logic* (London: George Allen and Unwin, 1965), 355.

[13] Hegel, *Aesthetik*, 3:155–7 and 164, Knox, 2:907–8 and 913; translation modified.

[14] See ibid., 3:135, Knox, 2:891.   [15] Ibid., 3:218, Knox, 2:955.

[16] See, for example, Adorno, *Introduction to the Sociology of Music*, 210, Philip Barford, 'The Approach to Beethoven's Late Music', *Music Review*, vol. 30 (1969), Christopher Ballantine, 'Beethoven, Hegel and Marx', *The Musical Review*, vol. 33 (1972), the exchange between Robert C. Solomon and Maynard Solomon in 'Beethoven and the Sonata Form' and 'Beethoven and the Enlightenment', *Telos*, vol. 19 (Spring, 1974), and Janet Schmalfeldt, 'Form as the Process of Becoming: The Beethoven-Hegelian Tradition and the "Tempest" Sonata', *Beethoven Forum 4*, ed. C. Reynolds, L. Lockwood and J. Webster (Lincoln: University of Nebraska Press, 1995).

[17] Hegel, *Aesthetik*, 1:134, Knox, 1:97.

negated form, in its search for spiritual freedom, transcending the beautiful to leave the aesthetic behind for a synthesis *beyond* art; the reflective consciousness of modernity requires philosophy and not art to articulate its freedom.[18] But the early Romantics, deaf to the spirit of history, insist that one should form 'one's life *artistically'*,[19] which, in Hegel's aesthetics, is like pouring modernity into old wineskins. Consequently, their aspiration to freedom will end up as a contradiction between reality and the unity they desire. The disintegration of modern art is therefore symptomatic of a society populated by Romantic individuals where universal freedom is merely a formal concept imposed on reality, but is not found in actual experience.[20] Modern man projects an aesthetic totality, thinking himself free only because he is blind to his unfreedom.[21] So instead of synthesising the divisions of modernity, modern music merely enacts them, covering up the cracks with a façade of abstract freedom. 'If music is to be nothing but music', comments Hegel, then it is 'entirely free'; but this 'unfettered freedom' is simply a tautology in which music declares itself to be music – its freedom is 'in and for itself'.[22] Like the ironic subject, music discovers its being only to find its freedom locked in the 'self-seclusion of the ego . . . void of externality';[23] instead of grasping the universal (*All-gemeine*), it represents the delusion of the isolated individual, spurning the outside world to vanish inside the 'empty self'.[24] And if the ego is empty, then 'music is empty' too,[25] or rather, its content is 'the self without any further content'.[26] Thus for Hegel, instrumental music has nothing definite to say in the unfolding of time, so it might as well bow out of history to make way for something more articulate – namely, religion and philosophy. The end of music is therefore nothing more than a loose end that must be pulled out of the fabric of history, for instead of seizing time as *kairos*, instrumental music seems to simulate the aimless, endless succession which Hegel derides as 'bad infinity'.[27] The empty sign has rendered the apocalyptic thrust of the aesthetic meaningless, and so signals the death of music history. The end.

Despite issuing these death sentences, Hegel is not indicating the death of art as an absolute; he is not even suggesting that music should cease to exist. He is merely announcing the dissolution of Romanticism as a necessary demise in modern society. Art remains an absolute for Hegel – 'the divine . . . closes itself in a work of art',[28] he says – but since there is nothing divine about instrumental music or the Romantic

---

[18] See ibid., 1:127–44, Knox 1:91–105.   [19] Ibid., 1:94, Knox, 1:65.

[20] See Rose, *Hegel Contra Sociology*, 72–7.

[21] See Hegel, *Aesthetik*, 3:142–4, Knox, 2:896–8.   [22] Ibid., 3:214, Le Huray and Day, 351.

[23] Ibid., 3:150, Osmaston, 358.   [24] Ibid., 3:135, Knox, 2:891.

[25] Ibid., 3:148, Osmaston, 357.   [26] Ibid., 3:135, Knox, 2:891.

[27] See Desmond, *Art and the Absolute*, 67.   [28] Hegel, *Aesthetik*, 1:50, Knox, 1:30

subject, they are not absolute.[29] They are finite, lopsided, blind and merely fake the absolute. And if an art is not absolute, then for Hegel, it is not art. 'Pure music', says Hegel, 'is empty, without significance, and is . . . not strictly art at all.'[30]

The issue is eschatological. Hegel and the early Romantics agreed that instrumental music is abstract and independent, but they differed on its apocalyptic function. The Romantics had no intention of objectifying music as reality, for its conceptual emptiness is precisely the promise of a Utopia that must not be prematurely reified and preferably left ineffable. But for Hegel, reality cannot be deferred forever in the hope of some secular *parousia* that may never materialise. This kind of aesthetic is merely the excuse of an inept subject that asserts its absolute status by making everything in its own image. The Utopian vision of secular humanity fails for Hegel precisely because it is all too *human*. There is no agency in a profane eschatology except the restless subjectivity of the ego. The idea of this subject saving itself from itself is about as empty as the tautology of the musical sign. Hence Hegel asserts that it is the lack of '*spiritual* content' that renders instrumental music neither art nor true music;[31] it fails to bring the Idea, that is God, into consciousness. If Romantic art is to disclose truth for Hegel, then it needs to be sacred. This is why he names the entire Christian era 'Romantic'; the name is a blatant anachronism, but in this way, Hegel is able to blame the secular Romantics of his day for the dissolution of Romantic art. True Romanticism, says Hegel, is the 'self-transcendence of art . . . in the form of art itself';[32] it is meant to disclose intimations of the divine *within* the aesthetic sphere. But the moment Romanticism severs itself from God, it merely reveals the limitations of humanity and locks the aesthetic into an inarticulate world symbolised by instrumental music, rendering both humanity and the aesthetic impotent in their autonomy. Hence art no longer transcends but can only negate itself in a process as dialectical as the monologue of a schizophrenic trying to talk his way out of reality. Hegel's farewell to the aesthetic is therefore an attempt to undercut the very agency of Romantic radicalism. He reverses the Romantic manifesto: modern consciousness as ironic and modern music as instrumental exhaust rather than maintain the revolutionary energy; instead of shaping the world, they merely annihilate themselves.

Perhaps Hegel does an injustice to Romantic irony.[33] It is true that he misrepresents Schlegel. But why? Maybe it is because Hegel catches in the Schlegelian mirror a glimpse of his own end – indeed, the demise of his entire metaphysical system. To this extent Hegel is a prophet: he

---

[29] See ibid., 1:93–5, Knox, 1:64–6.   [30] Ibid., 148–9; my translation.
[31] Ibid., 148, Knox, 2:902.   [32] Ibid., 1:113, Knox, 1:80.
[33] See Rose, *Hegel Contra Sociology*, 146–7.

foresees catastrophe and declares it dead in the hope that he might vanquish the Schlegelian beast. His aesthetics, in retrospect, functions as a warning: the play of ironic illusion will end in disillusion; what should be the infinite progress of art will backfire as an infinite regress in which art begins to tear itself apart; the Utopian dream will realise itself as disaster. Humanity will eat away its metaphysical supports in its hunger for truth, and will end up swallowing itself, unaware of its own destruction because it can shelter in the false haven of aesthetic nothingness. It is better to declare the death of this aesthetic before the aesthetic declares the 'death of God' (Nietzsche) or the 'death of Man' (Foucault) or 'the death of the subject' (Adorno, Barthes, Derrida), until every metaphysical notion has been ground out of existence to leave humanity and its aesthetic groundless. Hegel's prophecy is correct: the metaphysics of instrumental music already signals the death of metaphysics.

The Romantics, however, were not unaware of this possibility. They did not need Hegel to write their epitaph; in a sense, they wrote their own. After all, their system was designed to self-destruct. It was a kind of terrorist aesthetic that gambled everything for a stake in Utopia. 'Romanticism has the keenest knowledge of the narrow margin in which it can affirm itself', writes Maurice Blanchot: 'neither in the world nor outside the world; master of everything, but on the condition that the whole contain[s] nothing; pure consciousness without content, a pure speech that can say nothing. A situation in which failure and success are in strict reciprocity, fortune and misfortune indiscernible.'[34] Indeed, death stalks Romanticism as the Terror follows the revolution. And like the Terror, its secular death on the scaffolds of modernity was both heroic and meaningless. It was a sorry if principled end. 'Romanticism, it is true, ends badly', says Blanchot, 'but this is because it is essentially what begins and what cannot finish but badly: an end that is called suicide, loss, forgetting.'[35]

Romanticism ends badly in two ways. In the first case, Romanticism fizzles out and flops into the lethargy of post-apocalyptic depression, and betrays its own ideals. Hegel should not have bothered venting his hatred for Schlegel, he only needed to look at the man to see how the radical Romantic had become a fat slob. At least, that is Blanchot's verdict: 'as a young man [Schlegel] is an atheist, a radical, and an individualist', he writes. 'Some years pass: the same Schlegel, converted to Catholicism, a diplomat and journalist in the service of Metternich, surrounded by monks and pious men of society, is no longer anything but a fat philistine of uncouth speech, lazy, empty, his mind on food, and incapable of remembering the young man who had written: "A single absolute law: 'the free spirit always triumphs over nature'."' Which is

---

[34] Blanchot, 'The Athenaeum', *The Infinite Conversation*, 356.   [35] Ibid., 352–3.

the real Romanticism? asks Blanchot. Should it be defined by its premise or its result? Its birth or its death? 'Is the later Schlegel the truth of the first? Does the struggle against the bourgeois who is banal engender no more than a bourgeois who is exalted, then weary, and finally only contributes to an exaltation of the bourgeoisie? Where is Romanticism? In Iena [sic!] or Vienna?'[36]

Perhaps Blanchot would have said the same about Beethoven had the composer died at the height of his popularity in the years surrounding the Congress of Vienna (1815). Here was a man who ten years earlier had immortalised, however ambivalently, Napoleon as the hero in a symphony of hitherto unknown violence, and now, in 1813, he was celebrating the anticipated defeat of the same hero in a piece so banal as to be a parody of the *Eroica*; not that *Wellington's Victory* was meant to be a parody – banality is simply the price of reifying Utopia on earth in concrete images of bugle calls, war songs and cannon balls. And since the work is already Utopia, the teleological drama associated with Beethovenian symphonic structures is no longer necessary. In fact, the material has no necessity about it at all; it is devoid of tonal and thematic appetency. Humanity has arrived not as an organic totality, but as snatches of tunes all jumbled together in a jamboree of political flattery. Beethoven's ineluctable logic and formal virtuosity is negated by a style of monumental triviality,[37] that sounds remarkably like the patch-work politics that was the truth behind the unity of the Congress. It is true that Johann Nepomuk Mälzel drafted the idea for the piece, but Beethoven composed it and claimed it: 'I had long cherished the desire to be able to place some important work of mine on the altar of our Fatherland', he said.[38] In fact, Beethoven composed quite a few of these patriotic pieces over the period of the Congress.[39]

With these works, the unending finality of the Fifth Symphony, that haunted Hoffmann with its Utopian longings, has exhausted itself in the bombastic reality of the political 'now'. Beethoven's heroic period has come to a close. Is this what the apocalyptic energy of the Fifth Symphony struggled for? Romanticism, it is true, ends badly, but apparently the 'applause . . . reached the highest ecstasy' at the first performance of *Wellington's Victory*.[40] But then, it was given to an audience so besotted with patriotic pride that it could not distinguish the sublime from the ridiculous. Beethoven, of course, was under no delusions of grandeur, but he cashed in anyway on the festivities of a congress that sealed the

---

[36] Ibid., 352.   [37] See Solomon, *Beethoven*, 223.

[38] Emily Anderson, trans. and ed., *The Letters of Beethoven* (London: Macmillan, 1961), 3:1438.

[39] For example, *Namensfeier*, Op. 115; *Der glorreiche Augenblick*, Op. 136; *Chor auf die verbündeten Fürsten*, WoO 95; incidental music to the drama *Leonore Prohaska*, WoO 98.

[40] *Wiener Zeitung* (9 January 1814), cited in Thayer, *Thayer's Life of Beethoven*, 571.

end of the Napoleonic wars and initiated the Biedermeier world of sausages, beer and kitsch.

Obviously, as Maynard Solomon points out, this was not a time for political reflection but for celebration.[41] Beethoven's monumental contribution to the Congress was the cantata 'Der glorreiche Augenblick' – the glorious moment – which was not so glorious for the history of music, and whose aura thankfully lasted for only a moment, along with Beethoven's popularity in Vienna and the euphoria of the Congress. So which is the real Romanticism? The *Eroica* Symphony or *Wellington's Victory*? Is the later Beethoven the truth of the first? Does the struggle against the bourgeois who is banal engender no more than a bourgeois who is exalted, then weary, and finally only contributes to an exaltation of the bourgeoisie?

The heroic banality of *Wellington's Victory* is a kind of death. It is not the type of death that immortalises the hero, as in the *Eroica*, but an end so insignificant that no one notices: instrumental music evaporates into the ephemeral, and it is business as usual. Hegel was right. Music must pale into insignificance to banish the weight of an absolute that is *beyond* reality, so that life can get back to normal. After the festivities of the Congress, Vienna, under Metternich, slunk back with relief into the mundane existence of petty bureaucratic controls, without the apocalyptic nightmare stalking its conscience. Beethoven's bombastic compositions, that had united the Viennese public into a spontaneous community of celebration, were simply domesticated by a Biedermeier society into the conviviality of a *musikalische Gesellschaft*. By dispensing with the absolute, music returned from theory back into social praxis in which songs, both with and without words, became the harmonic structure for an honest, stable bourgeois life. Biedermeier music has no significant history in the Hegelian sense, because it did not wish to write one.[42] There was no longer any need for a crisis history of music. Normality was novel enough. The everyday can overcome the failure of humanity. The storm that Schlegel predicted at the dawn of the nineteenth century that would set the world ablaze with its flashes of lightning, turned out to be little more than a cold, damp drizzle.

Maybe that was not such a bad ending after all. Life goes on and society elaborates. 'In Gramsci's usage', explains Edward Said, 'elaboration equals maintenance, that is, the work done by members of society that keeps things going.'[43] So music returns to normal. After all, if Utopia has come, then absolute music must vanish into insignificance. Why criticise Beethoven for carrying out the logic to its conclusion.

---

[41] Solomon, *Beethoven*, 222–3.

[42] See Carl Dahlhaus, *Nineteenth-Century Music*, trans. J. B. Robinson (Berkeley: University of California Press, 1989), 168–78.

[43] Edward W. Said, *Musical Elaborations* (London: Chatto and Windus, 1991), 15.

Absolute music has exhausted itself. So let's call it a day and make peace with reality. Let music give up its pretensions of 'Truth'. Let art dissolve. Let Hegel create its tombstone as a *tabula rasa* in which all claims of truth have been erased. This does not mean that art is no longer produced, it just ceases to be the 'highest mode in which truth secures its existence'.[44] Art just elaborates. And why not? – for the alternative ending is suicide.

[44] Hegel, *Aesthetik*, 141; my translation.

33

On suicide

> The individual in Beethoven is indeed insignificant [nichtig] . . . the
> late style is the self-awareness of the insignificance of the individual
> . . . Herein lies the relationship of the late style to *death*.
>
> (Adorno)[1]

'There is a bullet in his head on the left side', said his mother. Karl had
shot himself on the Sunday, but the bullet did not penetrate the skull.
Beethoven was distraught: 'My Karl has shot himself', he said, 'there's
hope that he can be saved; – but the disgrace that he has brought me;
and I loved him so.'[2] Beethoven's love for his nephew, however, was an
obsessive one. His suffocating embrace had driven Karl to the hills of
Baden in the summer of 1826 to take his own life.[3] The suicide attempt
had the desired effect – the composer's life was shattered. Some commentators claim to hear the repercussions of this ordeal in Beethoven's
last quartet,[4] but in fact it is the other way around: Beethoven had
already driven his music to self destruction – Karl, in a sense, was enacting the music. And the motive for suicide? Karl mentions the 'weariness
of imprisonment'.[5]

It is an apt phrase: the weariness of imprisonment. Adorno could
have uttered these words, except they would have been universal – the
absolute suffering of history and the *total* incarceration of humanity. And
of course, like many before him, Adorno elects Beethoven to speak these
words through the mouth of absolute music. As far as Adorno is concerned, Beethoven had driven his music to existential despair. In the late
style, the music begins to mutilate itself and so marks the suicidal twist
in the Utopian thrust of modernity. These fractured pieces happen to
coincide with Hegel's death sentence over instrumental music, but the
death that Adorno imagines is not the quiet exhaustion of art in the

---

[1] Adorno, *Beethoven: The Philosophy of Music*, 161.
[2] Thayer, *Thayer's Life of Beethoven*, 997 and 1000.
[3] See Solomon, *Beethoven*, 231–55.
[4] See, for example, Christopher Reynolds, 'The Representational Impulse in Late
Beethoven, II: String Quartet in F Major, Op. 135', *Acta Musicologica*, vol. 60 no. 2 (1988).
[5] Thayer, *Thayer's Life of Beethoven*, 999.

dialectic of history, in which aesthetic truth is sublated by philosophy to unburden the weight of meaning that modernity had foisted upon music; rather Adorno stretches out the dissolution of art as a kind of suicide in slow motion.[6] And the reason for this interminable suffering is that Adorno, in contrast to Hegel, refuses to let go of truth.[7] He holds on to Schiller's apocalyptic declaration that 'truth lives on in the illusion of art . . . preparing the shape of things to come',[8] in the full knowledge that the vision of a new humanity has not come, but has 'progressed' into the hell of Auschwitz.[9] History reverses Hegel's idealism: 'The whole is the untrue', writes Adorno, and the only way in which art can hold on to truth is to destroy itself as the unwhole.[10] The apocalypse lives on as negation.

Adorno replays Hegel's dissolution of art. This time round, however, the Schlegelian abyss that Hegel dreaded has become reality. Adorno therefore reverses Hegel's aesthetics, making human freedom the negative apotheosis of history. 'Absolute freedom in art', writes Adorno, 'contradicts the abiding unfreedom of the social whole.' The autonomy of art, he adds, 'depended on the idea of humanity', but since society has become inhuman, 'there is no point trying to allay the self-doubt of art'.[11] To restage the dissolution, Adorno transfers the reconciliation of spirit and matter, which Hegel saw in the sculpture of Greek classicism, to the autonomy of music in Viennese classicism, which Hegel heard as empty. The end has become the beginning for Adorno, because his vision of Utopia is the Hegelian catastrophe of the purely human. For Adorno, the idea of human freedom, promised by the French Revolution, is reflected in absolute music, particularly in what he calls the 'dynamic unfolding totality' of Beethoven's middle-period works.[12] He means by this the harmonisation of the free individual within the necessary structures of society. In a Beethoven symphony, for example, the play of motivic particulars and the laws of formal construction seem to shape each other freely into a self-legislating organism, that conjures

---

[6] On the connection between Beethoven and death in Adorno's philosophy, see Stephen Hinton, 'Adorno's Unfinished Beethoven', in *Beethoven Forum 5*, eds. C. Reynolds, L. Lockwood and J. Webster (Lincoln: University of Nebraska Press, 1996).

[7] See Adorno, *Aesthetische Theorie*, 12–14. On the question of the English translations by C. Lenhardt and R. Hullot-Kentor see chapter 1, 'On History', note 13.

[8] Schiller, *On the Aesthetic Education of Man*, 57.

[9] See, for example, Adorno and Horkheimer, *Dialectic of Enlightenment*, Theodor W. Adorno, *Negative Dialectics*, trans. E. B. Ashton (New York: Seabury, 1973), 361–8, *Prisms*, trans. S. and S. Weber (Cambridge, MA: MIT Press, 1981), 19–34, and *Aesthetische Theorie*, 35–6; Hullot-Kentor, 18–19.

[10] Theodor W. Adorno, *Minima Moralia* (Frankfurt am Main: Suhrkamp, 1951), 80. Also see Adorno, *Beethoven*, 122. [11] Adorno, *Aesthetische Theorie*, 9; Lenhardt, 1–2.

[12] Adorno, *Introduction to the Sociology of Music*, 209.

up the image of humanity reconciled within itself and with nature. Adorno grasps the historical meaning of absolute music in technical terms, but the historical consequence of this insight is devastating: since humanity has failed, Adorno makes music bear 'all the darkness and guilt of the world'.[13] Absolute music becomes a secular Christ for him in order that it might preserve the remote possibility of redemption through death. From now on, music can only overcome the world negatively; thus late Beethoven is made by Adorno to annihilate the revolutionary ideals by destroying itself. But this is only the beginning of a long crucifixion in which the human subject, alienated in Beethoven's late works, is eventually buried in the cold objectivity of a dodecaphonic tomb – with no sign, as yet, of a resurrection. 'Modern music', writes Adorno, 'sees oblivion as its goal. It is the surviving message of despair from the shipwrecked.'[14]

As proof, Adorno dredges up the *Missa Solemnis*; it is a message in a bottle, washed up on the shore of a culture so jaded that he has to salvage the meaning of the message. That at least is his claim. The work, he explains, carries a secret which can only be unravelled if one reflects historically and philosophically on the structure of the work.[15] The historical truth of the work is that it is historically untrue; the *Missa Solemnis*, for Adorno, jars against history as an anachronistic text with its sacred meanings displaced to articulate the contradictions of humanity in a demythologised world.[16] It decentres the mystery of transubstantiation to declare 'the hope of eternal life for humanity' – *Et vitam venturi* – but it is a hope negated by the impossibility of a secular *parousia*.[17] The tragedy is that the *Missa Solemnis* is a human work without humanity.[18] Technically, Adorno puts this down to a change in Beethoven's motivic process; the composer has erased the Utopian thrust of the subject, suppressing its motivic identity by imposing cold, archaic abstractions that paralyse the work into a totality that crushes all particulars;[19] the 'subjective dynamic' of Beethoven's heroic period is negated by the anonymity of a stylised, architectonic structure. Consequently, the *Missa Solemnis* cannot affirm the absolute as either God or man, but leaves humanity and the divine order alienated and purposeless. The moral law within and the starry heavens above no

---

[13] Adorno, *Philosophy of Modern Music*, 133.   [14] Ibid.

[15] See Theodor W. Adorno, 'Alienated Masterpiece: The *Missa Solemnis*', trans. Duncan Smith, *Telos* (1976), 113 and 124.

[16] On Beethoven's search for a modern faith and how it might be reflected in the *Missa Solemnis*, see Birgit Lodes, '"When I try, now and then, to give musical form to my turbulent feelings": The Human and the Divine in the Gloria of Beethoven's *Missa Solemnis*', in *Beethoven Forum 6*, ed. L. Lockwood, M. Evan Bonds, C. Reynolds and E. R. Sisman (Lincoln: University of Nebraska Press, 1998).

[17] Adorno, 'Alienated Masterpiece', 119.   [18] See ibid., 114–17.   [19] Ibid., 122.

longer harmonise in Kant's teleology.[20] 'The subject', writes Adorno, 'remains exiled in its finiteness. The objective cosmos can no longer be imagined as an obligatory construct. Thus the *Missa* balances on the point of effectivity which approaches nothingness.'[21] Humanity has lost faith. And music can only maintain its integrity by destroying it.

Strangely, Adorno does not highlight the disintegration that disturbs the end of the work. The *Dona Nobis Pacem* commits aesthetic suicide. Perhaps it should really be called a 'sacrifice' since it comes after the *Agnus Dei*, but the music is too secular in Adorno's reading to merit the blood of redemption. If the movement sacrifices itself instead of Christ, it is only as a profane absurdity. The music verges on madness. In fact, it is almost schizophrenic, for Beethoven splits the music into forces that collide against each other to destroy the 'inner and outer peace' – the very words which Beethoven has marked into the score The internal and external order are made to tear each other apart, so that society can neither sing of the divine nor instrumental music express the human without contradiction. There is no reconciliation; peace, even with the receding rumbles of war in the coda (b. 406ff), remains outside the work.

Beethoven divides. He divides the vocal subject within itself by severing the 'dona' from the 'pacem', motivically, texturally and temporally (see example 37); the segregation of these words symbolises the alienation between the desire for peace and its realisation – give/peace.[22]

Moreover, the vocal subject is pitted against an instrumental world of war, conjured up by the same banalities that had rendered *Wellington's Victory* a travesty of the *Eroica*. The music of the Congress returns not as victory but mockery, for the battery of instruments deliberately disrupt the prayer of humanity. The whole parade, with its drums and trumpets, is a state of emergency that incites the singers to break into 'ängstlich' recitatives (bs 164–89). Thus the movement forces the sacred into the secular and turns the peace promised by the Congress into the horrors of despair. This is no longer the facile jingoism of 1815, but a critique honed against the Congress and the revolutionary fervour that preceded it. Inevitably, with these divisions, the movement, in Adorno's words, 'transcends into the fragmentary'.[23]

---

[20] Beethoven actually quotes Kant's phrase in his notebook: 'The starry heaven's above and the moral law within!!!' For a positive interpretation of this quote, see William Kinderman, 'Beethoven's Symbol for the Deity in the *Missa Solemnis* and the Ninth Symphony', *Nineteenth-Century Music*, vol. 11 (1985), and *Beethoven* (Oxford: Oxford University Press, 1995), 238–52. It is difficult to ascertain what Beethoven means by this quote. The three exclamation marks may express doubt as much as certainty, that is, either Adorno's reading or Kinderman's.   [21] Adorno, 'Alienated Masterpiece', 126.

[22] See William Drabkin, *Beethoven: Missa Solemnis* (Cambridge: Cambridge University Press, 1991), 88.   [23] Adorno, 'Alienated Masterpiece', 123.

Ex. 37 Beethoven, *Missa Solemnis*, Agnus Dei, bs 107–12, 131–4, 127–30 and 139–41.

(a) Pacem

(b) Dona

The most bizarre moment of disintegration occurs in an instrumental fugue (Presto, bs 266–350) that apes, with absolute disdain, a vocal fugue that had earlier tried to reconcile the stratification of 'dona' and 'pacem' by weaving their themes as subject and countersubject (bs 216–40, see example 38a). This instrumental fugue mangles the original subjects into such disfigured and inarticulate gestures that the harmony reacts by going haywire (bs 266–325, see example 38b).

To put it bluntly, this fugue is a technical disaster; there are kinks in its counterpoint, the modulations are out of control, the rhythms misalign – there are even parallel fifths. Absolute music has become perverse and deformed, and what should have been vocalised as a prayer for peace has mutated into a grotesque indictment against modern culture. A barbaric fugue, after all, is a contradiction in terms. The very symbol of cosmic order for Bach and social cohesion for Forkel is dismantled by a contrapuntal process that can only overcome the world by destroying itself. Consequently, 'dona nobis pacem' is negated and the attempt to synthesise peace is mocked out of court. It is only the sheer force of the military that eventually calls the fugue to order with its bel-

Ex. 38 Beethoven, *Missa Solemnis*, Agnus Dei, bs 216–22 and 266–71.

licose fanfares, but this merely has the effect of terrifying the singers into a solidarity of fear and anguish (bs 326–53). 'In the history of art', writes Adorno, 'late works are catastrophes.'[24]

Perhaps this fugue is meant to be a heroic suicide on the altar of the aesthetic. But it is a heroism without hope, because the death secures no certainty of future happiness. Beethoven had to 'dredge up the past in the anguish of the present as a sacrifice to the future', says Adorno.[25] But is there any efficacy in the sacrifice? he asks. From the perspective of Auschwitz, it is clear to Adorno that the aesthetic is no longer a viable means of keeping the revolutionary dream alive. 'To write poetry after Auschwitz is barbaric.'[26] A Beethoven symphony may document the hope of humanity, but that is over now. The *Missa Solemnis* may sacrifice itself, but it is not a sinless offering. Culture is not independent from history, but is complicit with it, and given the 'total aestheticisation' of fascism in Adorno's day, art is radically guilty. In the *Dialectic of Enlightenment*, humanism leads to the inhumane.[27] The failure of secular humanism, from Metternich's police state to Hitler's gas chambers, forces art to face the scum of its origins. Forget *Bildung*. Music has never been innocent. As Brecht puts it: the palace of culture is built out of dogshit. 'Years after that line was written', says Adorno, 'Auschwitz demonstrated irrefutably the failure of culture . . . All culture after

---

[24] Theodor W. Adorno, 'Spätstil Beethovens', *Moments Musicaux* (Frankfurt am Main, 1964), 17; also quoted in *Philosophy of Modern Music*, 119–20. This dysfunctional fugue is not unique among the late works; the *Hammerklavier* fugue and the *Grosse* fugue, for example, are also finales that obliterate the tranquil and transcendent with an aggressive critique. [25] Adorno, 'Alienated Masterpiece', 124. [26] Adorno, *Prisms*, 34.
[27] See ibid., 58–9. See also the chapter 'On Heroes' in this volume.

Auschwitz, including its urgent critique, is garbage.' So Adorno commands culture to rail against false consciousness, like a hunger-striker smearing his faeces on the walls of civilisation, then he makes it recognise its own complicity and guilt even in the act of protest, so that art forever dithers in a contradiction that is no longer the ironic hovering of Romanticism but an eternal suicide attempt. Anyone who maintains 'this radically guilty and shabby culture becomes an accomplice', declares Adorno, 'while anyone who rejects culture is directly furthering the barbarism that culture showed itself to be'.[28] Adorno puts the aesthetic in Auschwitz: there is no escape. You may speak or remain silent, either way, it is a load of shit. In Adorno's aesthetic theory, there is no real difference between scatology and eschatology.

Thus Adorno implicates his own critical stance in this cesspool of *écriture excrément*.[29] All who hope in humanity, even those who see through the delusions, are dragged into the bottomless pit of aesthetic torment. This is the moral pose of an intellectual Marxist in despair. 'How high-mindedly he shits on art!' says Adrian Leverkühn in *Dr Faustus*. Leverkühn was talking to the devil, who seemed to be uttering words straight out of Adorno's mouth (or rather, his backside, since Leverkühn accuses his visitor of 'devil-farting').[30] It was a bit of an odd conversation, because the devil had transformed himself into a 'theoretician and critic who sometimes composes', as he sat on the sofa in a manner disconcertingly cool for a being from hell. 'What is art today?' he asks, as if he were about to elaborate upon the *Philosophy of New Music*.[31] In Thomas Mann's novel, not only is Leverkühn 'to be read in filigree . . . [as] Adolf Hitler' in the form of Schoenberg,[32] but Adorno is the devil to whom music sells its soul.[33] The suicide of art, announced by Adorno, is played out in the novel as the end of culture, the end of humanity and the end of Germany. And Adorno is as guilty as hell.

It is not that Thomas Mann unequivocally consigns Schoenberg and Adorno to the abyss; he merely registers the paradox in Adorno's narrative of history in which his very attempt to save humanity can only damn it. Adorno is the devil that gives music no choice, but to 'hold itself inside nihilism, to assume it and to manifest it'.[34] In the *Philosophy of New Music*, Adorno writes: 'In an historical hour, when the reconciliation of the subject and object has been perverted to a satanic parody – to the liquidation of the subject in object presentation – the only philosophy which still serves this reconciliation is one which despises this illusion of reconciliation and – against universal self-alienation –

---

[28] Adorno, *Negative Dialectics*, 366–7; translation modified.
[29] See Adorno, *Prisms*, 34.   [30] Mann, *Doctor Faustus*, 241.   [31] Ibid., 240.
[32] Blanchot, 'Ars Nova', *The Infinite Conversation*, 345.
[33] See Jean-François Lyotard, 'Adorno as the Devil', *Telos*, vol. 19 (1974).   [34] Ibid., 127.

establishes the validity of the hopelessly alienated.'[35] What Adorno argues is this: totality has become a parody of itself; God is replaced by the devil; music, unless it is blind, must speak this reality; only then can humanity, if it has ears, know the truth; but the truth will not set it free.

This is the fate of absolute music. When the devil turned up on the sofa for a bit of negative dialectics, his task was to seal Leverkühn's fate as the one who would subject music to its most dazzling abstractions, only to see in its absolute construction and total rationalisation the emptiness of humanity. This fate is in the form of serialism, for fate, according to Adorno, 'is domination reduced to its pure abstraction, and the measure of its destruction is equal to that of its domination; fate is disaster'.[36] In Adorno's eyes, serialism is a paradox; it 'enchains music by liberating it';[37] it gains the absolute autonomy of music through the total organisation of the material, only to suppress all that is non-identical to it and therefore eliminates the possibility of freedom.[38] 'It is not only that all dimensions are developed to an equal degree', writes Adorno, 'but further that all of them evolve out of one another to such an extent that they all converge.'[39] There is no longer any difference in the music; the freedom of the subject is fossilised in the blank equality of the object, which renders human freedom meaningless. In this way, Adorno rehearses Hegel's pronouncement on absolute music, but this time it is on the side of *objectivity*; the musical structure, in articulating the cold totality of the object, has in fact made its content absolutely arbitrary. Hegel cannot even accuse instrumental music of subjective impotence, because there is no subject to accuse. 'Beethoven', remarks Adorno, 'reproduced the meaning of tonality out of subjective freedom. The new ordering of twelve-tone technique virtually extinguishes the subject.'[40] This is why Leverkühn's syphilitic life is reduced to a desensualised existence, alienated from humanity. The devil decrees it so:

'Thy life shall be cold, therefore thou shalt love no human being . . . Cold we want you to be that the fire of creation shall not be enough to warm yourself in. In them you will flee out of the cold of your life.'

'And from the burning back to ice', replies Leverkühn. 'It seems to be hell in advance', he protests.

These feverish extremes, to which Leverkühn is subjected, are the dialectics of hell on earth. The apocalypse of absolute music has come, and just to make it clear, Leverkühn writes a cantata called the *Apocalypse* in which the dodecaphonic cackle of hell and the songs of the angels are created out of the same musical substance.[41] The material no

---

[35] Adorno, *Philosophy of Modern Music*, 27–8.   [36] Ibid., 67.   [37] Ibid., 68.
[38] See ibid., 68–9, and Mann, *Doctor Faustus*, 488.
[39] Adorno, *Philosophy of Modern Music*, 53.   [40] Ibid., 69.
[41] Mann, *Doctor Faustus*, 486–91.

longer expresses anything.[42] If in the *Missa Solemnis* the irreconcilability of subject and object produces a glaze over the music that 'approaches nothingness',[43] then in Schoenberg that nothingness has arrived as something which Adorno erects as a tombstone to absolute music.[44]

And so, in the demonic calculations of Adorno's dialectic, the devil dares to speak of salvation: 'The inhumanity of art must triumph over the inhumanity of the world for the sake of the humane.'[45] To escape the weariness of imprisonment, absolute music, like Beethoven's nephew, must put a bullet through its skull and fall unheard 'into empty time like an impotent bullet'. Suicide is the truth of music. 'Modern music sees absolute oblivion as its goal.'[46]

Inevitably, many critics have condemned Adorno's secular eschatology as fatalistic and naïvely messianic; they deride his militant aesthetic as useless, hopeless and bogus.[47] He is blinded by an absolute history which he fails to deconstruct,[48] and an absolute music which he fails to historicise.[49] He takes German culture to be the measure of all things and 'shits on art' only to constipate his own aesthetic praxis. And besides, he is a bigot. All this may be true, perhaps. But it also misses the point. Adorno has no intention of standing outside history to pick up music with the tweezers of instrumental reason. He belongs to a tradition and interrogates it from within, for he has placed his faith in the music of secular humanism. He dares to be committed – a foolish act in the eyes of the post-modern age that only wants to play with the past as though it were plasticine. But that for Adorno is to forget: it is to forget the apocalyptic origins of Romanticism, and to deny the eschatological hope of humanity; it is to wash one's hands of complicity with the past, wipe out the meaning of absolute music and to erase the function of the aesthetic. If absolute music is born in the revolutionary fervour, then Adorno aligns himself with it. If it fails and Auschwitz is the reality, then Adorno chooses to bear the consequences, because someone has to take the responsibility. This is the price of a secular apocalypse: there is no God to blame. Is there an alternative if humanity is to keep its integrity? Adorno is simply being consistent. He is driven to hell by the logic of hope. In fact, his negations merely serve to intensify the desire for salvation; 'in the face of despair', remarks Adorno, 'the only philosophy

---

[42] See Adorno, *Philosophy of Modern Music*, 61 and 77–80.

[43] Adorno, 'Alienated Masterpiece', 120.

[44] See Adorno, *Philosophy of Modern Music*, 77.   [45] Ibid., 132.   [46] Ibid., 133.

[47] See, for example, Said, *Musical Elaborations*, Szondi, *On Textual Understanding and Other Essays*, Bürger, *Theory of the Avant-Garde*, Lyotard, 'Adorno as the Devil', and Albrecht Wellmar, 'Truth, Semblance, Reconciliation: Adorno's Aesthetic Redemption of Modernity', *Telos*, no. 62 (1984–5) and 'Reason, Utopia, and the Dialectic of Enlightenment', *Praxis International* 3 (1983).   [48] See Lyotard, 'Adorno as the Devil'.

[49] See Bürger, *Theory of the Avant-Garde*.

which can be responsibly practised is the attempt to consider all things as they would present themselves from the standpoint of salvation'.[50]

Adorno, the atheist, is really a theologian after all. Thomas Mann knew that, which is why the devil in *Dr Faustus* claims himself to be the sole custodian of a modern theology in which God has been declared dead.[51] This is precisely the dilemma for Adorno. How can Beethoven write a *Missa Solemnis* without God? How is salvation possible if there is no God and if Adorno is the devil? For the knowledge of salvation is not fact but means. As Adorno perused the dunghill of art, he could see no agency that could rescue the world.[52] This means that the Enlightenment with its instrumental powers of reason has proved that humanity cannot save itself. And yet Adorno cannot relinquish the hope of redemption; 'the divine name is maintained . . . by him who does not believe', he writes, for there is no other hope – however empty.[53] All that the aesthetic can do now is to resist ideology in order to prevent the onset of social amnesia, but it can no longer shape reality – it can only replay it. If the Romantics considered the empty sign of music as the agency of its Utopian visions, then for Adorno, the empty sign has simply emptied itself as a gaping abyss.[54] Absolute music becomes rebellion without praxis, a consolation not a solution,[55] a heroic suicide worthy of the revolution but without any consequence. This is the terrible truth that humanity must swallow. Adorno inverts Schlegel's fragment: music hibernates as a hedgehog with its spikes of autonomy turned inwards to destroy itself. 'The fragment is the intrusion of death into the work.'[56]

---

[50] Adorno, *Minima Moralia*, 480–1; the translation is modified from *Minima Moralia*, trans. E. F. N. Jephcott (London: Verso, 1978), 247.   [51] Mann, *Doctor Faustus*, 243.

[52] See Jochen Schulte-Sasse's introduction in Bürger, *Theory of the Avant-Garde*, xviii and xxv.   [53] Adorno, *Negative Dialectics*, 402.

[54] See Adorno, *Philosophy of Modern Music*, 67.

[55] See Adorno, *Aesthetische Theorie*, 55; Hullot-Kentor, 32.

[56] Ibid., 537; Hullot-Kentor, 361.

34

On absolute drivel

Absolute music has yet to die. The problem is, it only talks about dying. And if it is talking, it is obviously not dead. In fact, absolute music probably sustains its eternal existence by endlessly nattering on about its own demise. This performative contradiction is a typical tactic of late modernity: first, announce your own death, then try and conjure up a rebirth, which can always be re-phrased as an abortion if the 'new' fails to live up to the progress of history. So music constantly dies to resurrect itself as a new language that overcomes the past. Of course, if music fails to overcome the past, then music is just terminally ill forever. But at least the spectre of death gives music something meaningful to moan about: heroic deaths, ironic self-annihilation, apocalyptic destruction, structural calcification, suicide, entropy, hell – you name it, music has been there, done it and has survived to tell the tale. If only music would stop talking like a hypochondriac and get on with the silence that it threatens to fall into, then perhaps it would really die. At least one would think so, but, in fact, having acquired a certain existential charm, even its silence would be too eloquent a testimony of its own destruction.

Absolute music is doomed – whatever it says. It is consigned to talk itself to death, which is to say that it lives in the meaning of its own catastrophic statements. It assumes, of course, that it has always spoken with such weight, as if its words were born pregnant with their own fatality, but that is only because it has forgotten the accusations of gibberish that the eighteenth century use to hurl at instrumental music. In order for the vacant tones of instrumental music to speak with substance, they had to acquire a language of weight and amass enough power to make the kind of authoritative pronouncements that finally silenced its audience: by the 1840s, no one spoke when music spoke. What was accused by the eighteenth century of meaningless talk, by the nineteenth century had erased the chatter of the very society that had ridiculed it.[1] And it was the Beethoven symphony – the paradigm of absolute music – that first imposed this silence across the concert halls of Europe. It was the 'endless melodies' of these symphonies, says

---

[1] See Johnson, *Listening in Paris*, 257–80.

Wagner, that eliminated the social chattering which he could still imagine between the notes of a Mozart symphony.[2] So significant was the message for Wagner that he could no longer countenance any humour in these works;[3] Schumann could hear the symphonies as ironic,[4] but reality had become so painful for the disciple of Schopenhauer that this music could only speak with a metaphysical heaviness. A Beethoven symphony speaks for the world, because, as Schopenhauer explains, it reveals the essence of the world.[5] Or as Nietzsche puts it in a polemic against Wagner: the composer has become the 'mouthpiece of the "in-itself" of things, a telephone from beyond . . . [a] ventriloquist of God'.[6]

The question is: who is the authority speaking on the other end of the telephone? Certainly not God, for God was rumoured to have lost possession of the divine *logos* long before Nietzsche made the fatal mistake of pronouncing him dead.[7] And neither is the ventriloquist the composer; he merely mediates the message. Whoever this impersonator is, he would have to be foolish enough not only to steal the authority of the divine word, but to use it to pronounce himself dead. Who else could this ventriloquist be but the modern ego, which, having displayed its poetic prowess, flatters itself with the profundity of its own sufferings in the safe knowledge that its death-wish will remain only a wish in the fiction of the aesthetic? Music's death-rattle is merely the displaced discourse of the moaning ego.

Is absolute music doomed forever by the ventriloquism of the ego? Can it talk back? Can it wangle its way out of the significance of its speech? What would this language be like if even its confused stutterings are venerated as truth? Music would have to find a way of talking around the metaphysics of language and the histrionics of the subject and so slip out of their vicarious grip. Language and subjectivity would have to be suspended in a speech without origin or *telos*. The subjective presence ascribed to music by Rousseau would simply evaporate into anonymous chit-chat; the poetic chemistry of language assigned to music by the Romantics would calcify into clichés;[8] the seriousness of

---

[2] Wagner, 'Zukunftsmusik', *Sämtliche Schriften*, 7:126–7; an English translation is available in *Judaism in Music and Other Essays*, 334–5 and 338.

[3] So serious was Wagner's notion of music that he called the Beethoven symphonies 'the most unwitty thing conceivable'. See Richard Wagner, 'Über das Dichten und Komponieren', *Sämtliche Schriften*, 10:147; an English translation is available in *Religion and Art*, trans. W. Ashton Ellis (Lincoln: University of Nebraska Press, 1994), 142; also see Nietzsche, 'Richard Wagner in Bayreuth', *Unfashionable Observations*, 262.

[4] Schumann, *On Music and Musicians*, 57–9.

[5] Schopenhauer, *The World as Will and Representation*, 2:450–1.

[6] Nietzsche, *On the Genealogy of Morality*, 78.

[7] See, for example, Behler, *Irony and the Discourse of Modernity*, 91–4.

[8] See the chapters in this volume 'On the Body' and 'On Conscious Life-forms'.

its message would become sheer nonsense. Music would continue to speak, but somehow its talk would cease to function and the work would fall into idle chatter. Absolute music would have to aspire to the condition of absolute drivel – the kind of *Wettergespräch* (weather talk) which for Schleiermacher constitutes the zero-point of hermeneutics, where the repetition of language no longer develops but simply reiterates 'what has already been said'.[9] He writes:

Someone knows nothing of their inner development, and has never felt the depths of humanity in themselves, if the foundation stones of their language have crumbled into dust, if the power of their speech has dissolved into empty phrases and superficial polish, and if their loftiest rhetoric degenerates into an idle play of sound.[10]

In such cases, music would degenerate, but not by destroying itself, for that would merely demand a hermeneutics; rather it would communicate in a language so facile that it would cease to say anything at all.

Of course, blathering on about nothing would still constitute a death, but at least it would be a death without talking about death. The demise of meaning would no longer be meaningful; the destruction of music would not make music immortal. It would be a death without negation, a martyrdom without canonisation. Of all the disasters that Adorno documents in the late works of Beethoven, he fails to mention the catastrophe of chattering – but this is because it is a catastrophe without catastrophe.

Beethoven's late quartets talk a lot. Kerman calls it 'vocality'.[11] This talk is mostly of the seriously catastrophic type – interruptions, protestations, stammerings, outbursts. These are simulations of speech, and although they are Babelic in the way they disrupt the formal coherence, they actually derive their meaning from the very dispersal of language: the 'scream', as Kerman calls it, that tears through the polyphony in the opening of the A minor Quartet (bs 9–10), the stuttering arioso of the *Cavatina* (Op. 130), the impassioned recitative that falls out of rank to protest against the march of Op. 132,[12] are all voices that locate their significance in the breakdown of language, where the gaps disclose the emotional articulation of a subject battering against the linguistic barriers to gesture to a condition beyond words. But these structural fissures are not as subversive as the discrete chattering that babbles its way through these works, particularly as its most pronounced manifestation

---

[9] Friedrich Schleiermacher, *Hermeneutik und Kritik*, ed. M. Frank (Frankfurt am Main: Suhrkamp, 1977), 82–3. See Peter Fenves, *'Chatter': Language and History in Kierkegaard* (Stanford: Stanford University Press, 1993), 8–10. Many of the ideas in this chapter are indebted to Fenves' book.

[10] Friedrich Schleiermacher, *Monologue III*, trans. Beiser in *The Early Political Writings of the German Romantics*, 197.

[11] Joseph Kerman, *The Beethoven Quartets* (Oxford: Oxford University Press, 1967), 191–222. [12] See ibid., 244, and Chua, *The 'Galitzin' Quartets of Beethoven*, 108 and 196.

Ex. 39 Beethoven, String Quartet in C♯ minor, Op. 131, third movement.

is found in what is commonly regarded as the most structurally coherent of the late quartets – Op. 131 in C♯ minor.[13] It is true, of course, that Beethoven has removed the thick double barlines between the seven movements to connect the work as one harmonic entity and interwoven the quartet with a network of motivic connections. But despite these conciliatory gestures, something peculiar happens in the third movement (see example 39).

[13] See, for example, Kerman, *The Beethoven Quartets*, 326, and Amanda Glauert, 'The Double Perspective in Beethoven's Opus 131', *Nineteenth-Century Music*, vol. 4 (1980).

It comes as something of an interruption, as if Beethoven had suddenly 'grown conscious of his art', writes Wagner.[14] After the abstractions of the first two movements, the music begins to simulate speech. It makes operatic noises. But this new consciousness that Wagner registers is not simply an ironic awareness. For a start, the conversation seems to say nothing; the chattering suspends the teleological coherence of the work with a disruption that does not disclose the emotive state of a subject clawing beyond words. It is just talk – and rather formal at that. It is as if the quartet has suddenly started to impersonate the frivolous Viennese public that was still prone to chatter during performances. The first two chords function like a dry cough (b. 1), a polite clearing of the throat designed to disrupt the proceedings. The instruments begin to speak to one another in stiff sentences that sound like an exchange of opinion across the auditorium (bs 2–6). Then, after the initial discussion, the first violin has an idea, and judging by the bout of coloratura, it is a rather flowery and vacuous one (bs 7–9). What is the quartet talking about? Most probably about the quartet itself, for the work suddenly changes direction. It is as if the clichés of the 'cultured' have sabotaged the abstractions of the quartet; instead of continuing the work, the recitative seems to set the stage for some alternative Biedermeier fun. It becomes another piece, as it were. The curtains rise in the next movement to reveal a touch of home-spun operetta, a duet with variations, whose strategically silly pizzicatos (b. 130ff), canonic blunders (b. 114ff) and impertinent 'wiggles' (b. 195ff) mimic the taste of the chattering classes.

The recitative even has the structure of chattering – *non sequiturs*, inattentive comments, distracted clichés. In bar five there is a note missing in the conversation (viola). The first violin messes up its own speech with a coloratura so overblown that it destabilises the structure; it ends on the wrong beat like a grammatical mistake. And besides, this extravagant flourish does not know where it is going, despite its pretence at some kind of teleological gesture; the movement according to the key-signature is supposed to be in A major, but it only gets there by 'accident'. Admittedly, the recitative is meant to be a transition from the second to the fourth movement, but since the flourish ends up in the wrong key, the transition does not really work – the coloratura is functionally empty. Bar ten, the *telos* of the gesture, wants to cadence in E major, and it is only by an awkward harmonic hiccup in the next bar, with a flattened sixth in the bass to delineate the correct dominant, that the recitative suddenly turns towards the key of the fourth movement – A major.

---

[14] Wagner, 'Beethoven' (1870), *Sämtliche Schriften*, 9:97; an English translation is available in *Singers and Actors*, trans. W. Ashton Ellis (Lincoln: University of Nebraska Press, 1993), 97.

And all this is merely the beginning of a string of 'inept' transitions inspired by the recitative. Music, which for Schleiermacher 'consists of nothing but transitions',[15] seems to trip itself up in the attempt to connect ideas together. If the set of variations in the fourth movement is supposed to be 'the illusion of art concealing art', as Kerman claims, then Beethoven makes a pretty bad job of it. In fact, there is no concealment at all; the idea of integration is the butt of a recurring joke in which the transitions between variations simply fail to connect as the variations flit from one tempo to another. The texture will suddenly change, for example, so that the transition sticks out as an anomaly (bs 63–4). Sometimes Beethoven refuses to arrest the momentum; he lets the variation go on until it collides at an angle to the next one (bs 129, 161, 186). He even starts a theme in the bar of transition, creating a disjunction as two antecedent phrases knock into each other (bs 161–2). These inept linkages culminate in a coda that takes the idea of 'bad transitions' as a theme for variation. And what better agent to introduce this theme than the chatterings of the third movement; they reappear with the same 'dry cough', stiff exchanges and flowery flourishes (b. 220ff). Beethoven even repeats the cadential hiccup, with the flattened sixth inflection, in the final bars.

This coda consists of transitions of the most clichéd type. First, the terse exchanges of the recitative slacken into the 'loose-talk' of triplet figurations, followed by the prattle of trills and endless arpeggios (b. 227ff) that merely lead to an acceleration that seems to be a rhythmic transition to nowhere (b. 231ff); there are just more trills – more transitions. When the original theme finally arrives, it is in the worst possible taste, as though it were mimicking an over-decorated hurdy-gurdy, flaunting its vacuity with yet more trills, frills and arpeggios (b. 243ff). But this theme is just another 'inept' transition, for it fails to cadence and starts the entire process off again (b. 250ff). These bizarre oscillations of transitional textures, with slippages into C and F major that seem to have no structural function except to make more transitions, turn the very agent of Classical integration into a source of disintegration.[16] If, as Peter Fenves suggests, to chatter is to suspend the teleological fulfilment of language, then this coda is pure chattering, where the transitions no longer go anywhere, but idly wend their way through various clichés. What had started out as a polite enough conversation between the violins in the opening theme has degenerated into small-talk. *Wettergespräch.*

Another example of chattering is the finale of Beethoven's last

[15] Friedrich Schleiermacher, *Vorlesungen über die Ästhetik*, ed. C. Lommatzsch (Berlin, 1974), 642, quoted in Bowie, *Aesthetics and Subjectivity*, 169.

[16] See Rosen, *The Classical Style*, 57–74.

Ex. 40 Beethoven, String Quartet in F major, Op. 135, finale.

quartet, Op. 135 in F major. It announces itself as a hermeneutic problem
by attaching an enigmatic epigram in the score – *Der schwer gefasste
Entschluss: Muss es sein? Es muss sein!* (see example 40).

Beethoven has borrowed language, but far from using words to stabilise or conceptualise the piece, he renders them meaningless through
music. The question–answer dialogue is caught in that condition of misunderstanding which for Schleiermacher is the automatic premise of all
conversations.[17] There is an exchange of words, but what do they mean?
Is a hermeneutic even possible under these conditions? The notes
explain nothing semantically. Rather, this 'hard-won decision' is merely
a grammatical play, a purely musical logic that abstracts the meaning of
the words into kaleidoscopic patterns of difference. What Beethoven
emphasises in the epigram is the oppositional structure of the conversation, by dissecting and labelling the elements as a table of contrasts
before the movement begins: bass and treble clef, question and exclamation mark, triple and duple time, Grave and Allegro, up and down, single and double statements, 'atonal' and diatonic intervals, statement
and sequence (see example 40). The list could go on, but what would it
tell you? These contrasts are merely shapes, grammatical arrangements
designed to preclude meaning. Indeed, the double barline that divides
'Muss es sein?' from 'Es muss sein!' symbolises the binary blockage
between them – there is no mediation of meaning.

Of course, the words *appear* to make sense, since they are weighted
down (*schwer*) with the philosophical ideas of necessity (*muss*) and
being (*sein*), as if Beethoven were posing an authentic statement that
rises 'atonally' from the depth of the hermeneutic subject and answered
sequentially with the ineluctable closure of fate (*Entschluss*). It is the sort
of heavy talk that one would expect from absolute music. But what actually happens is chatter; the notes have no substance. Indeed, the story
that is often told to explain the incongruity of the words and music is a
tale born out of idle talk. They were all chattering away – Beethoven,
Karl Holz, Ignaz Dembscher. Holz told Dembscher that Beethoven

---

[17] Friedrich Schleiermacher, *Sämtliche Werke* (Berlin, 1834–84), 1:30, quoted in Gadamer,
Truth and Method, 185.

Ex. 41 Canonic chattering.

would not let him have any more music because Dembscher had failed to attend Schuppanzigh's concert of Beethoven's B♭ major Quartet, Op. 130. Dembscher was horrified. The only way out of the problem, suggested Holz, was for Dembscher to send fifty florins to Schuppanzigh, which was the price of the concert subscription. Dembscher laughed: 'Must it be?' he said. Beethoven laughed too when he heard the story from Holz and instantly preserved the conversation as a piece of canonic chattering: 'It must be! Yes, yes, yes. It must be! Out, out with the money, yes, yes, yes' (see example 41).

Beethoven, however, does not provide this story to explain the finale of the F major Quartet. He merely provides the form – pure prattle. The words mean nothing because the subject of conversation is not disclosed. What is this 'it' that must or must not be? And besides, who is asking the question? Because there is no meaningful answer, the teleology of language is suspended. What takes place is a finale where the music simply plays with the arrangements of words as a kind of linguistic *Schein*, and so robs the dialogue of any authenticity. This is particularly poignant at the start because the question and answer structure is presented as a dialectic of the serious and the silly. The Grave introduction is melodramatically grave, with dissonances that try to simulate the profundity of the question. But its pretensions to meaning are subverted by an Allegro that turns the question into the gibberish of a vacant subject who talks merely for the sake of talking. It jabbers away, answering the question by simply rearranging the order of words, as if it could solve the problems of existence as a play of musical grammar.[18]

Consequently, the hermeneutic process flounders in all this palaver.

---

[18] The contrast becomes more banal in the recapitulation (b. 161ff), where the Grave is weighted down with ominous tremolos followed by an Allegro that banters mindlessly with a ditty pinched from the codetta (b. 76, cello).

Ex. 42 Beethoven, String Quartet in F major, Op. 135, finale – bs 14–20.

Beethoven is not playing the game according to Gadamer's rules of hermeneutics. The question is not genuine; it does not exist authentically, but has its substance dispossessed by an answer that is not real, for it refuses to engage in a conversation that would draw out a sense of meaning.[19] So instead of negotiating language, the music defers the process of question-and-answer by scrambling the motifs of the epigram. First, it takes the interval content of the answer and rearranges it in the shape of the question (see example 42):

Then it creates a new theme by reordering 'Es muss sein' nonsensically into 'Muss sein es.' Moreover, this grammatical suspension is paralleled by a topological levelling with the rising question and falling answer flattened out into a static pentatonic tune that falls between the antitonal and diatonic gestures in the epigram (see example 43).

The dialogue is postponed by a kind of idle nonsense that babbles around the hermeneutic process, as if the 'difficult, heavy resolution' stated in the epigram were a piece of cake. In the coda – the final solution of the work – Beethoven makes this clear. 'Es muss sein!' suddenly undergoes a crisis of indecision; its diatonic motif is harmonised by the augmented triad latent in the melodic contour of the question 'Es muss sein?', turning 'Es muss sein!' into 'Es muss sein?' (b. 244ff). The answer to the dilemma is played pianissimo and pizzicato: 'Muss sein es.' The difficult decision of the pentatonic theme seems to tinkle out of a music box, with the first violin chirping like a mechanical bird (see example 44).

Of course, the early Romantics delighted in this kind of twittering nonsense. Language, as Novalis says, has the habit of tripping up communication; the moment anyone tries to say something determined 'language makes him say the most ridiculous and perverse stuff'.[20] It is better to chatter, he suggests, in the 'spirit of music', for the Babelic utterances will somehow find their meaning in the magic of tones. But when music itself begins to impersonate chatter, returning voluntarily to the empty talk it was once accused of, then it is no longer a solution to Babel but a simulation of it. Chattering music registers a collapse of the Romantic project; poesis is not the backdoor to paradise; the urban-

---

[19] See Peter Fenves, *'Chatter'*, 19–27, on Gadamer.
[20] Novalis (Friedrich von Hardenberg), 'Monolog', *Schriften*, 2:672.

Ex. 43 Beethoven, String Quartet in F major, Op. 135, finale, bs 53–60.

(muss   sein   es)

Ex. 44 Beethoven, String Quartet in F major, Op. 135, finale, bs 258–65.

isation of Eden has merely re-enacted the folly of Babel; *Bildung* crumbles in the very activity of self-creation as semiotic fiction. The ego has been taken over by mechanised speech.

In a letter to Tieck, Henrik Steffens wrote:

Certain as it is that the time which Goethe, Fichte, Schelling, the Schlegels, you, Novalis[,] Richter and I dreamt in unison, was rich in *seeds* of all kinds, yet there was something pointless about it all. A spiritual tower of Babel was to be erected to which all spirits should come from afar. But the confusion of speech buried the ambitious work in its own débris. 'Are you he with whom I thought myself one?' each asked of the other. 'I no longer know the fashion of your face, your words are incomprehensible to me', and each separated to the opposite parts of the Earth, most of them to erect, out of madness, a tower of Babel of their own![21]

In other words: Babel became Babel.

And it is not difficult to hear in the late quartets the accusation of 'Babel' that one early reviewer levelled at the *Grosse Fuge*.[22] The heterogeneous language and disintegrative structures gesture to a crisis history, that is, a history that makes sense of itself as catastrophe.

---

[21] Quoted in Una Birch's introduction in Novalis, *The Disciples at Saïs and Other Fragments* (London: Methuen, 1903), 9–10; slightly modified.

[22] *Allgemeine Musikalische Zeitung*, vol. 28 (1826), 310. See Schindler, *Beethoven as I Knew Him*, 307.

Decision and disaster are the tale they tell. In fact, all the late quartets should carry the epithet 'Der schwer gefasste Entschluss', for their finales fail to close the form. They are all forced to make decisions which cannot salvage the work, by trying to assert the tonic (Op. 131), the major (Op. 132) or a victory (Op. 133) as necessary but impossible solutions. *Es muss sein!* But perhaps Beethoven knew that the hardest decision was in his last quartet – hence the epigram. He decides to have a chat instead of a crisis, to undergo a metaphysical deflation instead of flaunting death as some heroic act from beyond. In Op. 135, Babel is blasé. If the late works are catastrophes, as Adorno claims, then they are catastrophes of the everyday.

35

On Babel

Fine art . . . is a mode of representation which is intrinsically final, and which, although devoid of any end, has the effect of advancing the culture of the mental powers in the interest of social communication.

(Kant)[1]

Now the whole world had one language and a common speech. As men moved eastward, they found a plain in Shinar [Babylonia] and settled there.

They said to each other, 'Come, let us make bricks and bake them thoroughly.' They used brick instead of stone and tar for mortar. Then they said, 'Come, let us build ourselves a city, with a tower that reaches to the heavens, so that we may make a name for ourselves and not be scattered over the face of the whole earth.'

But the LORD [*YHWH*] came down to see the city and the tower that the men were building. The LORD said, 'If as one people speaking the same language they have begun to do this, then nothing they plan to do will be impossible for them. Come, let us go down and confuse their language so they will not understand each other.'

So the LORD scattered them from there over all the earth, and they stopped building the city. That is why it was called Babel – because there the LORD confused the language of the whole world. From there the LORD scattered them over the face of the whole earth.

(Genesis 11:1–9. NIV)

Modernity set itself an impossible task: it wanted to eat from the tree of knowledge *and* remain in the garden.

But you cannot have it both ways: to 'be like God' was the promise of knowledge;[2] separation, however, was the price. The divine pronouncement 'you will surely die'[3] is the law that connects expulsion with death, and the knowledge that is gained is precisely the experience of this law; division and alienation are therefore the fatal wounds of knowledge which modernity licks to console itself. There is, however, no question of modernity returning to Eden, as if history could simply swivel round and submit itself to the heavens again. Modern humanity is too proud to turn back and forsake the knowledge it has gained by believing itself sovereign; the thrust of its own narrative can only propel it forward. 'We have eaten from the tree of knowledge', writes Kleist, 'paradise is locked

---

[1] Kant, *Critique of Judgement*, 166.   [2] Genesis 3:5.   [3] Genesis 2:17.

and the angel is behind us; we have to travel the whole way round the world and see if perhaps we might find a back entrance open on the other side.'[4] Modernity tries to work its way around the world to earn its own salvation; the redemption-history it writes is a defiant detour charted by the tools of knowledge that have colonised and devoured man and nature in their voracious pursuit of happiness. After all, if the fruit of knowledge has been eaten, then that knowledge must be *put to work*; the very agent of alienation must be harnessed to redevelop paradise. The critical task of modernity is therefore one of cultivation; technology would overcome the divine curse on the ground and human knowledge would till the soil to produce a culture so trimmed and clipped by the tools of reason that God would no longer be necessary. Indeed, the divine expulsion would be reversed; man would slip back into the garden and God would be engineered out. This is the elusive entrance on the other side of Eden.

The trouble is, having cultivated its way round the world, modernity discovers that the backgate of Eden is called 'Babel'. The division of meaning, as Max Weber explains, is 'the fate of an epoch that has eaten of the tree of knowledge'.[5] Instrumental knowledge cannot unify humanity and reconcile the world to itself; it only knows how to divide and confuse.

This journey from knowledge to confusion is the path that instrumental music traces. Whether reviled or revered, instrumental music has accompanied the pilgrimage of modernity, articulating its Utopian delusions and deferrals, as humanity progresses towards Babel. This is a journey from the absolute project ('Come, let us build ourselves . . . a tower that reaches to the heavens') to the meaningless ruin ('Come, let us . . . confuse their language'). Instrumental music simultaneously promises the technology of total identity ('Come let us make bricks . . . and build a city . . . [to] make a name for ourselves') and threatens to disperse the centre of the subject ('the Lord scattered them'). Of course, no one sets out to replay the tower of Babel; it just happens. Modernity plans the project of its own transcendence, but a divine inversion suddenly seizes its strategies and scatters its meaning like chaff, leaving the folly of a tower as an eternal monument to the impotence of man. The process is necessarily blind and the revelation too late. What the empty sign of instrumental music reflects is precisely this double process of blindness and revelation. It is blind because its dazzling abstractions are used to erase history at points where modernity wants to forget its failures and atrocities; absolute music is that which bears 'no history' in

---

[4] Heinrich von Kleist, 'Über das Marionettentheater' (1810), trans. D. Frank in *The Question of Style in Philosophy and the Arts*, ed. C. van Eck, J. Mcallister and R. van de Vall (Cambridge: Cambridge University Press, 1995), 240.

[5] Weber, *Methodology of the Social Sciences*, 57; see also the chapter in this volume 'On Disenchantment'.

times of catastrophe; it surfaces after 1789 in Romanticism, after 1848 as formalism, after 1918 as neo-classicism, after 1945 as total serialism. Absolute music forgets in order to allow humanity to make its name again in that all-encompassing fullness of the vacant sign that can dispense with the details of ideology and the burden of the past. After all, making the Name was the original project of Babel, to construct with the technology of bricks and bitumen a transcendental signifier that would fix the identity of a nomadic race.[6] But the attempt of instrumental music 'to name the Name', as Adorno puts it,[7] ended up re-inscribing the hieroglyph of Babel against the skyline of modernity. This is because the totality of its sign is also its emptiness, its centre is also the circumference, its universal utterance is also the Diaspora of meaning. The Babelic revelation of absolute music resides in the blindness itself, for the one sign contains both the delusion of Eden and the seed of Babel. The meaning of instrumental music is either/or in the dialectic of history.

This either/or structure enables absolute music to play out the ironic inversion of the name 'Babel'. The name itself is a word game only made possible *after* the confusion of tongues: 'Babel' sounds like 'Bālel', the Hebraic root for confusion – 'that is why it is called Babel', says the author of Genesis.[8] The name registers the ironic condition of language that has lost its grip on reality and can no longer speak clearly. Instead, language cleverly comments on itself, in a play that merely gestures to its own opacity; this is the wit that the early Romantics heard in instrumental music, an organic internet that teeters precariously on the edge of Babelic nonsense. Thus 'Babel' is not just another name; it is a new kind of name that enacts the condition of language at the very moment of its dispersal, the point where humanity loses its Adamic privilege to name things with total transparency and so discovers the irony latent in all its Utopian projects. Babel is the vacant sign – the sound of absolute music – that stands in the place of the Name that is now forever lost, because humanity never built it, and, after the confusion of tongues, can never be known. Babel is therefore transcendental absence, the negative absolute that is the motor of late modernity and all that follows in its wake. *Pace* Habermas, modernity will remain an 'incomplete project', however much it tries to communicate;[9] post-modernity merely plays with this as fact.[10]

---

[6] Genesis 11:4.   [7] Adorno, 'Music and Language', *Quasi una Fantasia*, 2.

[8] Genesis 11:9.

[9] See Jürgen Habermas, 'Modernity – An Incomplete Project', in *Postmodern Culture*, ed. H. Foster (London: Pluto Press, 1985).

[10] For Roland Barthes the name Babel is a kind of *jouissance*, a celebration of confusion designed to turn the punishment into bliss: 'The Biblical myth is reversed', says Barthes, 'the confusion of tongues is no longer a punishment, the subject gains access to bliss [*jouissance*] by the cohabitation of languages *working side by side*: the text of pleasure is a sanctioned Babel.' See Roland Barthes, *The Pleasure of the Text*, trans. R. Miller (Oxford: Blackwell, 1990), 3–4.

So, if Max Weber is correct, instrumental knowledge cannot rebuild Eden – only Babel; and instrumental music cannot solve the problem – it can only rehearse the dilemma. Modern society has forced instrumental music to travel the journey from Eden to Babel time and again in the hope that humanity might re-enter the garden. History will probably repeat itself and the empty sign will no doubt continue to beat with the push and pull of modernity and its post-modern side-kick, promising 'everything and nothing' in that vacant plenitude of meaning so peculiar to its utterance.[11] Perhaps, if lucky, absolute music may drop out of circulation, and settle somewhere else in another history less deluded and traumatic. But the temptation to recycle the empty sign may prove too strong for those who have invested too much in the project of humanity. Their voices may rise again as the louder narrative, drowning out other histories and possibilities, as in the past, to justify its brave and tragic story as necessary.[12] But there is nothing inevitable about it. So why repeat history? Why write the same narrative again if the music has said it so many times already? After all, Eden to Babel is only the beginning of Genesis; history has hardly got going. If absolute music is to escape the cage of repetition then it needs to move beyond Babel. But there is an impasse. The issue is not so much 'what happens after Babel?' – that we already know;[13] the real question is whether humanity can face up to redemption.

ISDG

[11] Wackenroder and Tieck, *Phantasien über die Kunst für Freunde der Kunst*, in *Werke und Briefe von Wilhelm Heinrich Wackenroder*, 190.
[12] See Cascardi, *The Subject of Modernity*, 5, 28–9.
[13] Genesis 12ff.

BIBLIOGRAPHY

Abrams, M. H. *The Mirror and the Lamp: Romantic Theory and the Critical Tradition* (Oxford: Oxford University Press, 1953).

Adorno, Theodor W. *Negative Dialectics*, trans. E. B. Ashton (New York: Seabury, 1973).

Introduction to the Sociology of Music, trans. E. B. Ashton (New York: Seabury, 1976).

'Alienated Masterpiece: The *Missa Solemnis*', trans. Duncan Smith, *Telos* (1976).

Minima Moralia, trans. E. F. N. Jephcott (London: Verso, 1978).

In Search of Wagner, trans. Rodney Livingstone (London: NLB, 1981).

Prisms, trans. S. and S. Weber (Cambridge, MA: MIT Press, 1981).

Philosophy of Modern Music, trans. A. G. Mitchell and W. V. Blomster (London: Sheed and Ward, 1987).

Quasi una Fantasia: Essays on Modern Music, trans. R. Livingstone (London: Verso, 1992).

Hegel: Three Studies, trans. S. W. Nicholsen (Cambridge, MA: MIT, 1993).

Aesthetische Theorie, ed. G. Adorno and R. Tiedemann (Frankfurt am Main: Suhrkamp, 1970). *Aesthetic Theory*, trans. C. Lenhardt (London: Routledge, 1984), and trans. Robert Hullot-Kentor (Minneapolis: University of Minnesota Press, 1997).

Beethoven: The Philosophy of Music, ed. R. Tiedemann, trans. E. Jephcott (Cambridge: Polity Press, 1998).

Agawu, V. Kofi. *Playing with Signs* (Princeton: Princeton University Press, 1991).

Alberti, Leon Battista. *On Painting*, trans. J. R. Spencer (New Haven: Yale University Press, 1966).

Allanbrook, Wye J. 'Two Threads in the Labyrinth: Topic and Process in the First Movements of K.332 and K.333', *Convention in Eighteenth- and Nineteenth-Century Music*, ed. W. J. Allanbrook, J. M. Levy and W. P. Mahrt (New York: Pendragon Press, 1992).

Apostolidès, Jean-Marie. *Le roi-machine: Spectacle et politique au temps de Louis XIV* (Paris: Les Éditions de Minuit, 1981).

Attali, Jacques. *Noise: The Political Economy of Music*, trans. B. Massumi (Manchester: Manchester University Press, 1985).

Bach, Carl Philipp Emanuel. *Essay on the True Art of Playing Keyboard Instruments*, trans. and ed. W. J. Mitchell (London: Cassell, 1949).

Ballantine, Christopher. 'Beethoven, Hegel and Marx', *The Musical Review*, vol. 33 (1972).

Barford, Philip. 'The Approach to Beethoven's Late Music', *Music Review*, vol. 30 (1969).

Barry, Kevin. *Language, Music and the Sign* (Cambridge: Cambridge University Press, 1987).

'Paper Money and English Romanticism: Literary Side-Effects of the Last Invasion of Britain', *The Times Literary Supplement* (21 February 1997).

Barthes, Roland. *The Responsibility of Forms*, trans. R. Howard (Oxford: Blackwell, 1986).

The Pleasure of the Text, trans. R. Miller (Oxford: Blackwell, 1990).

Battersby, Christine. *Gender and Genius: Towards a Feminist Aesthetics* (Bloomington: Indiana University Press, 1989).

Beethoven, Ludwig van. *The Letters of Beethoven*, trans. and ed. Emily Anderson, (London: Macmillan, 1961).

Begbie, Jeremy. *The Sound of God: Resonances between Music and Theology* (Cambridge: Cambridge University Press, forthcoming).

Behler, Ernst. *Irony and the Discourse of Modernity* (Seattle: University of Washington Press, 1990).

Beiser, Frederick C., ed. *The Early Political Writings of the German Romantics* (Cambridge: Cambridge University Press, 1996).

Benjamin, Walter. *Gesammelte Schriften* (Frankfurt: Suhrkamp, 1972–9).

Illuminations, trans. H. Zohn (London: Fontana, 1992).

Bent, Ian, ed. *Music Theory in the Age of Romanticism* (Cambridge: Cambridge University Press, 1996).

Bent, Margaret. 'Some Factors in the Control of Consonance and Sonority: Successive Composition and the Solus Tenor', *International Musicological Society: Report of the Twelfth Congress, Berkeley 1977*, ed. D. Heartz and B. Wade (Kassel: Bärenreiter, 1981).

'Resfacta and Cantare Super Librum', *Journal of the American Musicological Society*, vol. 36 (1983).

Benz, Ernst. *The Mystical Sources of German Romantic Philosophy*, trans. B. R. Reynolds and E. M. Paul (Allison Park, PA: Pickwick Publications, 1983).

Berger, Peter. *The Heretical Imperative: Contemporary Possibilities of Religious Affirmation* (New York: Anchor Press, 1979).

Berlioz, Hector. *Les soirées de l'orchestre* (Paris: Gründ, 1968). *Evenings with the Orchestra*, trans. J. Barzun (Chicago: Chicago University Press, 1973).

Bernstein, J. M. *The Fate of Art: Aesthetic Alienation from Kant to Derrida and Adorno* (Cambridge: Polity Press, 1992).

Bianconi, Lorenzo. *Music in the Seventeenth Century*, trans. D. Bryant (Cambridge: Cambridge University Press, 1987).

Biddle, Ian. 'F. W. J. Schelling's *Philosophie der Kunst*: An Emergent Semiology of Music', in *Music Theory in the Age of Romanticism*, ed. Ian Bent (Cambridge: Cambridge University Press, 1996).

Blanchot, Maurice. *The Infinite Conversation*, trans. S. Hanson (Minneapolis: University of Minnesota Press, 1993).

Blume, Friedrich. *Protestant Church Music: A History* (London: Victor Gollancz, 1975).

Boethius, Anicius Manlius Severinus. *De institutione musica*, translated by C. M. Bower as *Fundamentals of Music* (New Haven: Yale University Press, 1989).

Bonds, Mark Evan. *Wordless Rhetoric: Musical Form and the Metaphor of the Oration* (Cambridge, MA: Harvard University Press, 1991).

'Haydn, Laurence Sterne, and the Origins of Musical Irony', *Journal of the American Musicological Society*, vol. 44 no. 1 (1991).

'Idealism and the Aesthetic of Instrumental Music at the Turn of the Nineteenth Century', *Journal of the American Musicological Society*, vol. 50 nos. 2–3 (1997).

Bowie, Andrew. *Aesthetics and Subjectivity* (Manchester: Manchester University Press, 1990).

Boyd, Malcolm, ed. *Music and the French Revolution,* (Cambridge: Cambridge University Press, 1992).

Breuning, Gerhard von. *Memories of Beethoven*, trans. H. Mins and M. Solomon (Cambridge: Cambridge University Press, 1992).

Brown, Roger Langham. *Wilhelm von Humboldt's Conception of Linguistic Relativity* (The Hague: Mouton, 1967).

Bruford, W. N. *Culture and Society in Classical Weimar 1775–1806* (Cambridge: Cambridge University Press, 1962).

Bryson, Norman. *Vision and Painting: The Logic of the Gaze* (New Haven: Yale University Press, 1983).

Bryson, Norman, Michael Ann Holly and Keith Moxey, eds. *Visual Theory* (Cambridge: Polity Press, 1991).

Buelow, George J. *Thorough-Bass Accompaniment according to Johann David Heinichen* (Michigan: UMI Research Press, 1986).

Bürger, Peter. *Theory of the Avant-Garde*, trans. M. Shaw (Minneapolis: University of Minnesota Press, 1984).

Burke, Edmund. *A Philosophical Enquiry into the Origin of our Ideas of the Sublime and the Beautiful* (1757: reprinted London, 1906).

Burnett, Charles. 'Sound and its Perception in the Middle Ages', *The Second Sense: Studies in Hearing and Musical Judgement from Antiquity to the Seventeenth Century*, ed. C. Burnett, M. Fend and P. Gouk (London: Warburg Institute, University of London, 1991).

Burnham, Scott. 'On the Programmatic Reception of Beethoven's Eroica Symphony', *Beethoven Forum 1*, ed. C. Reynolds, L. Lockwood and J. Webster (Lincoln: University of Nebraska Press, 1992).

Beethoven Hero (Princeton: Princeton University Press, 1995).

Caccini, Giulio. *Le nuove musiche* (Florence, 1602), ed. H. W. Hitchcock (Madison: A-R Editions, 1970).

Carlerius, Egidius. *Tractatus de duplici ritu cantus ecclesiastici in divinis officiis* (c.1470), *On the Dignity and the Effects of Music*, trans. J. D. Cullington, ed. R. Strohm (London: Institute of Advanced Musical Studies, King's College London, 1996).

Carter, Tim. *Music in Late Renaissance and Early Baroque Italy* (London: B. T. Batsford, 1992).

'Printing the New Music', *Music and the Cultures of Print*, ed. Kate van Orden (New York: Garland Press, forthcoming).

Cascardi, Anthony J. *The Subject of Modernity* (Cambridge: Cambridge University Press, 1992).

Cassirer, Ernst. *The Philosophy of the Enlightenment*, trans. F. C. A. Koelln and J. Pettgrove (Princeton: Princeton University Press, 1951).

The Platonic Renaissance in England (Edinburgh: Nelson, 1953).

The Question of Jean-Jacques Rousseau, trans. P. Gay (Bloomington: Indiana University Press, 1954).

Chabanon, Michel-Paul Guy de. *Observations sur la musique et principalement sur la metaphysique de l'art* (Paris, 1764 and 1779).

Chafe, Eric T. *Monteverdi's Tonal Language* (New York: Schirmer, 1992).

Chiapusso, Jan. *Bach's World* (Bloomington: Indiana University Press, 1968).

Christensen, Thomas. *Rameau and Musical Thought in the Enlightenment* (Cambridge: Cambridge University Press, 1993).

Christensen, Thomas and Nancy K. Baker, eds. *Aesthetics and the Art of Musical Composition in the German Enlightenment* (Cambridge: Cambridge University Press, 1995).

Chua, Daniel K. L. *The 'Galitzin' Quartets of Beethoven* (Princeton: Princeton University Press, 1995).
  'Haydn as Romantic: A Chemical Experiment with Instrumental Music', *Haydn Studies*, ed. W. D. Sutcliffe (Cambridge: Cambridge University Press, 1998).
  'Vincenzo Galilei, Modernity and the Division of Nature', *Music Theory and Natural Order: From the Renaissance to the Early Twentieth Century*, ed. S. Clark and A. Rehding (Cambridge: Cambridge University Press, forthcoming).

Chung, David Y. S. *Keyboard Arrangements of Lully's Music and their Significance for French Harpsichord Music* (Ph.D. University of Cambridge, 1996).

Comini, Alessandra. *The Changing Image of Beethoven: A Study in Mythmaking* (New York: Rizzoli, 1987).

Cook, Nicholas. *Beethoven: Symphony No. 9* (Cambridge: Cambridge University Press, 1993).

Cooper, Grosvenor W. and Leonard B. Meyer. *The Rhythmic Structure of Music* (Chicago: Chicago University Press, 1960).

Cowart, Georgia. *The Origins of Modern Musical Criticism: French and Italian Music, 1600–1750* (Ann Arbor: UMI Research Press, 1981).
  'Sense and Sensibility in Eighteenth-Century Musical Thought', *Acta Musicologica* vol. 45 (1984),

Crowther, Paul. *The Kantian Sublime: From Morality to Art* (Oxford: Clarendon Press, 1989).

Dahlhaus, Carl. 'The Twofold Truth in Wagner's Aesthetics', *Between Romanticism and Modernism*, trans. M. Whittall (Berkeley: University of California Press, 1980).
  Foundations of Music History, trans. J. B. Robinson (Cambridge: Cambridge University Press, 1983).
  The Idea of Absolute Music, trans. R. Lustig (London and Chicago: University of Chicago Press, 1989).
  Nineteenth-Century Music, trans. J. B. Robinson (Berkeley: University of California Press, 1989).

Darbellay, Etienne. 'C. P. E. Bach's Aesthetic as Reflected in his Notation', *C. P. E. Bach Studies*, ed. S. L. Clark (Oxford: Clarendon Press, 1988).

Deathridge, John. 'Wagner and the Post-Modern', *Cambridge Opera Journal*, vol. 4 no. 2 (1992).
  'Post-Mortem on Isolde', *New German Critique*, vol. 69 (1996).

de Man, Paul. *Blindness and Insight: Essays in the Rhetoric of Contemporary Criticism* (New York: Oxford University Press, 1971).

Derrida, Jacques. *Of Grammatology*, trans. G. C. Spivak (Baltimore: Johns Hopkins University Press, 1976).

D'un ton apocalyptique adopté naguère en philosophie (Paris: Editions Galilée, 1983).

Descartes, René. *Compendium of Music*, trans. W. Roberts (American Institute of Musicology, 1961).

Discourse on Method, Optics, Geometry, and Meteorology, trans. P. J. Olscamp (Indianapolis: Bobbs-Merrill, 1965).

Meditations on First Philosophy, trans. J. Cottingham (Cambridge: Cambridge University Press, 1986).

Desmond, William. *Art and the Absolute: A Study of Hegel's Aesthetics* (Albany: State University of New York Press, 1986).

Deutsch, Otto Erich. *Mozart: A Documentary Biography* (Stanford: Stanford University Press, 1965).

Diderot, Denis. *Diderot's Selected Writings*, ed. L. G. Crocker, trans. D. Coltman (New York: Macmillan, 1966).

Œuvres complètes, ed. H. Dieckmann and J. Varloot (Paris: Hermann, 1978).

Di Stefano, Christine. *Configurations of Masculinity: A Feminist Perspective on Modern Political Theory* (Ithaca: Cornell University Press, 1991).

Drabkin, William. *Beethoven: Missa Solemnis* (Cambridge: Cambridge University Press, 1991).

Drake, Stillman. *Galileo at Work, His Scientific Biography* (Chicago: University of Chicago Press, 1970).

'Renaissance Music and Experimental Science', *Journal of the History of Ideas*, vol. 31 (1970).

Dreyfus, Laurence. *Bach and the Patterns of Invention* (Cambridge, MA: Harvard University Press, 1996).

Dubos, Jean-Batiste. *Réflexions critiques sur la poésie, la peinture et la musique* (Paris, 1740).

Eagleton, Terry. *The Ideology of the Aesthetic* (Oxford: Blackwell, 1990).

Edgerton Jr., Samuel Y. *The Renaissance Rediscovery of Linear Perspective* (New York: Basic Books, 1975).

Ellis, Katherine. 'Female Pianists and the Male Critics in Nineteenth-Century Paris', *Journal of the American Musicological Society*, vol. 50 nos. 2–3 (1997).

Epstein, David. *Beyond Orpheus* (Cambridge, MA: MIT Press, 1979).

Fend, Michael. 'The Changing Function of *Senso* and *Ragione* in Italian Music Theory of the Late Sixteenth Century', *The Second Sense: Studies in Hearing and Musical Judgement from Antiquity to the Seventeenth Century*, ed. C. Burnett, M. Fend and P. Gouk (London: Warburg Institute, University of London, 1991).

Fenlon, Iain and Peter N. Miller, *The Song of the Soul: Understanding Poppea* (London: Royal Musical Association, 1992).

Fenves, Peter. *'Chatter': Language and History in Kierkegaard* (Stanford: Stanford University Press, 1993).

Fichte, Johann Gottlieb. *The Science of Knowledge*, trans. P. Heath and J. Lachs (Cambridge: Cambridge University Press, 1982).

Fichte: Early Philosophical Writings, trans. D. Breazedale (Ithaca: Cornell University Press, 1988).

Forkel, Johann Nikolaus. *Musikalischer Almanach für Deutschland auf das Jahr 1784* (Leipzig, 1784).

Allgemeine Geschichte der Musik (Leipzig, 1788–1801).

Forstman, Jack. *A Romantic Triangle: Schleiermacher and Early German Romanticism* (Missoula, MT: Scholars Press, 1977).

Foucault, Michel. *The Order of Things: An Archaeology of the Human Sciences* (London: Tavistock/Routledge, 1974).

Discipline and Punish: The Birth of the Prison, trans. A. Sheridan (New York: Vintage Books, 1977).

Madness and Civilization, trans. R. Howard (London: Routledge, 1989).

Fubini, Enrico. *Music and Culture in Eighteenth-Century Europe* (London and Chicago: University of Chicago Press, 1994).

Gadamer, Hans Georg. *Truth and Method*, trans. J. Weinsheimer and D. G. Marshall (London: Sheed and Ward, 1975).

Galkin, Elliot W. *The History of Orchestral Conducting: Theory and Practice* (New York: Pendragon Press, 1988).

Geyer-Ryan, Helga. *Fables of Desire* (Cambridge: Polity Press, 1994).

Gillespie, Michael Allen and Tracy B. Strong, eds. *Nietzsche's New Seas: Explorations in Philosophy, Aesthetics and Politics* (Chicago: University of Chicago Press, 1988).

Glauert, Amanda. 'The Double Perspective in Beethoven's Opus 131', *Nineteenth-Century Music*, vol. 4 (1980).

Godwin, Joscelyn. *Music, Mysticism and Magic* (London: Routledge, 1986).

Goehr, Lydia. 'Being True to the Work', *Journal of Aesthetics and Art Criticism*, vol. 47 (1989).

The Imaginary Museum of Musical Works (Oxford: Clarendon Press, 1992).

'Writing Music History', *History and Theory*, vol. 31 no. 1 (1992).

Goldstein, Leonard. *The Social and Cultural Roots of Linear Perspective* (Minnesota: MEP Publications, 1988).

Gottsched, Johann Christoph. *Versuch einer critischen Dichtkunst* (Leipzig, 1742).

Auszug aus des Herrn Batteux schönen Künsten aus dem einzigen Grundsatze der Nachahmung hergeleitet (Leipzig, 1754).

Grey, Thomas S. *Wagner's Musical Prose: Texts and Contexts* (Cambridge: Cambridge University Press, 1995).

Griepenkerl, Wolfgang Robert. *Das Musikfest oder die Beethovener* (Braunschweig: Eduard Leibrock, 1841).

Gross, Kenneth. *The Dream of the Moving Statue* (Ithaca: Cornell University Press, 1992).

Habermas, Jürgen. *The Philosophical Discourse of Modernity*, trans. F. Lawrence (Cambridge: Polity Press, 1987).

The Structural Transformation of the Public Sphere, trans. T. Burger (Cambridge, MA: MIT Press, 1991).

Hankin, Thomas L. *Science and the Enlightenment* (Cambridge: Cambridge University Press, 1985).

Hannah, Richard W. *The Fichtean Dynamic of Novalis' Poetics* (Bern: Peter Lang, 1981).

Hanslick, Eduard. *The Beautiful in Music* (1854), trans. G. Cohen (New York: The Liberal Arts Press, 1957).

Harrán, Don. *Word-tone Relations in Musical Thought from Antiquity to the Seventeenth Century* (Neuhausen-Stuttgart: American Institute of Musicology and Hänssler-Verlag, 1986).

Harris, Ellen. *Handel and the Pastoral Tradition* (London: Oxford University Press, 1980).

Head, Matthew. "'Like Beauty Spots on the Face of Man'": Gender in 18th-Century North-German Discourse on Genre', *The Journal of Musicology*, vol. 8 no. 2 (Spring, 1995).

Hegel, Georg Wilhelm Friedrich. *The Philosophy of History*, trans. J. Sibree (New York: Dover, 1956).

Vorlesungen über die Aesthetik (Frankfurt am Main: Suhrkamp, 1970). *Aesthetics: Lectures on Fine Art*, trans. T. M. Knox (Oxford: Clarendon Press, 1975). *The Philosophy of Fine Art*, trans. F. P. B. Osmaston (New York: Hacker, 1975).

Heidegger, Martin. *The Question Concerning Technology and Other Essays*, trans. W. Lovitt (New York: Harper and Row, 1977).

Henrich, Dieter. *Aesthetic Judgement and the Moral Image of the World* (Stanford: Stanford University Press, 1992).

Herder, Johann Gottfried. *Sämmtliche Werke*, ed. B. Suphan (Berlin: Weidmann, 1877–1913).

Hiller, Johann Adam. *Wöchentliche Nachrichten und Anmerkungen die Musik betreffend* (Leipzig, 1766–70).

Hinton, Stephen. 'Adorno's Unfinished Beethoven', in *Beethoven Forum 5*, ed. C. Reynolds, L. Lockwood and J. Webster (Lincoln: University of Nebraska Press, 1996).

Hobbes, Thomas. *Leviathan* (1651), ed. C. B. Macpherson (London: Penguin, 1968).

Hoffmann, E. T. A. *E. T. A. Hoffmann's Musical Writings: Kreisleriana, The Poet and the Composer, Music Criticism*, ed. D. Charlton, trans. M. Clarke (Cambridge: Cambridge University Press, 1989).

Hogwood, Christopher. 'Frescobaldi on Performance', in *Italian Music at the Fitzwilliam* (Cambridge: Fitzwilliam Museum, 1976).

Hölderlin, Friedrich. *Sämtliche Werke*, ed. F. Beissner (Stuttgart: Cotta, 1946–77).

Hollander, John. *The Untuning of the Sky* (Princeton: Princeton University Press, 1961).

Horkheimer, Max and Theodor W. Adorno. *Dialectic of Enlightenment*, trans. John Cumming (London: Verso, 1979).

Hosler, Bellamy. *Changing Aesthetic Views of Instrumental Music in 18th-Century Germany* (Michigan: UMI Research Press, 1981).

Houle, George. *Meter in Music, 1600–1800: Performance, Perception, and Notation* (Bloomington and Indianapolis: Indiana University Press, 1987).

Humboldt, Wilhelm von. *On Language: The Diversity of Human Language-Structure and its Influence on the Mental Development of Mankind*, trans. P. Heath (Cambridge: Cambridge University Press, 1988).

Humphreys, David. *The Esoteric Structure of Bach's Clavierübung III* (Cardiff: University of Cardiff Press, 1983).

Hyer, Brian. 'Before Rameau and After', *Music Analysis*, vol. 5 no. 1 (1996).

James, Jamie. *The Music of the Spheres* (London: Little, Brown and Company, 1994).

Jay, Martin. *Downcast Eyes: The Degeneration of Vision in Twentieth-Century French Thought* (Berkeley: University of California Press, 1993).

Johnson, James H. *Listening in Paris: A Cultural History* (Berkeley: University of California Press, 1995).

Jones, William. *Treatise on the Art of Music* (Colchester, 1784).

Kallberg, Jeffrey. *Chopin at the Boundaries: Sex, History, and Musical Genre* (Cambridge, MA.: Harvard University Press, 1996).

Kant, Immanuel. *Critique of Practical Reason*, trans. L. W. Beck (Chicago: University of Chicago Press, 1949).

Critique of Pure Reason (1781), trans. N. Kemp Smith (New York: St Martin's Press, 1965).

Critique of Judgement (1790), trans. J. C. Meredith (Oxford: Oxford University Press, 1973).

Perpetual Peace and Other Essays, trans. T. Humphrey (Indianapolis: Hackett, 1983).

Katz, Ruth. *The Powers of Music: Aesthetic Theory and the Invention of Opera* (New Brunswick: Transaction Publishers, 1994).

Kauffman, Linda, ed. *Gender and Theory: Dialogues on Feminist Criticism* (Oxford: Blackwell, 1989).

Keller, Hans. *The Great Haydn Quartets* (London: Dent, 1986).

Keller, Hermann. *Thorough Bass Method*, trans. C. Parish (New York: Columbia University Press, 1990).

Kemp, Martin. 'The Mean and Measure of All Things', in *Circa 1492: Art in the Age of Exploration*, ed. J. A. Levenson (New Haven: Yale University Press, 1991).

Kerman, Joseph. *The Beethoven Quartets* (Oxford: Oxford University Press, 1967). 'A Few Canonic Variations', *Critical Inquiry*, vol. 10 no. 1 (1983).

Kermode, Frank. *The Sense of an Ending: Studies in the Theory of Fiction* (Oxford: Oxford University Press, 1966).

English Pastoral Poetry from the Beginning to Marvell (London: Harraps, 1972).

Kinderman, William. 'Beethoven's Symbol for the Deity in the *Missa Solemnis* and the Ninth Symphony', *Nineteenth-Century Music*, vol. 11 (1985).

Beethoven (Oxford: Oxford University Press, 1995).

'Beethoven's High Comic Style in Piano Sonatas of the 1790s, or Beethoven, Uncle Toby, and the "Muckcart-driver"', *Beethoven Forum 5*, ed. C. Reynolds, L. Lockwood and J. Webster (Lincoln: University of Nebraska Press, 1996).

Knighton, Tess and David Fallows, eds. *Companion to Medieval and Renaissance Music* (New York: Schirmer, 1992).

Koyré, Alexandre. *Metaphysics and Measurement: Essays in Scientific Revolution* (London: Chapman and Hall, 1968).

Kramer, Lawrence. *Music as Cultural Practice: 1800–1900* (Berkeley: University of California Press, 1990).

Kraus, Beate Angelika. 'Beethoven and the Revolution: The View of the French Musical Press', in *Music and the French Revolution,* ed. M. Boyd (Cambridge: Cambridge University Press, 1992).

Kropfinger, Klaus. *Wagner and Beethoven: Richard Wagner's Reception of Beethoven* (1974), trans. P. Palmer (Cambridge: Cambridge University Press, 1991).

Lacoue-Labarthe, Philippe. *Heidegger, Art and Politics,* trans. C. Turner (Oxford: Blackwell, 1990).

Musica Ficta, trans. F. McCarren (Stanford: Stanford University Press, 1994).

Lacoue-Labarthe, Philippe and Jean-Luc Nancy. *The Literary Absolute: The Theory of Literature in German Romanticism,* trans. P. Barnard and C. Lester (Albany: State University of New York Press, 1988).

La Mettrie, Julien Offray de. *Man as Machine* (Illinois: Open Court, 1912).

Laqueur, Thomas. 'Orgasm, Generation and the Politics of Reproductive Biology', *The Making of the Modern Body,* ed. C. Gallagher and T. Laqueur (Berkeley: University of California Press, 1987).

Lavater, Johann Caspar. *Physiognomische Fragmente, zur Beförderung der Menschenkenntnis und Menschenliebe* (Leipzig und Winterthur, 1775–8).

Lawrence, Christopher. 'The Nervous System and Society in the Scottish Enlightenment', *Natural Order,* ed. B. Barnes and S. Shapin (Beverly Hills: Sage, 1979).

Le Gallois, Pierre. *Lettre de M. Le Gallois à Mlle Regnault de Solier touchant la musique* (Paris, Michallet, 1680), in Louis Couperin, *Pièces de Clavecin* (Monaco: L'Oiseau-Lyre, 1985).

Le Huray, Peter and James Day. *Music Aesthetics in the Eighteenth and Early-Nineteenth Centuries* (Cambridge: Cambridge University Press, 1981).

Lenhoff, Sylvia G. and Howard M. Lenhoff. *Hydra and the Birth of Experimental Biology – 1744* (Pacific Grove, CA: Boxwood Press, 1988).

Lenz, Wilhelm von. *Beethoven: Eine Kunststudie* (Hamburg, 1855–60).

Leopold, Silke. *Monteverdi: Music in Transition,* trans. A. Smith (Oxford: Clarendon Press, 1991).

Leppert, Richard. *Music and Image* (Cambridge: Cambridge University Press, 1988).

Lester, Joel. *Compositional Theory in the Eighteenth Century* (Cambridge, MA: Harvard University Press, 1992).

Lestringant, Frank. *Mapping the Renaissance World: Geographical Imagination in the Age of Discovery,* trans. D. Fausett (Cambridge: Polity Press, 1994).

Levarie, Siegmund. 'Noise', *Critical Inquiry,* vol. 4 no. 1 (1977).

Levy, Janet M. '"Something Mechanical Encrusted on the Living": A Source of Musical Wit and Humor', in *Convention in Eighteenth- and Nineteenth-Century Music,* ed. W. J. Allanbrook, J. M. Levy and W. P. Mahrt (New York: Pendragon Press, 1992).

Lewin, David. 'Women's Voices and the Fundamental Bass', *The Journal of Musicology,* vol. 10 no. 4 (Fall, 1992).

Lippman, Edward. *A History of Western Aesthetics* (Lincoln: University of Nebraska Press, 1992).

Lockwood, Lewis. '"Eroica" Perspectives: Strategy and Design in the First Movement', *Beethoven Studies 3,* ed. A. Tyson (Cambridge: Cambridge University Press, 1982).

Lodes, Birgit. '"When I try, now and then, to give musical form to my turbulent feelings": The Human and the Divine in the Gloria of Beethoven's *Missa Solemnis*', *Beethoven Forum 6*, ed. L. Lockwood, M. Evan Bonds, C. Reynolds and E. R. Sisman (Lincoln: University of Nebraska Press, 1998).

Longyear, Rey. *Schiller and Music* (Chapel Hill: University of North Carolina Press, 1966).

Lowinsky, Edward E. 'The Concept of Physical and Musical Space in the Renaissance (A Preliminary Sketch)', in *Papers of the American Musicological Society*, ed. G. Reese (1946).

'On the Use of Scores by Sixteenth-Century Musicians', *Journal of the American Musicological Society*, vol. 1 (1948).

'Early Scores in Manuscript', *Journal of the American Musicological Society*, vol. 13 (1960).

Lukács, Georg. *The Theory of the Novel*, trans. A. Bostock (Cambridge, MA: MIT Press, 1994).

Lyotard, Jean-François. 'Adorno as the Devil', *Telos*, vol. 19 (1974).

'The Idea of History', *Post-Structuralism and the Question of History*, ed. D. Attridge, G. Bennington and R. Young (Cambridge: Cambridge University Press, 1989).

MacDonell, Diane. *Theories of Discourse: An Introduction* (Oxford: Blackwell, 1986).

MacIntyre, Alasdair. *After Virtue* (London: Duckworth, 1981).

Mandrou, Robert. *Introduction to Modern France 1500–1640: An Essay in Historical Psychology*, trans. R. E. Hallmark (London: Edward Arnold, 1975).

Maniates, Maria Rika. '*Sonata, que me veux-tu?*: The Enigma of French Musical Aesthetics in the 18th Century', *Current Musicology*, vol. 9 (1969).

Mann, Thomas. *Doctor Faustus*, trans. H. T. Lowe-Porter (London: Secker and Warburg, 1949).

Marx, Adolf Bernhard. *Ludwig van Beethoven: Leben und Schaffen* (Berlin, 1859).

Mattheson, Johann. *Der vollkommene Capellmeister* (Hamburg, 1739), trans. E. C. Harriss (Ann Arbor: UMI Research Press, 1981).

McClary, Susan. *Feminine Endings: Music, Gender and Sexuality* (Minneapolis: University of Minnesota Press, 1991).

Meconi, Honey. 'Is Underlay Necessary?', *Companion to Medieval and Renaissance Music*, ed. T. Knighton and D. Fallows (New York: Schirmer, 1992).

Mendelssohn, Felix. *Letters*, ed. G. Seldon-Goth (London: Paul Elek, 1946).

Mitchell, W. J. T. *Picture Theory* (Chicago: University of Chicago Press, 1994).

Morrow, Mary Sue. *German Music Criticism in the Late Eighteenth Century: Aesthetic Issues in Instrumental Music* (Cambridge: Cambridge University Press, 1998).

Moyer, Birgitte. '*Ombra* and Fantasia in late Eighteenth-Century Theory and Practice', *Convention in Eighteenth- and Nineteenth-Century Music*, ed. W. J. Allanbrook, J. M. Levy and W. P. Mahrt (New York: Pendragon Press, 1992).

Muecke, D. C. *Irony and the Ironic* (Methuen: London, 1982).

Nagler, A. M. *Theatre Festivals of the Medici: 1539–1637* (New Haven: Yale University Press, 1964).

Nattiez, Jean-Jacques. *Wagner Androgyne*, trans. S. Spencer (Princeton: Princeton University Press, 1993).

Neubauer, John. *The Emancipation of Music from Language: Departure from Mimesis in Eighteenth-Century Aesthetic* (New Haven: Yale University Press, 1986).

Newbegin, Lesslie. *Foolishness to the Greeks: The Gospel and Western Culture* (London: SPCK, 1986).

Newcomb, Anthony. 'Those Images That Yet Fresh Images Beget', *The Journal of Musicology*, vol. 2 (1983).

'Once More "Between Absolute and Program Music": Schumann's Second Symphony"', *Nineteenth-Century Music*, vol. 7 no. 3 (1984).

Nietzsche, Friedrich. *The Portable Nietzsche*, ed. and trans. W. Kaufmann (New York: Viking Press, 1954).

The Birth of Tragedy and The Case of Wagner, trans. W. Kaufmann (New York: Random House, 1967).

Human, All Too Human: A Book for Free Spirits, trans. R. J. Hollingdale (Cambridge: Cambridge University Press, 1986).

On the Genealogy of Morality, ed. K. Ansell-Pearson, trans. C. Diethe (Cambridge: Cambridge University Press, 1994).

Unfashionable Observations, trans. R. T. Gray (Stanford: Stanford University Press, 1995).

Nochlin, Linda. 'Women, Art and Power', *Visual Theory*, ed. N. Bryson, M. A. Holly and K. Moxey (Cambridge: Polity Press, 1991).

Norris, Christopher. *What's Wrong with Postmodernism* (Baltimore: Johns Hopkins University Press, 1990).

Novalis (Friedrich von Hardenberg), *Schriften*, second edition, ed. P. Kluckhohn and R. Samuel (Stuttgart: Kohlhammer, 1960–1975), third edition, ed. P. Kluchhohn, R. Samuel and H-J. Mähl (Stuttgart: Kohlhammer, 1977–88).

O'Brien, Wm. Arctander. *Novalis: Signs of Revolution* (Durham: Duke University Press, 1995).

Olender, Maurice. *The Language of Paradise: Race, Religion, and Philosophy in the Nineteenth Century*, trans. A. Goldhammer (Cambridge, MA: Harvard University Press, 1992).

Ottenburg, Hans-Günter. *Carl Philipp Emanuel Bach*, trans. P. J. Whitmore (Oxford: Oxford University Press, 1987).

Outram, Dorinda. *The Body and the French Revolution* (New Haven: Yale University Press, 1989).

Owens, Jessie Ann. *Composers at Work: The Craft of Musical Composition 1450–1600* (Oxford: Oxford University Press, 1997).

Paddison, Max. *Adorno's Aesthetics of Music* (Cambridge: Cambridge University Press, 1993).

Palisca, Claude V. 'Vincenzo Galilei's Counterpoint Treatise: A Code for the *Seconda Pratica*', *Journal of the American Musicological Society*, vol. 9 (1956).

'The Alterati of Florence, Pioneers in the Theory of Dramatic Music', *New Looks at Italian Opera: Essays in Honor of Donald J. Grout*, ed. W. W. Austin (Ithaca: Cornell University Press, 1968).

Baroque Music (Englewood Cliffs, NJ: Prentice Hall, 1981).

Humanism in Italian Renaissance Musical Thought (New Haven: Yale University Press, 1985).

The Florentine Camerata: Documentary Studies and Translations (New Haven: Yale University Press, 1989).

Panofsky, Erwin. *Perspective as Symbolic Form* (1927), trans. C. S. Wood (New York: Urzone, 1991).

Pederson, Sanna. 'Romantic Music Under Siege in 1848', in *Music Theory in the Age of Romanticism*, ed. Ian Bent (Cambridge: Cambridge University Press, 1996).

Pestelli, Georgio. *The Age of Mozart and Beethoven*, trans. E. Cross (Cambridge: Cambridge University Press, 1984).

Pfefferkorn, Kristin. *Novalis: A Romantic's Theory of Language and Poetry* (New Haven: Yale University Press, 1988).

Pirrotta, Nino. 'Early Opera and Aria', *New Looks at Italian Opera: Essays in Honor of Donald J. Grout*, ed. W. W. Austin (Ithaca: Cornell University Press, 1968).

Pirrotta, Nino and Elena Povoledo, *Music and Theatre from Poliziano to Monteverdi*, trans. K. Eales (Cambridge: Cambridge University Press, 1982).

Pluche, Nöel-Antoine. *Le Spectacle de la nature, ou Entretiens sur les particularités de l'histoire naturelle, qui ont paru les plus propres à rendre les jeunes-gens curieux, et à leur former l'esprit* (Paris, 1732–50).

Polanyi, Michael. *Personal Knowledge: Towards a Post-Critical Philosophy* (Chicago: University of Chicago Press, 1958).

Quantz, Johann Joachim. *On Playing the Flute*, trans. E. R. Reilly (London: Faber, 1966).

Rameau, Jean-Philippe. *Traité de l'harmonie réduite à ses principes naturels* (Paris, 1722).

Rasch, Rudolph. 'Johann Jakob Froberger and the Netherlands', in *The Harpsichord and its Repertoire: Proceedings of the International Harpsichord Symposium*, ed. P. Dirksen (Utrecht: STIMU, 1992).

Ratner, Leonard G. *Classic Music: Expression, Form, and Style* (New York: Schirmer, 1980).

Reese, Gustave. *Music in the Renaissance* (New York: Norton, 1954).

Reiss, Timothy J. 'Revolution in Bounds: Wollstonecraft, Women, and Reason', *Gender and Theory: Dialogues on Feminist Criticism*, ed. L Kauffman (Oxford: Blackwell, 1989).

Reynolds, Christopher. 'The Representational Impulse in Late Beethoven, II: String Quartet in F Major, Op. 135', *Acta Musicologica*, vol. 60 no. 2 (1988).

Reynolds, Christopher, Lewis Lockwood and James Webster, eds. *Beethoven Forum 1–5* (Lincoln: University of Nebraska Press, 1992–5).

Robbins Landon, H. C. *Haydn, Chronicle and Works* (London: Thames and Hudson, 1978).

Roberts, David. *Art and Enlightenment* (Lincoln: University of Nebraska Press, 1992).

Rolland, Romain. *Musicien d'autrefois* (Paris: Librairie Hachette, 1908).

Rose, Gillian. *Hegel Contra Sociology* (London: Athlone, 1981).

Rose, Paul Lawrence. *Wagner: Race and Revolution* (London: Faber, 1992).

Rosen, Charles. *The Classical Style* (London: Faber, 1971).

Sonata Forms (New York: Norton, 1988).

The Romantic Generation (Cambridge, MA: Harvard University Press, 1995).

Rotman, Brian. *Signifying Nothing: The Semiotics of Zero* (London: Macmillan, 1987).

Rousseau, Jean-Jacques. *Dictionnaire de musique* (Geneva, 1781).

Œuvres complètes (Paris: Pleiade, 1959).

The First and Second Discourses together with the Replies to Critics and Essay on the Origin of Languages, ed. and trans. V. Gourevitch (New York: Harper & Row, 1986).

The Creed of a Priest of Savoy, trans. A. H. Beattie (New York: Continuum, 1990).

The Social Contract and Discourses, trans. G. D. H. Cole (London: Dent, 1993).

Sachs, Klaus-Jürgen. 'Boethius and the Judgement of the Ears: A Hidden Challenge in Medieval and Renaissance Music', *The Second Sense: Studies in Hearing and Musical Judgement from Antiquity to the Seventeenth Century*, ed. C. Burnett, M. Fend and P. Gouk (London: Warburg Institute, University of London, 1991).

Said, Edward W. *Orientalism* (London: Penguin, 1995).

Musical Elaborations (London: Chatto and Windus, 1991).

Schama, Simon. *Landscape and Memory* (London: HarperCollins, 1995).

Schelling, Friedrich Wilhelm Joseph von. *System of Transcendental Idealism*, trans. P. Heath (Charlottesville: University Press of Virginia, 1978).

Ideas for a Philosophy of Nature (1797), trans. E. E. Harris and P. Heath (Cambridge: Cambridge University Press, 1988).

Schenker, Heinrich. 'Beethovens dritte Sinfonie, in ihrem wahren Inhalt zum erstenmal dargestellt', *Das Meisterwerk in der Musik* (Munich: Drei Masken, 1930).

Schiebinger, Londa. 'Skeletons in the Closet: The First Illustrations of the Female Skeleton in Eighteenth-Century Anatomy', *The Making of the Modern Body*, ed. C. Gallagher and T. Laqueur (Berkeley: University of California Press, 1987).

'The Private Life of Plants: Sexual Politics in Carl Linnaeus and Erasmus Darwin', *Science and Sensibility*, ed. M. Benjamin (Oxford: Blackwell, 1991).

Schiller, Friedrich von. *On the Naive and Sentimental in Literature*, trans. H. Watanabe-O'Kelly (Manchester: Carcanet Press, 1981).

On the Aesthetic Education of Man: In a Series of Letters, trans. E. Wilkinson and L. A. Willoughby (Oxford: Clarendon Press, 1967; reprinted 1985).

Schindler, A. F. *Beethoven as I Knew Him*, ed. D. W. MacArdle, trans. C. Jolly (London: Faber, 1966).

Schlegel, August and Friedrich Schlegel. *Athenaeum: Eine Zeitschrift von August Wilhelm Schlegel und Friedrich Schlegel*, ed. B. Sorg (Dortmund: Harenberg Edition, 1989).

Schlegel, Friedrich. *Literary Notebooks, 1797–1801*, ed. H. Eichner (London: The Athlone Press, 1957).

Dialogue on Poetry and Literary Aphorisms, trans. E. Behler and R. Struc (University Park: The Pennsylvania State University Press, 1968).

Lucinde and the Fragments, trans. P. Firchow (Minneapolis: University of Minnesota Press, 1971).

Kritische Schriften und Fragmente, ed. E. Behler and H. Eichner (Munich, 1988).

Philosophical Fragments, trans. P. Firchow (Minneapolis: University of Minnesota Press, 1991).

303

Schleiermacher, Friedrich. *Hermeneutik und Kritik*, ed. M. Frank (Frankfurt am Main: Suhrkamp, 1977).

Schmalfeldt, Janet. 'Form as the Process of Becoming: The Beethoven-Hegelian Tradition and the "Tempest" Sonata', *Beethoven Forum 4*, ed. C. Reynolds, L. Lockwood and J. Webster (Lincoln: University of Nebraska Press, 1995).

Schopenhauer, Arthur. *The World as Will and Representation*, trans. E. F. J. Payne (New York: Dover, 1969).

Schumann, Robert. *On Music and Musicians*, trans. R. Rosenfeld (New York: Pantheon, 1946).

  The Musical World of Robert Schumann: A Selection from his own Writings, trans. H. Pleasants (London: Gollancz, 1965).

Shell, Marc. *Money, Language, and Thought* (Baltimore: Johns Hopkins University Press, 1982).

Showalter, Elaine. *The Female Malady: Women, Madness and English Culture, 1830–1980* (London: Virago Press, 1987).

Simpson, David. *The Origins of Modern Critical Thought: German Aesthetic and Literary Criticism from Lessing to Hegel* (Cambridge: Cambridge University Press, 1988).

Smart, Ninian, John Clayton, Patrick Sherry and Steven T. Katz, eds. *Nineteenth Century Religious Thought in the West* (Cambridge: Cambridge University Press, 1985).

Solie, Ruth A. 'Beethoven as Secular Humanist: Ideology and the Ninth Symphony in Nineteenth-Century Criticism', *Explorations in Music, the Arts and Ideas*, ed. Eugene Narmour and Ruth A. Solie (Stuyvesant: Pendragon Press, 1988).

Solomon, Maynard. 'Beethoven, Sonata and Utopia', *Telos*, vol. 9 (Fall, 1971).

  Beethoven (New York: Schirmer, 1977).

  'Beethoven's Tagebuch of 1812–18', *Beethoven Studies 3*, ed. A. Tyson (Cambridge: Cambridge University Press, 1995).

Stafford, Barbara Maria. *Body Criticism: Imagining the Unseen in Enlightenment Art and Medicine* (Cambridge, MA: MIT Press, 1991).

Starobinski, Jean. *Jean-Jacques Rousseau: Transparency and Obstruction*, trans. A. Goldhammer (Chicago: University of Chicago Press, 1988).

Steigerwald, Joan. *Lebenskraft in Reflection: German Perspectives in the Late Eighteenth and Early Nineteenth Centuries* (King's London Ph.D., 1998).

Stepelevich, Lawrence S. *The Young Hegelians* (Cambridge: Cambridge University Press, 1983).

Sterne, Laurence. *A Sentimental Journey through France and Italy* (1786: reprinted London: Dent, 1960).

Stevenson, Robert M. *Patterns of Protestant Church Music* (Durham, NC: Duke University Press, 1953).

Strong, Roy. *Art and Power: Renaissance Festivals 1450–1650* (Woodbridge: Boydell Press, 1973).

Strong, Tracy B. 'Nietzsche's Political Aesthetics', *Nietzsche's New Seas: Explorations in Philosophy, Aesthetics and Politics*, ed. M. A. Gillespie and T. B. Strong (Chicago: University of Chicago Press, 1988).

Strunk, Oliver. *Source Readings in Music History* (New York: Norton, 1950).

Subotnik, Rose Rosengard. 'Adorno's Diagnosis of Beethoven's Late Style: Early Symptom of a Fatal Condition', *Journal of the American Musicological Society*, vol. 29 (1976).

Developing Variations (Minneapolis: University of Minnesota Press, 1991).

Sulzer, Johann Georg. *Allgemeine Theorie der schönen Künste* (1771–4), second edition (Leipzig, 1792–4).

Swack, Jeanne. *The Solo Sonatas of Georg Philipp Telemann: A Study of the Sources and Musical Style* (Ph.D. Yale, 1988).

Sydie, Rosalind A. 'The Female Body in Eighteenth-Century Art', *The Anatomy of Gender*, ed. D. H. Currie and V. Raoul (Ottawa: Carleton University Press, 1992).

Szondi, Peter. *On Textual Understanding and Other Essays*, trans. H. Mendelsohn (Manchester: Manchester University Press, 1986).

Taylor, Charles. *Sources of the Self* (Cambridge: Cambridge University Press, 1989).

Thayer, Alexander Wheelock. *Ludwig van Beethovens Leben* (Berlin, 1866–79), rev. and ed. Elliot Forbes as *Thayer's Life of Beethoven* (Princeton: Princeton University Press, 1964/1970).

Thomas, Downing A. *Music and the Origins of Language* (Cambridge: Cambridge University Press, 1995).

Tissot, Simon-André. 'On the Diseases of Literary and Sedentary Persons' (1766) trans. in *Three Essays* (Dublin, 1772).

'An Essay on Onanism, or A Treatise upon the Disorders Produced By Masturbation', trans. in *Three Essays* (Dublin, 1772).

Todd, Janet. *Sensibility: An Introduction* (London: Methuen, 1986).

Toews, John. 'Musical Historicism and the Transcendental Foundation of Community: Mendelssohn's *Lobgesang* and the "Christian German" Cultural Politics of Frederick William IV', *Rediscovering History: Culture, Politics and the Psyche*, ed. M. S. Roth (Stanford: Stanford University Press, 1994).

Tomlinson, Gary. *Monteverdi and the End of the Renaissance* (Berkeley: University of California Press, 1987).

Music in Renaissance Magic (London and Chicago: University of Chicago Press, 1993).

'Pastoral and Musical Magic in the Birth of Opera', *Opera and the Enlightenment*, ed. T. Bauman and M. P. McClymonds (Cambridge: Cambridge University Press, 1995).

Trembley, Abraham. *Mémoires pour servir à l'histoire d'un genre de polypes d'eau douce, à bras en forme de cornes* (Leiden, 1744).

Vattimo, Gianni. *The End of Modernity: Nihilism and Hermeneutics in Post-Modern Culture*, trans. J. R. Snyder (Cambridge: Polity Press, 1988).

Wackenroder, Wilhelm Heinrich. *Werke und Briefe von Wilhelm Heinrich Wackenroder* (Berlin: Verlag Lambert Schneider, 1938).

Confessions and Fantasies (Berlin, 1797), trans. M. H. Schubert (University Park and London: The Pennsylvania State University Press, 1971).

Wagner, Cosima. *Cosima Wagner's Diary*, trans. G. Skelton (London: Collins, 1978).

Wagner, Richard. *Sämtliche Schriften und Dichtungen* (Leipzig, 1911–16).
   Judaism in Music and Other Essays, trans. W. Ashton Ellis (Lincoln: University of Nebraska Press, 1993).
   Pilgrimage to Beethoven and Other Essays, trans. W. Ashton Ellis (Lincoln: University of Nebraska Press, 1994).
Walker, D. P. *Studies in Musical Science in the Late Renaissance* (London: The Warburg Institute, 1978; Leiden: E. J. Brill, 1978).
   Music, Spirit and Language in the Renaissance, ed. P. Gouk (London: Variorum Reprints, 1985).
Webb, Daniel. *Observations on the Correspondence Between Poetry and Music* (London, 1769).
Weber, Max. *From Max Weber*, ed. H. H. Mills and C. Wright Mills (New York: Oxford University Press, 1946).
   Methodology of the Social Sciences, ed. E. A. Shils and H. A. Finch (New York: The Free Press, 1949).
   The Rational and Social Foundations of Music, trans. D. Martindale, J. Riedel and G. Neuwirth (Carbondale and Edwardsville: Southern Illinois University Press, 1958).
   The Protestant Work Ethic and the Spirit of Capitalism, trans. T. Parsons (London: George Allen and Unwin, 1976).
Webster, James. *Haydn's 'Farewell' Symphony and the Idea of Classical Style* (Cambridge: Cambridge University Press, 1991).
   'The Form of the Finale of Beethoven's Ninth Symphony', *Beethoven Forum 1*, ed. C. Reynolds, L. Lockwood and J. Webster (Lincoln: University of Nebraska Press, 1992).
Weiskel, Thomas. *The Romantic Sublime* (Baltimore: The Johns Hopkins University Press, 1976).
Wheeler, Kathleen M. *German Aesthetic and Literary Criticism: The Romantic Ironists and Goethe* (Cambridge: Cambridge University Press, 1984).
Wheelock, Gretchen A. *Haydn's Ingenious Jesting with Art* (New York: Schirmer, 1992).
Winter, Alison. *Mesmerized: Powers of Mind in Victorian Britain* (Chicago: University of Chicago Press, 1998).
Wokler, Robert. *Rousseau on Society, Politics, Music and Language* (New York: Garland, 1987).
Woodward, David. 'Maps and the Rationalization of Geographic Space', in *Circa 1492: Art in the Age of Exploration*, ed. J. A. Levenson (New Haven: Yale University Press, 1991).
Young, Julian. *Nietzsche's Philosophy of Art* (Cambridge: Cambridge University Press, 1992).
Zaslaw, Neal. *Mozart's Symphonies: Context, Performance Practice, Reception* (Oxford: Clarendon Press, 1989).
Ziolkowski, Theodore. *German Romanticism and its Institutions* (Princeton: Princeton University Press, 1990).
Zuidervaart, Lambert. *Adorno's Aesthetic Theory* (Cambridge, MA: MIT Press, 1991).

INDEX

Index

Cramer, Carl Friedrich, 141–2
critic (music), 68
critic (Romantic), 185, 186, 188, 201, 203
critique, 5–6, 126, 166, 190, 207, 217, 257, 259, 269, 271n.24, 272
cross-dressing, 87, 145

Dahlhaus, Carl, 6, 75, 174, 231, 241
death, 82–4, 92, 95–6, 102, 151, 155, 157, 159–61, 168–9, 221–78; death of art, 257–75
Deathridge, John, 232, 256n.41
de Man, Paul, 244
Dembscher, Ignaz, 282–3
Derrida, Jacques, 85, 88, 245, 262
Descartes, René, 48, 78, 82–8, 96, 98–9, 107, 124, 130, 146, 148, 191
devil, 272–5
dialectic, xii, 23, 100, 155, 289; dialectic of Enlightenment, 153–4, 161, 162n.5, 164; Wagner, 224–7, 228–9; Hegel, 187, 258–9, 261; Adorno, 266, 271, 273–4
Diderot, Denis, 97–9, 105, 123, 128, 130–2
discourse, 6, 75, 125–7, 135, 140, 142–4, 149, 178, 212, 222–3, 241, 243
disenchantment, 12–60, 79, 268
disinterested contemplation, 145, 150, 229, 234
Di Stefano, Christine, 150
Dittersdorf, Karl Ditters von, 191
division, 20–1, 23–30, 40, 48–50, 53, 145, 148, 164, 190, 192, 200, 204, 209, 213, 216, 229, 248, 258, 260, 268–9, 272–3, 287–90
domination of nature. See instrumental reason
Doni, Giambattista, 37
Drake, Stillman, 18
Dreyfus, Laurence, 70
Dubos, Jean-Baptiste, 88

Eagleton, Terry, 93, 96, 249
Eckhart, Master, 183
economics, 7, 28, 33, 48, 251. See also money
Eden, 12–13, 29, 32, 36, 100, 103, 114–16, 124–5, 212, 216, 285, 287–90. See also Arcadia
effeminate music, 87, 126, 131–5, 137
Empedocles, 31
Empfindsamkeit, 107, 112, 119, 123, 125, 133–5, 135n.37, 138, 141, 144, 146, 154, 165, 178, 191, 204, 213
Empfindung, 107, 109, 134, 137, 186
Empfindungssprache, 107, 114
empiricism, 80, 84, 88, 100, 109, 112, 146, 148, 163, 164, 178, 181, 191–2; scientific, 18–20

emptiness (existential), 11, 32, 39, 48–9, 76, 99, 192, 224, 258, 260, 267, 273, 275, 289
empty sign, 4–5, 32, 37–9, 51–3, 75–6, 126, 168, 170, 172, 178–81, 187–92, 216, 221, 231, 234, 244, 250, 255, 260–1, 275–6, 288–90. See also nothing
Enlightenment, 8, 76–81, 114–17, 126–7, 136, 142, 163–4, 200, 216, 245, 248, 275
equal temperament, 13–22
eschatology, 164, 246, 249, 257, 261, 272, 274. See also apocalypse
eudomonism, 101, 114, 164, 216, 251, 288
Euridice, 39–41, 48–9
excrement, 199, 271–2, 274–5
existentialism, 266, 276
extra-musical, 4–7. See also purity

facts v. values, 12, 18, 21, 49, 61–2
fantasia, 119–21
fashion, 8–9, 66, 236
Febvre, Lucien, 51–2
Fenves, Peter, 281
Feuerbach, Ludwig, 225
Fichte, Johann Gottlieb, 162, 165, 211, 258, 285
Ficino, Marsilio, 16, 25, 31, 41, 43, 77
figured bass. See basso continuo
figures (Baroque), 63–4, 110–12, 123. See also Affektenlehre and stile rappresentativo
Filz, Johann Anton, 91n.38
Florentine Camerata, 31–4, 58, 61, 63
Fludd, Robert, 17
Fontenelle, Bernard le Bovier de, 62–3
Forkel, Johann Nikolaus, 105–25, 134, 195, 240, 270
form, 151–2, 164–5, 179, 187–8, 193, 195, 201–2, 204–11, 226, 228–9, 255, 267. See also sonata form
formalism, 228–9, 289
Formenlehre, 64, 226
Foucault, Michel, xii, 6, 16, 24, 27, 35, 47, 78–9, 115–16, 119, 262
fragment (Romantic), 170, 177–8, 187, 193, 202, 244, 269, 275
freedom (moral and political), 134, 147, 153, 161–3, 166, 188, 192, 246, 249, 258–60, 267, 273. See also autonomy
French Revolution. See revolution
Frescobaldi, Girolamo, 62, 71
Froberger, Johann Jakob
  WORKS
  Toccata I, *Livre de 1649*
Füger, G. C., 130
fugue, 114, 117–18, 217, 270–1, 271n.24
fundamental bass, 78
Fux, Johann Joseph, 69n.39

309

311

Index

music of the spheres, 14–22, 24–5, 34, 41–7, 52, 77–8, 117, 169–70, 172, 174, 183–4, 197, 206, 222, 230
musicology, 75, 182, 243–4

naïve art, 164, 191, 212–13, 216
Napoleon, 150, 152, 153n.12, 160, 165, 237, 245, 263–4
natural history 87–8, 105–10, 115–16
nature v. artificiality, 9, 29, 32–3, 34, 39, 41, 61, 79, 99–104, 115–25, 148
negation, 10–11, 177, 179–82, 193, 224–5, 250–1, 256–61, 267–8, 273, 274, 278, 289
neo-classicism, 289
Neo-Platonic thought, 16, 22, 42–4, 51
Newton, Isaac, 80
Nietzsche, Friedrich, 221, 225, 227, 229–37, 256, 262, 277
nihilism, 76, 169, 217, 225, 272
notation, 54–7, 65, 110, 121, 186
nothing, 4, 38–9, 75, 103, 131, 147, 155, 166–70, 183, 187, 192, 195, 197, 212, 221, 233, 244, 250, 262, 269, 274. See also emptiness and empty sign
Novalis (Friedrich von Hardenberg), 22, 153, 162, 172, 175, 178–9, 181, 183, 192, 196, 203, 244, 284–5
novel, 72, 118, 131, 201n.6, 212
numbers (musical), 16, 18–19, 25, 52. See also music of the spheres; quadrivium

object v. subject, 21, 44, 49, 53, 84, 145, 167, 169, 186–9, 192, 200–1, 203, 209, 211, 213, 215, 225, 258, 273–4. See also division; instrumental reason; irony; perspectivism
Ockeghem, Johannes, 55, 57
WORKS
Missa prolationum, 55, 57
ontology, 35, 61, 63, 75–81, 91, 103, 147, 170, 173, 230
opera, 29–50, 60, 202, 209, 280
orchestral lay-out, 59, 59n.25
Orfeo. See Monteverdi; Poliziano
organicism, 92, 99, 105–14, 123, 146, 148, 152, 177, 181, 186, 195–7, 199–202, 205, 208–9, 215, 248–9, 259, 263, 267, 289
orientalism, 90–1
Orpheus, 29–30, 41–2, 44, 48
Outram, Dorinda, 150
Ovid, 30

Palestrina, Giovanni Pierluigi, 28, 251
Panofsky, Erwin, 44, 53
panopticism, 46, 58–60
Pareia, Ramos de, 16, 22

passions, 81, 84–8, 96, 112, 119
pastoral, 29–32, 49. See also Arcadia
performance practice, xi, 64–7, 122
Peri, Jacopo, 32, 47, 57, 65n.18, 67n.25
WORKS
Euridice, 57
perspectivism, 44–60; perspectivism and polyphony, 51, 51n.3, 54n.15, 167–8
Petrarch, 61
phallus, 126, 143, 146, 149, 179
philosophy, 7
physics, 18, 78, 80–1
physiology, 7, 80–104
Plato, 15, 25
Pluche, Noël Antoine, 85
pneuma (cosmic), 99–100
poesis, 173–4, 185, 187, 189, 196–7, 246, 284
politics, 7, 117, 150–3, 162–6, 198, 224–6, 228–9, 245–6, 249–50, 263–4
Poliziano, Angelo, 30, 41
polyps, 105–13, 200
post-modernity, 244, 256n.41, 274, 289–90
presence (metaphysical), 35, 37, 49–50, 58–9, 67, 84, 88, 102–3, 119, 121, 148, 163, 174, 188–9, 196, 277. See also monodic self; subjectivity
progress, 8, 11, 13, 31, 67. See also modernity and history
Protestant work ethic, 23, 28, 33
Ptolemy, 43, 55, 80
public sphere, 68–9, 71
Pugnani, Gaetano, 91n.38
Puritanism, 23, 28, 33
purity, 4–7, 24, 75, 101, 103, 108, 165, 171, 174, 189, 191, 195, 197, 229, 250
Pygmalion, 99–100, 102, 118, 132–3
Pythagoras, 15, 16, 18–22, 31–2

quadrivium, 15–16, 35, 41, 61–2, 68
Quantz, Johann Joachim, 118
querelle des anciens et des modernes, 67–9, 247

Rameau, Jean-Philippe, 61, 67, 77–9, 99–103, 107, 132–3, 140, 197
WORKS
Pygmalion, 99–100, 132–3
reason, 10, 12, 14, 78–9, 81, 84–5, 88, 90, 101, 116, 123, 126–7, 130–2, 137, 173, 229, 246. See also Enlightenment; instrumental reason
redemption, 268–9, 272, 274–5, 288, 290
Reformation, 10, 23–8
Reichardt, Johann, 209
religion. See ancestral worship, art religion, Christianity, God
Renaissance, 10, 16, 82; festivals, 41–50